BALLET ART

BALLET ART

From the Renaissance to the Present

by Mary Clarke
and Clement Crisp

Clarkson N. Potter, Inc./Publishers NEW YORK

DISTRIBUTED BY CROWN PUBLISHERS, INC.

For Nadia Nerina
a ballerina who loves art

First published in the U.S.A. in 1978 by
Clarkson N. Potter Inc.
One Park Avenue, New York, N.Y. 10016

Produced by Ash & Grant Limited
120B Pentonville Road, London N1 9JB

Printed by Balding + Mansell Limited
Wisbech, Cambridgeshire

Library of Congress Cataloging in Publication Data

Clarke, Mary 1923–
Ballet Art
1. Ballet in Art   2. Art. I. Crisp, Clement II. Title.
N8217 .B35C55 1978   704.94′9′7928   78–7195
ISBN 0 517 53454 1
ISBN 0 517 53455 X pbk.

CONTENTS

INTRODUCTION

Maria Medina Viganò as
Terpsichore

*It is the movement of people which consoles us; if the
leaves on the trees did not move, how sad the trees would
be, and so should we.*

Edgar Degas

Ever since man learned to make graphic representations of the
world that surrounded him he has
sought to capture on an
immobile surface the movement
he observed. The earliest
surviving cave paintings show this in their portrayal of hunting or
of tribal activity. It is a commonplace that in the art of the ancient
world we find depicted ritual and celebration in which dance is a
crucial factor. The purpose of this book, however, is to offer some
insights into the most sophisticated and stylised form of dancing
that has been devised by Western civilisation. This is the classic
academic dance – the 'Ballet' of today's vocabulary. It is an art
which has its most evident origins in the court life of the
Renaissance, where dance was an essential part of the education of
the aristocracy. The festivities of the Renaissance were all aspects
of the elaborate machinery of state whose aim was the glorification
of the prince and of the idea of monarchy. The court provided the
setting; the courtiers provided both performers and audience.

In displays of every kind, in tournaments, in explosions of
fireworks (the artist Bernardo Buontalenti was nicknamed *delle
Girandole* – 'of the fireworks' – because he devised, among other
and more important decorative matters, firework displays for the
Medici festivities in Florence), in water pageants, in danced
intermezzi introduced into plays, in masquerades and in horse
ballets, as well as in the court ballets in which the monarch and his
nobles participated, we can trace a variety of elements which were
eventually to contribute to the emergence of 'Ballet' as a theatrical
form in the latter part of the seventeenth century. At this moment,
when the last of the noble amateurs – Louis XIV – had ceased to
perform, there came an important divide in the history of dancing.
The advent of professional training provided the foundation for
the development of ballet in the theatre; for the amateurs there
remained the various and rich forms of social dance.

The correspondence between ballet and its audience can be
identified in differing degrees through the iconography of artists
of all kinds who recorded it. Sometimes the most pertinent and

revealing view of an epoch may be found in caricature, in which the sharp eye of satire penetrates layers of pretence to capture some essential fact – as in certain Russian caricatures at the end of the nineteenth century. These saw through the elaborate paraphernalia of the ballerina as virtuoso and goddess to the dancer as a charmer decked with jewels.

More usually the representations of dancers were simply portraits, celebrating their beauty and charm as human beings rather than their identity as performing artists: Gainsborough's painting of Giovanna Baccelli is a case in point. Occasionally a major artist became deeply involved with the dancer as athlete, as the figure of stretched muscles and aching back – the often contorted and unexpected shape to be seen in a fleeting moment in class. Such was Degas. His multitudinous studies of dancers remain the supreme commentary upon the dancer as paradigm and symbol of movement.

Between the poles of caricature and great painting there lies an extraordinary range of representation of ballet. We have been concerned wherever possible with paintings, sculptures, drawings and engravings which capture performance rather than the static performer. Nevertheless, such curiosities as an eighteenth-century paper doll, a nineteenth-century soap wrapper featuring Marie Taglioni, the greatest divinity of the Romantic era, and twentieth-century postage stamps all suggest odd ways in which ballet has impinged upon society. The relationship of ballet to the society which gave it birth and nutured it can be inferred from the ways in which it was represented to the public of its time. How dancers were dressed tells us not only about the possibilities of their technique but also of their sexual identity: we have but to consider the elaborate skirts of the ballerina in the middle of the eighteenth century to understand how restricted was both her dancing and her role in society. Within fifty years the draperies of the Neoclassic period show how the *ancien régime* had given way to a very different political and social milieu. The etherealisation of the ballerina in the Romantic period, when lithographs reveal her poised like a wisp of mist in the night air, tells how ballet itself had changed in the public imagination and had become an art of escape, of fugitive images and impossible love. The steady decline – with a few very honourable exceptions – in the representation of dancing in the twentieth century reflects not a decline in the importance of ballet but the arrival of the camera as the ideal medium for capturing movement. The work of such exceptional camera artists as Baron de Meyer at the beginning of the century, and Anthony Crickmay today, can take us so near the very heart of performance that the painter or sculptor has far less incentive to treat of ballet.

Émile-Antoine Bourdelle, *Nijinsky as Harlequin in 'Le Carnaval'*

RENAISSANCE SPECTACLE

Nothing is so necessary to men as dancing.

Molière *Le Bourgeois Gentilhomme*

The aristocratic view of the human body which lies at the root of the training in the classic academic dance is attributable to the princely origins of ballet itself in the entertainments of the Renaissance. The court spectacles which developed in Italy in the fifteenth century, and which spread from there throughout Europe, were designed to glorify the image of the prince as ruler. By every form of display, from jousts to banquets, the *persona* of the ruler was subject to an aggrandisement which was intended to dazzle and impress courtiers and public. The celebrations of dynastic marriages, of triumphal entries, of alliances, were seen as metaphors of royal power and they served to stress the importance of the central figure in the eyes of other rulers as well as of the general populace. The festivities served also to propagate the idea of the quasi-divine nature of the prince.

Transitory though these spectacles were, they employed many of the finest artists available, whose gifts were best rewarded in the service of the prince: Tintoretto and Veronese, Holbein, Leonardo and Inigo Jones were all concerned at one time or another with providing decorative material for royal progresses. The development of the theatre in western Europe, following the rediscovery of Vitruvius' principles of the classic stage, owes much to the intermezzi and ballets that were the ephemeral celebrations of some royal event.

The festivals of the Medici in Florence made use for sixty years of the work of Buontalenti. The Florentine Catherine de'Medici, as Queen of France, provided a vital impulse to the expansion of court festivities in Paris and throughout France. Two of the most significant court ballets – the *Ballet des Polonais* of 1573 and the *Ballet Comique de la Reine* of 1581 – were to establish a tradition in France of *ballet de cour* which was to reach its apogee under Louis XIV and then lead on to the establishment of the professional ballet in 1670.

The form of the emergent court ballet in France was a combination of speech and declamation, music and song, machines (whereby divinities might descend among the mortals) and social dance. The vocabulary of movement used was quite simply that of the court dances of the period; the interest lay in the

1 Jacques Patin, Frontispiece to *Le Ballet Comique de la Reine*. Etching, 1582. *Le Ballet Comique de la Reine*, a five-hour entertainment, is celebrated in dance history as being the first ballet for which a published libretto is generally known. Patin, who was *peintre du Roi*, decorated this dramatic spectacle and his etching gives a fair indication of the scene in the Grand Salle de Bourbon in the Louvre in September 1581. This opening scene shows a courtier addressing the Royal party. The audience viewed the progress of the piece, an allegory about the freeing of enslaved man by royal power, from tiered seats on either side of the hall.

9

2 Pellegrino Tibaldi, *A Dancing Genius*. Pen and wash.

patterning and pulse of the steps rather than in any complexity of individual footwork. These entertainments paid obvious tribute to their presiding royal genius by being performed to 'the presence'. The royal party was to be found in a central and sometimes raised location. To them the entire entertainment was directed; the attendant courtiers would watch in tiered and serried ranks around the main performance area in a palace hall, or deferentially fanned out around the presence of the monarch.

The fact that the monarch and his courtiers performed suggests something of the importance attributed to these dance spectacles. Behind the most elaborate of these there often lay a very clear political message. The *Ballet des Polonais* was presented expressly to consolidate the position of the Duc d'Anjou, third son of Catherine de'Medici, as newly elected King of Poland. The Polish Ambassadors, arrived in Paris, were presented with this entertainment in which ladies of Catherine's household appeared on a silver-gilt rock, each representing one of the French regions and each paying tribute in verse to Henri d'Anjou. Descending from the rock, the ladies moved through carefully ordered patterns of movement devised by Belgioioso, Catherine's Italian dancing master. It was Belgioioso, whose name was adapted for the French to Beaujoyeulx, who was to devise the greatest of these early court ballets, the *Ballet Comique de la Reine*. This five-hour spectacle was presented as part of a sequence of festivities lasting two weeks which celebrated the marriage of the King of France's favourite, the Duc de Joyeuse, to the King's sister-in-law, Marguerite of Lorraine. So important was this *Ballet Comique* felt to be in suggesting the monarch's supremacy at a time of political unrest that a careful description was printed and circulated round the major royal houses of Europe. It survives as the most fascinating and complete record of an early French court spectacle.

The representations of court entertainments of every kind give us an invaluable insight into the attitudes as well as the appearance of Renaissance magnificences. Design drawings, official records of the wide range of royal entertainments, indicate how prodigal was the expenditure and no less extreme the ingenuity with which these affairs were presented. The Valois tapestries provide some indication of what was felt to be a most important enterprise. The illustrations to the *Ballet Comique de la Reine*; the series of design paintings by Buontalenti; the engravings by Cantagallina after Parigi of Florentine intermezzi; Callot's closely detailed observation of princely entertainments; indeed, the whole vast corpus of records of royal entertainments, all tell of the way in which public imagination was caught and stimulated.

The culminating days of court ballet came with Louis XIV of France. It is worth recording that his title of *Le Roi Soleil* came to him initially from his appearance as the Sun in the *Ballet Royal de la Nuit* in 1653. By now the *ballet de cour* was at its most complex: a series of entries upon a theme might serve merely to amuse an audience, but sometimes political motivation was retained. So it was in the *Ballet Royal de la Nuit*, where the young king's unassailable power and the blaze of his majesty were symbolised in his role as the Sun itself.

In this greatest age of the arts in France, the King's love of dancing and his participation in all forms of court display inspired remarkable illustrations of royal entertainments. In June 1662 a carrousel (a horse ballet) was staged in Paris – hence today's Place du Carrousel – to celebrate the birth of the Dauphin. The engraver Chauveau's record of this event is one of the most splendid annals of the period. Two years later, a series of entertainments in the grounds of the Palace of Versailles were staged under the title *Les Plaisirs de l'Ile Enchantée*, when for three days the court enjoyed comedies, ballets, banquets and equestrian displays, all dutifully fixed for posterity by Israel Silvestre. The portrayal of these opulent displays, and of the no less splendid entertainments with which the Habsburg court sought to make Vienna a rival to Versailles, indicates the imaginative fantasy as well as the vast extravagance with which the last years of the court ballets were illuminated.

The artist's view of these events – Küsel's engravings of Burnacini's designs for *Il Pomo d'Oro* in Vienna in 1668, Chauveau's and Silvestre's records of the work of the designers Gissey and Vigarani at Versailles – capture all that is best and most entrancing. They are, of course, in many ways idealised as views of performance. Nevertheless, contemporary descriptions indicate that huge sums were to be spent on the caparisoning of horse and rider in the carrousels, and immense ingenuity went into the creation of the world of fantastic illusion in the Baroque theatre exemplified by Burnacini. There were no fewer than twenty-one scene changes in *Il Pomo d'Oro*, each as prodigious as the last. Because these displays were intended to dazzle and excite, and to reiterate to the public the theme of royal power, iconography of the period offers precious testimony to a monarch's aspirations, to his way of life.

At the end of the 1660s Louis XIV gave up his participation in court ballets. This decision has been variously ascribed to his increasing portliness, but whatever the reason, it is significant that at this time the production of ballet passed into the hands of professionals. More especially there emerged the form of the opera-ballet staged at the Académie Royale de Musique in Paris under the absolute command of Jean-Baptiste Lully. Lully, sometime a dancer and later violinist to the King, obtained the royal *privilège* which enabled him alone to present lyric works. With the King's ballet master, Pierre Beauchamps, he codified the entertainment of opera-ballet into a combination of sung scenes interspersed with danced interludes. Lully's successors developed and extended the form of the opera-ballet without radically altering it. The emergence of a dance school at the Académie Royale de Musique was in due time to guarantee a supply of well trained dancers, and the later development of ballet as an art on its own drew upon the dance traditions of both France and Italy.

3 Henri Gissey, Costume for a male dancer representing a ship. This design comes from a book of costume drawings.

4 Carrousel in the Place Royale, Paris

4 Anonymous German engraving of the Carrousel given in April 1612 in the Place Royale, Paris. The medieval tradition of knightly jousting gradually became refined into a decorative display of horsemanship known as a Carrousel. Elaborated into a processional form, calling upon all the arts of designers to produce decorated cars and fantasy of costuming for horse as well as rider, the Carrousel, like other court entertainments, was used to proclaim the splendour of the monarchy. In 1612 the cementing of an alliance between France and Spain was marked by the double betrothal of Louis XIII to Anne of Austria, Infanta of Spain, and of Philip, Prince of the Asturias, heir to the Spanish throne, to Elisabeth of France. This engraving provides a magnificent, if slightly innocent, record of the various cars which joined the quadrilles of horsemen, and it shows the culminating effect of the firework display in which royal emblems (and later, royal portraits) blazed out.

5 Jacques Callot after Giulio Parigi, *La Guerra de Bellezza*. Engraving, 1616. The arrival of the Prince of Urbino in Florence as bridegroom to Claudia de' Medici was celebrated with much pomp, culminating in the tremendous public spectacle of a horse ballet on the Piazza Santa Croce. In this, as in the *ballet de cour*, part of the interest lay in what we would now describe as floor patterns. Complication of step mattered not at all. Like the courtier, whose vocabulary of movement was limited to the steps of the social dance of his time, the horse and its rider had but a limited range of trotting or galloping steps. For the audience the excitement lay in fantasy of costuming, in elaboration of symbolism and allegory, and in the fascination of the patterns created. Callot's magnificent engraving catches all the popular excitement (it was reported that more than 25,000 spectators viewed the ballet from the grandstands, or from roof tops) of this display.

6 Bonnart, *Monsieur Ballon*. Engraving. Jean Ballon was a principal dancer at the Paris Opéra at the beginning of the eighteenth century. He was famous for the buoyant quality in his dancing and he enjoyed the patronage of the King.

5 Jacques Callott after Giulio Parigi, *La Guerra de Bellezza*

6 Bonnart, *Monsieur Ballon*

7 Aveline after Giacomo Torelli, *Les Noces de Pélée et de Thétis*

7 Aveline after Giacomo Torelli, Scene from *Les Noces de Pélée et de Thétis*. Engraving. Torelli was one of the greatest designers of the mid-seventeenth century, celebrated for his brilliance in the use of stage machinery. The emergence of a framed, proscenium stage encouraged Torelli during his early years in Venice in experiments which were to create a remarkably fluid stage area. Summoned to France in 1645 to work for Anne of Austria, Torelli was one of the founders of the French 'theatre of machines'. In this engraving, of one of the most important ballets of the early years of Louis XIV's reign (in which the King took the role of Apollo in the first scene), Torelli's architectural skill and feeling for perspective is evident. The ballet was first staged in the Salle du Palais Bourbon in Paris in 1654. The engraving was made slightly later. As records of performance such prints served to disseminate through Europe the ideas of splendour and opulence associated with the French court theatre.

8 Jacques Callot after Giulio Parigi, View of the first intermezzo in *La Liberazione di Tireno e d'Arnea*. Etching. Callot's etchings are among the most intriguing views we have of court entertainments of the early seventeenth century, in both France and Italy. His own sense of the dramatic brings great immediacy to his presentation of these spectacles. *La Liberazione* was a *veglia*, or vigil, in which the interpolated dance scenes were considered particularly remarkable. This illustration shows the inside of the Teatro Medici, designed by Buontalenti, in the Uffizi Palace. It depicts the first intermezzo, in which a volcano is erupting above the body of a giant. The performance was given in honour of the marriage of the Duke of Mantua to Catherine de' Medici in February 1617. Callot indicates the way in which the stage performance was brought into the auditorium and, as in the *ballet de cour*, the final *grand ballet* united performers and audience.

8 Jacques Callot after Giulio Parigi, *La Liberazione di Tireno e d'Arnea*

9 Matthaus Küsel after Lodovico Burnacini, *Il Pomo d'Oro*

9 Matthaus Küsel after Lodovico Burnacini, *Il Pomo d'Oro*. Engraving. The political rivalry between France and Austria was reflected in the elaboration of spectacle in Versailles and Vienna. Greatest and most extravagant of the Viennese stagings at the end of the seventeenth century was the amazing production given of Antonio Cesti's opera *Il Pomo d'Oro*, with its danced interludes. It was presented in 1667 as the culmination of the marriage celebrations between the Emperor Leopold I and the Infanta Margareta Theresa. Burnacini, pre-eminent stage designer of his time, achieved in this production the consummation of high Baroque design. The theme of the Judgement of Paris was an excuse for a virtuoso presentation whose twenty-one scenes piled stage miracle upon stage miracle. The brilliance of mechanics in Baroque theatrecraft encouraged a designer like Burnacini to dazzle his audience, very necessarily, with scenes which reflected the magnificence of his royal master, while also flattering royal pretensions to quasi-divinity. The engraving shows an apotheosis which suggests the martial triumphs to be associated with Leopold I.

10 *Mademoiselle Subligny dancing at the Paris Opéra*. Engraving, c. 1700. Marie Subligny was a principal dancer at the Paris Opéra, succeeding in this position Mademoiselle Lafontaine, one of the first four professional female dancers. Subligny was noted for the grace and nobility of her style, qualities which marked the French manner of dancing at this time

and remained its distinguishing characteristic during the eighteenth century. The image presented in this engraving is entirely just: stage dress was at this time a heightened form of court dress. In this it reflected the attitudes of the *ballet de cour*, wherein the noble amateur wore his best for even an unimportant role.

11 *Le Ballet de la Délivrance de Renaud*. Wood engraving from the libretto. During the early years of the reign of Louis XIII a series of remarkably extravagant court ballets were staged under the influence of the King's favourite, the Duc de Luynes. Highly dramatic, these lavish enterprises also served a political purpose: the production of *Renaud* was intended to indicate that the King was asserting his authority instead of allowing his mother, Marie de' Medici, to direct affairs of state. The theme of the ballet came from that fruitful source of dramatic ideas, Tasso's *Gerusalemme Liberata*, and was concerned with the freeing of Renaud from the enchantments of the sorceress Armida. In the scene illustrated, Armida has summoned up her demons and they appear first in the form of crayfish, turtles and snails. Throwing off these disguises, they are next seen as old women. This wood engraving from the account of the ballet published at the time of its first performance was meant to suggest to a larger public the theme rather than the actuality of the performance.

10 *Mademoiselle Subligny dancing at the Paris Opéra*

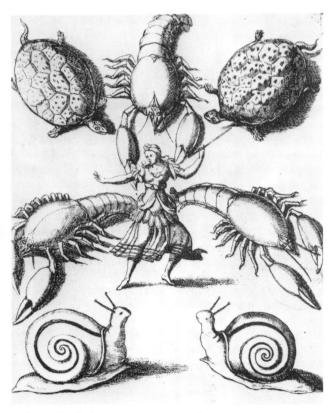

11 *Le Ballet de la Délivrance de Renaud*

Pages 18–19

12 *The Valois tapestries: the reception of the Polish ambassadors.* c. 1580. Among the most remarkable testimonies to the court life and the political ambitions of the House of Valois are the eight tapestries woven in Brussels which feature Catherine de' Medici and her sons who were successively kings of France. Though each tapestry ostensibly relates to a single event, collectively they represent a summation of the use of spectacle for propaganda purposes. In one tapestry we are shown the reception in 1573 of the Polish ambassadors who had come to France to invite Catherine de' Medici's third son, Henri d'Anjou, to rule Poland. The occasion was celebrated by a 'ballet' on August 19 in the Palace of the Tuileries. The panoramic view of court behaviour is here transferred to the open air so that the formal gardens may be admired; the style of court dancing is excellently depicted in the foreground figures who are seen in the general dance that habitually ended a court ballet, while the figure of Catherine is the focal point of the whole design, indicating her political importance.

13 Bernardo Buontalenti, Designs for the costumes of two female dancers. For nearly sixty years Bernardo Buontalenti acted as a designer and master of theatrical crafts for the Medici in Florence. These costumes indicate both the beauty and complexity of design and the freedom which they yet allowed for movement. They were also to be 'read' by the public as illustrating certain moral or physical qualities.

14 Herman van der Most (attrib.), *Ball at the court of Henri III.* The occasion of the marriage in 1581 of the King's favourite Anne, Duc de Joyeuse, to Marguerite of Lorraine, sister of Queen Louise, was celebrated by one of the greatest series of festivities in France in the sixteenth century. These are known as the Joyeuse 'Magnificences' and they lasted for two weeks, during which time a different entertainment was given on each day. The most celebrated of these was the *Ballet Comique de la Reine* (plate 1). The political motivation behind these 'Magnificences' lay in the profound unease in religious matters then affecting France: the question was not of conciliating the Reformed Church as represented by the Huguenots, but of pacifying the ultra-Catholic 'league'. This Counter-Reformation movement centred on the House of Lorraine and besides marrying into that House, King Henri – shown at the extreme left, near dowager Queen Catherine – sought to strengthen his connection by doing great honour to his favourite, the Duc of Joyeuse, who was also allying himself with the House of Lorraine. The Joyeuse 'Magnificences' were thus a studied political action.

12 *The Valois tapestries: The reception of the Polish Ambassadors*

13 Bernardo Buontalenti, Costumes for two dancers.

15 *Il Carnevale Languente.* 1647. Count Filippo d'Aglié was a nobleman turned theatrical producer. He was responsible during a period of three decades for ballet productions at the Court of Savoy. Here, in court theatres and also in princely castles, d'Aglié was master of design, production and machines, and sometimes librettist and musician for court entertainments. These excited great popular acclaim and are a most interesting development of the *ballet de cour* in Italy. Our illustration from the entertainment staged for the Duchess of Savoy, sister of Louis XIII of France, shows Count Giorgio di Mombasilio dancing the part of the melancholic earthy humour.

14 Herman van der Most (attrib.), *Ball at The Court of Henri III*

15 *Il Carnevale Languente*

BALLET INTO
THE THEATRE

A ballet is a picture, or rather a series of pictures connected one with the other by the plot which provides the theme of the ballet; the stage is, as it were, the canvas on which the composer expresses his ideas; the choice of the music, scenery and costumes are his colours; the composer is the painter.

Jean-Georges Noverre

The advent of professional dancers brought the rise of the star performer who triumphed through skill rather than through social position, as had happened in the *ballet de cour*. But social dress remained the basic shape of theatrical costume, and men's clothes allowed for more freedom of movement than did the long and heavily draped skirts of women performers. It was thus inevitable that throughout the century the male dancer was to be the dominant figure technically, and the few main traditions of eighteenth-century theatrical dance are those associated with men. The greatest figure of the early years of the century was Louis Dupré, Le Grand Dupré, the first *danseur noble* to earn that illustrious soubriquet, *Le Dieu de la danse*. His pupil Gaetano Vestris was Italian born but made his name in France and succeeded Dupré as a principal of the Paris Opéra where he was no less celebrated as a master of the *style noble*, considered the highest pinnacle of the art of dancing. Auguste Vestris, his son by his mistress the ballerina Marie Allard, followed him as the foremost male star in Europe, albeit his style was the more brilliant but less grand *demi-caractère*.

With these three dancers we bridge the entire history of dancing, from the opera-ballet to the dawn of the Romantic movement and that moment when the ballerina finally comes into her own. Even so, the female dancer was early to make her mark in the theatre. The first professional female dancers had been seen in 1681, but, like their immediate successors, their dancing was constricted by the conventions of dress which required them to appear in elaborated versions of court clothing. Yet female vanity being what it is, the first notable development in the costume of the *danseuse* came when Marie Camargo shortened her skirts to just above the ankles so that the public might admire her feet twinkling in an *entrechat*. For more serious artistic reasons her contemporary

16 Nicolas Lancret, *Le Moulinet devant la Charmille*. This enchanting picture is a study of dancing as part of a *fête galante*. The *Moulinet* of the title is the figure formed by the four dancers whose hands are crossed. The entire scene speaks of untrammelled pleasure: as in Watteau's *Le Bal*, the dancing figures are a pivot for the charmed world that is so beguilingly presented. The theatre – both the Italian comedy and the legitimate drama – was a fruitful source of inspiration for Watteau and his spiritual heirs, and in the dream-like world of the *fête galante* there seems no clear dividing line between 'amateur' and 'professional' performers.

17 Jean Raoux, *Mademoiselle Prévost as a Bacchante*. Françoise Prévost made her début at the Paris Opéra in 1699 and was soon recognised as the greatest dancer of her time, succeeding Mademoiselle Subligny (plate 10). This portrait by Raoux is not a literal representation of Prévost as a performer. It subscribes to the mythological conventions which had earned Raoux some of his public favour as a portraitist. The dance attitudes suggested in Prévost's pose and that of the group of bacchantes and satyrs are conventionally antique ones. More than anything else the picture celebrates the delicious femininity of its subject and a discreetly stated sexual charm. Something of the moral standing of the female performer is implied in the identification of Prévost as a bacchante.

18 De Vinck (attrib.), *Court Ballet given at Schonbrunn on January 23, 1765*. In celebration of the marriage of the Emperor Joseph II to Marie Josephine Antoinette of Bavaria in 1765, an allegorical ballet was given by the young members of the royal household. The three central figures are identified as the Archduke Ferdinand, the Archduke Maximilien and the Archduchess Marie Antoinette, while the attendant children are members of the Clary and Auersberg families. The painting is an unusual record of a court 'ballet' after the middle of the eighteenth century. In this case it probably amounted to no more than polite amateur theatricals, in which the royal children and their friends could demonstrate their skill in dancing. The line dividing theatrical dance from social dance was still imprecise.

19 Carle van Loo, *Portrait of Marie Sallé*. Marie Sallé was the contemporary of La Camargo and her exact opposite as an artist. This polarity was best expressed by Voltaire in his famous verses:

> *Ah, Camargo, que vous êtes brillante,*
> *Mais que Sallé, grands dieux, est ravissante,*
> *Que vos pas sont légers, et que les siens sont doux.*
> *Elle est inimitable et vous toujours nouvelle.*
> *Les nymphes sautent comme vous*
> *Et les graces dansent comme elle.*

Sallé, a dramatic dancer, was one of the first to seek some greater truth in stage dress than was habitual at this time: when she staged her own *Pygmalion* in London in 1732 her hair fell naturally on her shoulders and 'Grecian' draperies replaced the traditionally opulent outer garment. Like Camargo she sought reform of dress, but for reasons of artistic conscience rather than vanity. This portrait, variously attributed to Carle van Loo and to his nephew Louis Michel van Loo, reveals the serene charm of a clearly intelligent woman – qualities which impressed her contemporaries.

17 Jean Raoux, *Mademoiselle Prévost as a Bacchante*

18 De Vinck (attrib.), *Court Ballet at Schonbrunn*

19 Carle van Loo, *Portrait of Marie Sallé*

20 J. F. Schall, *Marie-Madeleine Guimard*

and rival Marie Sallé made a more radical change in stage dress. Appearing in her own ballet, *Pygmalion*, in London in 1734 she softened formal costume with lighter draperies and dressed her hair in accordance with the antique style in order to suggest some greater realism of character than was usual at this time. This quest for truth was to be a recurring theme of eighteenth-century dance. The attitudes of the opera-ballet had become so rigid that any sort of expressive truth was impossible. Innovators like Sallé, like the Englishman John Weaver, the Austrian Franz Hilferding, his pupil the Italian Gasparo Angiolini and, supremely, the French Jean-Georges Noverre were to strive for the establishment of a freer and more dramatically expressive form by which narrative might be explored in dance. This is the *ballet d'action*, whose theories were to mark the emergence of the choreographer as an important figure in ballet.

The breaking away from the rigid formulae of the opera-ballet can be seen as a reflection of the larger intellectual movement of the Enlightenment in the latter part of the eighteenth century and of the softening of late Baroque grandeur into the charm and delicacy of Rococo. But court attitudes still dominated dance. The male dancer of noble roles was trapped in the ludicrous *tonnelet*, a panniered skirt which might stretch the width of his arms and which had been adapted from the undergarments of medieval knights-at-arms. The female dancer was imprisoned in the ever-widening skirts which reflected the fashion of court dress of the time. The artists' view of dancers was still that of agreeable and highly decorative figures caught in the fantasy landscapes of Watteau, Lancret and Fragonard.

Albeit dance was now officially liberated from the court, its links with court spectacle still remained. The performance in 1745 of *La Princesse de Navarre*, a *comédie-ballet* staged to celebrate the marriage of Louis XV's son to an Infanta of Spain, and immortalised in Cochin's engraving, indicates how magnificent was the theatrical setting for court festivities and how intimate still was the link between the world of the monarchy and its reflection in stage spectacle.

No less flattering to the aspirations of the monarchy were the late Baroque decorations produced by the Bibiena family who, for more than a hundred years, propagated a grandiose style of stage architecture throughout Europe. The soaring, colonnaded complexities that can be seen in the designs by Giuseppe Galli Bibiena presented a magnificent view of palaces which reflected the monarchic ideal of the Habsburgs, whose entertainments he decorated. The collected architectural and perspective designs which Giuseppe Galli dedicated in 1740 to Charles VI, the Holy Roman Emperor, tell a great deal about the princely illusions fostered by the Bibienas. Beautiful, ingenious, they are like superb cages in which the ideas of monarchy were kept.

By the end of the century the theories of Noverre and his colleagues had spread throughout Europe. But at this time the emergence of Neoclassicism as an artistic movement must have seemed inimical to the quest for dramatic truth that lay at the heart of the *ballet d'action*. The ordered calm of Neoclassicism and its reflection of the ideals of the Napoleonic Empire are best seen in the monumental stagings which were given at the Teatro alla Scala in Milan during the early years of the nineteenth century.

The choreographies of Salvatore Viganò, vast heroic mime spectacles, and the designs of Alessandro Sanquirico which so aptly framed them, were based on huge themes like those of *The Titans*, *Joan of Arc* and *Othello*. The true forerunners of Romanticism, however, were Jean Dauberval, the first choreographer of the comic ballet *La Fille mal gardée*, and Charles-Louis Didelot. Didelot's career, spent chiefly in Russia, is a first indication of the quest for aerial flight as an attribute of dancing: in his *Flore et Zéphire*, in which dancers were made to fly on wires, one of the key images of Romanticism is seen for the first time.

The portrayal of dancing by artists at the beginning of the nineteenth century reveals how vast had been the change in costume with the emergence of Neoclassicism and the fashions in dress of Napoleon's Empire. Gone are the huge skirts for women and the decorative exuberance of male costume; instead, an elegant simplicity informs both male and female dress for the stage. Schadow's drawings of Viganò and his wife Maria Medina, Gillray's and Cruickshank's cartoons of Didelot's ballets in London, show how gauzy the ballerina's costumes had now become. The element of lubricity that we sometimes find in Rowlandson is amply evident in the pretty breasts that peep through the dancers' draperies, and the delight in such improbable incidents as members of the bench of bishops inspecting dancers' clothes in the interests of propriety. This alleged immodesty of female dancers' dress caused Captain Gronow, the English diarist, to note on a visit to Milan in 1821 that the dancers at La Scala 'were obliged to wear by order of the [Austrian] police, skyblue pantaloons which reached down to their knees, but were so tight that the outline of the figure was more apparent, and the effect produced more indelicate, than if the usual gauze inexpressibles had been used. What bullies and savages these Austrians are – they even make the dancing girls put on the breeches of their Hungarian infantry.'

21 L. Legoux, *Complimentary ticket for a benefit by Rose Didelot*. 1796. The choreographer Charles-Louis Didelot was one of the most influential figures in the first decades of the nineteenth century. His ballets provided an essential bridge between the eighteenth-century dance and the invasion of the air by the Romantic ballet. Though the crucial years of his career were spent in Russia, he made a series of appearances in London accompanied by his first wife, the radiantly pretty Mademoiselle Rose. For her first benefit performance in London in 1796 a special ticket was engraved. It shows Rose Didelot in the new style of Neoclassic costuming which allowed greater freedom of movement for the female dancer.

22 Gabriel de St Aubin, *Le Bal Paré* (detail)

23 Nicolas Lancret, *Mademoiselle Camargo*

23 Nicolas Lancret, *Mademoiselle Camargo*. Marie-Anne de Cupis de Camargo was born in Brussels and made her début in 1726 at the Paris Opéra where she had been a pupil of Mademoiselle Prévost. A woman of great beauty, charm, vivacity, she was celebrated for the lightness and brilliance of her style as a dancer. Her technical excellence was so considerable that her one time teacher was forced to retire when faced with such competition, and Camargo reigned very prettily in the hearts of her audience. A pride in her technical ability brought about the reform for which she is best remembered: the shortening of floor length skirts to a discreet mid-calf so that her skill in footwork could be seen. Lancret's portrait places her in a Watteauesque setting and offers a convincing record of the dance style of the period and of the costuming.

24 Antoine Pesne, *Portrait of Barbara Campanini*. La Barberina, as she was known, was an Italian dancer of brilliant technique and no less brilliant liaisons. Her lovers ranged from Frederick the Great, for whom she danced in Berlin, to Lord Stuart

24 Antoine Pesne, *Portrait of Barbara Campanini*

25 Thomas Gainsborough, *Giovanna Baccelli*

Mackenzie, with whom she eloped to Venice. It was while she was in Berlin that her undoubted beauty was captured by Pesne, at that time chief painter to Frederick the Great and director of the Berlin Academy. He presents her against a garden setting in the elaborate and ravishing costume of a bacchante, an identification due more to the leopardskin overskirt than to anything else.

25 Thomas Gainsborough, *Giovanna Baccelli*. Giovanna Zanerini, who was born in Venice and made her London début in 1774, was known under her stage name as La Baccelli. Acknowledged as a brilliant dancer as well as a creature of great charm and allure, she is remembered today chiefly through this magnificent portrait by Gainsborough, and through the enchanting marble by Locatelli which shows her reclining nude on a couch. This statue is found at Knole and her connection with that great house comes from her lengthy association with the Duke of Dorset. When the Duke was posted to Paris as British Ambassador, La Baccelli accompanied him and she celebrated his acquisition of the Order of the

Garter in 1788 by appearing on stage with its ribbon as a bandeau round her head. Gainsborough's portrait offers little testimony to her dance ability beyond the delicacy of her pose, but it says everything about her style and the elegance of her appearance for which she was justly celebrated.

26 Louis René Boquet, Costume design

27 P. Lior (attrib.), Costume design

28 Bernardo Bellotto, *Le Turc généreux*

26 Louis René Boquet, Costume design. c. 1750. The exaggerated span of this skirt suggests how formalised had become the dress of the female performer by the mid-eighteenth century. We can assume that Boquet made this design for some royal figure in an opera-ballet of the period and it indicates the fantastication of which Rococo design was capable. The vast panniered skirts of the female performer were matched by the *tonnelet* of the male dancer – small wonder that Noverre was to inveigh against the improbability of dancers' apparel when he sought some kind of dramatic reality in ballet. Boquet's design is typical of the unthinking development of stage costume to a point where it leaves any sort of truth behind.

27 P. Lior (attrib.), Design for a male dancer. c. 1750. Lior, who provided designs for the opera-ballets of the mid-eighteenth century, has here pinpointed much of the improbability in the appearance of the male performer. The *tonnelet*, a wired skirt which harked back to the under-garments of knights at arms, was built out on a frame and at its most extreme could extend to arm's

width. Its effect in performance, as Noverre pointed out, was to bounce up and down and to distort the movement of the body. This seemed to matter little to an audience who accepted this codified appearance of singers and dancers. The adaptation of Roman armour atop the *tonnelet* only increases the unlikeliness of this attire.

28 Bernardo Bellotto, *Le Turc généreux*. Engraving. Bernardo Bellotto, nephew and pupil of Canaletto, lived in Italy and Prussia before going to Poland, where he settled in Warsaw and worked for the King until his death. *Le Turc généreux* was a scene from *Les Indes galantes*, one of the grandest of Jean-Phillipe Rameau's opera-ballets. It was first given in Paris in 1735 and was revived in Vienna in 1758 with choreography by Franz Hilferding. Staged in honour of the Turkish envoys' visit to that city, it remained in the repertory at the Theater am Kartnertor and so impressed Bellotto when he saw it on his arrival in Vienna in 1759 that he made a rapid sketch of its central action in his notebook. This was incorporated in his finished engraving, a highly skilled representation of theatrical dance.

29 Gian Domenico Tiepolo, *The Minuet*

30 Carolina Lose after Alessandro Sanquirico, *Interior of a Greenhouse*

31 Jean-Louis Desprez, Setting for *Christine*

29 Gian Domenico Tiepolo, *The Minuet*. Oil. Son of the more celebrated Giovanni Battista, G. D. Tiepolo responded with great affection to the popular theatre and popular entertainments of his time in Venice. In the lovely *Minuet*, now in the Louvre, he presents a whirlpool of activity – of maskers, musicians and observers – round the ravishing central figure of the beautiful girl who gazes so serenely out from the background of grotesques. The sense of movement and the excitement of the scene are most stylishly caught. Tiepolo *fils* is here inspired by one of his father's paintings, dated 1756, now in the Catalonian Museum in Barcelona, in which a very similar Venetian carnival scene is depicted.

30 Carolina Lose after Alessandro Sanquirico, *Interior of a Greenhouse*. Etching and aquatint, 1827. Greatest master of stage design of the Neoclassic period was Alessandro Sanquirico, whose decorations for the operas and ballets staged at the Teatro alla Scala, Milan, in the first decades of the nineteenth century offer brave evidence of the theatre of the time. Completely in harmony with the grandiose aspirations of Neoclassicism, Sanquirico produced decors that can still amaze and delight the eye. This scene from Luigi Henry's ballet *Elerz and Zulmida* of 1826 shows a mime scene set in a gigantic conservatory. The figures of the performers are dwarfed not only by the architectural splendour of the building but also by the exuberance of the plants on the right hand side, which effectively balance the composition of the picture.

31 Jean-Louis Desprez, Setting for *Christine*. The French artist Jean-Louis Desprez went to Stockholm as designer for the court theatre under Gustave III and his watercolour of *Christine*, a comedy with songs and dance, shows the production as it was seen at the Gripsholm Palace Theatre in 1784. Far more than a simple design drawing, the watercolour is valuable testimony to the qualities of court entertainment at the end of the eighteenth century.

32 Gabriel de St Aubin, *Momus*

33 F. Basan after Gabriel de St Aubin, *La Guinguette*

32 Gabriel de St Aubin, *Momus*. Chalk drawing. De St Aubin here presents us with one of the most credible representations of a dancer in the full splendour of feathers and *tonnelet,* which were characteristic of the male dancer's garb in the middle of the eighteenth century. Momus serves to introduce, as his scroll announces, a collection of drawings of the fancy dress worn at a ball at Saint Cloud in 1752.

33 F. Basan after Gabriel de St Aubin, *La Guinguette*. Engraving. De St Aubin was one of the most compelling and lively analysts of Parisian life. The engraving of *La Guinguette* by Basan preserves a scene from a burlesque work with choreography by Jean François de Hesse, which was performed at the Théâtre Italien, in 1750. The Guinguette, a tavern scene, had long been the subject for dance – John Weaver's *Tavern Bilkers* of 1708 is an early fore-runner. De Hesse plainly made this scene more polite than earlier, ruder versions, and de St Aubin has also polished the appearance of the performers so that they seem relations of court play-actors who impersonated shepherds and shepherdesses.

34 Guiseppe Galli Bibiena,
Theatrical setting. The Bibiena
family were a dynasty of designers
whose four generations influenced
the appearance of the stage for a
hundred years from the end of the
seventeenth century. The grandeur
and tremendous power of high
Baroque decoration can be
particularly appreciated in the work
of Giuseppe, whose designs for
theatrical performances, for
monuments, and for every kind of
court display, seem to capture the
very spirit of the House of
Habsburg. His setting for the
entertainment staged on the
occasion of the marriage of the
Prince of Poland, Prince Elector of
Saxony, reflects exactly the
grandiose aspirations of his royal
masters. The setting became a
mirror in which the palace itself
acquired a heightened reality.
Against colonnades of false
perspective, the royal audience
could watch their own magnificence
being honoured. Bibiena created a
world of illusion which in turn
fostered the illusions of his princely
employers. This design comes from
a book of architectural and
perspective designs dedicated in
1740 to Charles VI, the Holy
Roman Emperor.

34 Guiseppe Galli Bibiena, Theatrical setting

35 After Carmontelle (Louis Carrogis), *Pas de deux from 'Sylvie'*

35 After Carmontelle (Louis Carrogis), *Pas de deux from 'Sylvie'*. Engraving. Carmontelle was both an author and a painter. His enthusiasm for the world in which he lived and his ability to move from the court to the fairground resulted, as Marian Hannah Winter notes in her invaluable *Pre-Romantic Ballet* (London, 1974), in 'a series of gouaches and watercolour sketches which are a unique record of the *ancien régime*'. This engraving of a watercolour sketch shows Jean Dauberval and Marie Allard in the pantomimic duet of the Scythians from the opera-ballet *Sylvie* first produced at the Paris Opéra in 1766, with choreography by Dauberval. Carmontelle records a scene in which the two characters were reportedly declaring their mutual affection. The stylisation of gesture as well as the improbability of costuming reveal how formal and stultified the conventions of theatrical performance had become. Plumes and trailing ivy leaves, leopard skins and elaborate hair styles, still reflect the complexity of performing dress. Each age per-petuates certain conventions about historical appearance. These supposedly antique figures are no more improbable, in fact, than some nineteenth-century versions of the classical world or, indeed, those of our own time in ballet or in the cinema.

36 Charles Nicolas Cochin, *La Princesse de Navarre*. Engraving. The marriage in February 1745 of the Dauphin, son of Louis XV, to the Infanta Marie Thérèse of Spain occasioned a magnificent spectacle. This was *La Princesse de Navarre*, a combination of drama, opera and dance, with a text by Voltaire and music by Rameau. The work was staged in the Riding School of the Grandes Écuries at Versailles and Cochin's engraving is a brilliant record of the final moments of the performance. Splendour is all: the worlds of court and theatre hardly seem separated by the proscenium arch, and the stage spectacle is like a looking glass in which the court may see a flattering reflection of itself.

36 Charles Nicolas Cochin, *La Princesse de Navarre*

37 Francesco Bartolozzi after Nathaniel Dance, *Jason and Medea*

38 Francesco Bartolozzi and Benedetto Pastorini after
Nathaniel Dance, *Auguste Vestris*

37 Francesco Bartolozzi after Nathaniel Dance, *Jason and Medea*. Etching and aquatint. The presence in London of Gaetano Vestris and Auguste Vestris, his son by Marie Allard, during the season of 1781 was sufficiently important to produce a considerable series of satirical drawings of them. Their dominant position in European dance could not be more clearly illustrated: both were insufferably vain, but their vanity was excused by their supremacy as performers. In the winter of 1780 father and son appeared at the King's Theatre in the Haymarket. Horace Walpole noted: '. . . It is the universal voice that he (Vestris *père*) is the only perfect being that has dropped from the clouds within the memory of man or woman.' The presence of these two extraordinary dancers (and the public's delight in satiric records of events) occasioned a sequence of broadsheets that testify to their extreme popular impact. Gilray, Sandby and Dance all produced drawings which poke fun at the pair. The illustration opposite is a slightly mocking view of Gaetano as he appeared in Noverre's *Jason and Medea* in June 1781.

38 Francesco Bartolozzi and Benedetto Pastorini after Nathaniel Dance, *Auguste Vestris*. Etching and engraving. Unlike his father, who was a *danseur noble*, Auguste Vestris, with his greater virtuosity, was a *danseur de demi-caractère*. Two engravings show Auguste in this pose: the first, a front view, finds him holding only his hat; the second, illustrated here, is a back view in which the dancer also clutches a bag labelled 'English guineas', while his hat is full of bank notes. The engraving is captioned *Oh qui goose-toe*. The reference to the goose comes from Plutarch's apothegm: a stranger at Sparta standing long on one leg, said to a Lacedaemonian, 'I do not believe you can do as much.' 'True', said he, 'but every goose can.'

A rhyme underneath reads:
He danc'd like a Monkey, his pockets well cramm'd:
Caper'd off with a Grin; 'Kiss my A . . . & be D . . .'

Despite its intentions as caricature, Dance's drawing is a fine evocation of the agility and technical exuberance that made Auguste the darling of his age and was also to make him one of the most influential teachers in the history of ballet. His life spans the last great years of eighteenth-century dance and the Romantic movement. His final appearance on stage was in a minuet with Marie Taglioni in 1834: the ages of Louis XVI and Louis Philippe were united.

39 Marie-Madeleine Guimard visiting the sick

39 *Marie-Madeleine Guimard visiting the sick*. Engraving. Marie-Madeleine Guimard was one of the most remarkable dancers of her time. Her professional career brought her early stardom at the age of twenty as a principal dancer at the Paris Opéra, despite a thinness which had earned her the nickname *La Squelette des Grâces*. Privately she was notorious for the succession of rich lovers who kept her in the most splendid luxury, which allowed her to play Lady Bountiful. This print is unusual in that it commemorates a totally untheatrical side of a dancer's life: Guimard's acts of charity were many.

40 James Gillray, *Operational Reform*

41 French paper doll

42 Thomas Rowlandson, *The Prospect Before Us*

40 James Gillray, *Operational Reform*. Engraving, 1798. Gillray's cartoon refers to the scandal when the Bench of Bishops were involved in deciding whether the French dancers at the King's Theatre in London were decently clothed.

41 French paper doll. c. 1750. The *Pantin* – a cut-out paper doll – took its name from a village near Paris in which these toys were first made. Originally intended for children, the *pantin* became a plaything for adults and soon achieved a vogue among the aristocracy in Paris, who were amused to cut out these figures printed on heavy paper or card and then transform them into dancing homuncules by means of thread. The fashion for them became so extreme that even François Boucher was called upon to decorate one, and they were sometimes shown dressed in imitation of the clothing of their owners. Eventually they developed into the more celebrated cut-out toys of the *Imagerie d'Épinal*. The doll reproduced is unusual in that it is made in the image of a *danseur noble* of the mid-eighteenth century – probably a *berger galant* – decked in *tonnelet* and feathered head-dress.

42 Thomas Rowlandson, *The Prospect Before Us*. Coloured etching. Thomas Rowlandson is one of the best guides to the social scene at the turn of the

nineteenth century. No aspect of contemporary life escaped his sharp eye and his even sharper pencil. A master draughtsman, he was also a master of observation. In *The Prospect Before Us* he shows Didelot dancing with Madame Théodore in *Amphion and Thalia* at the Pantheon. The satirical point of this print was the fact that two theatres, the Pantheon and the Haymarket, both claimed royal patronage and the coveted title of 'King's' Theatre. The rivalry between their respective managers, Mr Taylor and Mr O'Reilly, excited a good deal of public amusement. (This competition was to provide even more amusement when used by Ninette de Valois as the subject for her comedy ballet, *The Prospect Before Us*, in 1940.) Rowlandson's view of the scene is characteristically lively, and crammed with grotesque detail. In the royal box, just above Mme Théodore's head, George III, the theatre's patron, is using a spyglass, while his consort Queen Charlotte sits at his side.

43, 44 Gottfried Schadow, Salvatore Viganò and his wife Maria Medina

43, 44 Gottfried Schadow, Salvatore Viganò and his wife Maria Medina. Drawings, c. 1793. Salvatore Viganò is acknowledged as one of the great masters of Italian ballet: his staging of massive mimetic spectacles at the Teatro alla Scala, Milan, established a vogue for such entertainments, which were enhanced by the decoration of Sanquirico (plate 30). His early career was spent touring Europe and he first achieved fame as a dancer with his wife, Maria Medina, in their pantomimic duets which they performed in Vienna. In Schadow's drawings we sense a new elegance of costuming and a new freedom of movement. Neoclassicism has brought gauzy draperies and laced sandals for Maria Medina, and an admirable simplicity to Viganò's dress.

45 Johann Heinrich Füssli (Fuseli), *Two dancers*. Pencil and black chalk, c. 1814. Fuseli, who was Swiss-born but made his career in England, is one of the most interesting forerunners of Romanticism. In his paintings many of the night-mare and irrational aspects of Romanticism are to be seen, but he was also an outstanding illustrator of works of literature, being inspired by Shakespeare, Milton, the Bible and Dante. And it is from Dante that he took the idea of the two figures shown in this pencil and black chalk drawing. It is noteworthy for an observer today in the modernity of its pose and in its suggestion of very advanced *pas de deux* work. The position is not one lightly taken even now and the drawing represents an imaginative rather than an actual view of a performance. It is prophetic, and like the many dance poses that can be seen in the drawings of Fuseli's contemporary, William Blake, it shows beautiful movement 'frozen' at its most essential moment.

45 Johann Heinrich Fuseli, *Two dancers*

THE ROMANTIC MOVEMENT

The week I arrived in Petersburg was the last of the season at the Grand Opera; I had the pleasure of enjoying some toe-pointed stanzas of the poetry of motion as rendered by the agile limbs of the renowned Russian dancer, Mlle Bagdanov. The Russians are deliriously proud of this favoured child of Terpsichore . . . Last spring she was more the rage than ever. Her portrait, lithographed, was in all the printsellers' windows.

George Augustus Sala *A Journey due North*

Romanticism came late to ballet. The Romantic movement had its roots in the eighteenth century; in music, literature and painting its fine fervours can be traced to the last years of Napoleon's reign as master of Europe. The writings and compositions of E. T. A. Hoffman, the paintings of Géricault, the *Fantastic Symphony* of Berlioz, the *Meditations* of Lamartine and the piano music of Chopin had all established the ideals of Romanticism long before Marie Taglioni, the presiding divinity of the Romantic ballet, appeared on stage. The battle call of Romanticism in the theatre came with the celebrated first night of Victor Hugo's *Hernani* in 1830. In the following year the ballet scene in Meyerbeer's opera *Robert the Devil* showed the spectral figures of white-clad nuns, led by Taglioni, dancing in the moonlight in a ruined cloister. Here were the ingredients for the Romantic ballet: the female form swathed in gauze; mystery and the supernatural. Adolphe Nourrit, the leading tenor in the opera, had the wit to see that Taglioni seemed the very incarnation of the Romantic female. He suggested to Taglioni's choreographer father an idea for a ballet which took practical form in the following year with the first performance of *La Sylphide* at the Paris Opéra. For the next twenty years, during the heyday of the Romantic dance, the ballerina was to reign supreme. Such divinities as Taglioni, Carlotta Grisi, Fanny Elssler, Fanny Cerrito and Lucile Grahn dominated the stages of Europe, and imposed an image upon dancing which has yet to be totally dispelled. The pictorial records of the ballet of this period give a marvellously precise idea of the impact which the ballerina had upon the public. Gone was the dominance of the male dancer in the eighteenth century. The new, often bourgeois

46 John Brandard, *Lucile Grahn in 'Catarina'*. Lithograph, 1846. *Catarina or The Bandit's Daughter* was one of the several important full-length ballets staged in London by Jules Perrot at Her Majesty's Theatre. It was inspired by an incident in the life of the painter Salvatore Rosa, and its most famous dance was the *Pas Stratégique* in which the heroine, as Ivor Guest vividly describes in his *Romantic Ballet in England* (London, 1954), 'instructs her brigands in musket drill and military evolutions, which ended with the *corps de ballet* climbing up the rocks, then rushing down fiercely towards the audience, pointing their muskets at the unfortunate Monsieur Nadaud, who was conducting the orchestra'. Brandard was one of several artists producing very appealing records of the Romantic ballet.

47 *Marie Taglioni in 'La Sylphide'*

audience sought a theatre of heightened emotion and escapism, and this the Romantic ballet gave them, and this the artists of the period in turn depicted. The etherealisation of the female was reflected in the gradual emergence of *pointe* work – dancing on the very tips of the toes – which was intended to show the Romantic ballerina maintaining minimum contact with the ground. The popularity of ballet is reflected in the massive output of lithographs and prints which celebrate the imponderable charms of these goddesses of the age. Floating through the air, poised weightless upon a flower, caught in a variety of enchanting attitudes as supposed gypsies or Lithuanians or Spanish beauties, as ondines and naiads and wilis, the Romantic dancer is a creature of entrancing grace and prettiness, and complete improbability. Her dress is formalised in its reliance upon a bell-shaped skirt and light slippers upon her ideally narrow feet; the addition of a pair of wings, a saucy hat or a coronet of flowers, a beribboned bodice or pearl bracelets, are token suggestions of national or magical identity. But essentially and inescapably she is the ballerina, the adorable female, doe-eyed and deliciously rounded of forearm. As partner, or set discreetly in the background, the male dancer had been put in his place – a place he did not leave for nearly a hundred years, when Vaslav Nijinsky and Adolf Bolm announced, during the *Saison Russe* of 1909, that the *danseur* had a positive identity in ballet once again.

In an age when most women were trapped in the home as wives and mothers, the 'liberated' figure of the ballerina reflects both her unusual physical freedom and also the fact of her dubious social position. It was a commonplace that dancers were not 'respectable', yet nevertheless their popularity was intense. Their image was to be found in prints, in porcelain; the name of the Sylphide advertised parasols; stage coaches were called after dancers; the ballerinas were fêted wherever they went. Even Queen Victoria doted upon the ballet, and at her behest two of the most celebrated ballerinas were brought together in the delicate rivalry of a *pas de deux*.

From its initial burst of activity in Paris the ideals of the Romantic ballet spread swiftly throughout Europe and to the United States, thanks to the peregrinations of ballerinas and choreographers. In London during the 1840s the presence of Jules Perrot, greatest choreographer of the period, brought a golden age of ballet which was not to return for another hundred years. Taglioni's visits to Russia were generally accredited with having revived a flagging public interest in the ballet, and when Jules Perrot worked at the Bolshoy Theatre in St Petersburg for a decade in the 1850s he initiated the greatest era of the Imperial Ballet. Fanny Elssler excited vast admiration wherever she travelled: in Washington, Congress adjourned its sessions early so that its members might attend her performances. In Moscow her final appearance earned her more than three hundred bouquets and the attentions of the secret police into the verses celebrating her talents.

The prints and lithographs of the Romantic ballet that emerged during the heyday of the 1830s and 1840s represent, inevitably, something of what we may call Victorian taste. Certainly some of the finest examples – the work of Chalon and Brandard – proclaim those virtues of poetical grace and airy delicacy which we can also find in the music of that darling of the early Victorians, Felix Mendelssohn-Bartholdy. With their remarkable technical finesse, their clear, light colours and apposite pinpointing of a pose or a movement, these lithographs are works of art of unquestioned merit. Brandard and Chalon were both adept at catching what we assume to be a very good 'likeness' of the dancer; other artists – Bouvier, for example – tend rather more to generalisation, in an art form which at worst we must reproach with generalising about the identity of the ballerina as a symbol of femininity. But the delicious freedom of some of the poses, the happy way in which movement has often been captured, mark these lithographs as convincing testimony to the gifts of the performers they hymn. At their very finest, in Chalon's series of portraits of Marie Taglioni, we do indeed know something about 'Marie pleine de grace', about her gentleness and sweetness of expression, about her phenomenal lightness and the lovely fragility of her style. Like Baron de Meyer's superb sequence of photographs of Nijinsky taken in London during 1911, we sense the reality of movement, and the force of a temperament uniquely great which still haunts dancers and audiences today.

In Italy, as in France, Romanticism lost its impetus by the mid-century. Curiously, in the backwater of Denmark the presence of a great choreographer and dancer, August Bournonville, ensured a continuity of interest through his considerable output of ballets and the great system of training – inherited from his teacher Auguste Vestris – that he established in the Royal Theatre in Copenhagen.

In Russia the entire development of choreography during the nineteenth century was due to a series of French ballet masters. Didelot had created major works in the early years of the century; Jules Perrot and Arthur Saint-Léon enriched the repertory in subsequent years; in 1869 Marius Petipa became chief ballet master and ruled with absolute power until 1903. Petipa had arrived in Russia as a dancer in 1847; thereafter his career was placed entirely at the service of the Imperial Ballet and it is to him that we must ascribe the supremacy of the Russian Ballet in the last years of the nineteenth century.

The waning of interest in ballet as an art form in much of western Europe, which came with the fading of the Romantic movement, is reflected in the absence of any really significant pictorial material. It was only with the emergence of Impressionism and the desire to depict what the eye actually sees that we find artists, fascinated in recording the complexities of movement, renewing an interest in dance and the dancer. It is ironic that what Degas was to record was ballet in decline.

48 Constantin Guys, *Dans les Coulisses*. Pen and wash. Guys was one of the most perceptive analysts of nineteenth-century life. Baudelaire, in his study, *The Painter of Modern Life*, said of him: 'His interest is the whole world; he wants to know, understand and appreciate everything that happens on the surface of our globe . . . The crowd is his element, as the air is that of birds and water of fishes. His passion and his profession are to become one flesh with the crowd.' Guys captured both the pageantry and squalor of Parisian life during the period of the Second Empire, and inevitably the women of that world – both the whores and the grand ladies in their crinolines – are immortalised in his work.

49 Jules Collignon, *Giselle*

49 Jules Collignon, *The Second Act of 'Giselle'*.
Steel engraving, 1844. *Giselle* is the apogee of
Romanticism. In its second act the midnight forest,
the mysterious Wilis and the floating figure of the
lost beloved epitomise the Romantic ideal. This
engraving, though not literal, conveys exactly the
spirit of the work. *Les Beautés de l'Opéra*, from which
this illustration comes, was a souvenir book
produced in Paris which contained illustrated essays
on nine of the most famous operas and ballets of the
Romantic period. The great popularity of these same
works in London occasioned an English edition
which was dedicated 'with the profoundest respect'
to Queen Victoria. Her Majesty's affection for the
ballet dated from her childhood and in 1843, when
asked what items it would please her to see on a
State visit to the theatre, she requested a *pas de deux*
which would feature two of London's darlings,
Fanny Elssler and Fanny Cerrito. This sparked off
the succession of ballerina displays which took place
later in the decade, when Taglioni, Grisi, Cerrito,
Grahn and Rosati were all variously deployed in
those *divertissements* by Jules Perrot that were
described by the rival choreographer Saint Léon as
'steeple-chases'.

50 Eichens after Paul Bürde, *Marie-Paul Taglioni*. Lithograph. Marie-Paul Taglioni was the daughter of Paul Taglioni and niece of the greater Marie whose name she bears. Her father presented her in London in several ballets, among which *Thea or the Flower Fairy* (1847) was the most successful. Eichens' lithograph of Bürde's painting accepts the Romantic convention of showing the dancer barefoot. Marie-Paul Taglioni's role as the flower fairy is charmingly suggested in her costuming and in the slightly sentimentalised setting among bedewed roses. Yet the innocence of the presentation avoids any suggestion of kitsch. In an unsophisticated age both artist and public were prepared to believe in this identification of a dancer with her role. It is nice to record that Marie-Paul Taglioni married extremely well, becoming the wife of the immensely noble Prince Joseph Windisch-Grätz.

51 Angelo Inganni, Portrait captioned 'La danzatrice Maria Taglioni'. This mysterious portrait of a dancer in her dressing room is improbably identified as Marie Taglioni. In a discussion of the painting in *Dance and Dancers* in May 1963, the late Cyril Beaumont made out a very good case for its being Marie-Paul Taglioni. It is an unexpectedly frank portrayal of a dancer, more an excuse for a study of a beautiful nude than a record of a performer. The dancer, preparing for a performance, has been cast as Venus in what must have seemed an updated version of the Toilet of Venus. The duenna and the attendant dresser all contribute to the erotic quality of the painting.

50 Eichens after Paul Bürde, *Marie-Paul Taglioni*

51 Angelo Inganni, *La danzatrice Maria Taglioni*

52 *The Wags of Wapping*

52 *The Wags of Wapping*. Engraving, 1846. *The Illustrated London News* published this record of the ballet staged at the Theatre Royal, Drury Lane, London in the mid century. The ballerina is Sophia Fucco, who was nicknamed *La Pointue* because of the strength of her *pointe* work.

53 Achille Devéria, *La Gipsy*, Act II. Lithograph. First staged at the Paris Opéra in January 1839, the immensely successful *La Gipsy*, a ballet by Joseph Mazilier, was conceived as a vehicle for Fanny Elssler. Elssler was Marie Taglioni's only real rival, offering the other side of the Romantic coin, dramatic vivacity and a lustrous physical presence: Gautier spoke of Taglioni as a 'Christian' and of Elssler as a 'Pagan' dancer. *La Gipsy* was no more silly in its plot than many another work of the period. It involved gypsies, a stolen baby, the market place in Edinburgh and one of the most intriguing characters in all ballet, Narcisse de Crakentorp – 'Lord Campbell's nephew and a conceited fool'. Devéria's lithograph is of a later cast – Adèle Dumilâtre and Eugène Coralli – and it conveys something of the dramatic vitality and

energy which marked this ballet. It is a compelling record of stage action and without the marmorial daintiness of some Romantic iconography.

54 *Fanny Cerrito in 'Ondine'*. Steel engraving from the *Illustrated London News*, 1843. Baudelaire records that Guys provided drawings which were engraved for the *Illustrated London News*, a journal which regularly depicted the theatrical events of the time. It remains a treasure house for the historian concerned with ballet. The conventions of its ballet drawings during the Romantic period were fantasticated – the ballerinas had feet which were shaped to perfect and delicate points – but nevertheless the atmosphere of the performance was captured. In 1843 Fanny Cerrito, the darling of London, appeared in *Ondine*, a ballet by Jules Perrot. Its *pas de l'ombre*, in which the water sprite danced with her own shadow, was an instant sensation and became a favourite subject for artists of the period.

53 Achille Devéria, *La Gipsy*

54 *Fanny Cerrito in 'Ondine'*

55 Marie-Alexandre Alophe, *Carlotta Grisi and Lucien Petipa in 'La Péri'*

55 Marie-Alexandre Alophe, *Carlotta Grisi and Lucien Petipa in 'La Péri'*. Lithograph. *La Péri* was first staged at the Paris Opéra in 1843 and its most exciting moment was that in which Grisi had to leap from a six foot platform into the arms of Petipa. The public became obsessed with this feat of derring-do and Ivor Guest in his *Romantic Ballet in Paris* (London, 1966) records that on one occasion when the leap failed to come off the audience obliged Grisi to repeat it three times before they would applaud her. In London, on the other hand, the public begged her not to repeat it when it had misfired. Guest also notes that one gentleman was so convinced that the leap would prove fatal that he would not miss a single performance at the Opéra so that he might be present at her death. Alophe's lithograph captures the moment of this leap which became an understandably popular subject for print-makers.

56 J. Arnout, *The Interior of the Paris Opéra*. Lithograph, c. 1860. A series of handsome coloured lithographs of Paris buildings at the time of the Second Empire by the Arnout family are impressive records of the life in that gilded age. This interior of the Paris Opéra shows the ballet of the nuns from the fourth act of Meyerbeer's opera *Robert le Diable* which had remained in the repertory since 1831. It is worth noting that the stalls were exclusively given over to the gentlemen, while the fashionable ladies disposed themselves in the loges.

57 *Fanny Elssler*. Popular print, c. 1850. Fanny Elssler's triumphs throughout her career were as prodigious as those of any Romantic star. The illustration is a German popular print which satirises that ideal tribute to an artist when the horses are unhitched from her coach and she is drawn in triumph through the streets by an army of admirers.

56 J. Arnout, *The Interior of the Paris Opéra*

57 *Fanny Elssler*

58 J. Bouvier, *Adèle Dumilâtre and Henri Desplaces in 'Le Corsaire'*

59 Edward Morton after S. M. Joy, *Lucile Grahn in 'Eoline, ou la Dryade'*

58 J. Bouvier, *Adèle Dumilâtre and Henri Desplaces in 'Le Corsaire'*. Lithograph, 1844. *The Corsair* was adapted from Byron's poem by several choreographers for the ballet stage. Bouvier's lithograph is of especial interest in that it shows two dancers in correct academic positions and it illuminates the partnering of the period – the pose is unusual for its time. Bouvier has caught the dancers with almost photographic precision in a difficult lift. The absence of any kind of effort and a certain naïveté of style suggest yet again the supposedly imponderable nature of the ballerina.

59 Edward Morton after S. M. Joy, *Lucile Grahn in 'Eoline, ou la Dryade'*. Lithograph, 1845. Another of the divinities of the Romantic Ballet was Lucile Grahn. Danish-born, Grahn was a pupil of August Bournonville and it was for her that he staged his version of *La Sylphide* in Copenhagen in 1836. *Eoline* was one of the ballets in which she endeared herself to the London audience – it was staged at Her Majesty's Theatre in 1845 – and it tells of a wood sprite who falls in love with a mortal and dies on her wedding day. The lithograph presents an entirely typical view of a Romantic ballerina: it is not 'true' to Grahn save in its approximation of her features, but it is true to the image which her dancing was supposed to arouse in the public mind and true to

the qualities of the character she interpreted. Lithographs such as these abounded, serving as reminders of a theatrical experience. In her later years Grahn lived in Germany where she choreographed the dance scenes in some of Wagner's operas – and the master approved of her work.

60 John Brandard, Carlotta Grisi in *La Péri*. Lithograph. The Italian-born ballerina, Carlotta Grisi, was the pupil and mistress of Jules Perrot and the favourite dancer of the poet Théophile Gautier. He wrote for her the libretto of *Giselle* in which she created the title role.

60 John Brandard, *Carlotta Grisi in 'La Péri'*

61 Eugène Lami, *Au foyer de l'Opéra*

61 Eugène Lami, *Au foyer de l'Opéra*. 1841. Lami's view of the green room of the Paris Opéra is an imaginary gathering which provides a souvenir of the Romantic movement at its height. Bringing together some of the dancers and the habitués of the *foyer de la danse*, as well as the administrators, it pinpoints more accurately than strict representation the atmosphere of what must have seemed in later years a golden age. Among the personalities involved are Alfred de Musset, Dr Véron, formerly director of the Opera, Fanny Elssler and Adèle Dumilâtre.

62 Marie-Alexandre Alophe, *Carolina Rosati in 'Le Corsaire'*. Lithograph, c. 1856. With the decline of the Romantic movement in the middle of the nineteenth century, ballet performances in Western Europe stood a poor second to opera. An important series of lithographs of the ballerinas at the Paris Opéra appeared in the 1850s, but they were expressly offered as portrayals of the costumes of the principal ballets of the time and were sold by the fashion magazine *Les Modes Parisiennes*. In this opulent period of the Second Empire, the ballerina was acquiring public status as an obvious clothes horse.

63 Richard Buckner, *Adeline Plunkett*. Oil, 1844. The Belgian dancer Adeline Plunkett was a visitor to London in the 1840s and 1850s where her dancing, her temperament and her beauty were equally newsworthy.

62 Marie-Alexandre Alophe, *Carolina Rosati in 'Le Corsaire'*

63 Richard Buckner, *Adeline Plunkett*

64 Borrell after Charlemagne, *The Naiad and the Fisherman*

65 Paul Gavarni, *In The Wings*

66 Regnier after Belin, *L'Opéra*

64 Borrell after Charlemagne, *The Naiad and the Fisherman*. Lithograph. This Russian lithograph provides a charming record of an incident of royal patronage. On June 16, 1851, the artists of the Imperial Ballet were commissioned to appear in the gardens of the Peterhof outside St Petersburg. A small stage had been built over the surface of the lake in the palace's grounds and Jules Perrot, then a ballet master in St Petersburg, revived part of his *Ondine* for this open air performance in honour of the birthday of the Grand Duchess Olga. Carlotta Grisi, who had been discovered in Naples as a young dancer by Perrot and whose career had been launched by him, was a guest artist with the Imperial Ballet and she appeared in the role of the Ondine, with Perrot himself as the fisherman who loves her. The natural charm of the setting gave a very special attraction to the performance, and the *corps de ballet* of naiads were brought across the lake in little boats shaped like shells.

65 Paul Gavarni, *In the Wings*. Lithograph. Gavarni's record of the world of the Second Empire is frank and unembarrassed in presenting the moral climate of its time. His revellers at public balls, his artists and models and grisettes, are the stuff of *La Vie de Bohème*. The interview that he captures in the wings of a popular theatre is entirely unromantic. The ballet girl's gauzy skirt reveals everything of her limbs, and we may assume that the gentleman's interest is not only in her dancing. 'Twas ever thus.

66 Regnier after Belin, *L'Opéra*. Lithograph, c. 1850. This is one of a pair of lithographs produced in the 1850s and published both in Paris and New York, which offer scenes from an unidentified Spanish ballet. The purpose of the lithograph is to capitalise on a good deal of Spanish posing by very attractive girls. The deliciously rounded arms and bosoms and calves, the prettiness of the costuming, are far more the subject of the artist's attention than the dance itself. Ballet is now being offered to a wider public as a sanctification of voyeurism.

67 Alfred Edward Chalon, *At the Opera*

68 Bettanier frères after Teichel, *A Roomful of Rats*

67 Alfred Edward Chalon, *At the Opera*. Engraving, 1839. A less enchanted view of the Romantic goddesses than that presented in the lithographs of the period comes from a literary curiosity of the time. The relationship between Lady Blessington and the dandyish Count d'Orsay was somewhat frayed by d'Orsay's predilection for actresses and ballerinas. Lady Blessington took some slight revenge in her lengthy ode *The Belle of the Season*:

Brisk music gayer scenes announces,
And in a half dressed danseuse bounces,
With arms that wreathe, and eyes that swim,
And drapery that scarce shades each limb . . .
When Mary saw her vault in air,
Her snow white tunic leaving bare
Her limbs – and heard the deafening shout
Grow louder as she twirled about,
With one leg pointing towards the sky
As if the gallery to defy:
Surprised, and shocked, she turned away,
Wondering how woman e'er could stay,
And thinking men must sure be frantic
Who patronised such postures antic:

She felt abashed to meet the eye
Of every fop that loitered by:
And, oh! how rudely did it vex
Her fresh, pure heart, to mark her sex
Thus outraged, while the noblest came
To gaze and revel in their shame . . .

Chalon provided a not inapposite contrast between the Victorian young lady sniffing her bouquet and the figure of Fanny Cerrito who is seen in a characteristic pose.

68 Bettanier frères after Teichel, *A Roomful of Rats*. Lithograph, c. 1860. The Paris Opéra was notoriously a happy hunting ground for men of all ages in search of female companionship. The liaisons that resulted were to provide material for novels, plays and a cascade of lithographs which pinpointed exactly contemporary morality. For the girls, the opportunity of a rich lover was sometimes the main reason for their entering the dancing profession. The 'rats' of Teichel's title were the *corps de ballet* girls, and the double demands of a ballet master and of an admirer are cleverly indicated.

69 Gustave Doré, *The Lions' Pit*

69 Gustave Doré, *The Lions' Pit*. Lithograph.
Balletomania had two distinct forms in the
nineteenth century. In Russia, where the word
originated in the 1800s, it implied an obsession with
ballet and with certain dancers whose careers were
followed with intense and all consuming enthusiasm.
In St Petersburg balletomanes acquired a pair of
Taglioni's shoes, had them cooked with a special
sauce and consumed them as best they could. In
Paris, the word suggested rather the Jockey Club's
attitude to dance: a show by pretty girls who were
variously mistresses and mothers but never wives. It
was the Jockey Club who disrupted the first Paris
performance of *Tannhäuser* with determined shouts
for 'le bal-let: le bal-let', because they had arrived
too late at the theatre to witness the dancing that had
been interpolated early in the opera for their benefit.
Doré captures the fanatical enthusiasm and the
sexual interest of the *abonnés* (the season ticket
holders) in the dancing girls.

70 Gustave Doré, *Les Rats de l'Opéra*. Lithograph.
Doré's caricature speaks for itself: a line of pretty
girls fully aware of the gentlemen in the box and the
gentlemen no less aware of the girls. It is an entirely
realistic view of the relationship between dancers
and audience in the middle of the nineteenth
century. Gavarni, Daumier and de Beaumont, as
well as Doré, all produced lithographs which
explored this relationship.

71 William Makepeace Thackeray, *Flora Bemoans the
Absence of Zephyr*, 1836. Unexpectedly, Thackeray
was a balletomane and he gave practical evidence of
this enthusiasm in a small book of caricatures
entitled *Flore et Zephyr* which was published in
London in 1836, supposedly drawn by 'Theophile
Wagstaff'. Like *The Yellowplush Papers* and *The Rose
and the Ring*, it shows Thackeray's delight in satiric
fantasy. Ivor Guest has identified the performances
which inspired Thackeray as those which featured
Taglioni in London in the early 1830s. In a letter
Thackeray noted that Taglioni had 'the most superb
pair of pins', and his drawing of her bewailing
Zephyr's absence conveys very accurately something
of the ritual aspect of dancing, whereby an extension
of the leg into second position is supposed to
express an emotion.

70 Gustave Doré, *Les Rats de l'Opéra*

71 Thackeray, *Flora Bemoans the Absence of Zephyr*

72 George Cruickshank, *Maria Mercandotti*

73 Lorenz, *Giselle*

72 George Cruikshank, *Maria Mercandotti*. Satiric print, 1823. The Earl of Fife was a great admirer of ballet and of ballet dancers. During his service in the Peninsular War he made the acquaintance of a Spanish lady and in 1819 he brought her daughter, the fifteen-year old dancer, Maria Mercandotti, to England. His relationship with her is not clear, but he certainly acted as her patron, and her subsequent success owed much to Lord Fife's protection and interest. Mercandotti's beauty attracted a good many suitors, some encouraged by the fact that Lord Fife had announced that he would settle £15,000 on her when she made a suitable marriage. A leading contender was Mr Hughes Ball who initially offered her an annual income of £2,000. Successive rejections of his offers increased his bids and eventually drove him to tendering both his hand and his entire fortune, which amounted to the then astronomical sum of £25,000 a year (hence his nickname 'Golden Balls'). Mercandotti accepted. The whole intrigue was, of course, public know-ledge and occasioned a series of gleeful prints which delighted in Lord Fife's canniness, Hughes' ardour (there is a nice *double entendre* in 'Golden Balls'' supposed comment) and Mercandotti's astuteness.

73 Lorenz, *Giselle* parody. 1841. The excesses of the ballet were meat and drink to the satiric papers in Paris, and in one of them – *The Musée Philipon* – a

74 Alfred Edward Chalon, *Mademoiselle Athalie and Josephine Hullin in 'Le Carnaval de Venise'*

whole section was devoted to *Giselle* when the ballet was first staged. The illustration, which affords a welcome counterbalance to the idealisation of dancers in lithographs, shows a view of the *pas de deux* in Act I between Giselle and Loys. The accompanying text reads '*Oh, la la!* It's stylish dancing, expressive dancing . . . sobbing kneecaps, impassioned calves, weeping arms. It's cramped feet, elegaic ronds de jambes; it's fudge! – fudge, the delight of young ladies in boarding schools, but calm fudge, grand, noble and imposing!'

74 Alfred Edward Chalon, *Mademoiselle Athalie and Josephine Hullin in 'Le Carnaval de Venise'*. Drawing, 1830. Besides providing a beautiful record of the divinities of the Romantic period, Alfred Chalon reveals another side of his character in a series of lampoons which he made in the years immediately before Taglioni altered the course of dancing. Without being savage, and sustained by a very nice understanding of dance technique, Chalon pinpoints some of the posturings and affectations of the dancers and singers of the time. The caricature of Athalie and Hullin is arguably more accurate – because less idealised – than the polished and proper records that were later to be made of the Romantic dance.

Marie Taglioni. Pages 66–67

Marie Taglioni was the incarnation of Romanticism in dance. Her style, her physical appearance, her qualities as an artist, were to be responsible for a most profound change in the art of dancing. The thin and delicately boned daughter born to Filippo Taglioni, an Italian ballet master, must have seemed improbable material from which a great dancer was to be made. Yet rigorous training and an extremely acute understanding of what she could do best, as well as a flawless technique, eventually made Taglioni the supreme dancer of her time, and one whose image is still today central to the dancing of every ballerina. Taglioni's lightness, her ease, her grace of manner and demure charm, seemed the most beautiful realisation of the Romantic dream of spiritualised femininity. When in 1832 she appeared as La Sylphide she established an image for ballet dancing which it has not yet cast off.

To the new middle class audience of the 1830s Taglioni's qualities were exactly right as an example of womanhood: grace, delicacy, respectability were the chaste aspects of her style. That she floated and barely touched the ground suggests how unreal was man's vision of an unattainable beloved. Every representation we have of her argues a delicious modesty – she was the Victorian Miss etherealised. Her dancing was unquestionably sustained by the most brilliant and carefully studied technique of her time – she would labour half an hour in class repeating a single step – but its effects were not for bravura, but for ease, lightness and that quality, which first beguiled her viewers, of 'a young girl dancing in the ballroom of her father's house'. This intriguing combination of theatrical magic and eminently respectable presence (a marked contrast to the boisterous charms of the ladies who preceded and followed her) caught the public's imagination throughout Europe, and held it. Her career, spanning twenty-five years, found her supremacy as a dancer unchallenged. After her retirement, she was seen as a highly respectable figure (her brief marriage to the unappealing Count Gilbert des Voisins produced one daughter) but her later years were haunted by poverty. A few years before her death she was reduced to teaching the politer ballroom dances to well born English girls.

75 François G. G. Le Paulle, *Marie Taglioni and her brother James in 'La Sylphide'*. Oil, 1834

76 Achille Devéria and Henri Grevedon after August Barre, *Marie Taglioni as La Sylphide*. Lithograph, c. 1837

77 Templeton after Alfred Edward Chalon, *Marie Taglioni as La Sylphide*. Lithograph, 1845

78 *Taglioni*. Stained glass window, c. 1850

79 August Barre, *Marie Taglioni as La Sylphide*. Bronze, 1837

80 *Lola Montez sails for America.* Popular print. Lola Montez was an Irish adventuress and self-styled Spanish dancer who had a vastly successful career as a courtesan. The highpoint of her life was her liaison with King Ludwig I of Bavaria. Thereafter she travelled the world lecturing on the care of the bust, horsewhipping an Australian editor and finally devoting herself to care of fallen women. This cartoon contains some very astute comments upon Lola's character. In the swan boat, with Cupid at the stern aiming his arrows at moping European royalties, Lola blows farewell kisses to the Old World. Her life style in the New World was described by Dr Thomas Nichols, who met her in New York in 1852, as bizarre. 'In the first floor drawing room I found a monkey, three dogs, a parrot, a mocking bird, a Polish prince, a Hungarian count, a bundle of cigarettes, a box of cigars, a decanter of brandy, and Lola Montez, Countess of Landsfeldt . . . who, between puffs of her cigarette, conversed with her visitors in three or four languages, caressed her dogs, scolded her monkey, and was as lively, sparkling, amiable, and rattle-headed as she knew how to be.'

81 Eugenio Latilla, *Three Siamese Grotesques.* 1825. The tradition of grotesque dancing dates back to the very origins of ballet, when acrobatics were introduced as a contrast to nobler forms of dance. This nineteenth-century print by a dancer-turned-artist is of three grotesques in 'The Funeral Dance of Siamese Jugglers' which could have featured in pantomimes well into the present century.

82 *The Black Crook.* Poster, c. 1866. *The Black Crook* must go down in history as the longest running musical entertainment of all time, having notched up forty years of performances in New York. Based upon a nonsensical melodrama, it was developed into an extravaganza of song and dance which opened in Niblo's Gardens in New York in 1866. Its appeal to the public was that irresistible combination of spectacle and naughtiness. Considerable sums were spent on scenery and a 'great Parisienne ballet troupe' was much touted. Rumours that something like nudity would be on view attracted an eager male audience and any female members of the public were reported to be wearing heavy veils to conceal their faces. The poster indicates how costuming for the chorus was as explicit as possible in revealing the nether limbs. Plainly it was the element of 'boldness' that ensured public interest. That some of the dancing might have merit was almost incidental.

80 *Lola Montez sails for America*

81 Eugenio Latilla, *Three Siamese Grotesques*

82 *The Black Crook*

83 Alfred Edward Chalon (attrib.), *The Three Graces*

84 *Behind the Curtain*

83 Alfred Edward Chalon (attrib.), *The Three Graces*.
Lithograph, c. 1840. This charming group is not
from any one ballet. It is a fantasy representing the
three chief graces of the Romantic era as London
best loved them. On the left Taglioni is seen as the
Sylphide; in the centre is Fanny Elssler dressed in
her Cachucha costume from *Le Diable boîteux*; and
on the right Carlotta Grisi is seen in the *Pas de Diane*
from *La Jolie Fille de Gand*. The lithograph is
something of a curiosity. The imaginary linking of
these three dancers is not surprising – during the
1840s concatenations of stars were brought on to the
stage of Her Majesty's Theatre to vast public
enthusiasm – but the costuming of both Taglioni
and Grisi has been much amended. Taglioni's dress
is shorter; Grisi's is abbreviated to a point of
immodesty to Victorian eyes and her bared breast is
unthinkable on the stage at that time. The bare feet
of these two dancers represent a convention rather
than actuality. The public eye was prepared to accept
this fantastication of the female performer. No
lithographs of the Romantic era pretend to truth of
representation. The exquisitely tapered feet, the
delicate balance, the notions of flight and the prettily
rounded but unmuscular limbs foster illusions about
dancing and about womanhood. The Romantic
ballerina was never truthfully represented save in the
occasional portrait of her as a woman rather than a
dancing character.

84 *Behind the Curtain*. Popular print, c. 1880. There
was no continuity of ballet tradition in London, and
after the high summer of Romanticism stage dancing
swiftly fell into bad habits as part of the entertainment in pantomime and music halls. Albert Smith's
Natural History of the Ballet Girl (London, 1847) is a
curious and very revealing document which gives
intriguing insights into the drudgery and pathos of
dancers' lives, those 'pretty trim-built girls, with
sallow faces and large eyes – the pallor that
overspreads their features resulting from cosmetics
and late hours'.

85 C. Mittag after Paul Bürde, *Fanny Cerrito in 'La
Esmeralda'*. Lithograph, 1847. *La Esmeralda* was one
of the greatest of Jules Perrot's ballets, inspired by
Victor Hugo's novel *Notre Dame de Paris*. Bürde's
deliciously improbable painting shows Fanny
Cerrito with various appurtenances of the drama:
Esmeralda's pet goat; the letters with which she has
spelled out the name of her beloved, Phoebus; a
distant prospect of Notre Dame itself through the
archway and a small dagger tucked into the
waistband of her dress. It is an appealing evocation
of a radiantly pretty woman who was a darling of
the Romantic Age and who did not die until the
spring of 1909 – at the moment when Diaghilev
brought the Russian Ballet to Paris.

85 C. Mittag after Paul Bürde, *Fanny Cerrito in 'La Esmeralda'*

THE WORLD OF DEGAS

In the evening the Muses do not discuss, they dance.
Paul Valéry quoting Edgar Degas

The Impressionist movement in the 1860s sought to capture what the eye sees. Of one of its founders Cézanne said, 'Monet is only an eye. But what an eye!' For the Impressionist painter the transient moment, the impact of light, was of prime importance. In recording ballet and dancers Edgar Degas accepted the Impressionist ideal of trying to seize the instant, but for him this meant an attempt to catch the immediacy of movement seen in the bodies of the dancers of the Paris Opéra. Lillian Browse observes in her masterly *Degas Dancers* (London 1949): 'The dancers had come into their own. Degas had discovered another art through the exploration of which his own was to find fulfilment. No other field allowed such unlimited possibilities of form in movement, a fact which he himself admitted by his relatively small series of Horses, Blanchisseuses and Modistes . . . It must be emphasised how inevitable was his choice, for dancing is the fundamental expression of the human body, and the human body the fundamental form in European art.'

Degas' obsession with the dancer began in the 1870s in the first days of the Third Republic. The Paris Opéra was no longer of any real importance in the world of ballet – that position was to be occupied by the ballet in St Petersburg – but Degas was not interested in ballet as such. He was concerned with the dancers as bodies. As E. H. Gombrich observes, 'He was not interested in the ballerinas because they were pretty girls. He did not seem to care for their moods. He looked at them with the same dispassionate objectivity with which the Impressionists looked at the landscape around them. What mattered to him was the interplay of light and shade on the human form, and the way in which he could suggest movement or space. He proved to the academic world that, far from being incompatible with perfect draughtsmanship, the new principles of the young artists were posing new problems which only the most consummate master of design could solve.'

Here came a vital break in the representation of the dancer by artists. Previously painting, lithography and sculpture were concerned with personality, or with idealising the figure. The dancers were essentially individuals with whom the public might be thought to identify – and later, more indifferent artists, such as

86 Edgar Degas, *Danseuse à la barre*. Pastel and crayon. The image of the dancer stretching and limbering at the *barre* recurs through the entire corpus of Degas' paintings of the dance. The daily labours of class, the basis of the ballet dancer's whole existence, inevitably attracted Degas' attention. In it he could see most clearly the bodily mechanics which so fascinated him. His drawings and sketches of class work show how complete was his understanding of the reality of the dancer's body.

87 Edgar Degas, *Before the Performance*. Oil, c. 1882. Against an unidentified background the dancers are seen in archetypal poses, fiddling with shoes and preparing themselves during those nervous moments before the curtain goes up. The richness of the colouring conveys the intense lighting that obtains on stage before curtain rise.

87 Edgar Degas, *Before the Performance*

88 Honoré Daumier, *La Danseuse*. Drawing. Daumier's massive output of lithographs is a resolutely honest and sometimes very bitter view of the France of the middle years of the nineteenth century. This drawing of the dancer is a record of action seized at the very minute – the quick pencil line is eager to catch the flurry of movement as the *danseuse* flutters her skirts.

Clairin, Forain, Bertier and Laurent-Desrousseaux, reverted to this cult. For Degas the dancers served chiefly as abstractions in which movement could be observed at its most refined and disciplined. He was plainly fascinated by the rules of the classic academic dance. The exploration of these rules by the dancer finds its parallel in Degas' reliance upon the rules of draughtsmanship. Any representation of a dancer which does not understand the vital disciplines of turn out, of positions of the feet, of the hard won evolution of the classic technique, all implicit in the dancer's body, must inevitably fail. The average run of depictions of dancers in posters, book illustrations and ephemera always betrays lack of this knowledge. The dancers are not dancers. But Degas – the supreme, the only artist really to have penetrated to the centre of the dancer's art – understood that the academic dance training radically alters the human body. In action the dancer's body 'speaks' differently from those of ordinary people and it is this which Degas shows us.

Other major painters of the period represented dancers merely as decorative figures. Manet's *Lola de Valence* which dates from 1861–62 is a portrait of a Spanish *danseuse* who performed at the Hippodrome in Paris. It is as ravishing in its way as Gainsborough's *Baccelli* – Baudelaire spoke of its 'unexpected charm as of a pink and black jewel' – but it says nothing about dancing.

No less delightful is Renoir's portrait of Rosita Mauri, the Spanish ballerina who was the darling of the Paris Opéra in the 1880s, but again it is a painting of an image seen from the outside rather than an observation based on acute understanding, such as Degas', of the dancer's physique. As a disciple of Degas, Toulouse-Lautrec brought a more sardonic eye to the depiction of all forms of dance. Chiefly concerned with the music hall, the café and the circus, in which he catches everything of the vivacity and sometimes grotesqueness of the popular performers, Toulouse-Lautrec made a few portraits of ballet dancers. In them we see his debt to Degas in the apparently accidental composition – the dancer caught as in a flash of observation.

By the end of the century and in the golden years of the Belle Époque the ballerina had become a symbol of all that was most lavish and worldly. The most celebrated of the *grandes horizontales* were titularly dancers, but such ravishing beauties as Cléo de Mérode and La Belle Otéro owed their fame more to their jewels and extravagance than to their art. The paintings, the postcards and posters which reflected their notoriety also reflected their beauty: as dancers they were hymned as lovely women. Ballet became merely the prettified excuse for the painting, rather than its inspiration.

Ballet itself was now completely moribund in the West, a dainty adjunct to opera performances, in which male roles were usually assigned to pretty girls; Degas never once included a male dancer in his work. It was not until the arrival of the Russian dancers from St Petersburg and Moscow in the first *Saison Russe* organised by Serge Diaghilev in Paris in 1909 that the West was to realise that ballet as an art was alive.

89 Edgar Degas, *Ballet dancer and studies of feet*

90 Edgar Degas, *La Grande Arabesque*

89 Edgar Degas, *Ballet dancer and studies of feet*. Chalk and crayon, 1878–80. In this drawing and its attendant studies of feet Degas demonstrates his interest in the mechanics of the foot in a turned-out position and the dancer's pose as she works on her *pointe*. The drawings show complete understanding of feet properly balanced in the turned-out position, which is the basis of classical ballet.

90 Edgar Degas, *La Grande Arabesque*. Bronze. Degas produced some seventy bronzes which seem both an extension and a commentary on his paintings and drawings of dancers. The most celebrated of these is *La Petite Danseuse de Quatorze Ans* which dates from 1880. During the following decade he also produced the series of studies of naked dancers in various academic positions. *La Grande Arabesque* embodies both the flow of movement and the careful balancing of weight that is an essential part of the arabesque itself.

91 Edgar Degas, *Eugénie Fiocre in 'La Source'*

92 Edgar Degas, *Dancers Resting*

91 Edgar Degas, *Eugénie Fiocre in 'La Source'*. Oil, 1866–67. This is probably the most static of all Degas' paintings of the dance and it is also only his second theatrical work. The ravishing Eugénie Fiocre appeared in Arthur Saint Léon's *La Source* when it was first produced at the Paris Opéra in 1866. The scene Degas recalls is the moment in the first act when the beautiful Nouredda (Fiocre) pauses by a stream. Degas has elaborated this incident by showing Fiocre paddling her feet in the water while her discarded shoes can be seen between the forelegs of a horse. The lack of animation in the painting and in the poses of the dancers was something Degas was soon to abandon.

92 Edgar Degas, *Dancers Resting*. Pastel, 1888–90. Degas found dancers as attractive in repose as in action. These four girls are caught in a shaft of light from a window and their preoccupation with shoes and the fan which one of them holds suggests a moment's break from a rehearsal.

93 Henri de Toulouse-Lautrec, *Dancer adjusting her costume*. Toulouse-Lautrec's world of *café concerts*, bars, brothels and music halls inevitably included dancers. But not for him the fustiness and ritual associated with the Paris Opéra. It was the popular world which fascinated him and his favourite dancing subjects were the figures at the Moulin Rouge, or Jane Avril, or Loie Fuller. There exist several Toulouse-Lautrec drawings showing dancers preparing for performance and adjusting their costumes as in this simple sketch 'after nature'.

94 P. Renouard, *Le Harpiste*. One of a series of engravings of scenes in the Paris Opéra.

95 Jean-Louis Forain, *Dancer and Patron*. Gouache over pencil sketch. Forain's interest in the social identity of the dancer is nowhere better caught than in this brilliant sketch whose subject is entirely self-explanatory. As in Degas' *Dancers Resting*, on the previous page, the backstage activities of the dancers have supplanted their more public image. Their double existence as performers both on and off stage has now entered the accepted canons of representation.

96 H. A. L. Laurent-Desrousseaux, *La Classe de Mme Théodore*. Oil, 1894. This representation of the classroom could not be more different than that provided by Degas. It is a view in which the reality of the dance class is reasonably conveyed, but which also capitalises on the pretty forms of the *danseuses*. Certain facts implied in the picture are of interest: the girls wear the obligatory bloomers which were supposed to maintain standards of decency; the accompaniment is still provided by a violin (the piano was not used in ballet classes until the turn of the century) and the girls at rest are preserving the freshness of their tarlatans by keeping the top layer of the skirt raised. It is, nonetheless, chocolate box art.

93 Henri de Toulouse-Lautrec, *Dancer adjusting her costume*

94 P. Renouard, *Le Harpiste*

95 Jean-Louis Forain, *Dancer and Patron*

96 H. A. L. Laurent-Desrousseaux, *La Classe de Mme Théodore*

97 Pierre Auguste Renoir, *The Young Dancer*. Oil. Renoir's delight in this young dancer is evident. The tenderness and warmth with which the girl is caught in a balletic stance (her feet are sketching a third position) suggest an idealisation of the *rat de l'Opéra*. But she is less a dancer than a very pretty girl in a ballet costume.

98 Edgar Degas, *The Ballet Scene from 'Robert le Diable'*. Oil, 1876. The informality with which Degas shows the figures in the audience and in the orchestra reflects his concern with light, and the dancing figures of the nuns, in the ballet scene from Meyerbeer's opera, are secondary to the heads in the foreground. See also plate 56.

99 Edgar Degas, *The Dance Class of Monsieur Perrot*. Oil, 1873–74. Of the several studies which Degas did of dancers in class, two are of particular interest for the ballet lover. Both produced in the early 1870s and both similar in structure, they show the venerable figure of Jules Perrot as teacher. This greatest choreographer of the Romantic period was no longer producing ballets; instead, he was passing on the dance traditions which he had inherited from his master Auguste Vestris. This version of the class catches a moment of repose as Perrot gestures to the dancer in front of him in explanation.

97 Pierre Auguste Renoir, *The Young Dancer*

98 Edgar Degas, *The Ballet Scene from 'Robert le Diable'*

99 Edgar Degas, *The Dance Class of Monsieur Perrot*

100 E. Debat-Ponsan, *La Maladetta*. 1893. *La Maladetta*, a ballet with choreography by Joseph Hansen and music by Paul Vidal, was first staged at the Paris Opéra in 1893. It starred Rosita Mauri, whose beauty and allure are admirably caught in this painting. It offers interesting testimony to the warmth of Mauri's personality: born in Spain, she excelled in roles which allowed her temperament full reign. Debat-Ponsan is plainly inspired by Mauri, and his painting does her far greater justice, as a portrait and as the record of an individual dancer, than was usual at the turn of the century.

101 Georges Clairin, *Virginia Zucchi*. Oil, 1884. Virginia Zucchi is one of the most exceptional of the virtuoso ballerinas who dominated dance at the end of the nineteenth century. Possessed of genius as a dramatic performer, her appearances in St Petersburg in the 1880s were responsible for the renewal of Russian interest in ballet at this time. At the Eden Theatre, Paris (a hall given over to musical extravaganzas), the Italian choreographer Manzotti staged a series of spectacles. Among them, *Siéba* featured Zucchi, and Clairin's portrait offers a slightly provocative view of a great dancer. She was far more serious an artist, and more important a performer, than this obviously alluring and essentially cheap representation suggests.

102 Nicolas and Serge Legat, *Marie M. Petipa*. Coloured lithograph. The Legat brothers were among the most brilliant male dancers of the Imperial Ballet in St Petersburg at the beginning of the twentieth century. Among their hobbies was that of caricature, in which they jointly excelled, and an album of some one hundred of these caricatures was produced in St Petersburg in 1900. The drawings mocked none too gently the foibles and qualities of the Legats' colleagues. The portrait of Marie Mariusovna Petipa, daughter of the great ballet master, shows her in *Paquita*, in ballet's idea of Spanish costume. It also celebrates a certain generosity of *embonpoint* and her affection for 'important' jewels – which were then sported by dancers on stage.

100 E. Debat-Ponsan, *La Maladetta*

101 Georges Clarin, *Virginia Zucchi*

102 Nicolas and Serge Legat, *Marie M. Petipa*

Pages 86–87

103 Jean-Louis Forain, *Danseuse*. Oil. Although he is more generally known as a master of etching and lithography, Forain also produced a series of paintings in which his concern with the immediate event was quite as brilliant as that of his friend and patron, Degas. Like Degas, he was fascinated by the world of the theatre, but his interest was not so much with the capturing of movement as with the social and moral identity of the dancer. The *danseuse* in plate 103 is pictured in the wings of the theatre and her dress suggests involvement in some pseudo-Spanish enterprise.

104 Jean Béraud, *Les Coulisses de l'Opéra*. Oil, 1889. Nothing more accurately conveys the state of ballet as an art at the end of the nineteenth century than this piece of reportage by Béraud. By now ballet and the ballet dancer had become totally debased in the public imagination. The *corps de ballet* of the Paris Opéra was a collection of young women as marketable as any other commodity. The cohorts of admirers who are seen in attentive poses are all too obviously concerned with life rather than art. It seems almost by accident that one of the girls is shown in a balletic pose. The excuse for their appearance is the obligatory ballet scene that was interpolated into every opera and interpolated late enough to allow the gentlemen of the Jockey Club to dine before coming in for the ballet scene and then leave to organize an intimate supper with the lady of their choice.

105 Henri de Toulouse-Lautrec, *Loie Fuller*. Sketch for a poster, 1893. The effect of Loie Fuller in Paris was instantaneous: her dances, by the swirling shapes created with skirts and draperies, were a realisation of the sinuous lines of *art nouveau*. In making his lithographic posters of her, Lautrec was at pains to ink his stones with several colours to capture the varying shades of La Loie's draperies on each impression, subsequently sprinkling them with gold dust. This first sketch exactly suggests the convolutions of La Loie's veil dancing.

103 Jean-Louis Forain, *Danseuse*

104 Jean Béraud, *Les Coulisses de l'Opéra*

105 Henri de Toulouse-Lautrec, *Loie Fuller*

THE DIAGHILEV YEARS

If it can be said at all that one man took ballet from the thin aristocratic stratum of society and gave it to the people at large, Diaghilev was the man who did it.

George Balanchine

The twenty years of the Diaghilev enterprise (1909–29) saw the life span of what is generally acknowledged as the single greatest artistic enterprise of this century. It is testimony to the stature of Diaghilev himself that at his death at the age of 57, in 1929, the Ballet Russe could no longer continue. The Ballet Russe was, though, only the culminating achievement of this exceptional man, who laboured long to serve the arts of his native Russia before his decision in 1906 to bring exhibitions of painting, then concerts, then operas and finally ballets to Paris, to reveal to the West the vitality of the arts in his homeland.

As a young man of good family Sergey Diaghilev had studied law, but his great love was music. When, in a brisk interview with Rimsky-Korsakov, he was disabused of his ambitions as a composer, he turned his phenomenal energies to a career as a promoter of painting. In this he was guided, and his taste encouraged, by two artists – Alexandre Benois and Léon Bakst – who remained central to his achievements for many years. The magazine *The World of Art*, which Diaghilev directed for ten years at the turn of the century, was vital in awakening Russian taste to what was new in art, and the exhibitions which he organised to show European painting in Russia were symptomatic of the growing awareness there of the newest currents in Western art.

Wealthy Muscovite collectors were among the first important patrons of the Fauve painters; the patronage of the millionaire industrialist Savva Mamontov brought such important Russian artists as Korovin and Golovin into the theatre as decorators for his private operatic performances. It is not unreasonable to assume that Diaghilev and his associates learnt from Mamontov's example, and when Diaghilev organised the first Russian season of opera in Paris in 1908 the decorative splendour of the works presented contributed greatly to their success.

Diaghilev's constant quest for the new made him the great explorer of ways in which painting could serve to enhance theatrical spectacle. It is to Diaghilev's example that we owe the

107 Léon Bakst, *Nijinsky as the Faun*

108 Léon Bakst, Design for a Bacchante in *Narcisse*

107 Léon Bakst, *Nijinsky as the Faun*. Watercolour, 1912. Bakst's Hellenism produced some magnificent stage décors – *Daphnis and Chloe*, *Hélène de Sparte*, *Narcisse*, *L'après-midi d'un faune* – as well as the painting *Terror Antiquus*. His design for Nijinsky as the Faun is far more than a mere working drawing: it is a telling portrait of the dancer as the character and also a masterly piece of decoration.

108 Léon Bakst, Design for a Bacchante in *Narcisse*. Watercolour, 1911. Although this is costume design for a Fokine ballet staged by Diaghilev in 1911, it is design raised to the level of high art. The eroticism of the girl's clothes and the sensuality with which Bakst has treated her body and its draperies are an extraordinary tribute to Bakst's power as a painter.

109 Léon Bakst, *Nijinsky in 'La Péri'*. Watercolour, 1911. Diaghilev had hoped to stage *La Péri*, the *poème dansée* by Paul Dukas, but in the event it was acquired by the indifferent dancer Natalia Trouhanova through her friendship with the composer. Nevertheless, Bakst had begun work on designs for the ballet and this portrait of Nijinsky in costume is both a design and an evocation.

90

109 Léon Bakst, *Nijinsky in 'La Péri'*

110 Émile-Antoine Bourdelle, *Nijinsky as Harlequin in 'Le Carnaval'*. Drawing. Bourdelle's drawing pinpoints the quality of malicious delight which is the essence of this role.

rebirth of ballet in the West, and his involvement of many of the greatest painters of the century as decorators means that the décors for ballets produced under his banner often survive as works of art in their own right. It suffices to list the painters employed by Diaghilev – some of them producing their first theatre work for him – to indicate the stature of design in the Ballet Russe. Diaghilev's Ballet Russe was in fact a travelling exhibition of the works of the following artists: Benois, Bakst, Korovin, Roerich, Golovin, Anisfeld, Sudeikin, Dobuzhinsky, Sert, Goncharova, Larionov, Balla, Picasso, Matisse, Derain, Gris, Laurencin, Braque, Laurens, Pruna, Utrillo, Ernst, Miró, Gabo, Pevsner, Yakulov, Tchelitchev, Bauchant, de Chirico, Rouault.

Vital to the understanding of Diaghilev's work is the fact that after the 1917 Revolution he and his ballet were émigrés. Moreover, while beginning as a Russian company, feeding on the greatest traditions of Russian art and music, Diaghilev's quest for the new brought him into contact with Parisian taste and with the artistic apparatus of the École de Paris. Furthermore, where he had been in the avant-garde before the Revolution, the last decade of his company's existence found him obliged to seek the new wherever he could find it, in an endeavour to keep up with his pre-war reputation. The undeniable chic of the company during the 1920s is reflected in such airy delights as *Les Biches*. The sometime desperate quest for novelty can be noted in the pseudo-Soviet disaster *Le Pas d'acier*, which provided salon communism for the Train Bleu audience (and the Train Bleu itself offered the excuse for an 'amusing' work by Jean Cocteau).

But whatever the straining after novel pleasures to delight a worldly audience, the solid basis of the repertory and the superlative standards of presentation remained. Throughout the entire twenty years of the Diaghilev Ballet it never ceased to attract and fascinate the foremost artists of the time. As collaborators with Diaghilev they became involved not only in designing works but also in the daily life of the company. And there results from this close communion a very rich gallery of portraits which celebrate the beauty of the dancers and the vitality of the company's creative ambience.

Ephemeral, but very pertinent, are the innumerable caricatures which survive as testimony to the daily activities of the collaborators. Mikhail Larionov was constantly drawing Diaghilev and his entourage – the last portrait we have of Diaghilev shows him in bed in the Grand Hotel, Paris in 1929, correcting a score. Benois could sketch Ravel standing on the beach at St Jean de Luz. Picasso, at the time of his collaboration on *Parade*, caught Massine, Diaghilev and Bakst sitting outside a café in Rome. Stravinsky caricatured Bakst. Bakst produced a magnificent head of Diaghilev on the writing paper of the Branksome Hotel, Bournemouth. Jean Cocteau was indefatigable in caricaturing everyone: Poulenc at the piano, Nijinsky in rehearsal, Stravinsky pounding out the rhythms of *Le Sacre du Printemps*, Stravinsky watching Nijinsky making up for *Le Carnaval*, Diaghilev as the Young Girl in *Spectre de la Rose* and Bakst as the Rose.

Once he was drawn into the world of the Ballet Russe, Pablo Picasso discovered a source of inspiration which was to last him until the end of his life. Quite apart from his theatre work, which extended to his redesigning of Serge Lifar's *Icare* in 1962, Picasso became even more intimate with the ballet through his meeting with a Ballet Russe dancer, Olga Khokhlova, in 1916 and their marriage a year later. His drawings of dancers which date from this period are marked by an almost classical approach in draughtsmanship. Such works as the portrait of Olga in Spanish costume and the depiction of three male dancers resting, from as late as 1925, are beautifully serene in execution. Like Degas before him, Picasso demonstrates that essential understanding of the dancers' physiques: his dancers are truly dancers. But Picasso also fed upon dancing to find his inspiration in very different ways, most significantly in the tremendous *Three Dancers*, also dating from 1925, a work which shows a significant change in his style, and whose ferocity and emotional violence mark it as one of his major creations. The figures are not recognisably classical ballet dancers, but they reaffirm Picasso's fascination with dance in his determination to show many facets of the human figure at the same time.

In 1954, to commemorate the twenty-fifth anniversary of Diaghilev's death, the ballet critic Richard Buckle organised a fine Diaghilev exhibition, seen first at the Edinburgh Festival and then in an enlarged form at Forbes House in London. The shade of Diaghilev himself seemed to pervade the enterprise. Buckle worked in the Diaghilev tradition, finding a new and creative way of displaying exhibits so that the actual life of the Ballet Russe could be sensed. The richness of the Ballet Russe activity was evident from the range and multiplicity of objects on display. The Ballet Russe itself, as well as the works it created, had offered constant inspiration to artists, as was evident from the extraordinary wealth of portraiture. In one gallery were portraits of the stars, collaborators and patrons of the Diaghilev Ballet, and it was possible to see nine different views of Tamara Karsavina, seven of Serge Lifar, six of Lydia Lopokova, seven of Leonid Massine and thirteen of Nijinsky. In his book about the exhibition, *In Search of Diaghilev* (London 1955) Buckle records how he had to resort to guile to obtain some of the material. Leonid Massine had failed to answer several requests for items from his collection. Buckle wrote a final plea: 'You must admit that it will be absurd if there are eight portraits of Lifar in the exhibition, and none of you.' Massine's reply then came by return of post: 'If you will guarantee to pay the costs of transport and insure the pictures for $1,000 each . . . I will order to be released for you one portrait of me by Bakst, one by Derain, one by Matisse, three by Picasso . . .'

The entire history of the Diaghilev Ballet can be traced both in portraiture and in caricature. Stravinsky noted that immediately after the first performance of *The Firebird* in Paris in 1910 Jacques-Émile Blanche, 'a *fine mouche* for a celebrity', came to make his portrait. The impact of Karsavina and Nijinsky can be found in the admirable drawings made by John Singer Sargent at the behest of Lady Ripon, an early patron of Diaghilev, and in their portraits by

111 Ludwig Kainer, *Karsavina in 'Le Dieu Bleu'*. Drawing, 1912. *Le Dieu Bleu* was a confection devised by Cocteau and Reynaldo Hahn, most charming of composers, to satisfy a continuing public demand for oriental fantasy in the manner of *Schéhérazade*. The ballet was not a success, despite the opulence of Bakst's designs, but Kainer's drawing – one of many he made of the Ballet Russe – does convey something of Karsavina's presence, playing a Young Girl who tries to stop her beloved from becoming a Hindu priest.

112 Spencer Frederick Gore, *Our Flag*. Oil, 1910. The English painter Spencer Frederick Gore was influenced both by the manner of Sickert and by late Impressionist painting. Like Sickert he was attracted to the theatre and in the early 1900s he made records of the ballet performances at the Alhambra and Empire Theatres in London. His view of *Our Flag* shows the Danish ballerina Britta as the Spirit of the Flag in one of the patriotic works which typified the miserable state of ballet in London before the arrival of Diaghilev. Spencer Gore catches everything of its hectic and inartistic manner.

113 Everett Shinn, *Ballet in the Park*. Oil. Everett Shinn was a member of that group of American painters at the turn of the twentieth century who sought a style of painting which was consonant with American life. Called 'The Ash Can School' because of their recognition of the importance of everyday subjects for art, many had begun working as illustrators for newspapers in the 1890s, making drawings of events to accompany press reports. In the days before photography was universally used in newspapers they developed a quick, almost shorthand style of recording. One of the leaders of the Ash Can School, Robert Henri, urged his colleagues to adopt this quickness of style in their paintings. Shinn demonstrates this skill in catching effects of light but for him, as for many other artists, painting was still essentially European and conservative, never totally accepting the socialism implicit in the Ash Can School's ideas. During the first few decades of the twentieth century, Shinn became attracted to the style of Degas and this painting of an open air ballet performance records an elegant audience watching a performance of *Les Sylphides*. The pose of the dancers is reminiscent of a celebrated early photograph of *Les Sylphides* in Paris in 1909.

112 Spencer Frederick Gore, *Our Flag*

113 Everett Shinn, *Ballet in the Park*

114 Natalia Goncharova, *Les Noces*.
Pen and ink, 1923. With music by
Igor Stravinsky, choreography by
Bronislava Nijinska and designs by
Natalia Goncharova, *Les Noces* was
an evocation of the peasant faith of
Holy Russia. Nijinska's dances were
conceived in monolithic architectural terms. This drawing is one of
several that Goncharova made: it
shows the bridesmaids holding the
long ritualistic braids of the bride
and it indicates one of the pyramidal
groupings of the choreography.

Blanche. In the latter years of the company the young English
artist Christopher Wood, who became involved with the
Diaghilev enterprise in 1926, produced some entertaining
caricatures and portraits.

Contemporary with Diaghilev, two great stars reflect the
extreme poles of the dancer's art: Anna Pavlova and Isadora
Duncan. Pavlova, briefly associated with Diaghilev in his first
seasons, went off to pursue a career of her own. The records of her
genius are few: the multitudinous portraits offer likenesses but not
insight. Valerian Svetlov's biography (Paris 1922) is crowded with
tasteless illustrations of her impact on the world. There are few
representations of her which do anything like justice to her
incomparable artistry.

Very different was the case of Isadora Duncan. Edward Gordon
Craig, in a BBC broadcast in 1952, best summed up the impact that
Duncan had upon those who watched her. 'Was it art? No, it was
not. It was something which inspires those men who labour in the
narrower fields of the arts, harder but more lasting. It released the
minds of hundreds of such men: one had but to see her dance for
one's thoughts to wing their way, as it were, with the fresh air. It
rid us of all nonsense we had been pondering so long. How is that
– for she said nothing? On the contrary, she said everything that
was worth hearing; and everything that anyone else but the poets
had forgotten to say.' Thus it is that we find Isadora recorded not
only by Craig, who loved her, but also by Bourdelle who
immortalised her in the reliefs he made for the Théâtre des Champs
Elysées in 1913, by Bakst, by Carrière, by Rodin and Jose Clara, by
Segonzac and many more.

In each representation, the passionate life of her art can be
perceived. Isadora the revolutionary attracted the more
adventurous artists; Pavlova's conservatism of taste – which had
alienated her from Diaghilev – is reflected in the many
conventional portrayals which minimise her genius. But it is to
Pavlova that we turn in gratitude as the greater propagandist for
ballet itself. She had started to travel at the beginning of the
century, while still a member of the Imperial Russian Ballet, and
from 1913 her journeyings were worldwide and ceaseless. She
took ballet where it had never been seen before; her image is the
popular one of the ballerina. She instilled a love and a feeling for
ballet in generations of admirers.

By taking ballet away from the institutionalised setting of the
opera house, Diaghilev and Pavlova were responsible for the first
increase in its popularity in the present century. But there is
nothing in the visual arts that reflects this popularity as did the
lithographs and prints that proliferated during the last high point
of public interest in ballet during the Romantic era. Dance now
seems to lie in the realm of the still and moving camera. It is tragic
to recall that there exists not one minute of film of the Diaghilev
Ballet or of its great stars, and that Anna Pavlova is known to us
only through ultimately unsatisfactory fragments. At a time when
artists were seeking new ways of revealing the world around them,
and nineteenth-century representationalism had been left to the
academies, the camera remained to record the dancer's art.

115 Léon Bakst, Design for *Le Festin (L'Oiseau d'or)*.
Used as a cover for the number of the magazine
Commoedia Illustré which commemorated the first
Russian season of the Ballet Russe in 1909.

116 Georges Barbier, *Nijinsky and Ida Rubinstein in 'Schéhérazade'*

Vaslav Nijinsky

Nijinsky remains the most celebrated male dancer of this century. At a time when male dancing had fallen into the worst disrepute in Western Europe, Nijinsky's genius – combining phenomenal technique and no less phenomenal dramatic power – reasserted the importance of men in ballet. His tragically short career as a performer lasted only ten years before the clouds of mental illness cut him off from the world in 1917. But from 1909, when he first appeared in Paris, until 1913, when he broke with Diaghilev, he proved an irresistible figure to artists of all kinds. From the many works inspired by him, the following six convey his range, his animal attraction and his magnetism, evident even in indifferent portrayals of him.

John Singer Sargent made a drawing (117) which fixes for us the allure and radiant beauty of the young Nijinsky as he appeared in *Le Pavillon d'Armide*. It catches particularly the extraordinary placing of Nijinsky's head on his neck and the vitality of presence which was Nijinsky's once he had put on a costume.

Georges Barbier's view of Nijinsky and Ida Rubinstein in *Schéhérazade* (116) is Beardsleyesque in its manipulation of black and white and it indicates how strongly Parisian taste had been caught by the exoticism of Bakst's designs.

In 1912 Jean Cocteau – a member of the Diaghilev entourage from the first *Saison Russe* – made one of his many caricatures (118) showing Nijinsky in the wings ready to go on as the Golden Slave in *Schéhérazade*, with behind him the dominating figure of Diaghilev. Diaghilev's features are exactly as Cocteau has recorded them in his prose: 'Eyes like Portuguese oysters and baby crocodile's teeth'.

117 John Singer Sargent, *Nijinsky in 'Le Pavillon d'Armide'*

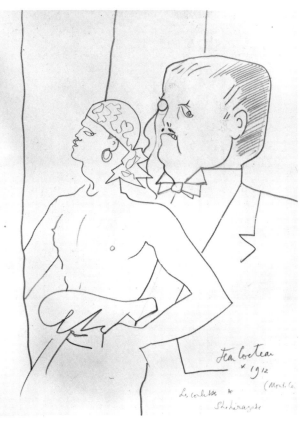

118 Jean Cocteau, Nijinsky and Diaghilev

Nijinsky (continued)

In the first season in Paris of the Russian dancers, Nijinsky appeared in the Bluebird *pas de deux* from the last act of *The Sleeping Beauty*. It formed part of a *divertissement* called *Le Festin*, and because Diaghilev had announced *The Firebird*, which was not to be created until the following season, Nijinsky was billed as '*l'oiseau d'or*'. Barbier's drawing (119) dates from three years later and is a fantasy upon the Bakst costume. It is one of a series of drawings made for a de luxe edition about Nijinsky published in Paris in 1913, and the pose is almost identical with that in a Barbier drawing of Nijinsky as the Favourite Slave in *Cléopâtre*.

Marc Chagall made a drawing in 1911 (120, Collection of the Museum of Modern Art, New York) in pen and ink and gouache of Nijinsky as the Rose. The Cocteau poster (106) and this drawing testify, as do many others, to the extraordinary impact that this brief duet, for Nijinsky and Karsavina, had upon artists.

In 1912 Nijinsky's first ballet, *L'après-midi d'un faune,* was publicly censured as obscene. Rodin leapt to Nijinsky's defence in a letter to the daily newspaper *Le Matin* and subsequently Nijinsky visited Rodin in his studio and danced for him. A result of this meeting was this bronze (121). Like the other sculptures of dancers made towards the end of Rodin's life, it was an entirely private piece of work – none of the dancing figures was cast or shown until after his death. They represent a final summation of his genius.

119 Georges Barbier, *Nijinsky in 'Le Festin'*

120 Marc Chagall, *Nijinsky in 'Le Spectre de la Rose'*

121 Auguste Rodin, *Nijinsky*

122 John Singer Sargent, *Karsavina in 'Le Dieu Bleu'*

123 Jacques-Émile Blanche, *Karsavina as The Firebird*

124 Paul Scheurich, *Karsavina and Nijinsky in 'Le Carnaval'*

125 Glyn Philpot, *Karsavina as Thamar*

126 Jean Cocteau, Poster for the Ballet Russe

Tamara Karsavina

Most loved of Diaghilev's ballerinas, Karsavina was a product of the Imperial Ballet School in St Petersburg. It was she, though, who best understood the ideals of the new ballet as propounded by Fokine and Diaghilev, and she was the female star of the Diaghilev seasons until the First World War. After a return to Russia, she married an English diplomat, H. J. Bruce, and settled in England, where her presence was an inspiration to everyone connected with ballet. Great artists of almost every European nationality created portraits of her: in her most famous roles, in her dressing room, in society. She was depicted in oils and watercolours, drawings, engravings, statuettes of porcelain, silver and bronze.

John Singer Sargent was plainly fascinated by Karsavina's beauty, notably the lustrous eyes which gave such expression to her performances. The head from *Le Dieu Bleu* (122), drawn in charcoal, tells us everything of the languorous grace of her interpretation.

Jacques-Émile Blanche was one of the most fashionable portraitists of his time and with the advent of the Diaghilev Russian seasons Blanche (whom Stravinsky observed had 'a keen nose for a celebrity') was quick to engage in a series of portraits of the most distinguished artists in the Russian Ballet. Karsavina is shown (123) in the pose the Firebird adopts in the Lullaby of the second scene, standing in front of a coromandel screen in Blanche's studio. The portrait is entirely faithful in capturing the beauty of the model and the exotic brilliance of the costume designed by Léon Bakst.

The popularity of the Ballet Russe also brought a revival in the manufacture of good porcelain models of dancers. The Meissen factory commissioned the artist Paul Scheurich to model a complete set of the characters in Fokine's ballet, *Le Carnaval*. The pair illustrated (124) shows Karsavina and Nijinsky as Columbine and Harlequin. The quality of these Meissen figures maintains the great tradition of modelling in this medium, a tradition which was to become appallingly debased in later years. Today, porcelain models of dancers are almost always masterpieces of kitsch in which vulgarity and physical improbability horridly combine.

Glyn Philpot was fascinated by Karsavina's appearance as Thamar. His brilliant study in oils (125) catches the ruthlessness of the Queen as she poses watchfully on the piled cushions which featured in the amazing Bakst design.

As a companion piece to his posters of Pavlova and Nijinsky, Jean Cocteau made delightful capital out of the figure of Karsavina as the Young Girl in *Le Spectre de la Rose* (126). Eyes shut, she seems to be dreaming of the ball.

127 André Dunoyer de Segonzac, *Fokine and Karsavina in 'Le Carnaval'*

128 Valentin Serov, *Portrait of Karsavina*

Karsavina (continued)

André Dunoyer de Segonzac produced a number of quick, almost calligraphic impressions of dancers, and this view (127) of Fokine and Karsavina is taken on the wing. No more than a caricature, it nonetheless captures the mischievous nature of the characters in *Le Carnaval*.

Valentin Serov's pencil drawing of Karsavina (128) dates from her early years in St Petersburg. With extreme simplicity it reveals the freshness of her beauty and the exquisite quality of her profile: no wonder the entire student population of St Petersburg was in love with her. Serov, a pupil of Repin, was a precociously brilliant draughtsman and around the turn of the century he became the most accomplished and successful portraitist in Russia.

Charles Hallo's affection for views from the wings of the Paris Opéra produced this atmospheric glimpse of Karsavina in performance as the Firebird (129).

129 Charles Hallo, *The Firebird*

Anna Pavlova

Sir John Lavery, one of the most successful and honoured painters of his time, made three fine studies of Anna Pavlova. *The Dying Swan* (131) was Pavlova's most celebrated solo, and Lavery offers an interpretation of her in this role. Pavlova's position is not one found in her dance and it seems as if Lavery has shown her in the grounds of her North London home, Ivy House, where the ballerina was much given to posing with her pet swan by the lake. The Pavlova in *Autumn Bacchanale* (130), with the grapes and vineleaves framing the beautiful face, is Pavlova the ballerina, the *assoluta* with the world at her feet.

Léon Bakst was a masterly portraitist and his drawings of members of the Diaghilev entourage are well known. The drawing of Pavlova (132) is a product of his last years and it reflects his deep understanding of his subject, whom he had known since her début in St Petersburg in 1899. In this drawing Bakst seems to have stripped away all the external glamour of the ballerina image to reveal something essential about a forty-year-old woman who is universally acclaimed. It is without question the best portrait of Pavlova, whose curse it is to have been celebrated in an infinity of indifferent works of art.

130 John Lavery, *Pavlova in 'Autumn Bacchanale'*

131 John Lavery, *The Dying Swan*

132 Léon Bakst, *Portrait of Anna Pavlova*

133 Auguste Rodin, *Isadora Duncan*

134, 135 Émile-Antoine Bourdelle, *Isadora Duncan*

133 Auguste Rodin, *Isadora Duncan*. Pencil and wash. In the last two decades of his life Rodin started to make an extraordinary series of drawings of dancers – both the exotics who visited Paris (Javanese dancers in 1896, Cambodian dancers ten years later) and, inevitably, Isadora Duncan. In Anthony Ludovici's *Personal Reminiscences of Auguste Rodin* (Philadelphia, 1926), the artist is quoted as saying, '. . . my drawings are only my way of testing myself. They are my way of proving to myself how far this incorporation of the subtle secrets of the human form has taken place within me. I try to see the figure as a mass, a volume. It is the voluminousness that I try to understand. That is why, as you see, I sometimes wash a tint over the drawings. This completes the feeling of massiveness, and helps me to ascertain how far I have succeeded in grasping the movement as a mass . . .'

134, 135 Émile-Antoine Bourdelle, *Isadora Duncan*. Pen and ink, 1909. Bourdelle has been attracted by the young Isadora at her most joyous. These drawings convey the quality that was so subtly evoked by Sir Frederick Ashton in his *Isadora Duncan Dances* created for Lynn Seymour in 1976.

Ida Rubinstein

Ida Rubinstein was one of the most mysterious figures in the ballet of the twentieth century. Of a wealthy Moscow family, she was a woman of stunning beauty whose ambitions as a performer were rarely realised on stage. A private pupil of Fokine, she appeared in mime roles during the early Diaghilev Ballet Russe seasons. Her striking appearance compensated for any lack of technique. At various times thereafter she formed companies in which she appeared, and sought to perpetuate her beauty in a variety of specially created roles.

Serov's portrait in oils (137) tells a great deal about the exoticism and glamour of her presence. It is a portrait very consciously arranged in its angular lines, which stress the sudden decorative moments of rings on toes and fingers and the conflicting mass of the russet hair which framed the ravishing face.

Romaine Brooks' etiolated portrait of Rubinstein (136) is sometimes known as *la femme morte*. It is a macabre view of its subject, painted in oils in 1911, owing something to the decadent art of the Symbolists. It suggests, though, the extraordinary attraction that Rubinstein had for her admirers.

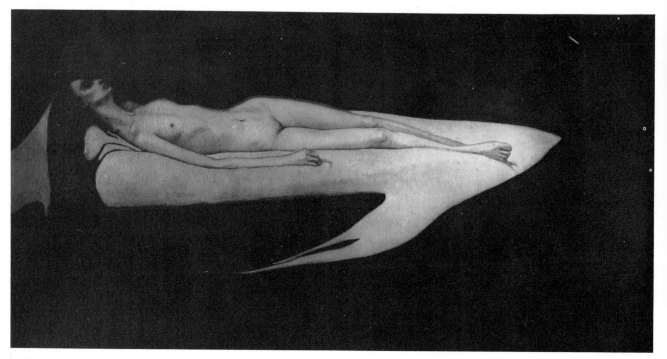

136 Romaine Brooks, *Le Trajet*

137 Valentin Serov, *Ida Rubinstein*

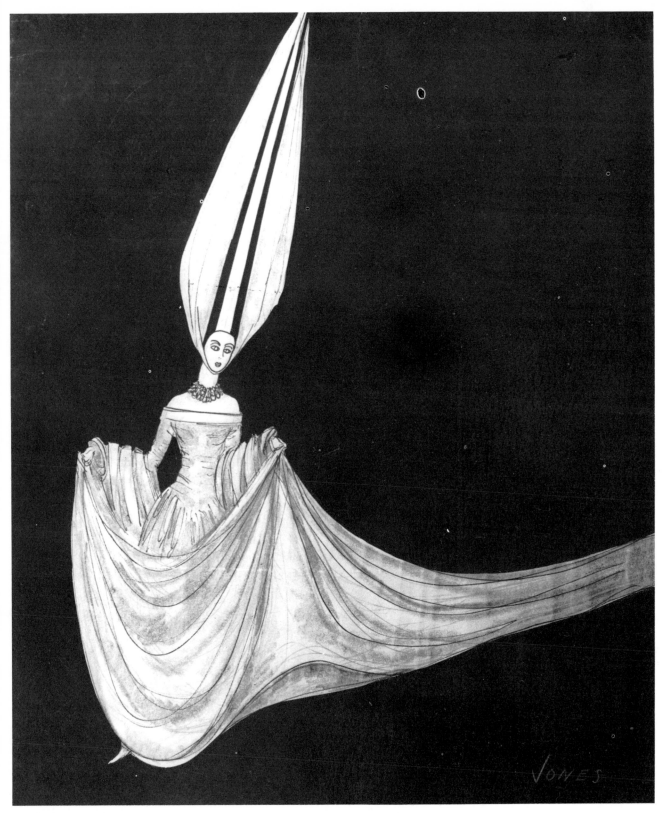

138 Robert Edmond Jones, Costume design

138 Robert Edmond Jones, Design for a Chateleine in *Tyl Eulenspiegel*. This ballet was staged by the Diaghilev Ballet Russe in New York in 1916 with choreography by Nijinsky.

139 Pablo Picasso, *Four Dancers*

139 Pablo Picasso, *Four Dancers*. Pen and ink, 1925. Museum of Modern Art, New York.

140 Pablo Picasso, *La Boutique fantasque*. Pen and sepia ink, 1919. In 1919 one of Leonid Massine's most enduring and delightful ballets was given its first performance in London. Picasso's page of quick sketches is a souvenir of a time when he was in London with the Ballet Russe for the staging of *Le Tricorne* which he had designed and which had its first performance in London on July 22, 1919. *Boutique* had been given its premiere just two weeks before. The sketches show Lydia Lopokova and

Massine as the Can-Can dancers. Dedicated by the artist to Massine, the sketches have a wonderful immediacy.

141 Pablo Picasso, *Two Dancers*. Ink, 1926. After his marriage to Olga Khokhlova and his involvement with first ballet design in 1917, for the Ballet Russe production of *Parade*, Picasso spent a decade immersed in the world of the Ballet Russe. He drew it repeatedly, making a series of brilliant portraits of the various members of the Diaghilev entourage and also immersing himself in the physical attitudes of dancers. Not since Degas had an artist

140 Pablo Picasso, *La Boutique fantasque*

been so obsessed with dance movement. The presence of dancers is found not only in his masterly drawings – which seem to prefer performers in rehearsal rather than in the theatre – but many of the paintings during this decade reflect, by attitudes and arrangements of limbs, the continued fact of the ballet world in Picasso's consciousness. In his definitive *Picasso Theatre* (Weidenfeld & Nicolson, London, 1968) Douglas Cooper observes: 'By 1925 Picasso was tired of his long association with the ballet, his marriage had become a source of irritation to him, he had found new artistic interests and he was determined to free himself from the claims of the theatre. In April of that year Picasso and Olga paid a last visit to Diaghilev and his Ballet Russe at Monte Carlo, where he made drawings of elegantly posed dancers as he had done previously. But when he got back to Paris a month later he painted *The Dance*, a climactic masterpiece in which the elation he had once felt is overlaid with pain and in which dancing and dancers are treated with bitter mockery. This painting was a true cry from the heart, a passionate and spontaneous outburst which marks the end of Picasso's interest in ballet for twenty years.'

141 Pablo Picasso, *Two Dancers*

142 Émile-Antoine Bourdelle, *Isadora Duncan*

142 Émile-Antoine Bourdelle, *Isadora Duncan*. Pen and wash. Isadora Duncan's impact upon European artists can be traced in the innumerable drawings and sculptures which exist of her. Like his master Rodin, Bourdelle was enraptured by her art; he told his students: 'All my muses in the theatre are movements seized during Isadora's flight; she was my principal source'. In his sketches, as in his sculptures, Bourdelle captured both the monumental quality of Isadora's dance and also its Dionysiac abandon. This drawing illustrates a pose expressive of grief: in it we sense, as always with Bourdelle, the actuality of Isadora.

143 Abraham Walkowitz, *Isadora Duncan*. Pen and watercolour. In a series of drawings dating from 1920 Abraham Walkowitz provided eloquent testimony to the grander impulses and more monumental tone of Duncan's dancing in the last, dark decades of her life.

144 Mikhail Larionov, *Soleil de Nuit*. Watercolour, 1915. This impression, by its designer, of Massine's first ballet for Diaghilev shows the peasant vitality which informed the early work of Larionov. He remained one of Diaghilev's closest associates.

143 Abraham Walkowitz, *Isadora Duncan*

144 Mikhail Larionov, *Soleil de Nuit*

145 Mikhail Larionov, *Diaghilev watching Lifar in rehearsal*

145 Mikhail Larionov, *Diaghilev watching Lifar in rehearsal*. Pen and ink, 1927. Larionov's rehearsal drawing says a great deal about the toil of a dancer's life, from the watering can with which the floor is kept damp and unslippery, to the looking glass against which Diaghilev is sitting, and the energetic figures of the dancers at work. Serge Lifar is seated in the foreground.

146 George William Bissill, *Anton Dolin in 'Le Train Bleu'*. Pen, Indian ink and water colour, 1924. *Le Train Bleu* was the quintessential *chic* ballet of the 1920s. With its music by Milhaud, choreography by Nijinska, decor by Laurens and costumes by Chanel, it typified the quest for the 'amusing'. It was inspired by Cocteau seeing Dolin performing hand-stands in Monte Carlo. From this there developed the idea of the ballet which was given its title because, as Diaghilev observed, 'the first point about *Le Train Bleu* is that there is no Blue Train in it'. Bissill's drawing shows Dolin in the acrobatic choreography which became so associated with him at this time.

147 Eileen Mayo, *Serge Lifar in 'La Chatte'*. Pencil and crayon, 1928. *La Chatte*, first produced by Diaghilev's Ballet Russe in Monte Carlo in 1927, was

146 George William Bissill, *Anton Dolin in 'Le Train Bleu'*

an updating of one of Aesop's fables, given a brilliant Constructivist decor and costumes by Naum Gabo and Antoine Pevsner. Eileen Mayo's drawing is a souvenir of the beauty of *le beau Serge* and of the extraordinary lighting effects obtained from the black floorcloth and transparent mica shapes of the setting.

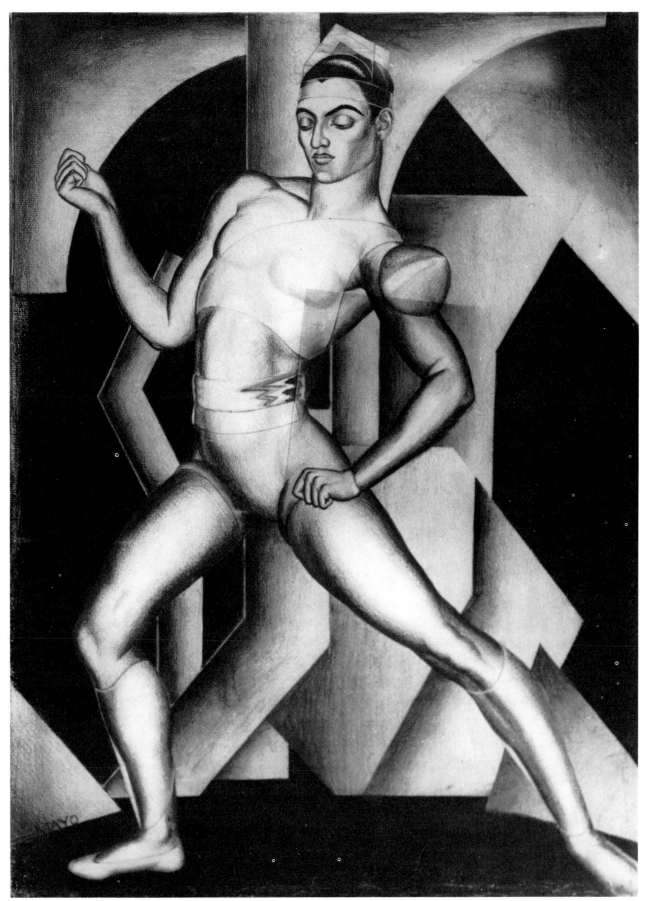

147 Eileen Mayo, *Serge Lifar in 'La Chatte'*

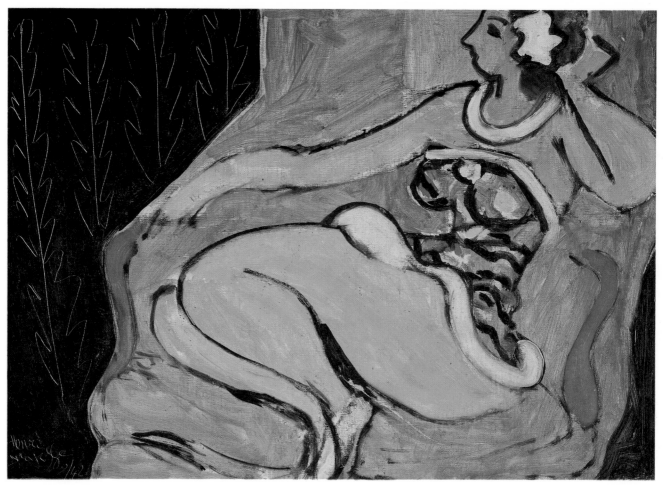

148 Henri Matisse, *Dancer and Armchair, black background*

148 Henri Matisse, *Dancer and Armchair, black background*. Oil, 1942. Matisse's involvement with the ballet started with his designs for *Le Chant du Rossignol* which he made for Diaghilev in 1920. After a later revival of the work in 1925, this exercise in Chinoiserie was his only connection with the ballet until he was invited to design Massine's *Rouge et Noir* in 1939. He turned, instead, to dancers as subjects for painting and during the 1920s and 1930s he celebrated the female form in a sequence of oil paintings of voluptuous beauty. Talking of his work at this time he said, 'I depend entirely on my model whom I observe at liberty, and then I decide on the pose that best suits her nature. When I take a new model I guess the appropriate position from the abandoned attitudes of repose, and then I become the slave of that pose'.

149 Marie Laurencin. *Le Déjeuner sur l'herbe*. Watercolour, 1945. In 1944 an explosion of talent occurred in Paris which seemed to represent the lightening of spirits that followed the ending of the Occupation. A group of young dancers from the Paris Opéra, led by Roland Petit and with the patronage and guidance of Christian Bérard and

Boris Kochno, emerged as the freshest of young companies, Les Ballets des Champs Elysées. Following the Diaghilev example, Petit invited the collaboration of the finest artists – a procedure he has maintained to this day – and the work of Bérard, Clavé, Cocteau, André Beaurepaire, Wakhevitch, and many more, enhanced the productions. This watercolour by Marie Laurencin is an impression of the ballet which she decorated for Petit. As with *Les Biches*, which she designed for Diaghilev in 1924, it makes entrancing use of light, clear colours and the delicious qualities of *jeunes filles en fleurs*.

150 Paul Colin, *Jean Börlin*. Poster, 1925. Colin is one of the masters of the poster, as well as being a fine stage designer, and this early example of his poster work celebrates an appearance by Jean Börlin. Börlin was principal dancer and sole choreographer of the Ballets Suédois, a company financed by the Swedish millionaire Rolf de Maré, which for five years emulated the Diaghilev ideal. Colin's poster is striking in its economy and clarity and the vitality with which the ideas of Art Deco are used.

149 Marie Laurencin, *Le Déjeuner sur l'herbe*

150 Paul Colin, *Jean Börlin*

MODERN TIMES AND MODERN CRIMES

Ballet today exists as something on its own, quite separate from the theatre, the art-gallery and the concert hall. It has no influence on anything but itself.

Arnold L. Haskell

The vast change in styles of painting, and the diverse ways of making them in recent decades, have brought the literal, veristic representation of dancing into some disrepute. Few are the artists like Picasso or Degas who have found in ballet, or dance in any of its forms, some consistent inspiration. There has been, in past years, a nasty flurry of activity supposedly showing dancers and the dance – smudged 'impressions' of movement; deadly drawings that look as if someone has industriously copied over a photograph with tracing paper; sculpture like a haphazard agglomeration of animal concretions; smarmy delineations of dancers that copy every superficial procedure of Degas with not one iota of his anatomical understanding; portrayals of dancers, photographically exact in showing their bodies, which are akin to soft porn.

This distressing state of affairs reflects the fact that ballet itself has undergone a crisis of identity. Is it the respectable middle-brow art, found in opera houses, which beguiles its devotees with Tchaikovsky and cohorts of young women impersonating swans? Is it, rather, the portentous spectacles of Maurice Béjart for the devoted legion of the young who follow him to sports stadia and tents in search of messages about life? Or is it the truly adventurous work of American modern dancers and the uncompromising brilliance of Balanchine's New York City Ballet? Because ballet has acquired so confused an image in the public mind, it has lost its attraction for most artists and has become almost exclusively the province of the camera. The camera's effect has furthermore been to exclude the artist from any need for strict representation, and this at a time when representation itself has been so widely rejected by the most honoured and publicised artists of this century.

The result is that many literal representations of ballet are excruciatingly bad, and paintings of ballet are often at the level of chocolate box art, rehashing yet again clichés based upon Degas' paintings. Magnificent exceptions there are. We would cite the

151 Paul Colin, *Serge Lifar*. Poster, 1935. Colin's mastery of the poster is nowhere more apparent than in this large three-colour design for a recital by Lifar. It combines the bold image of Lifar's face – very stylised but utterly true – with the simplified figure of the dancer leaping in an *attitude*. The contrast between the stillness of the face and the upward movement of the body, the use of the surrounding blackness and the beautifully placed scarlet lettering, are very remarkable. See also plate 150.

152 Leslie Hurry, *Robert Helpmann*

152 Leslie Hurry, *Robert Helpmann*. Pen, ink and wash, 1942. The then Sadler's Wells (now Royal) Ballet staged Robert Helpmann's *Hamlet*, a noteworthy production, in 1942. The work was brilliantly theatrical, not least because of the superb designs by Leslie Hurry – his first work for the theatre. In 1941 Hurry had exhibited at the Redfern Gallery, showing paintings which explored an imaginative world by means of an extended Surrealist manner. Robert Helpmann visited this show and invited Hurry to decorate his forthcoming *Hamlet*. For a study of Robert Helpmann's work by Caryl Brahms (published in London in 1943) Leslie Hurry provided the dust jacket which is illustrated. It features a double portrait of Helpmann as Comus (left) and as Hamlet, in a fantasy world of ballet.

153 Bryan Organ, *Portrait of Nadia Nerina*. Oil, 1969. Bryan Organ's portrait of Nadia Nerina catches her in a pose from *The Dragonfly*. Nerina had danced this Pavlova solo with great success, and Organ fixes the essence of the movement in what seems a brilliantly immediate succession of brush strokes. The play of light through the filmy costume and its reflection on the dancer's face and breast suggest the speed of movement which is so essentially a part of this dazzling solo.

154 Marc Chagall, *Aleko: Alicia Markova as Zemphira*. Watercolour drawing, 1942. Collection of the Museum of Modern Art, New York. In 1942 American Ballet Theatre was installed in Mexico City for a five month season. During this time Leonid Massine created a ballet, inspired by Pushkin's poem *The Gypsies*, which was designed by

153 Bryan Organ, *Portrait of Nadia Nerina*

Marc Chagall. For this *Aleko* he produced decor and costumes which were a most happy marriage of his own style with the ballet's theme. The leading role of Zemphira was created for Alicia Markova, and Dame Alicia records how Chagall himself painted the heart and the tree of life on to the bodice of her costume as she wore it.

154 Marc Chagall, *Aleko*

155 Charlotte Trowbridge, *Martha Graham in 'Letter to the World'*

156 Pavel Tchelitchev, *Serge Lifar as Albrecht in 'Giselle' Act II*. Sepia pen wash on paper. Serge Lifar acquired a great reputation during the 1930s as an interpreter of the role of Albrecht in *Giselle* in his staging of that Romantic masterpiece at the Paris Opéra. Tchelitchev's superb drawing provides beautiful testimony to the power and romantic ardour of Lifar's interpretation. It is a compelling likeness, not least in the very precise rendering of Lifar's hands. Tchelitchev pinpoints the despairing energy of the hapless hero as he soars in the air – exhausted, but forced to continue dancing by the relentless Queen of the Wilis.

work of Paul Cadmus and Pavel Tchelitchev, and also the less direct contributions of distinguished painters like Berman and Bérard who were primarily involved in ballet as decorators. Because so much portrayal of dancing today never gets beyond graphic cleverness, even at its best, it is all the more rewarding to find a sculptor like William Pye intrigued by the possibilities of dance and expressive movement. In our quest for examples of contemporary painting we have found that the work of many good artists in connection with ballet has seemed peripheral – decorative, amused footnotes to the art rather than deeply concerned involvement. For the most part the contact of major artists with ballet has been in the matter of decoration: Sutherland, Piper, Ayrton, Ceri Richards in Britain; Noguchi, Johns, Rauschenberg, Stella, Warhol in America; the galaxy of artists who have worked with Roland Petit – among them Clavé, Carzou, Ernst, Delvaux; and the no less exceptional catalogue of painters who have worked for the Ballet Théâtre Contemporain in France. This activity indicates that the connection between art and ballet maintains the practical relationship initiated by Diaghilev, rather than an imaginative involvement with ballet as a source of painterly inspiration.

Paradoxically, ballet today is enjoying a popularity unknown since the heyday of the Romantic era, and is far more widespread in its manifestations. To satisfy a public demand for souvenirs of their favourite dancers and companies there are, of course, a profusion of photographs and posters. There is also a new industry in footling statuettes and drawings, but far more relevant and 'of the period' are the T-shirts and lapel buttons on sale inside and outside theatres which celebrate the names or faces of the ballet company and its stars. Taglioni appeared on soap wrappers in the 1830s; Nureyev now appears on fake dollar bills; the Soviets, Cubans and Danes put their ballerinas on postage stamps; tablets of soap are imprinted with scenes from the classical ballets.

Yet the serious involvement of artists with ballet is not impossible and not totally extinct. The camera will naturally and rightly dominate the preservation of an essentially ephemeral art. Nevertheless, the challenge to the painter remains. We can but echo David Bomberg's dictum: 'Good judgement is through good drawing . . . and when the good draughtsman draws, the muses come to dance.'

156 Pavel Tchelitchev, *Serge Lifar as Albrecht in 'Giselle'*

157 Martin Battersby, *Lynn Seymour*

157 Martin Battersby, *Lynn Seymour*. Oil, 1961. In 1961 the English *tromp-l'oeil* artist Martin Battersby held an exhibition on the theme of sphinxes; among his subjects was the young Lynn Seymour, at that time first making her mark with the Royal Ballet. Battersby saw her as a sylphide sphinx and he placed her in a nocturnal setting of a ruined abbey. The painting is a delightful caprice which also provides a touching portrait of the twenty-year-old Seymour.

158 Andy Warhol, *Merce Cunningham*. Silkscreen print. The American modern dancer Merce Cunningham has been a vastly influential figure since his first works were staged in 1952. An important aspect of his creativity has been his constant co-operation with painters in the making of his dances: Robert Rauschenberg, Jasper Johns, Frank Stella, Andy Warhol, among others, have been vitally involved in the presentation of Cunningham pieces. On some occasions this has meant that the artists have been called upon to produce aleatory settings; at other moments, the designers have left a firm imprint upon the dance from its very inception – as in the case of Rauschenberg's pointillist setting for *Summer Space*. Andy Warhol decorated *Rainforest* for

the Cunningham company, and the silver helium-filled pillows which he devised floated over the stage making their own choreographic patterns. This portrait of Cunningham is a tribute to an early dance, of 1958, in which the choreographer appeared with a chair strapped to his back. Warhol has embellished the photograph by overprinting it with a Victorian wallpaper pattern. It seems entirely in accord with Cunningham's own procedures.

158 Andy Warhol, *Merce Cunningham*

159, 160, 161 Pavel Tchelitchev, Drawings for *Errante*. 1933. *Les Ballets 1933* was a short-lived company, financed by Edward James for his wife, the dancer Tilly Losch. James's unquestioned taste as a patron of the arts guaranteed the collaboration of some of the brightest talents of the time: Balanchine, Derain, Tchelitchev, Sauguet, Milhaud, Bérard, Weill and Brecht. Among the most mysterious works created by the company was *Errante*, danced to Schubert's *Wanderer Fantasy* with choreography by Balanchine. It was designed by Tchelitchev, who gave free rein to his bizarre personal mythology and created stage pictures of ravishing beauty. The drawings illustrated are impressions of the hermaphroditic angels guiding the heroine through the fantastic action of the piece; the heroine herself is seen on the right.

159–161 Pavel Tchelitchev, Drawings for *Errante*

160

161

162 André Derain, *Two Dancers*

163 Joseph Cornell, *Hotel de l'Etoile*

162 André Derain, *Two Dancers*. Drawing. André Derain was first involved with the ballet when Diaghilev commissioned him to provide the decor and costumes for Massine's *La Boutique fantasque* in 1919. Thereafter he worked for many companies, always producing distinguished decoration. This drawing was used for the cover of a souvenir book of the Original Ballet Russe for a number of years from the late 1930s. The two *danseuses* in their Romantic tarlatans represent a popular public image of ballet, but Derain's clean line does not prettify them.

163 Joseph Cornell, *Hôtel de l'Etoile*. Construction. The American Surrealist Joseph Cornell was particularly fascinated by the procedures of *trompe l'oeil*, and he took this idea further by devising 'boxes' in which real objects rather than painted representations were put to surreal use. These boxes are, in effect, collages in which fragments are juxtaposed to evoke other times or other places. They are irrational, but there arise from them allusions which excite the spectator's imagination. Cornell was a balletomane and especially fond of the Romantic ballet. He used issues of *Dance Index*, the distinguished series of monographs produced in New York between 1942 and 1948, as a source for some of his imagery in such creations as *Taglioni's Jewel Casket* and his several *Homages to the Romantic Ballet*. In the *Hôtel de L'Etoile* the dancer is Lucile Grahn in *La Sylphide*.

164 Boris Chaliapin, *Alicia Markova in 'Swan Lake'*. Gouache, 1941. The super-realism of this almost life-size portrait of Alicia Markova achieves an exceptional intensity of presence. A meticulous presentation of this great English ballerina as Odette in *Swan Lake*, it catches the spiritual concentration so essentially a part of a unique performer and celebrates the enormous popularity she enjoyed in the United States.

165 Ronald Searle, Margot Fonteyn in *Hamlet*

166 Philippe Jullian, *Romantic Agony*

165 Ronald Searle, Margot Fonteyn as Ophelia in Robert Helpmann's *Hamlet*, 1943.

166 Philippe Jullian, *Romantic Agony*. Pen and ink. The author Philippe Jullian showed an equally felicitous talent as an illustrator. To both sides of his talent he brought a most perceptive eye. He seemed to take a particular delight in some of the extravagances of the ballet world and for Richard Buckle's incomparable and much lamented magazine *Ballet*, which was so influential during the six years of its existence from 1946 to 1952, Jullian contributed several sequences of funny, cruel yet truthful drawings. Shown here is the final nail in the coffin of *Giselle* – the paraphernalia of the Gothic performance style is mercilessly revealed.

167 Edward Gorey, *The Gilded Bat*. Pen and ink. The American artist and writer Edward Gorey has earned a devoted following during the past two decades through a series of books which he has written and illustrated. These combine a macabre humour with a sense of mystery and unease: the result is often disquieting, highly poetic, as well as wildly funny. Gorey is also an astute observer of the

ballet – he reportedly never misses a performance by the New York City Ballet – and his *Gilded Bat*, from which this illustration comes, is a tragi-comedy of the progress of a child, Maudie Splaytoes, who embarks upon a ballet career, changes her name to Mirella Splatover, achieves world fame and meets her doom in an aeroplane accident.

168 Saul Steinberg, *Three Dancers*. Drawing, 1951. Saul Steinberg's caricatures are far more than ephemera; they remain some of the most pertinent and valuable of social comments upon American life. This drawing made on the former premises of the School of American Ballet appeared in the American magazine *Wake*, number 10, published in New York in 1951. Steinberg indicates a great deal about the brilliant and athletic style of the dancers of the New York City Ballet.

167 Edward Gorey, *The Gilded Bat*

168 Saul Steinberg, *Three Dancers*

169 Feliks Topolski, *Ballerina in her Dressing Room, Monte Carlo*

170 Christian Bérard, *Alice Nikitina in 'La Nuit'*

169 Feliks Topolski, *Ballerina in her Dressing Room, Monte Carlo*. In 1940 the leading ballet critic Arnold Haskell arranged the publication of a book, *Ballet – to Poland*, to be sold in aid of the Polish Relief Fund. It included contributions from some of the most distinguished dance figures of the time, all of whom gave their work in aid of this excellent cause. Feliks Topolski, himself Polish, donated a portfolio of drawings of the ballet, among which was this evocative portrait of the ballerina Vera Nemchinova in her dressing room during a performance of *Coppélia*. As in the Constantin Guys drawing, plate 48, the sense of the theatre is potent.

170 Christian Bérard, *Alice Nikitina in 'La Nuit'*. Pen and watercolour, 1930. A key figure in the French art scene for twenty-five years was Christian Bérard; as painter, designer, arbiter of taste, he held a unique position. A decorator of genius, he consistently produced magic in the theatre by the simplest means, while at the same time showing an ability to create decors and costumes of the most exquisite refinement and grandest luxury. Inevitably he was attracted to the ballet, illuminating a series of works for various companies. In 1930 C. B. Cochran invited him to decorate the short ballet, *La Nuit*, which Lifar choreographed for *Cochran's 1930 Revue*.

171 Paul Cadmus, *Arabesque*. Pencil drawing, 1947. The American artist Paul Cadmus is a member of the school of painting known as Symbolic Realism, whose work was given an exhibition of exceptional interest in London in 1950. Cadmus remains one of the few artists of recent years able accurately to represent classic dancing without either vulgarity or sentimentality. His studies of dancers, nearly always in the rehearsal studio, are exact in showing how bodies work and they achieve a poetic dimension: the atmosphere, so potently created in Jerome Robbins's masterly ballet *Afternoon of a Faun*, of young bodies discovering themselves in a studio, is exactly that found in Cadmus's drawings.

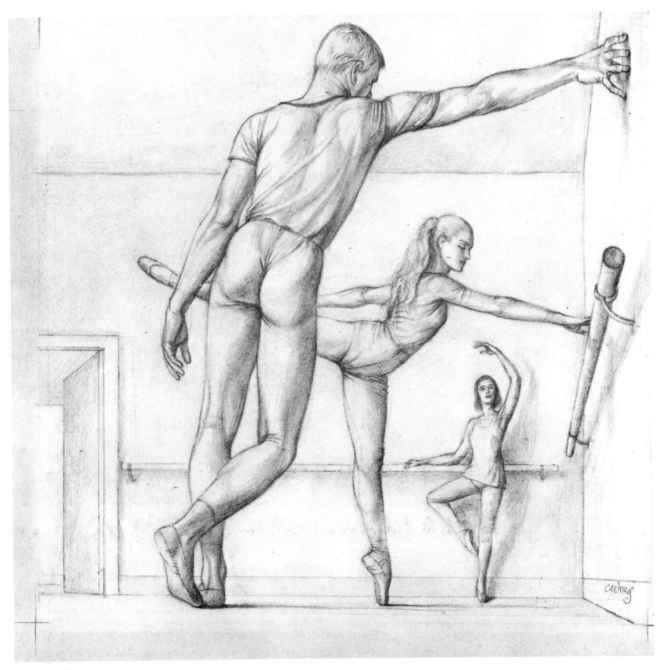

171 Paul Cadmus, *Arabesque*

172 Byrd, Poster for the Dance Theatre of Harlem.
1975. A design in electric blue and silver.

173 César, Poster for *Hopop*. 1969. Ballet Théâtre
Contemporain was founded to take up residence at
the Maison de la Culture in Amiens in 1968 as part
of André Malraux's grand scheme for the de-
centralisation of the arts in France. Director of the
company since its inception has been Jean-Albert
Cartier, whose distinguished career as an art critic
has had considerable influence upon the decorative
aspects of the works staged. Cartier commissioned
designs from many of the most interesting and
adventurous painters and sculptors working in
France. Among these was the sculptor César. His
designs for *Hopop*, for which he provided the decor,
reflect the Pop Art scene of the 1960s. His poster is a
bold and eye-catching arrangement of colour.

174 Donn Matus, *Jewels*. Poster. Matus created three
posters for the three sections of the New York City
Ballet's *Jewels*, identical except for their colours –
emeralds, rubies and diamonds.

172 Byrd, Poster for Dance Theatre of Harlem

173 César, Poster for *Hopop*

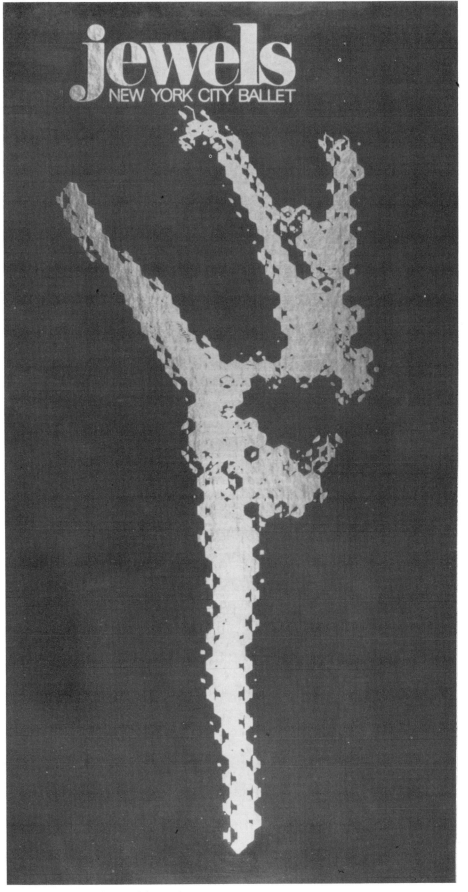

174 Donn Matus, Poster for *Jewels*

175 Enzio Frigerio, Designs for *Romeo and Juliet*

175 Ezio Frigerio, Designs for Escalus and attendants in *Romeo and Juliet*, as presented by London Festival Ballet in 1976.

176 Rex Whistler, Costume designs for *The Rake's Progress*. 1935. This ballet, by Ninette de Valois with music by Gavin Gordon, was first produced by the Sadler's Wells Ballet in 1935. Whistler's costume designs for *The Rake's Progress* were inspired by Hogarth's series of paintings.

177 Nadine Baylis, Designs for *Ziggurat*. This ballet by Glen Tetley was first produced by the Ballet Rambert in 1967. Nadine Baylis is one of the most distinguished designers working in the field of contemporary dance today.

176 Rex Whistler, Costume designs for *The Rake's Progress*

177 Nadine Baylis, Designs for *Ziggurat*

178, 179 Enzo Plazzotta, *Nadia Nerina*. Bronze, 1967. Among the earliest bronzes by the Italian-born sculptor Enzo Plazzotta were some studies he made in the 1960s of Nadia Nerina, then principal ballerina of the Royal Ballet. In the *Arabesque sur terre*, (179) the stretch of the body of a dancer in practice dress seems to sustain the bronze itself. Like its companion, which shows Nerina adjusting her leg warmers, this is in no sense a glamorised portrait, but an honest portrayal of a dancer at work. The hair is tied back in a bandeau; Nerina is wearing leg-warmers; the academic exactness of turn out and the anatomical logic behind it, is clearly to be seen. The bronzes also remind us of the strength and open quality of Nerina's dancing.

180 William Pye, *Nerina*. Steel sculpture, 1970. In making this standing form inspired by the dancing of Nadia Nerina, the sculptor William Pye has evoked a dancer's presence and the sense of movement inherent in a pose without sacrificing his own style. It is not a literal portrait of the dancer, but nevertheless the image of dancing, refined and transposed, is strongly present: it is rare today to find a non-representational sculptor willing and able to accept the challenge of dance.

178

178, 179 Enzo Plazzotta, *Nadia Nerina*

180 William Pye, *Nerina*

INDEX

Figures in **bold** type refer to illustrations

ACKNOWLEDGEMENTS

This book would not have been possible without the tireless help and research of Susan Hyman and Caroline Lucas. To both of them we owe an extreme debt of gratitude. We must also record our indebtedness to the generosity of Mrs Parmenia Migel Ekstrom of New York for lending so many treasures from her collection. Also in New York David Vaughan gave us valuable assistance, and we have to record our gratitude to the staff of many museums and galleries, most notably the Theatre Museum at the Victoria and Albert Museum, the Dance Collection of The Center for Performing Arts, Lincoln Center and Sotheby Parke-Bernet, New York. Christina Gascoigne kindly produced and identified gems from the Italian Renaissance theatre. To Angelo Hornak, John Webb and other photographers whose work is represented go our thanks. To Carol Venn, as always, gratitude for help in preparing the manuscript. Throughout our enterprise, Madame Maria Sackova was a constant source of inspiration.

Picture Credits

Numbers refer to plates except where marked.
Front cover: Edgar Degas, *La Danseuse au Bouquet*. Museum of Art, Rhode Island School of Design (Gift of Mrs Murray S. Danforth); Back cover: Edward Gorey, Poster for the New York City Ballet. Private collection; Page 1: Giacomo Pregliasco, *Designs for a Chinese Ballet*. Biblioteca Civica, Turin; Page 2: Eugene Berman, *Giselle*. Private collection; Page 4: John Brandard, *Carlotta Grisi in 'La Péri'*. Crown Copyright, Victoria and Albert Museum; Agence Topp, 109 (SPADEM); Bibliothèque de l'Opéra, 96 (Photo: Giraudon); Bibliothèque Nationale, 6; Birmingham Museums & Art Gallery, 63; The Brooklyn Museum (Gift of James H. Post, John T. Underwood and A. Augustus Healy), 91 (SPADEM); Bulloz, Page 7, 16, 18, 22, 100, 123 (SPADEM); Charlottenburg, 24 (Photo: Scala); Christina Gascoigne Photographs, 15; Collection Charles Gordon, 153, 179; Collection Parmenia Migel Ekstrom, Page 6, 20, 38, 55, 70, 80, 85; Crown Copyright, Victoria and Albert Museum, 1, 3, 11, 13, 26–7, 30 (Photo: Michael Holford), 36–9, 57, 60, 74 (Photo: Robert Harding), 77 (Photo: Michael Holford), 98 (Photo: Cooper-Bridgeman) (SPADEM); Dance Collection, The New York Public Library at Lincoln Center,

Astor, Lenox & Tilden Foundations, 40, 68–9, 144, 158–61, 171; Fine Art Society London, 108 (Photo: Cooper-Bridgeman) (SPADEM); Frederick Gore Collection, 112 (Photo: Robert Harding); Giraudon, 134 (ADAGP), 135 (ADAGP); Glasgow Art Gallery, 92 (Photo: Cooper Bridgeman (SPADEM); Harvard Theater Collection, 64; Jeu de Paume, Paris, 99 (Photo: Scala) (SPADEM); Kunstmuseum Basel, Kupferstichkabinett, 45; Los Angeles County Museum of Art, 2; Louvre, 14 (Photo: Giraudon), 103 (Photo: Giraudon) (SPADEM); Mander & Mitchenson Theatre Collection, 67, 71, 117; Mansell Collection, 130; Mary Evans Picture Library, 10, 59, 83; Musée Bourdelle, Paris, 142 (ADAGP); Musée Carnavalet, 66 (Photo: Bulloz), 76 (Photo: Bulloz), 105 (Photo: Snark) (ADAGP); Musée des Arts Decoratifs, 75 (Photo: Bulloz); Musée d'Art Moderne, Paris, 148 (Photo: Bulloz) (SPADEM); Musée des Beaux-Arts, 133 (Photo: Giraudon) (SPADEM); Musée des Beaux-Arts, Tours, 19 (Photo: Giraudon); Musée de Toulouse-Lautrec, Albi, 93; Musées Nationaux, Paris, 29; Museum of Modern Art, New York, 120 (Gift of Edward M. M. Warburg) (ADAGP), 139 (Gift of Abbey Aldrich Rockefeller) (SPADEM), 154 (Acquired through the Lillie P. Bliss Bequest) (ADAGP); National Gallery of Art, Washington, 88 (Rosenwald Collection), 89 (Gift of Myron A. Hofer) (SPADEM), 97 (Widener Collection) (SPADEM); National Gallery of Fine Arts, Smithsonian Institution, 136 (Gift of Romaine Brooks); National Gallery of Scotland, 87 (Photo: Cooper-Bridgeman) (SPADEM), 90 (SPADEM); Nationalmuseum, Stockholm, 31; Osterreichische Nationalbibliothek, Vienna, 50; Pictor Milano, 104; Pierpont Morgan Library, 32; Private collection, 7, 9, 21, 41, 43, 47–9. 51–4, 62, 65, 72–3, 79, 81, 84, 94, 102, 110–1, 122, 124, 125–9, 132, 137–8, 140–1, 149 (ADAGP), 152, 155, 162, 164 (Photo courtesy of Boris Chaliapin), 165–9, 172–8, 180; Radio Times Hulton Picture Library, 46, 58, 101; Roger-Viollet, 61 (SPADEM), 115 (SPADEM); Royal Academy of Dancing Library, 57, 78; Snark International, 107 (SPADEM), 116 (ADAGP), 118 (SPADEM), 143 (ADAGP), 150 (ADAGP); Sotheby & Co., 86 (SPADEM), 106 (SPADEM), 119 (ADAGP), 124, 146, 151 (ADAGP); Sterling & Francine Clark Art Institute, Williamstown, Massachusetts, 95 (SPADEM); Tacoma Art Museum, Tacoma, Washington, 113 (Photo courtesy of Chapellier Galleries, Inc., New York); The Tate Gallery, London, 25, 131; Theater & Music Collection, Museum of the City of New York, 82; Trustees of the British Museum, 5, 8 (Photo: Aldus Books), 28 (Photo: John Freeman), 33 (Photo: John Freeman), 34–5, 42; Uffizi, Florence, 12 (Photo: Scala); Wadsworth Atheneum, Hartford, Connecticut, 156 (Ella Gallup Sumner and Mary Catlin Sumner Collection), 170 (Ella Gallup Sumner and Mary Catlin Sumner Collection) (SPADEM); Wallace Collection, 23 (Reproduced by permission of the Trustees); Weidenfeld & Nicolson Archives, 4, 114, 121 (SPADEM), 145 (ADAGP).

FOR DUMMIES™

BUSINESS AND
GENERAL
REFERENCE
BOOK SERIES
FROM IDG

Politics For Dummies

Cheat Sheet

P9-DFY-653

Candidate Selection Checklist

Here are some tips on what you may want in a candidate, what you may want to avoid, and what to do when you find a candidate you like.

Things to Look For

- ✔ Does the candidate appear intelligent or is he just filling out the suit?
- ✔ Is the candidate qualified for the job?
- ✔ Does she have the education and experience to handle the job?
- ✔ Do you agree with the programs and ideas the candidate has proposed?
- ✔ Are you comfortable with the groups and the individuals who support the candidate?
- ✔ Can you trust the candidate?
- ✔ Does he pass the elevator test? (If an elevator door opened in front of you, and getting on meant you would ride alone with the candidate, would you get on?)
- ✔ Is the candidate a leader?
- ✔ Does she have ideas of her own?

Things to Watch Out For

- ✔ Candidates who make appeals to your emotions — *not* to your intelligence
- ✔ Candidates who identify problems — but don't propose realistic solutions
- ✔ Candidates who offer simple, no-sacrifice solutions to complex problems
- ✔ Candidates who talk exclusively about hot-button issues such as race, immigration, the flag, English as the official language, class warfare — and not about such issues as taxes, health care, the budget
- ✔ Candidates with shady dealings in their backgrounds
- ✔ Candidates who tell you what they think you want to hear
- ✔ Candidates who use negative campaign tactics to give you a false impression of the competition

Supporting a Candidate

- ✔ Volunteer your time — contact voters, organize events, distribute literature
- ✔ Contribute money or help the candidate raise money
- ✔ Urge others to support your candidate
- ✔ Remember to vote for your candidate on election day

BUSINESS AND
GENERAL
REFERENCE
BOOK SERIES
FROM IDG

Politics For Dummies™

Cheat Sheet

Contacting Elected Officials

To exercise your newfound political skills and tell the people who represent you what you want them to do, you have to know who your congressperson, state representative, or state senator is. To find out, call one of the following offices (you can find the numbers in the phone book):

- County board of elections or voter registration
- State election board
- Local office of the League of Women Voters
- Public library
- State or county headquarters of the Republican or Democratic parties

Ask the person to tell you (make sure you have your address with you):

- Your congressional district, congressperson, and the office phone number
- Your legislative district, state legislator, and the main number at the statehouse
- Your state senate district, state senator, and a phone number at the statehouse.

Ask whether the official has an 800 number and or an e-mail address.

Check your voter registration card; it may list your ward and precinct. That information makes it easier for the county office to determine which district you live in.

...For Dummies: The Best Selling Book Series

IDG BOOKS WORLDWIDE

When You Call Your Elected Officials

- Be prepared to give your name and address
- Tell the person precisely why you are calling
- If you are calling about a particular piece of legislation, give the number of the bill, if possible
- Tell the individual whether you are for or against the legislation and why
- Be patient; other voters may be calling to express their views, too

Steps to Getting Involved in Politics

- Register to vote
- Vote in every election
- Join a political party
- Vote in primaries
- Read and listen to the information about the candidates — cast an informed vote
- Ask questions of candidates and elected officials
- Don't hesitate to tell officials when they've done something you don't like
- Thank officals when they do something you do like
- Use your phone, the mail, your fax, your computer e-mail — let your representatives hear from you often
- Circulate petitions and join with others who think as you do
- Become a delegate to a national convention

What Readers Say About Politics For Dummies

"Ann's book explains politics in clear concise language that every one can understand."

— Mike McDaniel, Republican

"*Politics For Dummies* gets my vote for the best how-to political book on the market."

— Doug Richardson, Democratic Governor's Association

"How many people can say 'I truly made a difference?'
Politics For Dummies tells you how to do it."

— Rex C. Early, Republican Candidate for Governor of Indiana

What Readers Say About . . .For Dummies Business and General Reference Books

"Excellent! Informative! I liked the simple layman's terms and humor. I like this book <u>very</u>, <u>very</u>, <u>very</u>, <u>very</u>, <u>very</u>, <u>very</u>, <u>very</u>, <u>very</u> much!"

— Laura Goosby, Poughkeepsie, NY

"Clear, concise, informative, and humorous. I read it cover to cover."

— M. Byrne, Etobicoke, Ont.

"Easy to read and understandable. Everyone above the age of 14 should read and own this book!!!"

— John Cakars, Berkeley, CA

"Appreciated answers to all 'dumb' questions..."

— Lorraine Gosselin, Montreal, Que.

BUSINESS AND
GENERAL
REFERENCE
BOOK SERIES
FROM IDG

References for the Rest of Us!™

Do you find that traditional reference books are overloaded with technical details and advice you'll never use? Do you postpone important life decisions because you just don't want to deal with them? Then our ...*For Dummies*™ business and general reference book series is for you.

...*For Dummies* business and general reference books are written for those frustrated and hard-working souls who know they aren't dumb, but find that the myriad of personal and business issues and the accompanying horror stories make them feel helpless. ...*For Dummies* books use a lighthearted approach, a down-to-earth style, and even cartoons and humorous icons to diffuse fears and build confidence. Lighthearted but not lightweight, these books are perfect survival guides to solve your everyday personal and business problems.

> *"More than a publishing phenomenon, 'Dummies' is a sign of the times."*
> — *The New York Times*

> *"A world of detailed and authoritative information is packed into them..."*
> — *U.S. News and World Report*

> *"... you won't go wrong buying them."*
> — *Walter Mossberg, Wall Street Journal, on IDG's ...For Dummies™ books*

Already, hundreds of thousands of satisfied readers agree. They have made ...*For Dummies* the #1 introductory level computer book series and a best-selling business book series. They have written asking for more. So, if you're looking for the best and easiest way to learn about business and other general reference topics, look to ...*For Dummies* to give you a helping hand.

IDG
BOOKS
WORLDWIDE

POLITICS
FOR
DUMMIES™

POLITICS
FOR
DUMMIES™

by Ann DeLaney

IDG Books Worldwide, Inc.
An International Data Group Company

Foster City, CA ♦ Chicago, IL ♦ Indianapolis, IN ♦ Braintree, MA ♦ Dallas, TX

Politics For Dummies™

Published by
IDG Books Worldwide, Inc.
An International Data Group Company
919 E. Hillsdale Blvd.
Suite 400
Foster City, CA 94404

Library of Congress Catalog Card No.: 95-81097

ISBN: 1-56884-381-X

Printed in the United States of America

10 9 8 7 6 5 4 3 2 1

1A/SQ/RR/ZV

Distributed in the United States by IDG Books Worldwide, Inc.

Distributed by Macmillan Canada for Canada; by Computer and Technical Books for the Caribbean Basin; by Contemporanea de Ediciones for Venezuela; by Distribuidora Cuspide for Argentina; by CITEC for Brazil; by Ediciones ZETA S.C.R. Ltda. for Peru; by Editorial Limusa SA for Mexico; by Transworld Publishers Limited in the United Kingdom and Europe; by Al-Maiman Publishers & Distributors for Saudi Arabia; by Simron Pty. Ltd. for South Africa; by IDG Communications (HK) Ltd. for Hong Kong; by Toppan Company Ltd. for Japan; by Addison Wesley Publishing Company for Korea; by Longman Singapore Publishers Ltd. for Singapore, Malaysia, Thailand, and Indonesia; by Unalis Corporation for Taiwan; by WS Computer Publishing Company, Inc. for the Philippines; by WoodsLane Pty. Ltd. for Australia; by WoodsLane Enterprises Ltd. for New Zealand.

For general information on IDG Books Worldwide's books in the U.S., please call our Consumer Customer Service department at 800-762-2974. For reseller information, including discounts and premium sales, please call our Reseller Customer Service department at 800-434-3422.

For information on where to purchase IDG Books Worldwide's books outside the U.S., contact IDG Books Worldwide at 415-655-3021 or fax 415-655-3295.

For information on translations, contact Marc Jeffrey Mikulich, Director, Foreign & Subsidiary Rights, at IDG Books Worldwide, 415-655-3018 or fax 415-655-3295.

For sales inquiries and special prices for bulk quantities, write to the address above or call IDG Books Worldwide at 415-655-3200.

For information on using IDG Books Worldwide's books in the classroom, or ordering examination copies, contact Jim Kelly at 800-434-2086.

For authorization to photocopy items for corporate, personal, or educational use, please contact Copyright Clearance Center, 222 Rosewood Drive, Danvers, MA 01923, or fax 508-750-4470.

 is a trademark under exclusive license to IDG Books Worldwide, Inc., from International Data Group, Inc.

About the Author

Ann M. DeLaney began a long association with politics and political involvement as a political science graduate of the State University of New York at Binghamton, where she served as student-body president. She received her law degree from Indiana University and became a deputy prosecuting attorney specializing in rape and child abuse cases. Ann also served as Commissioner of the Marion Superior Court.

Ann knows all about campaigns and politics because she's been politically active as a precinct committeeperson, worker in voter registration drives, delegate to state and national party conventions, and a member of the Democratic National Committee.

Conventional political wisdom needs bucking now and again; Ann was the first woman nominated by a major party as a candidate for Lieutenant Governor of Indiana, running with Wayne Townsend who was willing to break the conventions. She was the Legislative Director for the first Democratic governor of Indiana in twenty years, Evan Bayh, serving when the House of the Indiana General Assembly was divided 50/50 between Democrats and Republicans and had dual Speakers of the House, a Democratic Speaker one day, a Republican speaker the next.

A former Executive Director of the Indiana Democratic Party, Ann served as the manager for the 1992 gubernatorial reelection campaign of Indiana's governor, Evan Bayh. Ann was also the first woman to serve as chair of a major political party in Indiana.

Ann continues her involvement in politics as a panelist on *Indiana Week in Review,* a weekly political talk show carried on public television and public radio in Indiana that has received public television's award for a best public affairs show two years in a row. She is also a regular panelist on *The Mike Pence Show,* a public affairs television show in Indiana. She frequently speaks on politics to civic and political groups and is a former columnist for the *Indianapolis Business Journal.*

Welcome to the world of IDG Books Worldwide.

IDG Books Worldwide, Inc., is a subsidiary of International Data Group, the world's largest publisher of computer-related information and the leading global provider of information services on information technology. IDG was founded more than 25 years ago and now employs more than 7,700 people worldwide. IDG publishes more than 250 computer publications in 67 countries (see listing below). More than 70 million people read one or more IDG publications each month.

Launched in 1990, IDG Books Worldwide is today the #1 publisher of best-selling computer books in the United States. We are proud to have received 8 awards from the Computer Press Association in recognition of editorial excellence and three from Computer Currents' First Annual Readers' Choice Awards, and our best-selling ...*For Dummies*® series has more than 19 million copies in print with translations in 28 languages. IDG Books Worldwide, through a joint venture with IDG's Hi-Tech Beijing, became the first U.S. publisher to publish a computer book in the People's Republic of China. In record time, IDG Books Worldwide has become the first choice for millions of readers around the world who want to learn how to better manage their businesses.

Our mission is simple: Every one of our books is designed to bring extra value and skill-building instructions to the reader. Our books are written by experts who understand and care about our readers. The knowledge base of our editorial staff comes from years of experience in publishing, education, and journalism — experience which we use to produce books for the '90s. In short, we care about books, so we attract the best people. We devote special attention to details such as audience, interior design, use of icons, and illustrations. And because we use an efficient process of authoring, editing, and desktop publishing our books electronically, we can spend more time ensuring superior content and spend less time on the technicalities of making books.

You can count on our commitment to deliver high-quality books at competitive prices on topics you want to read about. At IDG Books Worldwide, we continue in the IDG tradition of delivering quality for more than 25 years. You'll find no better book on a subject than one from IDG Books Worldwide.

John Kilcullen
President and CEO
IDG Books Worldwide, Inc.

IDG Books Worldwide, Inc., is a subsidiary of International Data Group, the world's largest publisher of computer-related information and the leading global provider of information services on information technology. International Data Group publishes over 250 computer publications in 67 countries. Seventy million people read one or more International Data Group publications each month. International Data Group's publications include: **ARGENTINA:** Computerworld Argentina, GamePro, Infoworld, PC World Argentina; **AUSTRALIA:** Australian Macworld, Client/Server Journal, Computer Living, Computerworld, Digital News, Network World, PC World, Publishing Essentials, Reseller; **AUSTRIA:** Computerwelt, PC TEST; **BELARUS:** PC World Belarus; **BELGIUM:** Data News; **BRAZIL:** Annuário de Informática, Computerworld Brazil, Connections, Super Game Power, Macworld, PC World Brazil, Publish Brazil, SUPERGAME; **BULGARIA:** Computerworld Bulgaria, Networkworld/Bulgaria, PC & MacWorld Bulgaria; **CANADA:** CIO Canada, ComputerWorld Canada, InfoCanada, Network World Canada, Reseller World; **CHILE:** Computerworld Chile, GamePro, PC World Chile; **COLUMBIA:** Computerworld Colombia, GamePro, PC World Colombia; **COSTA RICA:** PC World Costa Rica/Nicaragua; **THE CZECH AND SLOVAK REPUBLICS:** Computerworld Czechoslovakia, Elektronika Czechoslovakia, PC World Czechoslovakia; **DENMARK:** Communications World, Computerworld Danmark, Macworld Danmark, PC World Danmark, PC World Danmark Supplements, TECH World; **DOMINICAN REPUBLIC:** PC World Republica Dominicana; **ECUADOR:** PC World Ecuador, GamePro; **EGYPT:** Computerworld Middle East, PC World Middle East; **EL SALVADOR:** PC World Centro America; **FINLAND:** MikroPC, Tietoverkko, Tietoviikko; **FRANCE:** Distributique, Golden, Info PC, Le Guide du Monde Informatique, Le Monde Informatique, Reseaux & Telecoms; **GERMANY:** Computer Business, Computerwoche, Computerwoche Extra, Computerwoche Focus, Electronic Entertainment, GamePro, I/M Information Management, Macwelt, PC Welt; **GREECE:** GamePro, Macworld & Publish; **GUATEMALA:** PC World Centro America; **HONDURAS:** PC World Centro America; **HONG KONG:** Computerworld Hong Kong, PCWorld Hong Kong, Publish in Asia; **HUNGARY:** ABCD CD-ROM, Computerworld Szamitastechnika, PC & Mac World Hungary, PC-X Magazine; **INDIA:** Computerworld India, PC World India, Publish in Asia; **INDONESIA:** InfoKomputer PC World, Komputek Computerworld, Publish in Asia; **IRELAND:** ComputerScope, PC Live!; **ISRAEL:** PC World 32 BIT, People & Computers; **ITALY:** Computerworld Italia, Computerworld Italia Special Editions, Lotus Italia, Macworld Italia, Networking Italia, PC Shopping, PC World Italia, PC World/Walt Disney; **JAPAN:** Macworld Japan, Nikkei Personal Computing, SunWorld Japan, Windows World Japan; **KENYA:** East African Computer News; **KOREA:** Hi-Tech Information/Computerworld, Macworld Korea, PC World Korea; **MACEDONIA:** PC World Macedonia; **MALAYSIA:** Computerworld Malaysia, PC World Malaysia, Publish in Asia; **MEXICO:** Computerworld Mexico, GamePro, Macworld, PC World Mexico; **MYANMAR:** PC World Myanmar; **NETHERLANDS:** Computable, Computer! Totaal, LAN Magazine, Macworld, Net Magazine; **NEW ZEALAND:** Computer Buyer, Computerworld New Zealand, MTB, Network World, PC World New Zealand; **NICARAGUA:** PC World Costa Rica/Nicaragua; **NIGERIA:** PC World Africa; **NORWAY:** Computerworld Norge, Computerworld Privat, CW Rapport Klient/Tjener, CW Rapport Nettverk & Telecom, CW Rapport Offentlig Sektor, IDG's KURSGUIDE, Macworld Norge, Multimedia World, PC World Ekspress, PC World Nettverk, PC World Norge, PC World's Produktguide, Windows Spesial; **PAKISTAN:** Computerworld Pakistan, PC World Pakistan; **PANAMA:** GamePro, PC World Panama; **PARAGUAY:** PC World Paraguay; **P. R. OF CHINA:** China Computerworld, China Infoworld, Computer & Communication, Electronic Product World, Electronics Today, Game Camp, PC World China, Popular Computer Week, Software World, Telecom Product World; **PERU:** Computerworld Peru, GamePro, PC World Profesional Peru, PC World Peru; **POLAND:** Computerworld Poland, Computerworld Special Report, Macworld, Networld, PC World Komputer; **PHILIPPINES:** Computerworld Philippines, PC Digest, Publish in Asia; **PORTUGAL:** Cerebro/PC World, Correio Informático/Computerworld, Mac•In/PC•In Portugal; **PUERTO RICO:** PC World Puerto Rico; **ROMANIA:** Computerworld Romania, PC World Romania, Telecom Romania; **RUSSIA:** Computerworld Rossiya, Network World Russia, PC World Russia; **SINGAPORE:** Computerworld Singapore, PC World Singapore, Publish in Asia; **SLOVENIA:** MONITOR; **SOUTH AFRICA:** Computing S.A., Network World S.A., Software World; **SPAIN:** Computerworld España, COMUNICACIONES WORLD, Dealer World, Macworld España, PC World España; **SWEDEN:** CAP&Design, Computer Sweden, Corporate Computing, MacWorld, Maxi Data, MikroDatorn, Nätverk & Kommunikation, PC/Aktiv, PC World, Windows World; **SWITZERLAND:** Computerworld Schweiz, Macworld Schweiz, PCtip; **TAIWAN:** Computerworld Taiwan, Macworld Taiwan, PC World Taiwan, Publish Taiwan, Windows World; **THAILAND:** Thai Computerworld, Publish in Asia; **TURKEY:** Computerworld Monitör, MACWORLD Turkiye, PC WORLD Turkiye; **UKRAINE:** Computerworld Kiev, Computers & Software Magazine, PC World Ukraine; **UNITED KINGDOM:** Acorn User, Amiga Action, Amiga Computing, Amiga, Appletalk, CD Powerplay, CD-ROM Now, Computing, Connexion, GamePro, Lotus Magazine, Macaction, Macworld, Open Computing, Parents and Computers, PC Home, PC Works, The WEB; **UNITED STATES:** Cable in the Classroom, CD Review, CIO Magazine, Computerworld, Computerworld Client/Server Journal, Digital Video Magazine, DOS World, Electronic, InfoWorld, I-Way, Macworld, Maximize, MULTIMEDIA WORLD, Network World, PC World, PUBLISH, SWATPro Magazine, Video Event, WebMaster; **URUGUAY:** PC World Uruguay; **VENEZUELA:** Computerworld Venezuela, GamePro, PC World Venezuela; and **VIETNAM:** PC World Vietnam   10/17/95

Dedication

I dedicate this book to those people who work hard every election to make our political system the envy of the world — the unsung heroes of American politics, the party activists in all parties, such as Miles Lloyd, Owen Sweeney, and Stan Meng, who showed me what commitment meant, and to Harry Truman, who showed me that ordinary people can make a difference if they are willing to try.

I dedicate this book to my active, interesting, opinionated but very loving family, for whom I am very grateful: My wonderful husband of many years Ed; daughters Kathleen, the lawyer and new mother, and Jennifer, the doctor; teenaged son Tim, a budding biologist and guitarist; and my sons-in-law Jim and Chris. A mother-in-law could not ask for better. Without the encouragement, love, and support they gave me, this project would still be a concept. Their willingness to read and to listen, to do research, and to nag me about deadlines and find files I vaporized on our home computer — permitted me to complete this book reasonably on time. I'd also like to dedicate this book to the newest member of our family, born one week before deadline, whom I hope will be the first of several in her generation to carry the torch for political involvement, our first grandchild, Emma DeLaney Strenski.

Credits

Acknowledgments

I am also grateful to several friends and colleagues for their support, ideas and encouragement. I'd like to thank Bill Moreau, political strategist extraordinaire, for his generosity in spending hours reading the drafts and making suggestions. I'd like to thank Rodney Schmisseur for his help in suggesting ways to integrate computers and politics in Chapter 6. Thanks also to my colleague on the other side of the political aisle, Indiana Republican State Chairman Mike McDaniel, and to my friends, David Dawson, Fred J. Nation, John Dillon, Mike Draper, Brian Williams, Mary Murphy, Jo Ann Williams, and Richard Gordon for their ideas, contributions, and encouragement.

Thanks also to the Honorable Evan Bayh, Governor of Indiana, the Honorable Pamela Carter, Attorney-General of Indiana, former State Senator Wayne Townsend, pollster Doug Schoen, and media consultant Cindy Wall for assisting in my political education over the years.

To the excellent, and patient, IDG staff: First of all, Diane Steele and my nephew, the young but very talented, Greg Kilkenny, who conceived of the idea for this book and convinced me to write it; Stephanie Britt, my wonderful project editor who doesn't get rattled by anything, Diane Giangrossi, Shannon Ross, and Mike Kelly. Thank you as well to my wonderful technical reviewers, Reid Duffy and Doug Richardson.

(The Publisher would like to give special thanks to Patrick J. McGovern and Bill Murphy, without whom this book would not have been possible.)

Contents at a Glance

Cartoons at a Glance

By Rich Tennant

Table of Contents

· ·

Part VII: The Part of Tens 295

Introduction

● ●

Welcome to *Politics For Dummies*.

When I was growing up in a traditional two-parent family where my mother never worked outside the home, I was taught that a lady was mentioned in the newspaper when she was born, when she married, and when she died and certainly no other time. Politics was not something that was discussed in my home at the dinner table. I think my parents voted, but I couldn't tell you how, and I know they never went to a fund-raiser for a candidate or volunteered for a campaign.

When I became active in politics and began appearing in the press and on television with some regularity, my mother wondered where she and my father had gone wrong. What I had discovered, to my parents' dismay, was that politics wasn't all that complicated and actually could be fun. It could also be tough, even dirty and nasty at times, but winning and being part of something bigger than yourself brings with it a tremendous sense of satisfaction and control, even if your only involvement is to vote for the candidate of your choice. You're exercising your rights, and the candidates have to consider your views. You are in control!

What Is Politics?

What exactly is politics? That depends on who's doing the defining. Some people use the word *politics* as an expletive. Suppose you've just seen a particularly vicious negative political advertisement on TV, where one candidate challenged the honesty, patriotism, or parentage of the opposing candidate. You would not be alone if you dismissed the ad by saying, "That's just politics."

Many of us use the phrase "That's just politics" to express our displeasure with everything we see wrong with our system. We get disgusted with special legislation that gives expatriated Americans a $3.6 billion tax windfall. We dislike seeing officials get favorable treatment from regulatory agencies for constituents or contributors.

Many of us are offended by Congress's generosity to itself (pensions, free lunches, and golf trips from lobbyists). We disapprove of Members of Congress saying one thing and voting for another (such as supporting term limits but not retroactively). And we tend to condemn these activities with a disgusted "That's just politics!"

It may be "just politics," but once you learn the ropes, you can have an impact on politics. You can find out how candidates stand on issues of importance to you. You can make elected officials listen to your concerns and those of your neighbors. You can make a difference!

Politics is more than just what is wrong with our system. Politics *is* our system. It orders our lives. It determines who wins and who loses when governments make decisions. It determines whether the future will be brighter or bleaker for our children.

Here's just a sample of the many things that politics determines:

- Who serves in office and for how long
- The policies our governments enacts
- Who wins and who loses when groups compete for resources or favorable legislation
- Who pays taxes, how much, and what kind
- Whether a landfill opens near your neighborhood despite your concerns about having potentially toxic waste close to where your children play
- What your children are taught in school, what tests they take, and what scores they must achieve to graduate
- How much you pay to send your children to a state-supported college and whether student loans are available to help you pay the cost
- When your garbage is collected and what items are accepted

From the sublime to the ridiculous, politics is everywhere!

However you define it, politics is the glue keeping our entire society together and determining the relationships of all the members of that society. You can't avoid politics. You can refuse to participate in the process by not registering or voting, but the process will still affect you and your family every day of your lives, in ways you know and in ways you can't imagine.

You can't avoid it, no matter how far you try to bury your head in the sand. So you may as well find out enough about politics to understand what's really happening. Once you understand politics, you can act to improve your position in those decisions that have an impact on you, your family, and your neighborhood. Who knows, with *Politics For Dummies* at your side, you may decide to run for President of the United States — or at least for city council. Anyway, you can make politics work for you.

Why You Need This Book

Americans have been taught to think that politics is something that decent people don't know anything about and certainly don't participate in. The combination of late-night talk shows and jokes at the expense of politicians has convinced most of us that politics is dirty, sleazy, and incomprehensible to normal people.

Most people will never run for office. They will never work in a political campaign or directly give money to a political party or to a candidate. A substantial number of people in this country, more than one-third of our adult population, will never register to vote or vote on a regular basis. Most adults know little or nothing about politics, but they're not to blame. The process by which people serve in elected office, and what they do when they get there, remains a mystery to most of us. Whatever meager attempts are made to teach civics in schools are limited to how a bill becomes a law and the like. Schools make little if any effort to prepare students to understand politics.

This book can help you understand what's going on, how people are trying to influence or manipulate you, and what you can do about it. Whether you like it or not, politics affects your life, for better or worse, in many different ways. Wouldn't you like to have a voice in these decisions that have a direct effect on your life? You have opinions on these issues. Those opinions should be considered before such decisions are made. Because you can't avoid politics, you might as well understand it and make it work for you.

The key to understanding politics is to realize that it isn't all that complicated. Selling a candidate isn't really much different from selling a product, any product, even deodorant! The words the media uses on the nightly news and never bothers to define — such as *caucuses, primaries, pollsters,* and *political action committees* — are just jargon.

This book tells you what really happens starting from when you register to vote. It helps you sift through the many conflicting messages you see and hear in the media and from the campaigns. Then you can vote for the candidate who is right for you, the one you can trust with important decisions that affect your life.

I hope that this book will peel away the layers of misperception and distrust so that, once you understand politics, you can also understand how politics can work for you. Who knows, once you understand what's going on, you may decide that politics can be fun, even as a spectator sport!

How to Use This Book

This book is meant to be a reference that you can take off the shelf whenever you have questions about what's happening politically. You can read it through from cover to cover, if you like, and if your social life is at an unusual lull. But *Politics For Dummies* is designed to answer your questions by easy reference to the table of contents, the index, the icons, and the sidebars. As your questions arise, you can find exactly what you want to know without having to read the entire book.

This book answers the questions most frequently asked by intelligent people who have avoided the perils of politics to date. If you have little or no knowledge of politics, don't be embarrassed. You are like most people, and this book can help you understand and make politics work for you. If you have some knowledge and want to increase it, this book is the vehicle to do so.

How This Book Is Organized

Each chapter attempts to answer a frequently asked question about politics. The chapters are organized into parts, each of which covers an area of politics. Here's a summary of what you will find in each part.

Part I: Politics and You

This part is all you need for intelligent cocktail party conversation to demonstrate that you're in the know and taking the first step in any kind of political activity.

Part II: Making Your Voice Heard

This part tells you how to communicate with the big shots. How to start changing the world as we know it. How to become a political player. This is where you can find out how to start getting yourself involved in politics. The last chapter opens up the world of politics on the Internet. Politics is one of the top three topics on the Internet, so whatever your political beliefs, there's a Web site out there for you.

Part III: Politics Is a Team Sport

This part discusses why we have only two major parties and all sorts of minor parties and independent candidates. It tells you some of the differences between Democrats and Republicans, how to become a member of a political party, and what happens when you do. Also, the ever-popular special interest groups — are you part of one? Are you sure? This chapter tells you what special interest groups are, how to join one, and how to make them work for you.

Part IV: It's All Marketing

This part tells you how a campaign introduces and sells the candidates. It tells you how to separate the truth from the advertising run by the campaigns. All this should help you choose which candidate you want to vote for.

Part V: Let the Campaigns Begin!

This part talks about campaigns at the local, state, and national level. Find out where the money goes and where the special interests are. The parties also want to know what you think about everything under the sun, so there's a chapter telling you about all those polls the parties — and the media — like so much. Then there are the issues that candidates and parties don't want to discuss in public — because you might not like what they have to say. This part also explores the dark side of politics — the whys and wherefores behind negative campaigning and the reforms needed for politics to clean up its act.

Part VI: Presidential Politics

This part covers the presidential campaigns: from the New Hampshire primary to the national party conventions to the Electoral College. Turn here to find out what actually goes into electing a president.

Part VII: The Part of Tens

This is the famous ...*For Dummies* part that's all lists. Here, I've included the ten things you need to teach your kids or yourself about politics, the ten commandments of politics, and, of course, the ten most common political mistakes — just so you can see whether the latest candidate might have figured out a new way to screw up.

Icons in This Book

The little round pictures in the margins of the book point out really important information, warnings of thin ice, things you should remember, and ways you can become active in politics. Here's a list of the icons and a brief description of what each one does:

This icon highlights the interesting, technical parts in the book that are good to know, but that you can skip over. These are case studies, historical anecdotes, and all kinds of political trivia for the would-be political buff.

This icon flags ways you can find your own voice in politics and make politicians listen to what you have to say.

This icon highlights ways you can take action and become a political player.

This icon sheds light on stories about politics that are part of the common wisdom but may not be true. Look here to find out what the reality is.

This icon marks political words of wisdom that can help you navigate the system.

This icon alerts you to things to avoid and common mistakes people make.

This icon is a friendly reminder of information discussed elsewhere in the book or stuff you definitely want to keep in mind.

Where to Go from Here

You can either read this book straight through or you can skip from chapter to chapter. If you need to brush up on some of the political basics, turn the page. If becoming an active player in politics is what you're looking for, go straight to Part II. Use this book to find out about politics and become a player in your community, state, or the country itself.

Part I:
Politics and You

In this part...

This part has all you need to demonstrate your political savvy at weenie roasts and cocktail parties. Find out what *politics* really means and the critical role votes and money play in every political decision. Discover why, when it comes down to it, politics is all about you — the voter.

Chapter 1

"It's Politics, Stupid!"

● ●

In This Chapter

▶ Understanding local, state, and federal legislatures

▶ The difference between politics and government

▶ What politics really means for you

● ●

*P*olitics is that unique situation in which you choose people to run parts of your life — by choosing the people who run your government. Our government has all kinds of elected politicians, from the president down to the village animal-control officer. In most cases, you can choose whichever candidate you think will do the best job.

Elected Politicians — A Quick Look

Elected officials come in three levels: federal, state, and local. You have a role in determining who gets elected to all three. You can think of these officials as three tiers of a wedding cake: As you move down, each layer gets larger and larger, with more and more politicians. (See Figure 1-1.) The president and the vice president go on top of the cake of politicians. It's up to you whether or not they hold hands, or whether you want to file for divorce at the next election.

Federal elected officials

The federal government consists of three branches: judicial, legislative, and executive.

    ✔ The *judicial branch* consists of federal trial and appeals judges, including the U.S. Supreme Court. These judges are nominated by the president and confirmed by the Senate — you don't have a vote in the selection of federal judges. The judicial branch of government interprets federal laws when lawsuits are filed in federal courts. On occassion, it also decides whether state laws conform to the federal constitution.

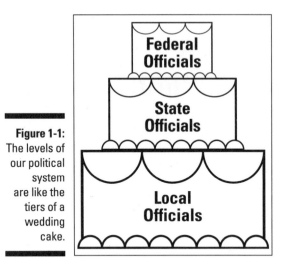

Federal
Officials

State
Officials

Local
Officials

✔ You do elect the members of the *legislative branch,* called Congress. (Congress includes both the U.S. Senate and the House of Representatives.) Congress makes the laws by passing bills.

✔ You also elect the heads of the *executive branch:* the president and the vice president. The executive branch of government plays a role in making laws by the use of the president's veto of legislation. The executive branch also carries out the laws that Congress enacts and the courts have clarified.

How we elect federal officials — the president, the vice president, senators, and representatives — is set by the U.S. Constitution, which has been changed several times to encourage more participation by voters.

The president and the vice president

The U.S. elects a president and the vice president every four years. They are elected together to avoid having the president from one party and the vice president from another serve together. This happened early in our country's history without damaging the republic, but it created enough fuss to suggest that it was not a good idea.

You don't elect the president and vice president directly, but you do have a role to play in their election. That's the topic of Chapter 22.

Senators

Each state, regardless of its population, elects two senators to serve six-year terms. Every two years, one-third of the Senate is elected, so your state may or may not have a Senate contest in a given *general election year,* which is a year in which candidates are elected in most constituencies. General elections are held in even-numbered years (1994,1996, 1998, and so forth).

Representatives

Each state also elects Members of Congress, called *representatives,* who serve in the House of Representatives in the Congress. The number of representatives in Congress is limited to 435. The census, taken every ten years, determines how many of those 435 representatives each state has. States with growing populations gain congressional seats after the census, and states with shrinking populations lose congressional seats.

After the census results are in, each state's legislature redraws the congressional districts for its state. The exact boundaries of these districts are the subject of much political fighting, turf warfare, and teeth gnashing, as incumbents try to sweet-talk their state legislatures into drawing districts that would allow them and their next of kin to maintain their current lifestyle.

A Member of Congress is elected every two years and represents roughly a half-million people in his or her district.

State elected officials

Each state is divided into three branches of state government, just like the federal government: judicial, legislative, and executive. The functions of these three branches are largely the same as they are with the three branches of the federal government.

- ✔ **Judicial:** Judges in state courts interpret state laws. Some states elect their trial court and appellate court judges; some don't. Some states permit citizens to vote to retain or remove judges but don't permit partisan elections for judicial positions. Whether you can play a role in the selection of judges depends on your state law.

- ✔ **Legislative:** State legislatures enact laws that apply to their state. In each state, voters are grouped into legislative districts for the state legislature or general assembly. You are assigned to a district for the *upper* and *lower* houses of your legislature. The upper house is usually called the *senate,* and the lower one, *the house of representatives.* You choose an official for each house of the state legislature. The terms vary from two to four years.

    The ever efficient and tidy state of Nebraska has only one house in its legislature consisting of 49 members with no party affiliations. (Parties and affiliations are discussed in Chapters 7 and 8.)

- ✔ **Executive:** The voters of each state elect a governor for their state. When the election takes place and how long the governor's term is depend on state law. Most states have four-year terms for their governors and elect them in general election years. Vermont and New Hampshire have two-year terms. A few states, like New Jersey, elect their governors in odd-numbered years.

> Most states elect a governor and a lieutenant governor on the same ticket, and many states limit the number of terms a governor can serve to two or even one.

Local elected officials

Cities, towns, and counties also have elections to choose officials for their legislative and executive branches. Some judicial offices may be elected at the local level, but these courts handle small-claims issues or local ordinances for minor matters. State law largely governs criminal and civil matters.

Mayors, city council members, county commissioners, and the like are elected at the local level. How, when, and for how long these officials are chosen depends on state law. Some states elect local officials in odd-numbered years, some in even-numbered years. Some officials have term limits; some don't. Your state or county election board or clerk's office can tell you how these elections work in your community.

Politics versus Government

Politics and government don't differ very much, but, the rhetoric changes somewhat. Politicians discuss things in governmental or policy-motivated terms and avoid partisanship. Rather than talk about a proposal benefiting Republican or Democratic constituencies. Republicans talk about getting government off the backs of small businesspeople and about adopting tax policies to encourage initiative. The Democrats discuss corporate welfare or the plight of the working man or woman. The terms, particularly the labels, may change, but the sides are basically the same. That's because *politics is the art of governing.*

Politics has spin doctors

When the forum shifts from government to politics, the spokespeople for or against the policies also change. In the heat of a political campaign, the campaign manager or the Democratic or Republican party official is the public spokesperson. He advances and defends ideas proposed by one side of the campaign, and the corresponding person on the opposite side responds.

The campaign or party spokesperson is responsible for controlling the *spin* of a story — in other words, trying to get the media to portray a story in a way favorable to the party official's campaign. The spin, or the way the media approaches a story, determines whether a story helps or hurts a campaign. A perfect example of a spin doctor's failure is a political joke making the rounds.

> President Clinton and the Pope went out on a lake in a rowboat to do some fishing. The Pope's hat fell into the water. President Clinton got out of the boat, walked across the water, retrieved the hat, and returned it to the Pope. The headline in the next day's newspaper was "President Clinton Can't Swim!"

President Clinton demonstrates an ability to walk on water, and the media interpretation is that the president can't swim. Obviously, this joke is extreme, but it does illustrate a point. Media portrayal can turn a perfectly positive story into a negative one and vice versa. Spin doctors play a very important role in campaigns. Every good campaign has a spin doctor, and the campaign attempts to make the spin doctor the only contact person for the media.

The government has spokespeople

In government, as opposed to politics, the spokesperson is the elected official or a third-party group. The recent national debate over health care provides a perfect example of this model. The Republican Party opposed President Clinton's proposal, but it was the financial interests — the insurance industry, the nursing home industry, and the hospital association — that attacked the proposal openly. The attacks came in the form of paid advertisements on television, in press conferences, and in public statements. Labor unions and liberal doctors groups defended the president's proposal.

The tactic of using nonpartisan groups rather than political parties to support or attack a proposal is very common because reactions of these groups have more credibility with the media and the public than do either party's reaction. Because the parties are trying to persuade the media and the public to a particular point of view, they'll use whatever tactic is most likely to get that goal accomplished.

No matter the label, no matter the spokesperson, the sides are basically the same. The Democrats are in favor of the proposal, and the Republicans are opposed to it, or vice versa. Politicians can wrap packages with pretty ribbons and call decisions by favored names, but the decisions made in the name of government remain political decisions. That's because the heart of any decision about how the government chooses among competing interests vying for scarce resources is political.

After all, that's what democracy is all about. The will of the majority is supposed to prevail, within the constraints of our constitutional protections of the rights of the minority.

Voters look with disfavor on elected officials who don't vote the way the voters want. You shouldn't be surprised when disgruntled voters "vote out" those who disagree with them by not reelecting them to office. It takes an exceptional officeholder or circumstance for someone to risk thwarting the will of a majority of voters on an issue of importance.

Officeholders don't remain in office for longer than one term if they fail to keep those risks in mind. Some other candidate will come forward and accuse the officeholder of failing to listen to the voters. That is an accusation that will stick with the voters. The campaign rhetoric will call for a new officeholder who will listen to what the voters want.

The same political calculation — where are the votes and where is the money — is done for almost every governmental decision. In that way, politics and government are the same. (See Chapter 2 for more on the money/vote analysis.)

The majority rules, but the Constitution controls

The Constitution restricts some of the effects of majority rule. If a right is protected by our Constitution, the majority cannot pass laws or adopt policies restricting that right. Our courts would declare such actions unconstitutional. The law or policy would be invalid and unenforceable. For example, the vast majority of citizens in this country violently disagree with the principles of the Ku Klux Klan. They are deeply disturbed by the hatred that the group preaches.

Say that I'm a spokesperson for that vast majority. I question whether Klan members have any place in American society. I recognize that the Klan is a very small segment of our population, and I don't believe that it should be able to disrupt our cities. We citizens shouldn't be required to pay for its police protection when it marches and spreads its venom. I would prefer not to hear it or see it march again. A majority of our citizens would like to see Klan rallies banned. A majority of Americans would favor outlawing the group itself.

Despite how most of us feel, the will of the majority cannot determine the treatment accorded the Klan. Our Constitution says that the Klan has rights whether we like it our not. The First Amendment to the Constitution states that Congress "shall make no law abridging the freedom of speech . . . or the right of the people peaceably to assemble." The Klan is free to march and speak, regardless of how violently the rest of us react to its message. The Constitution protects the rights of minorities no matter how unpopular they are. In fact, the more unpopular they are, the more they need the protections afforded by the Constitution.

When our Constitution protects a right or an action, government can't interfere with that right or action. Even if most voters want their elected officials to interfere, our system won't let that happen.

What Do You Want from Your Elected Officials?

It's pretty simple. You want your elected officials to be responsive to you. You may want them to lead, but first you want them to listen to what you have to say. On most issues, you know what you want and what is best for you. You want respect and attention to your point of view. There are very few issues that are so complicated that you need the official's expertise and experience to decide what you want. On those very few issues, you still want the elected official to use his insight and experience to do what you think should be done. You'll leave how to get what you want done to the official, but you know what it is you want.

When Representative Joe Schmoe does something that you, Jane Voter, are opposed to, he'd better have a very good reason for his action. And the reason had better not be that a well-heeled contributor asked him to do it! You have a right to ask Representative Joe what his reasons were for doing what he did. The explanation may convince you that what he did was the right thing; or it may only convince you that he did what he thought was the right thing. You don't have to agree with Joe's decisions 100 percent of the time to vote for his reelection. But you do need to tell him what you want and ask him to explain why you can't have it, if the answer is no.

Elected officials who don't listen to voters risk their political careers. That is true even when the elected official follows a course of conduct that later proves to be the right one. The political risk involved with being out of touch with voters helps to explain why pollsters have become so important in modern politics. Elected officials spend a great deal of time and money finding out what you and other voters think about an issue. More of that in Chapters 5 and 15.

You can force an elected official to do what is right, even if she or her campaign-finance chairman doesn't want to do it. You simply have to get enough people like you organized to get the job done. Having the energy and organization and being on the right side of an issue are enough if you know what you're doing. You can make the political system work for you. You can have clout. Chapter 5 has tips on how to organize to use your political clout.

POLITICAL STUFF

Do politicians ever become statesmen?

What is a *statesman,* anyway? Harry Truman said, "A statesman is a politician that has been dead 10 or 15 years."

I think of statesmen as people who put government and policy ahead of partisanship. They put the public good ahead of their own personal political survival. They make decisions based on what is right, not on what is popular. That means a statesman will vote the way she thinks is right, even if it means going against what you want. She will risk losing elections to vote the right way. In other words, a statesman will not always vote the way you want her to vote.

Maybe when they get old, before they fade away, or when they no longer hold office, politicians can become statesmen. But that phenomenon is quite rare. Occasionally, there are times when an honorable politician will risk his or her career to take an unpopular position on an issue.

One excellent example of statesmanship — of putting principle ahead of political self-interest — occurred in 1964 when the Civil Rights Act was passed. Through seniority, Southern conservative Democrats controlled the powerful Rules Committee of the U.S. House of Representatives and, thumbing their noses at the House Democratic leadership and President Johnson, kept civil rights legislation from getting to the House floor for a vote.

In order to break the logjam, the House leadership moved to expand the membership of the Rules Committee so civil rights supporters could be appointed to create a majority in favor of the legislation. When the resolution to expand the

Rules Committee was put to a vote, everyone knew the vote would be close. A key vote in support was cast by a first-term Democrat from rural Louisiana, Gillis W. Long. The Rules Committee expansion passed, Congress approved it, and the Civil Rights Act became law. When Representative Long ran for reelection in 1964, he was painted as a liberal and defeated.

But there's a happy ending. When the Representative who defeated Long retired in 1972, the voters of the district returned Long to Congress, where he served until his death in 1985.

And when Representative Long returned to Capitol Hill in 1973, to what key committee did the House leadership appoint him? That's right — the Rules Committee!

Sometimes, if a politician is sufficiently well thought of by her constituents, she can take an unpopular position on a volatile issue and survive the next election. Indeed, sometimes that politician can convince the voters of the rightness of her position, not simply convince the voters to support her despite it.

More often, a politician who swims against the tide to do the "right thing" on a tough issue finds that the cost of having a clear conscience may well be her elected position. That is one of the prices of majority rule. If the politician was correct on a matter of sufficient note to make the history books, that politician may be labeled a statesman by future voters. However, the politician will be known as a statesman only after she is gainfully employed in another field.

Chapter 2

The Money/Vote Analysis

• •

In This Chapter

▶ The reality behind taking a political stance — the money/vote analysis

▶ What does politics really mean for you?

▶ Figuring out your stake in the election

• •

*B*oth money and votes play starring roles in politics, whether the politics is local, state, or national. You need to know what determines the stances that politicians take on any and every issue so you can figure out how the politician's stance affects you.

Uncovering the Factors behind Any Political Stance

Most issues and campaigns have two sides: one side supporting a candidate or an issue and the other opposing it. But even if a campaign for election or legislation has more than two sides, a politician's analysis is the same. And it doesn't matter whether the issues are local, state, or national; the analysis works the same way at every level.

When legislators and candidates analyze an issue, they take into account what's at stake for them in terms of votes and money:

✔ They find out which side of a campaign for election or legislation is more popular with a large number of motivated voters.

✔ They take a close look at which side has the support of special interest groups that have money to contribute.

You should know how your elected officials are likely to behave given the vote/money analysis. That knowledge helps explain their conduct. It also explains why they sometimes don't behave as you would like them to. You may be on the losing end of the vote/money analysis. The other side may be better organized or more willing to spend money on campaigns or issues and better able to get the attention of the elected official. You need to know this so you can compensate. You may also become an advocate of campaign finance reform. More of that in Chapter 19.

The weight of public opinion

Be aware that when politicians analyze an issue, they weigh which stance will gain or lose them the most votes. Far from voting out of gut feeling or conscience, the first questions a politician needs to ask are these:

- Where are the votes?
- Who cares about a particular issue?
- Which side is better organized?
- Which side can turn out more voters or demonstrators in support of its position?
- Which side feels more strongly about the issue?
- Is one side or the other more likely to cast votes in the next election based on this issue alone?
- What are the risks to the official or the candidate in supporting one position or the other?

It doesn't matter whether these are local, state, or national campaigns or issues. The analysis is the same for all. Officials who desire reelection and candidates who want to win must have a majority of the voters supporting them. The composition of that majority may change many times during an official's term or the duration of a campaign, but having a majority is essential to any victory.

Officials and candidates are reluctant to take any action or position that could alienate large segments of the voting public, for obvious reasons. Once that segment is alienated, wooing it back is very difficult. Officials and candidates will take such action or articulate such positions when doing so is unavoidable, but usually only then. Sometimes, officials or candidates can get caught between the proverbial rock and the hard place. An issue can be so polarizing that politicians will alienate a significant segment of the voting population no matter which way they go.

Failing to act or to take a position has the potential of alienating everyone, so officials and candidates must go one way or the other — perhaps resorting to the coin-flip or the "voters-love-me, they-love-me-not" method.

Many times, the issues are not quite so volatile. In those cases, absent an overarching and strongly held philosophy, the candidate or official performs a vote/money analysis. Which position will cost more votes in the next election? Which position will gain more money in the next election?

Counting up the money

After looking at how his stance will affect votes, the next question that a politician must ask in assessing a political issue is: Who cares enough about this proposal to contribute substantial sums of money for its passage or defeat?

I am not suggesting that many elected officials or candidates benefit personally from this money. Some do, but they usually wind up under indictment. I'm not going to spend time talking about those officials here because, despite what you may hear, the vast majority of elected officials are honest people. They're too scared to be anything else!

Money plays a significant role in politics because elections cost so much. Because money is such an important factor in campaigns, it isn't surprising that, in addition to voting trends, the other question that candidates and elected officials are likely to consider is whether taking one position or the other will result in substantial contributions for or against their campaigns. Elected officials also consider whether one or another position will cause money to be spent against them indirectly.

The Abscam scandal

Since the sting operation known as Abscam (run by the FBI to catch senators and representatives taking bribes), congressional representatives have been either more honest or more cautious, or allergic to grand juries.

Abscam *(Arab Scam)* was a two-year sting operation where the FBI used a phony Arab sheik to offer bribes to federal elected officials. The "sheik" wanted the officials to obtain federal money or licenses or to set up real estate deals. When the operation was shut down in 1980, six representatives and one senator were indicted and convicted after exhibiting their greed on the FBI's candid camera.

POLITICAL STUFF

Candidates and touchy issues: striker replacements

Periodically, a debate arises on the national scene over *striker replacements,* which would allow employers to hire permanent replacements for striking workers. Businesses, chambers of commerce, and business associations favor striker replacement.

The bill is also a litmus test for organized labor, meaning that organized labor campaigns against anyone supporting striker replacement. Labor unions also support any candidate or official opposed to striker replacement legislation.

In a district or state where organized labor plays a significant role, supporting striker replacement can cost a candidate votes. In fact, supporting striker replacement legislation can mean losing the election in a heavily union district. Businesspeople may feel very strongly about this issue, but more voters will vote against the candidate because of his position than business can produce to vote *for* the candidate. Because businesses can't generate more votes for the candidate than will be lost by supporting striker replacement, they usually lose the debate with organized labor in a district with a significant organized-labor population.

When you analyze this issue to see what is really going on, you will understand what your elected official is likely to do and why. If you are opposed to the likely course of action for your elected official, you can begin to exert pressure on the official to vote the other way.

Many issues like this one must be subjected to both prongs of the vote/money analysis. In the section "The weight of public opinion," I discuss the votes component of this issue, but you need to know, if you don't already, that money is at the heart of this debate, as it is for many policy issues.

Employers want the ability to hire permanent replacements for striking workers for financial reasons. When an employer can fire strikers, her bargaining power in negotiations with labor unions is strengthened considerably. The employer is able to cut costs and stay competitive so that business can grow. The most significant weapon a union has to force an employer to bargain in good faith — the right to strike — is blunted. Fear of losing their jobs will force union members to settle for less money and benefits than they might otherwise negotiate.

The issue is a tug-of-war over who keeps more of the money, labor or management. Both sides argue that their position is righteous, pure, and above reproach.

The debate over striker replacement legislation is a fight over money. The decision by the elected official will probably be determined by the number of votes generated for or against him.

Before I get too cynical here, I am not suggesting that the issues of votes and money will always determine an official's or candidate's position on an issue, but they are factors that all successful politicians consider, whether they admit it or not. Candidates consider money and votes because they want to be reelected. No candidate likes to lose. It's like Abraham Lincoln said when asked how he felt after losing an election: "I'm too big to cry, but it hurts too much to laugh." No candidate wants that to happen to her, and so she weighs the risks of taking on the special interests, and possibly taking on the political unemployment line.

Money Makes the World Go 'Round

For you to assess the impact of proposed legislation on *you,* you first need to understand who benefits from the legislation. You can get a clue to who benefits by examining who is contributing big money to get the legislation enacted.

When you know which groups are bankrolling campaigns to pass certain laws, you can understand *why* the legislation is being pushed and, therefore, what is really happening. *Then* you're in a position to determine whether it affects you.

An example of how money can talk in the political process occurred recently in the New York legislature. A long-term debate on cutting certain New York taxes ended up benefiting the beverage industry of New York State, to the tune of a $40 million annual tax cut. Now, cutting taxes for the beverage industry had not been at the top of the list of possible cuts proposed by Governor George Pataki or the Business Council of New York State. So how did it happen? The beverage industry waged a four-year battle for tax cuts, spending between $2 million and $4 million on hiring high-powered lobbyists (see Chapter 9 for more on lobbyists) and wining and dining legislators. The industry made substantial contributions to political campaigns for both parties. In short, it demonstrated the power of money in directing policy decisions for governments.

Once you know the facts behind decisions like these, you can see the influence of money and votes. Decide whether this is the type of policy you want or not. You can make your elected officials accountable for these decisions if you determine that these are not the kinds of policies you want to see.

Raising money

The money politicians gain by supporting or opposing legislation goes into the campaign coffers of candidates — incumbents or challengers — not their pockets. Raising money is a significant part of any campaign. Congressional campaign spending for 1994 increased 17 percent over 1992's record levels. Spending totaled $693,500,000 for the 1994 election cycle in congressional races. All this for people who continually tell us how they are going to save our hard-earned tax dollars.

The largest increases in spending in 1994 occurred in House of Representative races involving Republican challengers, a category where median spending increased 66 percent. Republicans running for open House seats increased their spending by 35 percent. One in four Republican challengers for the House raised a minimum of $400,000 through the end of November 1994. In 1992, only one in ten Republican challengers reached that level of fund-raising (Federal Election Commission release, December 22, 1994).

The average representative in Congress represents approximately 500,000 citizens. Representatives run for election every two years. In terms of fund-raising, the top 50 incumbents in the House seeking reelection each raised more than $900,000 for the 1994 campaign. Thirty-three of them raised over $1 million. You can see why money plays such an important role in political campaigns when this performance is repeated every two years.

Leverage and money

Incumbents raise money year-round. They also spend a substantial amount of time fund-raising to come up with the amount of money I'm talking about here. That means our elected representatives and senators spend time with people and groups that have money to give and reasons to give it.

That is a political reality that should give all of us pause and make our wallets ache.

All this means that your elected official pays a great deal of attention to the wishes and opinions of large contributors. If the position that you want the elected official to take is at odds with one that a large contributor wants, you may lose the debate, all things being equal. The official may very well give more consideration to the opinion of the contributor than to you. That's true even if the contributor and his bank account don't live in your district or even your state.

That's the way it is now, but it doesn't have to be. Reading this book and doing your analysis are your ways of finding out what is really going on and what to do about it. You won't be fooled by the pious rhetoric about the issue.

Senate money

Senate campaigns are in a whole different league from House of Representative campaigns. Senators are elected by a majority of the voters of each state but only every six years. The 1994 spending for Senate campaigns increased 52 percent over 1992 (Federal Election Commission release, December 22, 1994).

The ridiculous cost of campaigns

Look at the California Senate race from 1994. The Democratic nominee, Dianne Feinstein, and the Republican nominee, Michael Huffington, raised more than $43,000,000 combined for their campaigns. Even more amazing than that sum is the fact that they went into debt besides. The two sides had a combined debt after that election totaling more than $15,000,000. The 1994 California Senate campaign cost over $58,000,000. All this for a job that pays $133,600 a year.

In the 1994 congressional elections, candidates raised $611,500,000, up 23 percent over the amount raised in 1992 (Federal Election Commission release, December 22, 1994). There is every indication that the cost of campaigns will continue to grow.

And to paraphrase the late Illinois Senator Everett Dirksen: pretty soon, we'll be talking about real money.

(Chapter 19 discusses campaign finance reform.)

It is not uncommon for Senate campaigns to spend millions of dollars each. In fact, the top 50 Senate campaigns in the 1994 election each raised more than $1,500,000 — and they didn't do it with bake sales and car washes.

Many times, the money is contributed in big chunks. Each federally qualified PAC can donate $5,000 per election per candidate. (See Chapter 14 for more on PACs, or *political action committees*.) That means $10,000 per PAC for the primary and general elections combined. PACs can also give to the national parties and their offshoots. The national parties are able to spend larger amounts to elect candidates for the House and the Senate than any PAC or individual can give.

Hatred Is a Greater Motivator than Love

Given human nature, it is easier to motivate voters to vote *against* than to vote *for* a candidate. Unfortunately, hatred continues to be a greater motivating force than love. An official or candidate must consider whether a PAC or group will spend money contacting its members with attacks on the official. Will these groups or PACs spend the resources necessary to cost the official votes in the next election?

Evil versus good

Politicians are more successful in getting voters' attention by emphasizing the divisions that separate rather than the ties that unify people behind a common cause or a common candidate. For people less involved in an issue or a campaign, the images that stick with them are those that arouse an emotional reaction. That is true in life as well as in politics. When you read or see the news, you'll probably remember the story of a firefighter killed in action more readily than the story about the opening of a new fire station.

When a candidate finds an issue to exploit or distort to make the opponent appear awful, evil, or even capable of tormenting puppies, voters' choice becomes clearer. Voters reject the awful or evil opponent and support the other candidate. The sharper the contrast a candidate is able to create between him and his opponent, the easier the choice (see Chapter 13 for more on how campaigns use comparative advertising). A candidate who demonizes his opponent is more likely to get attention and votes than a candidate who patiently explains the ten points that make her a slightly better candidate.

But who is the bad guy?

Many campaigns use warm and fuzzy positive images of the candidate they are marketing and hard, negative attacks on his opponent. You pay attention to the hard, negative attacks, which motivate you to vote for the candidate making them. You don't have to weigh the fine points of the backgrounds of the two candidates — you can react against the awful or evil opponent, just like in championship wrestling.

The religious right and the anti–gun control groups have used their financial resources very effectively to do just that to candidates who have opposed them. Their attacks have demonized the candidates who dared to oppose these special interests and encouraged those voters sympathetic to the special interests to vote against the candidates. An official or candidate must consider the effect of indirect money from these groups in her campaign as well as direct contributions to the opposition.

Your Stake in the Election

By completing the vote/money analysis, you can determine what is really happening. You can determine who is on which side of an issue and why.

The next questions you need to ask yourself are

- ✔ Does this issue matter to me at all?
- ✔ Will the issue have any impact on me?

Is the legislation good for you?

Many elected officials propose legislation because they believe it will be good for the country or the economy. Just because they honestly believe a bill is good doesn't mean they are right. Good-thinking, intelligent people can disagree about the nature of a problem as well as the solution to a problem. You need to make your own, independent decision on the wisdom of the legislation.

Occasionally, a public official sponsors a bill because a special interest group supportive of the official wants it. But the discussion of the merits of the bill will always be couched in terms of the good of the country or the state.

Don't listen to the rhetoric from the official. It is the rare public official who will tell you that he is sponsoring a bill because a well-heeled contributor wants it and just deposited $10,000 in his campaign coffers as a show of good faith. The bill will always have some lofty public purpose. You need to decide for yourself whether the bill is in your interest.

Because you can't count on the rhetoric of the official to tell you what's going on, how do you know if you have a dog in the fight?

Independent sources of information

In judging whether a bill is in your interest, look to independent sources. Analysis by government watchdog groups can help you understand what's going on. Taxpayer groups that analyze tax fairness and public interest groups that monitor the effects of tax changes on the deficit can be valuable sources of information on what is truly happening. The media reporting on the pros and cons of a proposal solicits comments from these independent groups. You are also free to contact these groups directly if you want additional information.

Don't rely on any single source of information for your opinions. Each group of independents and journalists can have its own slant on an issue. Look at all the information available and decide for yourself.

Who's on what side?

Another part of your assessment of whether an issue matters to you is to examine who is on which side of the issue and whether you are comfortable supporting one of those sides. For you to assess whether you are comfortable supporting one side of an issue, you should know as much as possible about who is contributing to that team. There is an old expression: "Politics makes strange bedfellows." Many people are uneasy aligning themselves on an issue or campaign with a group with which they would ordinarily be at odds.

After you have listened to the arguments from both sides, you will have a better idea of what is going on. Now you are in a position to trust your gut instincts. You're aware of many of the pros and cons of the legislation. You will probably never know all the facts. But, at some point, you decide which side of an issue you find most persuasive and then decide to act or not to act.

Surprising bedfellows

As an example of the tough "bedfellow" choices that politics requires, say that you are an advocate of the rights of nonsmokers. You have supported the restrictions imposed on smokers during airline flights and in public buildings. You are worried about the effects of secondary smoke on nonsmokers like yourself. You are more than willing to curtail the rights of smokers to protect yourself and your family from the dangers of exposure to secondary cigarette smoke and ugly ashtrays.

But you were raised on a family farm and believe that family farms should be protected, so you also support subsidies for farmers who restrict their production. You think that the federal government should do all it can to protect the existence of family farms by adopting policies to make farming profitable.

The Agriculture Committee of the U.S. Senate wants to reduce or eliminate subsidies, which make family farming profitable, in order to cut the deficit. A strong supporter of agricultural subsidies for farmers is the tobacco industry, because many of the farmers grow tobacco. However, the tobacco industry is also, naturally, one of the biggest opponents of smoking restrictions and ashtray control.

Do you participate in a campaign financed by the tobacco industry to defeat the plan to reduce agricultural subsidies? Does your shared opposition to repealing subsidies make you an ally of the tobacco industry? Does the enemy of your enemy suddenly become your friend? Food for thought! And, for some, grounds for a cigarette.

Does the legislation touch your life?

Take a close look at what the legislation says it will do and what other people say it will do.

- ✔ Listen to what all sides in the debate are saying.

- ✔ Read and watch news stories about the impact of the legislation.

- ✔ Review any analysis by independent people or groups concerned with the legislation, such as that provided by *think tanks* (research institutions) or the Congressional Budget Office.

- ✔ Determine the positions of groups you generally support — such as the chamber of commerce, senior citizens groups, public interest groups, women's groups, environmental organizations, church organizations, or labor unions.

- ✔ See where elected officials you trust and support stand on the issue.

- ✔ Trust your instincts and decide for yourself.

Part II:

Making Your Voice Heard

The 5th Wave   By Rich Tennant

In this part...

Sometimes it's easy to feel like you don't have a say in political decision-making. Some people just throw up their hands when it comes to contributing to politics because they don't know where to start.

This part tells you how to take your first steps into the world of politics by voting, how to become a political player by volunteering your time and money, how to get politicians to lend you their ears, and, perhaps, how to change the world as we know it. The last chapter opens up the world of politics on the Internet. Politics is one of the top three topics on the Internet, so whatever your political beliefs, there's a Web site out there for you.

Chapter 3
Vote — Be a Part of the Solution

● ●

In This Chapter

▶ Deciding to register to vote

▶ Registering by mail

▶ Voting in primaries

▶ Making elected officials care about what you think

▶ Telling focus groups and pollsters what you think

● ●

*E*leanor Roosevelt said

> *I'd rather light one candle than curse the darkness.*

The same is true for our government. Your vote counts. You may have noticed through the years that our system of government is not perfect — it has its warts and flaws — but it's still the best system in the world. Our country is the single most successful exercise in democracy in history. If it's not perfect, or even not as good as it could be, maybe that's because not enough good people like you are involved.

✔ Do you tell yourself that you're so busy you can't spare the 15 minutes it takes to vote in every election?

✔ Do you tell yourself that your vote doesn't count anyway?

✔ If you're critical of politics and government, do you use that criticism as an excuse not to participate?

If you answered *yes* to any of these questions — that's a cop-out. You need to participate, and this book can help you become more involved. Your participation *can* make a difference. Here's an opportunity where you and only you can be in control. You can decide what level of involvement you want to have. You can decide how much you want to do. You're the only one who knows how much time and money you have. You can decide what else you want to do. But there is one thing you must do no matter what else: *You must vote.* If you don't vote, you have no right to complain about politics, politicians, or government.

Should You Register to Vote?

Many of us — more than *50 million* citizens in this country — are eligible to vote but do not bother to register. Every citizen of the U. S. over the age of 18 is eligible to register and vote.

In all but four states, you must register *before* election day in order to vote. Maine, Minnesota, and Wisconsin allow their citizens to register on election day. North Dakota is the most voter-friendly of all — it doesn't require you to register at all!

Every other state requires registration in advance of election day. Most states close the registration period 30 days before they hold the election. You must be registered in order to vote for any elective office in the U. S., from president to township advisory board. You only have to register once as long as you live at the same address and vote now and again.

Upsides and downsides of registering

Maybe you're not registered because you've convinced yourself that you should avoid politics. Check out this book's Introduction — avoiding politics is not possible. Political decisions will be made for you even if you elect not to participate. You still have to pay taxes even if you don't vote. Elected officials make decisions about which streets get paved, which sidewalks get repaired, and which schools close without regard to your opinions, if you don't vote. There is no hole deep enough for you to bury your head in to avoid politics completely. You can't run, and you can't hide — so you may as well participate.

Make a difference

If you do participate, you can make the system better. It may never be perfect, but improvement is possible. With the knowledge you gain by reading this book, you can make your elected officials respond to you. Your voice will be loud enough to be heard by everyone.

Voting is a valuable right that you, as an American, have. Many Americans take that right for granted . . . even the politicians. In the 1994 elections, a wave of voter reaction — a "throw 'em all out" after years of inaction and deadlock by Congress — shook up both major political parties, changed the dominant party in Congress, and made the politicians brutally aware of the issues about which voters had been concerned for years, and which the politicians had bypassed. That reaction reminded every politician not to take the voters for granted. The politicians heard the discontentment among voters, and they had to respond.

Become important

Voting is not required in the U. S., as it is in some other countries. The former Soviet Union used to brag about its 98 percent voter turnout on election day — but citizens faced stiff fines and punishment if they didn't exercise their right to vote for the candidate their government told them to vote for. But, in truth, there are so many compelling reasons to vote in our country, it's a wonder the voting turnout here doesn't come close to approaching that of the countries that demand it.

When you vote and participate, elected officials have to consider what you think. They may not always do what you want, but they have to listen to your opinions. When you vote, you become someone important.

Cynics are probably saying, "Yeah, but not as important as PACs and special interest groups with money." (See Chapter 9 for more on PACs and special interests.) Keep in mind, though, that a district (be it a small town or the entire country) has only so many voters. Although money is in potentially limitless supply for a candidate (it can be raised from many sources), it's illegal to buy votes, and you can't give someone else your proxy to vote for you; so the number of votes cast in any election is finite. You and only you can cast your vote. Your vote has the same weight as the vote of every other citizen. Rich or poor, young or old, male or female, black or white, each vote is equally important.

Political power

Each one of us has the same number of votes. You may not have an equal share of the world's financial resources, but the secret ballot gives us all an equal amount of voting power. Each registered voter has one and only one vote to cast — regardless of what you hear to the contrary about certain big-city or downstate rural districts, where the concept of "vote early and vote often" is allegedly in force, or where that age-old question — "Is there voting after death?" — is supposedly answered in the affirmative.

The vote of a person who has contributed $1 million to a candidate counts for no more than the vote of the person who has given nothing to a campaign. After all, winning elections is all about getting a majority of the votes cast. Secret ballots like we have in this country do not permit unequal weight to be attached to a certain person's vote. Votes are one-size-fits-all. Politicians need the votes of the "little people," and there are more "little people" than there are rich and powerful ones.

Since John F. Kennedy was elected, the percentage of eligible voters participating in presidential elections has declined in almost every election. That is true in local elections as well.

When we all vote, we are a powerful force that can move mountains, or at least politicians. When we don't, the small number of special interest voters have more clout because they are a bigger percentage of a smaller pie.

Figure 3-1 illustrates just how few people who are eligible to vote actually do. The outer circle represents the number of people in the U. S. who are eligible to vote. The next circle in the figure is the number of people who registered to vote in the 1992 elections. The next circle represents the number of people who actually voted in the 1992 presidential election. The number of people who actually voted is the 1992 voting population. The smallest circle is the group of people who voted in the primaries. Think how different things might be if everybody who could vote actually voted.

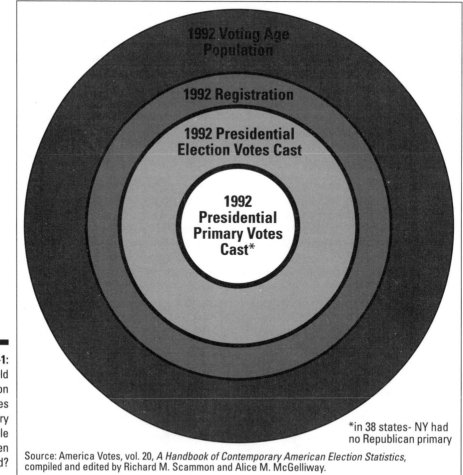

Figure 3-1:
What would election outcomes be if every eligible citizen voted?

*in 38 states- NY had no Republican primary

Source: America Votes, vol. 20, *A Handbook of Contemporary American Election Statistics*, compiled and edited by Richard M. Scammon and Alice M. McGelliway.

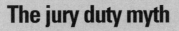

The jury duty myth

Some of us don't register to vote because we focus on the downside of registering. A common fear is that you'll be selected for jury duty if you register to vote. I can't blame you here. What's your worst fear — selection to the O.J. Simpson trial or the Menendez brothers Part II?

Some jurisdictions do rely on voter registration rolls to select their jury pools, but many more jurisdictions use motor vehicle and tax records (statistics) to select their jurors. Even if you don't believe that you have a civic responsibility to serve on a jury when your number comes up, not registering to vote does not give you the protection that you think it does!

Some people who have not registered to vote do get called for jury duty. These days, you'd be better off not getting a driver's license if you're so eager to avoid serving on a jury. I don't think you'll give up the car — but you're giving up much more than that if you don't register and vote.

What if registering to vote does get you selected for jury duty? Most of the time, you stand around at a courthouse for a day and go home at the end of the day. Most people called for jury duty don't serve on juries. The few people who do end up on juries serve for a trial that lasts a day, or maybe three days. A trial the length of O.J. Simpson's is rare — trials are not usually that long. The infamous Susan Smith trial only lasted three weeks — total.

The jury system works only when average citizens take their duty to serve on juries seriously. Everyone who is charged with a crime, no matter how important or unimportant that person is, is entitled to a trial by a jury. You have benefited greatly by living in this country. Isn't it time to take some responsibility for that citizenship?

Regardless of whether you take your citizenship responsibilities seriously, unless you are prepared to give up driving and risk not paying property taxes, you may as well register to vote. There's no reason for you to put up with the downside of not participating in the election of your representatives.

Motor Voter law

In 1994, Congress passed the *Motor Voter law,* which was designed to make voter registration easier. Congress hoped that simplifying the registration process would ultimately result in improved voter turnout for elections. Motor Voter requires that every motor vehicle office in every state offer voter registration to anyone obtaining or renewing a driver's license. Plus, each state must select other state offices to provide the same registration services. These state offices vary, but unemployment offices and welfare offices are common choices.

Each state must accept a national mail-in registration form approved by the Federal Election Commission and permit voters using it to vote in federal elections (a congressional, senatorial, or presidential contest). Most states also recognize the Motor Voter form to qualify citizens to vote in state elections (governor, legislature, local offices).

WARNING!

Roadblocks and detours in the Motor Voter law

Court challenges to the Motor Voter law are under way in South Carolina, Michigan, Virginia, Kansas, and Louisiana. The outcome of those lawsuits is uncertain as of publication of this book. Also, the governor of California has threatened a court appeal to block Motor Voter in California. If you live in one of these states, call your state election board or secretary of state's office to find out whether you can use the national mail-in registration form.

Idaho and New Hampshire are seeking to override the Motor Voter requirements by passing laws permitting same-day registrations in their states. New Hampshire's action is being challenged in court. If you live in one of these states, call your state election board or secretary of state's office to find out whether you can use the national mail-in registration form.

Four states are exempt from the requirements of Motor Voter because they enacted same-day registration or don't require registration at all. They are North Dakota, Maine, Minnesota, and Wisconsin.

Illinois and Mississippi have dual state and federal registrations. In Illinois and Mississippi, the national mail-in registration form merely registers a voter for federal elections. To vote in state and local elections in these states, you have to fill out a state registration form.

Historically, voter registration has always increased when hurdles to voting (such as lengthy residency requirements and proof of good moral character, which were hurdles in the nineteenth century) were removed. Motor Voter has been effective already: Early reports show an increase in the number of new registrants, which is encouraging news — even though it doesn't guarantee that those new voters will actually *vote*.

Some politicians don't actually want more people to vote. More voters means, to them, that they have to appeal to a larger and broader segment of the population. All they have to do now is keep one group of people, the registered voters, happy. That group has always been much smaller than the rest of the country. Now that group is going to become larger and less predictable because more people will be able to vote — if they take advantage of the Motor Voter law.

How Do You Register to Vote?

A copy of the national mail-in registration form that you can use to register for the next presidential election is in the back of this book. Just complete the form and mail it to the address for your state in advance of the election. See Appendix A for complete instructions, the registration deadline in your state, and the address to mail the form to.

POLITICAL STUFF

The poll tax: a hurdle overcome

One of the more recent voting hurdles to bite the dust was the use of a poll tax in many Southern states. The *poll tax* was a fee charged to everyone who voted in an election. The tax was cumulative. That is, if you failed to vote in one election, you had to pay the fee for that election as well as the current fee when you tried to vote in the next election.

The poll tax discouraged poorer voters, particularly African-Americans, from voting. Poll taxes were outlawed in federal elections by the 24th Amendment to the Constitution. The Supreme Court outlawed them in state elections. African-American participation increased after the poll taxes were outlawed.

Once you send in your national mail-in registration form, you will be able to vote for president, congressional representatives, and U. S. senators when your state has a contest. This form also enables you to vote in your state and local elections (in most states). Filling out this form only takes a couple of minutes, less time than it would take to call your mother-in-law and wish her a good day. And it will be time equally well spent — after all, how many people enjoy calling mothers-in-law? You make the call because you want to stay on your mother-in-law's good side. You fill out your national mail-in registration form because you want to be a good citizen.

Once you know all you need to know about politics from reading this book, you can put that knowledge to good use by voting. So fill out this form, mail it in, and go for it! Registering to vote does not *require* you to vote in any election; it's a *prerequisite* for voting in all elections. Register to vote now. You can always decide not to vote later. If you decide to vote later, it may be too late for you to register.

Voting in Primaries

I talk about primaries more in Chapter 20, but you should know about them when you register to vote because primaries are the first place you'll have an opportunity to vote and have an impact. Even so, most voters do not vote in primaries.

Primaries are one of the methods by which parties select candidates to represent them in the general election. Parties use primaries to select their nominees for important offices, such as governor, senator, and Member of Congress. Primaries are also commonly used to select legislative candidates, mayors, sheriffs, prosecuting attorneys, and other local officeholders.

The nominees of political parties for some statewide offices that are not as visible as governor and senator — like secretary of state, lieutenant governor, superintendent of public instruction, and attorney general — may be selected by a statewide convention convened by the political parties. Some states, like New Jersey, permit the governor to appoint some or all of these officeholders.

Your chance to choose the candidate

If you vote in a primary, you have a voice in choosing all your party's candidates, including president and vice president. Not only do you have a voice, but your voice is loud. So few people vote in primaries that your vote carries much more weight in a primary than it does in a general election. Primary voters definitely have clout!

If you don't have input into the selection of the nominees of the parties in a primary, your choices are limited in the general election to the two nominees already chosen in the primary election. You may be stuck choosing the lesser of two evils! And keep in mind, if you are dissatisfied with the incumbent and feel a new occupant is in order for that office, the primary gives you two shots, not just one, to send the incumbent into blissful retirement.

Besides, because so few people vote in the primaries, your vote can have a much more significant impact in a primary than in the general election. In fact, in many states, as few as 25 percent of the eligible voters vote in a primary election. Proportionately, your individual vote is much more important in a primary than in a general election.

Declaring your party affiliation

In many jurisdictions, when you vote in a primary, you have to declare your party affiliation. In other words, you must say that you want a Republican, Democratic, or some other party ballot. A few states permit what is called *crossover voting.* That means Republican primary voters can vote to select the Democratic party's candidate for one office or more and vice versa.

If you are reluctant to declare a party affiliation, you can avoid the primary process altogether. You also have the option of voting in the Republican primary one election year and the Democratic primary the next year and so on. That way, you can have a say in who is on the ballot for the final election and still maintain your position of independence.

Ordinarily, when you declare your party affiliation, you are given an opportunity to vote for the candidates of that party, but only that party, in the primary election. In other words, you cannot vote for one of the Republican candidates for governor and one of the Democratic candidates for Congress. You must make a choice between the parties. (To find out more about parties, see Chapter 7; for tips on choosing a party, skip to Chapter 8.)

Do Elected Officials Care What You Think?

The answer is a resounding *yes,* but only if you are registered to vote! If you do not register, you declare yourself out of the game, and no one makes any effort to find out what you think or what you want. Officials don't contact you to solicit your ideas or concerns because you don't show up on their lists at all. You must be registered if you want your opinions to count. Even if you don't vote, the fact that you're registered means that your support and opinions will still be solicited. If you don't register, you don't count, and you don't matter. Period.

Elected officials make real efforts to know what you, as a registered voter, want them to do and not do. They hold town meetings to interact with average voters like you and to find out what's on your mind and what worries you most about your city, state, or country. Successful elected officials — who, along with their families and staffs, have a deep and abiding interest and desire to keep their jobs — know that the key to reelection is knowing what the voters want and, within reason, delivering it.

Your opinions are worth real money

Your elected officials pay good money to pick your brain (provided you're a registered voter). They hire special consultants to organize focus groups and professional pollsters to conduct surveys. The burning question is this: "What's on *your* mind?" . . . followed by, "How can I get what's on your mind into my mind so you will keep me in mind come election day?"

Focus groups

Elected officials sometimes, particularly in an election cycle, pay large amounts of money to stage a cozy little get-together called a *focus group.* Focus groups are scientifically selected small groups of voters in the official's district. These voters are selected at random from the list of registered voters and are paid a small fee to meet for several hours with a political consultant to discuss issues and impressions in much greater depth than a poll allows.

Campaigns use focus groups to test "average" voters' reactions to campaign themes, plans of attack that the campaign is thinking of using on the opposition, and defenses that the campaign may use to fend off attacks from the opposition.

The small group doesn't even know who is paying for the session, which helps the consultant obtain candid responses from the group. These responses can help an official know whether the voters are paying attention to what he or she is saying and whether the right information is being communicated.

Because the focus group is such a small part of the electorate, usually no more than a dozen people, the campaign also conducts scientific polls on the information obtained in the focus group. But both of these expensive methods are used to discover what you think about the candidates and the issues. Elected officials and candidates spend all this time, money, and effort because they want to know what you want and think.

And you didn't think they cared.

Polling

Elected officials, particularly occupants of higher offices (governor, senator, congressperson, and so on), spend thousands of dollars every year trying to find out what you think about the issues and about the officials themselves. Pollsters even ask how you personally feel about the candidate (for example, is he honest? Does she care about people like you? Is he intelligent? Is she trustworthy?).

Those same pollsters ask what you think about all important policy issues. How do you feel the state or country is doing? Are you better off now than two or four years ago? Are you (or anyone in your family) afraid of losing a job? How do you feel about a particular tax increase proposal? Do you think education funding should be increased? Are you willing to increase sentences for violent crimes, even though the construction of more prisons will increase the tax burden? You get the idea.

Contrary to popular belief, officeholders, if they are smart, really want to do what most of the voters want done. If an officeholder can determine what you want and deliver that to you, the officeholder will keep getting elected and perhaps move on to higher office. That is why elected officials and candidates pay huge amounts of money to campaign consultants: to find out what you, as a registered voter, want.

Officials spend time and money inventing new ways or refining old ways of interacting with average voters in their districts. Pollsters are paid tens of thousands of dollars to select voters at random and question them. These voters are a cross section of the electorate in the official's or candidate's district. The pollsters are paid a great deal of money because of their expertise in drafting questions and analyzing the results of the interviews. This expensive expertise is just another way to permit the officeholder or candidate to know what you want.

The pollsters may not do a perfect job in finding out what you think and interpreting your opinions for the elected official. Sometimes the method of asking the questions influences the answers. Sometimes, accidentally, the sample that the pollster selected is biased in favor of one group of voters. Polling may not be a perfect way to determine what you and other registered voters think, but it's the preferred way. If you want to find out more about polling, flip ahead to Chapter 15.

Only if you vote

Elected officials spend a great deal of time and money determining what we want. These officials care very much about what you and the other people in their district or state think, but only if you care enough to vote in their elections.

The media's pollsters

It isn't just the elected officials and candidates who are extremely curious about what exactly you want them to do about the issues and problems you care deeply about. The news media also spends huge amounts of money to satisfy its abundant curiosity on these points, with extensive polling at the state and national level. Like the candidates, the media is way too impatient to wait until election night to get a handle on what you're thinking. The networks and major daily newspapers want to be able to stay on top of a campaign by trying to figure out the mood of the voters while they're still in the mood.

The media recognizes that the key to electoral success is identifying what a majority of the voters in a district, a state, or the country want or don't want.

Every poll screens people contacted to determine whether they are registered to vote and, if so, likely to vote. If your answer to either of these two questions is no, the interviewer assumes that you have no pulse, and finds inventive ways to terminate the interview immediately. Thus, the elected official won't know what you think about these issues, and, because you're not registered or not going to vote, the elected official will not care what you think. In fact, nobody will bother to ask.

If you're not registered, you don't have any voice at all!

At the risk of sounding spooky, politically, if you neither register nor intend to vote, you don't exist. You are a nonperson! That doesn't look good on a resume.

If you want to be heard and have your views considered, you must participate. One of the first questions a pollster asks is whether you are a registered voter. If you are not registered, the pollster isn't going to care what you say.

A statewide poll to determine voters' positions has a typical sample of 800 voters. (Statewide campaigns occasionally use samples as small as 400 to 600 voters.) Elected officials use the information gained from those 800 people to determine which policies to advocate, and that same information helps determine what their positions on the issues will be.

National polls taken by newspapers and the networks tell us what the entire country is thinking by interviewing fewer than 1,100 people! Primary voters and interviewees for polls are important people.

Of course, selection for poll interviews or focus groups is completely random; you may never be called. You can't guarantee yourself a voice through polls and focus groups, but you can be heard through the primary elections that come along almost every year. If you follow the suggestions for getting involved in Chapters 3 and 4 of this book, the role you play may increase in importance. You may never be selected for a poll or a focus group even if you register. The only thing you can guarantee is that you will never be selected if you don't register.

If you don't register, you shouldn't be surprised that elected officials and candidates aren't spending any time thinking about you. You shouldn't even complain about that lack of consideration. After all, you have declared yourself to be out of politics, and they have simply taken you at your word. You can't ask for much more than that. Although we all try to do so, you probably shouldn't expect to have it both ways: You can't be too good to be involved in the greedy and self-centered world of the politician and expect that greedy and self-centered politician to turn handsprings to figure out what you want and get it for you, no matter what the cost to him.

Giving voters what they say they want

Once candidates or officeholders accurately determine what the voters want, they can fashion a way to deliver it. Sometimes, of course, we want it all. We do have a tendency to ask our candidates to give us better roads, more prisons, extra dollars for education, and, while they're at it, lower taxes. Sometimes we want one thing one year and forget about it the next. Yes, as voters, we often have whims. And those whims can change as quickly as the length of women's skirts.

It's important to remember that no matter how hard officials try and how good they are, they're not magicians. Inconsistent goals may not be possible, no matter how much the voters want them. Scientists still haven't developed a tree that produces dollar bills. So, without making the thoroughly unappreciated decision to raise taxes, an official may not be able to provide for all the increased services that the voters want.

Elected officials face the challenge of determining which item is most important to a majority of us, whether they can deliver it, and how they can explain the impossibility of delivering on all goals. If delivering on the most important goal is not possible, officials still want to be in a position to demonstrate to us that they're fighting to get what we want and will keep doing so if we keep supporting them with our votes in the next election.

For example, Governor Jill Shmoe complains that too few of the dollars her state sends to Washington in taxes are returned by the federal government. She meets with the state's representatives and senators to ask for help in getting more federal dollars back to the state. She writes letters to the president. She complains about the federal government in speeches and press conferences.

Even if this state's share of federal funds remains constant year after year, Governor Jill Shmoe has demonstrated that she is willing to fight for what her constituents feel is the state's fair share of federal money. She is responsive. She is trying. This governor deserves reelection.

You may disagree completely with what the polls say "the people" want. You may think that Governor Shmoe is barking up the wrong tree completely. But (you know what's coming) you have no say if you are not registered to vote. If you are registered and you're still disgruntled, then it's time to take action. See Chapter 5 for ways to make your voice heard.

Chapter 4
Contributing Your Time or Money

● ●

In This Chapter

▶ Giving your time

▶ Giving your money

▶ Reaping your rewards

● ●

*A*re you looking for direct involvement in the game of politics, beyond simply exercising your constitutional right and civic duty to vote? If you've decided to take the plunge, this chapter tells you how to find the pool.

You can get involved in politics on a number of levels. Which one is right for you depends on how much time and effort you are willing to commit as well as how fat your wallet is and how willing you are to slenderize it on behalf of a candidate.

Donating Your Time

Campaigns need volunteers to drive candidates to events, monitor local newspapers, make phone calls, write letters to the editor, organize events, register voters, help raise money, and so on. Your involvement can be as simple as putting a candidate-support sign in your front yard or hosting a coffee at your home and inviting your neighbors and friends to meet the candidate. Or it can be as complicated as raising all the funds for the campaign or coordinating all the volunteer efforts. You know what your talents are and how much time you have available. Anything that you agree to do and do well is welcome.

As a volunteer, you can do many valuable things for a campaign:

✔ Research the press coverage that your candidate and the opponent are receiving

✔ Contact other voters to get your candidate's message to them

✔ Organize events

✔ Register voters

✔ Raise money

✔ Get your candidate's message out to the public

✔ Do opposition research to see whether anything the opponent said, did, or voted on in the past can be held against him

Finding your niche

When you contact the campaign, you should already have in mind several specific ways in which you can help. If you call simply to volunteer, you may be put to work stuffing envelopes, licking stamps, or picking up pizza. Not that there's anything wrong with stuffing envelopes — someone has to do it. But if you can write press releases, schedule a candidate's time efficiently and accurately, write position papers on issues, or raise a ton of campaign money, these are more important ways to assist the campaign.

Campaigns are always interested in volunteers with a knack for raising money. (Chapter 14 tells all the things campaigns do with that money.) If you demonstrate an ability to set a fund-raising goal and meet it or — better yet — exceed it, the candidate will value you and your support. We all know how well paved the road to hell is; when a candidate finds a volunteer who can deliver on her good intentions, he will ask her to do more fund-raising and perhaps to expand her role in the campaign.

Don't commit to more than you are certain you can do well and promptly. Nothing impresses a campaign manager more than a volunteer who can execute a plan successfully and quickly, but nothing is more frustrating than volunteers who call asking for assignments and then don't get those assignments done.

A campaign manager will be very impressed if you call to volunteer and have specific ideas in mind on things that you can do to help the candidate. For example, you can offer to take responsibility for placing yard signs in your neighborhood or a certain area of town. You can tell the campaign manager that you will obtain permission from the homeowners and place the signs yourself at, say, 50 or 100 homes.

If yard signs aren't your thing, or if the campaign you're supporting doesn't use them, think of other discreet tasks you can accomplish that will help the campaign gain momentum. One great idea is to offer to arrange several neighborhood coffees to permit voters who haven't made up their minds to meet your candidate.

If you want to arrange neighborhood coffees, here's what you do:

1. **Find people who can serve as hosts and hostesses.**

   These people should have homes that are comfortable meeting places for the candidate and the voters — in terms of both location and the layout of the house.

2. **Make the appointments with the candidate's secretary.**

   Don't forget to double-check the candidate's availability against that of your hosts' and hostesses'.

3. **Identify the voters you want to persuade.**

   The campaign manager can get that information for you.

4. **Invite the voters to attend.**

   Here's the real test of your powers of persuasion. You need to get enough firm commitments of attendance to make the meeting worthwhile.

5. **Follow up with your hosts and hostesses to make sure that the arrangements are complete, with the candidate's secretary to make sure that the date is still set, and with as many of the voters as you can to ensure their attendance.**

6. **Attend the coffees yourself.**

   Your presence reinforces the important role you played in getting these affairs arranged.

More, more, and more volunteers!

When a candidate is first starting out, she relies more on volunteers than paid staff. After all, paid staff is expensive, and new candidates are usually short on money. Even if a candidate is an incumbent or has run before, she relies more on volunteers if the office is less visible. That is both a function of the money available and the type of tasks that must be performed to run a successful campaign.

For example, a campaign for city council, except in a large metropolitan area like New York City or Los Angeles, probably won't have any paid campaign staff. Most city-council candidates rely on volunteers to place yard signs on the lawns of supporters. They use volunteers to distribute literature to potential voters. Volunteers call voters to tell them about the candidate and to urge

(continued)

(continued)

them to vote on election day. A well-run campaign of this type may use 10, 20, or more volunteers.

Volunteers also play a significant role in the campaigns for more-visible offices. Most statewide candidates — those who want to succeed, anyway — try to conserve their funds for TV ads, which go directly to voters. Any money they spend for staff reduces the money available to persuade voters to vote for the candidate. Most statewide or congressional candidates try to keep their paid staff to a half dozen or fewer people. They have many times that number of volunteers.

Time well spent

Why would you want to bother working for a political campaign without getting paid? The answer is that you *do* get paid. Not with money, of course, but with experience.

- ✔ Many people enjoy the team spirit and camaraderie that come with volunteering for a political campaign.

- ✔ Volunteering for a campaign is a great way to meet people who care about the same issues you do.

- ✔ Your experience working for a political campaign stands out on a resume. It shows not only that you have great organizational skills but also that you care about and get involved in your community.

- ✔ Especially in smaller, local campaigns, volunteering is a way to make your voice heard. You may be the reason a particular candidate gets elected. And, once elected, officials are likely to consider the opinions of those who helped them get there.

You've put in a lot of work to make your candidate successful. You ought to get credit for your volunteer efforts. Don't miss an opportunity to be at an event when the candidate is present. Once she sees you several times at successful events that you've put together, you can be certain she will remember who you are and how much you've helped to get her elected.

Hardworking volunteers who can accomplish tasks are worth their weight in gold. But you want to be sure the candidate knows that *you* are responsible for the success of the events . . . not the paid staff at headquarters.

Money Talks

For some of us, time is an even scarcer resource than money. You may find that you'd rather contribute to a campaign from your wallet than from your overbooked schedule.

If you decide to get involved in politics by contributing money, you may want to start with a fairly minimal level of involvement. If so, just pick a candidate you like (see the next section for help on identifying a candidate to contribute to) and make a small monetary contribution to that candidate.

What constitutes a small, medium, or large contribution in a political campaign depends on the office being sought. What is a large donation for a local race may not be significant in a statewide contest for governor or U. S. Senate. Usually, between $50 and $100 is a respectable sum. In some local races, that would be a very significant contribution — you could get by with $25. In some statewide elections, you need to give more to accomplish that goal. The key is giving enough to ensure that your donation is noticed.

If you want your donation to be noticed, always err on the side of a larger contribution. Any contribution over $100 results in invitations to most of the campaign fund-raisers. Very few candidates besides incumbent U.S. senators and presidential candidates have events with a price tag of $1,000. Candidates who have events with price tags over $100 have more than one tier of giving for such an event. For example, the base price may be $100 to a dinner. If you want to attend the cocktail party before the dinner, the price may increase to $250 or even $500 for a statewide candidate (for governor or U.S. senator).

Table 4-1	A General Range for Contributions in Some Types of Campaigns		
Type of Race	*Small*	*Medium*	*Large*
Local races (school board official, county officeholder, city or county council member, county commissioner)	$10–$15	$15–$50	>$50
Legislative races (general assembly member, state representative, state senator)	$25–$50	$50–$100	>$100

(continued)

Table 4-1 *(continued)*

Type of Race	Small	Medium	Large
Less visible statewide races (attorney-general, state treasurer, state auditor)	$50-$100	$100–$250	>$250
More-visible statewide races (governor, U.S. senator)	<$100	$250–$1,000	$1,000

The maximum contribution that a U.S. Senate candidate can accept is $1,000 per election. That means $1,000 for the primary and $1,000 for the general election. If you're married, your spouse can give the same $1,000 per election. And $4,000 is a very substantial contribution!

In many states those limits do not apply for state races (governor, lieutenant governor, attorney general), and some wealthy contributors give much more.

The money avenue does provide you with a ready entry into virtually every campaign. How do you decide which one to enter? Well, for starters, you can read the next section.

Deciding who should get your money

You've decided to get involved by contributing money. To whom do you give?

If you already think of yourself as a Republican or a Democrat, the answer to that question is easy. You pick the candidate of your party who has the most appeal to you.

- ✔ If you like to back a winner, you pick the favorite. Remember, though, that nothing in this life is certain but death and taxes. There are certainly no sure things in politics.

- ✔ If you aspire to be a kingmaker, you pick a candidate of your party who is seen as a long shot, provided that the candidate has potential. Look for a candidate who is telegenic, hardworking, and articulate and who also has an attractive family — a person you would be pleased to have your son or daughter marry.

Don't be afraid to trust your instincts. If you like the person, the odds are that other voters will, too. Of course, the campaign has to be run in an intelligent fashion to make the most of the attractive characteristics of your candidate. Your candidate may walk on water, but that does the campaign no good if the voters aren't aware of it!

The decision is more complicated if you don't have a predisposition to either party. In that case, your decision on the beneficiary of your contributions may take some independent research. See Chapter 13 for more on how to do that.

Putting your wallet away

If you've decided to make a contribution to a candidate or to raise money for that candidate, virtually every campaign will be eager to have you — with a few notable exceptions. If you make your money operating a brothel or have ties to organized crime, most campaigns won't touch your money with a ten-foot pole.

Even if your sources of income are perfectly legal and aboveboard, campaigns may be reluctant to accept your contribution if taking your money creates a political problem. For example, suppose you own a company that employs a substantial number of the voters in a candidate's district, but you are embroiled in a nasty dispute with the labor union representing the workers. Your candidate's opponent may use your contribution, which must be reported, to persuade those workers to vote against your candidate. As much as your candidate would like to have your money, he should refuse to accept it. Don't get upset by the refusal.

If the opponent attacks your candidate because of your contribution, there will be news stories. Those news stories will resurrect the labor unpleasantness and speculate as to whether you have an ulterior motive in making the contribution. Your candidate's refusal to accept your contribution also protects you from unfavorable publicity, even if the candidate was motivated purely by self-protection.

These are rare exceptions to the rule that money powers the political process. The vast majority of the time, campaign managers jump at the chance to take your contribution or fund-raising efforts.

What to expect

Once you are a donor, your support is solicited during the remainder of that campaign. You get invited to events, at additional cost. If your candidate is running a state-of-the-art campaign, you receive direct-mail solicitations. Your candidate considers your views on everything from her position on issues to the effectiveness of the campaign strategy. Because you helped finance the campaign, you now have a personal stake in the outcome of that election.

Which Kind of Contributor Are You?

The simple fact is that candidates need money in order to run a campaign. What's not so simple is where the money comes from and why it is donated.

Where the contributions come from varies with respect to the type of contributor, the amount donated, and the motivation behind the contribution. But every contributor — from the individual who gives $25 because she agrees with a candidate's ideas to the special interest group that gives tens of thousands of dollars to push for certain legislation — is warmly welcomed into a campaign.

Contributors fall into a few categories based on their style of contributing and their motivation: party supporters, ideological givers with or without a personal agenda, kingmakers (and queenmakers), and special interest groups.

What contributors expect in return for their contribution (if anything) depends on the contributor. The following sections give an overview of the contributors and their motivations, which may help you determine where you fall and what you should expect in return for your contribution.

Party backers

If you're a voter who identifies strongly with a political party, you are likely to contribute money to candidates of that party to help them win elections. You probably give over and over again to many different party candidates over the years. Your gifts are usually modest — less than $100 at a time. You are a *party backer;* you make these contributions because you're committed to the success of the party. And you measure that success by the number of officeholders a party has at any given time. Your contributions are meant to help increase the number of party officeholders.

It doesn't matter too much to you who the candidates are. What matters most is the party affiliation. People who support the party will give to almost any Democratic or any Republican candidate who asks them for contributions.

Individuals with strong party identification raise small contributions in any one of a hundred ways. Here are just a few of the things that they pay for:

- Tickets to hog roasts, fish fries, and bean dinners that honor a candidate or a party
- Buttons emblazoned with the candidate's name
- A chance in a raffle for a homemade quilt or pie

> ✓ A car wash performed by volunteers who give the money raised to a candidate or party

> ✓ Dues to a party organization

In local elections for county offices or small-town mayors, party backers may form the majority of givers. They may also represent the majority of the total campaign budget. In smaller towns and cities or rural counties, the entire campaign budget for an office may be less than $5,000, raised entirely or primarily from the party backers.

If you are a party backer and give to a candidate, you may expect that candidate to represent the party well during the campaign and, if successful, in office. Continued loyalty to the party and its people after the candidate is in office is a must. The officeholder is expected to "dance with the one which brung ya," which means that party supporters want policy and hiring decisions to reflect party affiliation. (See Chapter 23.)

Ideological givers

If you are an *ideological giver* with or without a personal agenda, you give to see that certain laws are passed or repealed; you expect the candidates you're supporting to vote a certain way on these issues while in office. You usually interview the candidate in depth before giving your support. The in-depth discussions assure you, as an ideological giver, that the candidate shares your concerns about issues of importance to you.

Ideological groups typically expect to have the officeholders they supported listen with a sympathetic ear to their arguments when legislation or policy is being decided. Contributors make their contributions with a goal in mind: for the officeholders to reflect their views when the time comes to pass laws or implement policy, whether their support was motivated by a personal agenda or not.

With no personal agenda

You may be a person who gives money for a completely unselfish reason: the desire for good government. Sometimes a candidate's background, qualifications, or ideas excite a particular group into contributing to the candidate's campaign with no other motivation than the hope that this person will be good for the city, state, or country. If you are this type of contributor, you expect and demand high standards from your officeholders. Because you don't have a specific purpose in mind — other than good government — when you give, you usually don't expect the officeholder to provide something in return for the contribution.

If you belong to this group, you give to candidates who support the same issues that you do. Ideological givers feel deeply about certain issues and want to elect officeholders who reflect those views.

An example of this type of ideological giver is an environmental activist. These activists contribute to and work for candidates who are committed to protecting the environment. They have nothing personal to gain from their support of candidates; they simply want to see that people who are committed to protecting the environment are in positions of power. The only thing they hope to gain is a cleaner, safer environment for themselves and future generations. That's the only way they benefit from their support.

Other groups that fit into this category are pro-choice and pro-life givers. These individuals may never be personally involved in an abortion decision themselves but feel strongly about protecting or restricting the right to abortions for others. These ideological givers give regularly to candidates who support the pro-choice or the pro-life position in the hope of protecting or restricting these legal rights.

With a personal agenda

If you are an ideological giver *with* a personal agenda, you support certain types of candidates committed to the same issues as you are. You have a more personal interest in the selection of officeholders than those with no personal agenda. You hope that the selection of candidates with a similar point of view will mean a government that shares your views and takes action consistent with those views, which will directly and personally benefit you. Examples of this type are business, labor, and some single-issue contributors.

Not all single-issue contributors have a personal agenda. For example, you may support a pro-choice or pro-life position without ever having to make a personal decision on that issue for yourself. If the law is changed, it doesn't affect your conduct or lifestyle. But, if you are a single issue contributor *with* a personal agenda, a change in the law would affect you personally. For example, you might be an anti–gun control single-issue contributor who owns guns. If the law changes, your ability to own weapons also changes. You are committed to opposing gun control, but you also have a personal stake in the issue.

Business groups such as chambers of commerce support general ideological principles that will also help their members financially if they become law. For example, laws making environmental regulations more difficult to issue and legislation shifting the property tax burden from businesses to individuals reflect the members' ideology and help their bottom lines.

Labor unions give their contributions in much the same way. They want officeholders who oppose laws such as striker replacement legislation and bills that tax health benefits to union workers. They want officeholders who support increases in the minimum wage and the right to organize.

Single-issue groups also include religious groups, which oppose government regulation of any aspect of their activities. If you are a member, you believe philosophically that the First Amendment to the Constitution makes you secure from any government interference in the way you run your church. Practically, you also have a second agenda. If you can keep government completely away from your organization, you can operate day care centers without bearing the cost of complying with governmental health and safety regulations. You believe in the issues you are fighting for, but winning the battle also has a direct benefit on your bottom line.

Kingmakers (and queenmakers)

Some wealthy contributors give to political candidates because they enjoy the power that comes from helping to create a political phenomenon.

You may be a kingmaker if

- You like being in the know.
- You like having calls returned by important people.
- You like having your favors and contributions sought.
- You are in a position to contribute and/or raise thousands or tens of thousands of dollars for a candidate.

Many wealthy contributors may like to be acknowledged by people in the know but may shun publicity. You may or may not seek any direct financial benefit from your role as kingmaker. You may simply enjoy the social part of your power — the invitations to special parties and receptions that come from being on the A-list of important and influential people. The prestige of creating a successful candidate may provide enough satisfaction for you.

If you're in this category, you seek the recognition that comes with your role in helping a candidate become an officeholder. You can expect to be stroked by the officeholder, to have your counsel sought and your advice heeded, and to help influence the decisions that the officeholder makes.

Many times, personal financial gain does not play a role in kingmaking because it's too risky for the officeholder to associate closely with an adviser who stands to gain from the association. Reporters love to do stories that detail a personal gain for a key financial backer and adviser to a visible elected official. So, if at all possible, politicians shy away from relationships with large contributors who may gain in personal, financial ways from those relationships.

Special interest groups

Special interest groups are bands of like-minded individuals who contribute to candidates in order to advance their positions or to protect themselves from assaults by other interests. Chapter 9 deals with special interest groups in more detail.

Chapter 5

Telling Politicians What's on Your Mind

In This Chapter

▶ Calling your congressperson

▶ Speaking up at town meetings

▶ Writing letters to your representatives

▶ Getting others to join you

▶ Changing the world as you know it

*W*hen you are no longer content to be buffeted like driftwood by the waves of political change, it's time to take the plunge and communicate with some of your elected officials.

How you communicate with elected officials depends on which ones you're trying to contact. Communication can be pretty informal when it comes to your local elected officials. Your city-council representative or county commissioner, small-town mayor, school board representative, or state representative is accustomed to receiving telephone calls at work or at home from voters who express their opinions and concerns directly.

The larger the size of the official's constituency, the more difficult that official is to contact directly. That stands to reason. Officials elected by the voters of an entire state answer to millions of voters. There are simply not enough hours in a day for statewide officials (officials whose constituency is a state's entire voting population) to speak with all the voters who want to express their views directly, even if the officials are inclined to listen.

The problem is much greater with national officials. The president wouldn't have much time to hold a state dinner for the ambassador from New Guinea or natter on with NATO if he were compelled to deal with Tom, Dick, and Mary Fenster from Des Moines, who just called to say that they're in town and would like to talk to him about that little farm bill that might adversely affect their 120 acres of soybeans.

Reaching Out and Touching Your Representatives

If you feel strongly about a local issue, whether it's the location of a liquor store or the construction of a new jail or the level of state funding for education, just pick up your phone and call the elected official whom you think has responsibility for that issue.

Calling an official's work number is more polite than calling at home, unless the official is part time and doesn't have an office. Believe it or not, your elected officials are people, too, with business and family demands that should be respected.

Phone numbers are listed in the government section of your phone book. If you can't find a phone number for the official, call the county or state party headquarters for the official's political party and ask how to reach him or her.

State legislatures have hot lines to the party caucuses, or meetings (see Chapter 21 for a full definition of *party caucuses*). You can call these hot lines to leave messages for your state representatives and state senators who are in session and are voting on bills that you read about in your morning newspaper.

You can also call the congressional office for your Members of Congress. You're less likely to speak to your national representative than to your local elected official, but it never hurts to ask. At the very least, you can leave your name and your message with a staff person who will see that the representative understands your position. Each representative has at least one district office. You can also call the representative's office in Washington and do the same thing.

I thought you'd never ask

Many legislators and Members of Congress send out questionnaires to voters in their districts soliciting their opinions on important issues or pending bills. If you are registered to vote, you probably receive these questionnaires from time to time. They usually take just a few minutes to complete. If you make the effort to return these questionnaires, the elected official conducting the mailing considers your answers.

Responding to questionnaires is a painless way for you to communicate with your elected official and let her know what you're thinking. See Chapter 15 for more on how elected officials pick your brain.

If you're not sure who your state representative or senator is, you can call any of the following places:

- ✔ Your county election board or Board of Elections for your state
- ✔ Your local office of the League of Women Voters
- ✔ The local headquarters for the Democratic or Republican parties
- ✔ Your local library — ask the reference librarian

Every Member of Congress has staff people who keep track of the number of phone calls received on an issue. The greater the number of calls, the more likely that the Member will pay attention to the issue and the views of the callers.

Every year, *Congressional Quarterly* publishes a Washington information directory that gives the exact address for your district's representative and your state's senators. It also includes direct phone numbers for each office. *Congressional Quarterly* is available at your local public library. In addition, at the start of each session of Congress, most newspapers publish addresses and phone numbers for Members of Congress and U.S. senators in their area. Cut that list out of your local newspaper and put it on your refrigerator. You never know when you may have an urge to call or write.

If it's too late to cut the phone list out of the paper, call or visit your local library. The reference librarian will be able to get that information for you in a matter of minutes.

Here are some tips for calling your Member of Congress:

- ✔ Be prepared to give your name, address, and phone number.
- ✔ Tell the staff person precisely why you are calling.
- ✔ Refer to the bill you're calling about by number, if you can.
- ✔ Tell the staffer whether you support or oppose the bill and why.
- ✔ Be patient. If an issue is hot enough, the phone lines may be busy.

Town Meetings

In addition to being available over the telephone, many legislators and Members of Congress regularly hold town meetings when the legislature or Congress is in session. These town meetings are conducted around the district to give all voters a chance to attend. Schedules are available from the official's office.

Town meetings allow you to ask questions directly of the officials on topics that you want discussed. Because these meetings are not always well attended, they provide a good opportunity for in-depth interaction with your elected officials.They also guarantee that your opinions won't be filtered or sanitized by a staff person. Your elected official will hear from you directly, like it or not.

If the elected official doesn't know the answer to your question during the meeting, you will be given a response later. Staff people will take down your name and address if your question requires further investigation. Be sure to get their business cards so you can follow up in case you don't hear from them.

For the most part, legislators and their staff make a point of paying dutiful attention to constituent problems and concerns; after all, legislators come up for a job-performance review with the voters every time there's an election. They can't afford to get a reputation for not getting back to constituents who call with a problem or question. Indeed, solid problem-solving work from the congressional staff is considered as crucial to a congressperson's reelection as his voting record.

If you are interested in attending a town meeting, here's what you do:

1. **Call the local office for your Member of Congress and ask for a schedule of town meetings.**

   or

   Call the main number for your state legislature and ask to speak with your representative or her staff person. Ask for a town meeting (sometimes called a *third house meeting*) schedule.

2. **Go to your local library and read all newspaper or magazine articles on the issue that you want to discuss so you're prepared to talk knowledgeably about the topic.**

3. **Get to the town meeting early to get a seat where you can be sure that the congressperson can't miss you when you raise your hand for questions.**

Don't worry that you may not know all the facts when you express your opinion to your elected official. Don't be afraid of feeling foolish. If you've done your homework but don't know all the facts, it's because the elected official and the media have not done a very good job communicating the facts to you. And that's certainly not your fault.

Putting it in Writing

You don't have to use the phone or attend a town meeting to put your opinions before your elected officials. You can always dash off a letter.

Say you noticed in today's paper that Senator Smith cast a vote in favor of aid to Freedonia. You are opposed to aid to Freedonia. You want Senator Smith to know of your displeasure with his vote. What do you do?

Sit down and write the good senator a letter about your feelings. When you've analyzed the issue and are confident that you've stated your position just the way you want, call the senator's office — the number should be in your phone book — and ask for the address to send your letter.

One of the fastest ways to get your letter to the senator's office is to fax it. Instead of asking for the senator's address, ask for his fax number. (Unfortunately, the phone company hasn't segregated fax lines from voice lines yet. Directory assistance can't give you the senator's fax number, but his office can.) Ask the receptionist whether the senator has a fax number and then write it down. He may have separate fax lines for his state office and his Washington office. Ask for all the numbers. You may decide to make a habit of sharing your views with the senator by fax.

While your displeasure with Senator Smith is in the front of your mind, you may want to see whether the senator's opponent in the upcoming election agrees with the vote on aid to Freedonia. Call her campaign headquarters and get the opponent's address or fax number and send or fax her a letter asking how she would have voted on this issue if she were in the U. S. Senate.

Remember to send letters complimenting your officials who vote the way you want them to. After all, positive reinforcement can work as well as criticism.

Faxing your way into talk radio

You can use the fax machine to make your views on issues and candidates heard on popular talk radio shows. Most of the national commentators and many local ones have fax numbers that they broadcast on the air. They regularly read the faxes their shows receive. Liddy, Limbaugh, and the rest may publicize your comments by reading your fax over the radio for everyone to hear.

More sometimes means less

The more local the office, the less likely that office is to receive a large volume of mail from voters. If an office doesn't receive a large volume of mail, the mail that the office does receive has a greater impact. The greater the impact, the higher the probability that the elected official will answer the mail personally.

Conversely, the more mail an elected official receives, the less significant the impact of one letter. Offices that receive volume mail have staff members whose sole responsibility is to answer that mail. The higher the volume, the less the likelihood that the official will ever see a particular piece of correspondence. But staff members keep track of the number of letters received for and against a bill or issue and then inform the official of those numbers. Sometimes, the size of those numbers may be persuasive to an official.

Multiplying your opinion

If writing a letter doesn't put your views in front of your official, what else can you do? The answer is *multiply*. Elected officials pay more attention to opinions that are not yours alone. For example, if your neighbors share your opinion that a liquor store should not be located on your corner, get them to sign your letter in support of that position. Or, better yet, get your neighbors to write letters, too.

The most effective way to multiply is to get others to write their own letters in their own words. Flooding the congressperson's office with form letters and postcards, while not without its attention-getting impact, is not considered as effective as that personal, heartfelt letter from the individual constituent.

Here are some more tips for getting others involved and achieving strength through numbers:

- ✔ Ask your neighbors, friends, coworkers, and relatives to write similar letters.

- ✔ Draft and reproduce a one-page flyer telling people why they should care about the issue. Distribute the flyer to possible letter writers or petition signers.

- ✔ Circulate petitions supporting your views to people you know.

- ✔ Recruit others to help you organize. These people can provide the core of your team and can approach *their* friends, relatives, coworkers, and neighbors for letter writing and petition signing.

✔ Think of all the places you go where you could approach people: church, work, Little League, the supermarket, your children's school events, and so on. Then be sure to take flyers along.

The first time you try to mobilize people on an issue, it seems impossible. You may be intimidated by asking five people to help. It gets easier. Those five people may provide the core and each find five others the next time you want to make your voices heard. The next time you flex your political muscle, you may get support from 25 others, and so on, and so on.

The key is picking an issue that you and your neighbors or friends think is important and then getting started. Before too long, you may have a grassroots movement that can move mountains — or at least politicians. Now the elected official is not simply dealing with one angry voter but with tens, hundreds, maybe thousands of voters, if the issue is hot enough, all united under one goal.

If you're successful in gathering substantial neighborhood support for your position, you may be able to request and get a meeting with the elected official to make your case in person. A personal meeting with the elected official allows you and your neighbors to convince the official that you feel strongly about the issue. Certainly, you and your neighbors care enough about the issue that you've taken time from your busy schedules to meet with the official. In other words, you mean business.

You are now in a position to prove the truth of the point that I make in Chapter 2 about the nature of politics. You can make the vote/money analysis that the official performs on this issue work for you. You are able to demonstrate to the official that opening the liquor store in your neighborhood (to continue this example) will cost that official a substantial number of votes in the next election.

When the elected official does his political analysis about the cost of opening the liquor store, he will have to weigh the effect of hundreds or thousands of votes cast against him in the next election. You have shown the elected official that you and hundreds or thousands of your neighbors feel so strongly about this liquor store that this issue alone will determine your votes in the next election. If the elected official is with you, he can count on your votes. If the elected official disregards your views, he will pay a substantial price at the voting booth.

You must realize that there will be pressure pulling the elected official in the opposite direction, coming from those who think that a liquor store in the neighborhood is a brilliant idea. You won't be able to tell how strong that pressure is, so you cannot know whether your side will prevail. Business groups may be behind the opening. The owners of the liquor store may have contributed to the official's campaign. You can't accurately assess the strength of the opposition, but you can make your side as strong and well organized as possible. In so doing, you ensure that your views are taken seriously. The threat of a voting bloc of that size in a local election is not one that a successful politician is likely to disregard.

The Name of the Game Is Teamwork

If the elected official doesn't read your letter, staff people intercept your calls, and the security guards don't let you get close enough to the official for a face-to-face conversation, how can you make certain that your opinion reaches that official? The answer is simply teamwork.

Teamwork means recruiting other interested parties to help you make your case to an official you can't reach by yourself. The more people or organizations you bring on board your issue, the more likely it is that you will be listened to. Reinforcements can be local organizations, local chapters of national organizations, or the ultimate big gun: the media.

Other officials

Other elected officials — particularly the more approachable ones, like your own state representative and state senator — are valuable potential team members. They can intercede to gain the higher official's attention. They may even be able to schedule you an appointment with the official you are attempting to persuade so you can make your case personally.

The local elected official may be willing to help you out once you have convinced her that many of her voters share your concerns. When you request your local official's intercession, you are subtly letting her know that you and your allies will remember her cooperation or lack of cooperation on election day. If the local official can gain the support of a group of voters, she may help you put the problem in the lap of an elected official higher up the political food chain.

Recognized organizations

Other well-known organizations can serve the same function as a local elected official in connecting you to the statewide official. Neighborhood organizations, the chamber of commerce, labor unions, community groups — any organizations with the credibility to obtain the higher official's attention can be useful allies and intermediaries. To form a team, you must recruit organizations that share your point of view.

Organizations are not going to assist you and your neighbors unless they share your goal. So don't try to enlist the National Rifle Association in your crusade to limit the sales of handguns in your community, or ask Greenpeace to help build a toxic waste dump near a fish hatchery.

The media

Another useful ally in the fight to get attention and results is the media. The media loves reporting on events organized by ordinary citizens trying to convince their government to do the right thing. The media is likely to cover your event if you organize it well and pick a day when not too much other news is happening.

Even television may cover your event if you remember to provide interesting and creative visuals for the cameras to shoot. Elected officials pay a great deal of attention to television coverage. If you can get the television reporters to cover your event, you may get a double hit out of it. If you indicate to the reporters that you are asking your governor, senator, or big-city mayor to do something, the reporters may go to the governor, senator, or big-city mayor and ask that person to comment on your request.

When you want media attention, you need to do the following:

✓ **Pick a location that will provide the television cameras with something interesting to shoot.**

An individual sitting at a desk or standing behind a podium is not nearly as interesting as a statement or demonstration in front of the public library if the issue is censorship of library books, or on a street filled with chuckholes if the issue is road maintenance. Television news departments like to shoot tape of images that help to convey the message effectively, and not just a picture of a spokesperson reading or delivering a statement, producing the dreaded "talking head."

Be creative. Think like a television producer and figure out ways to make your message more visually interesting and appealing. Also keep in mind that, in today's fast-paced newscasts, reporters will be using only 10- to 15-second excerpts, or *sound bites,* from your spokes- person's statement or answers to reporter's questions. So try to keep such statements and answers brief and to the point to help make sure that the meat of the message makes the air.

✓ **Pick a day and a time that make it easy for the media to attend.**

Day-shift reporters and news photographers generally come in around 9 a.m. So a good time to schedule your news conference or event is 9:30 a.m., which should put it among the first stories on a newsroom's daily assignment menu. Events at this time also allow the reporter to put your story on the station's noontime broadcast in addition to the early evening news shows.

Try to avoid scheduling your event after 3 p.m., when reporters and photographers are plunging into their hectic, bordering on maniacal, ordeal of writing and editing their stories in time for the 5 p.m. newscast.

✓ **If your goal is newspaper coverage, make sure that you find out the reporter's deadlines.**

Give the reporter time to cover your story and still make her deadline.

✓ **Give the reporters as much advance notice as possible of the event and remind them by calling the morning of the event.**

✓ **Tell the media in writing what the issue is all about. Draft a simple news release telling reporters**

- Who your group is

- Why you are having your event

- What you want officials to do or not to do

- A name and a phone number to contact for additional information

✓ **Organize the event to have as many people as possible there.**

The media views the number of supporters present as a sign of strength.

✓ **If you have any documents to support your position, make copies of them available to the press.**

✓ **If someone can shed additional light on the problem through personal experience, have him available to talk to the press.**

✓ **Identify a member of your group who will speak with the press and answer any questions.**

Be selective in choosing a spokesperson. It must be someone articulate who can make the necessary points directly and concisely.

✓ **Limit the number of speakers to the best one or two. Newspeople have deadlines and not much patience.**

Nothing is guaranteed to focus the attention of officials more quickly than a television camera in the face. With the help of the media, you can make almost any elected official sit up and take notice. One of the greatest things about this country is that any citizen with enough determination and organization and the right issue can become a force to be reckoned with. If you feel strongly about something, go for it. Make your officials listen to you. Tell them what you think!

Chapter 6
Getting Political on the Internet

In This Chapter

▶ Communicating with politicians via computer

▶ Using your computer to find out more about the candidates

▶ Using your computer to find out more about the issues

▶ Chatting with other voters by computer

*T*wenty years ago, what you knew as a citizen was limited to what you saw with your own eyes or held in your hands. If you watched the news, you had to rely on the information that the press chose to provide you. The ability to do research was normally severely limited to the printed text. You could go to the library to research newspaper and magazine articles, if you had the time. Or, if you wanted to have your voice heard by elected officials, you could sit down and write letters or try to call the politicians on the telephone. For many, that was about the extent of it.

Now all of that has changed. In the 1990s, computers have unleashed an avalanche of information. For the first time in many people's lives, Americans are inundated with a constant flow of information.

Many of us have access to a computer, either at work or at school. Many others have joined the ranks of the computer literate and have Macs or other PCs (personal computers) sitting in our homes. Your computer allows you to become politically active from your desk or den in a number of ways:

✔ You can obtain the information that you need in order to decide which candidate to support or which issues affect you.

✔ You can communicate your views to elected officials and candidates.

✔ You can discuss candidates and issues with other voters.

Your computer can be your ticket to becoming more politically involved without leaving the comfort of your own home. It can make your desire to be an informed voter come true. It can provide you with political clout.

Going Online

You don't have to go to the library or make it a point to listen to speeches in order to learn what candidates and interested groups are saying about campaigns or issues. You can find any information you need on your home computer screen.

Your computer can do the work for you by talking to other computers to get you the information you want. Computers use phone lines to call other computers that are programmed to hear their calls. When you dial out, you need to reach a line that has another computer at the other end waiting to accept your call. This technique is called *going online,* and it's not only a lot of fun but also a great way to communicate with elected officials and other voters.

You can go online in three major ways:

- ✔ **Commercial services:** These services, such as CompuServe and America Online, offer fairly comprehensive coverage on a wide variety of topics.

- ✔ **Private bulletin board systems:** These systems, also known as BBSs, can be as small as somebody just like yourself who has made his or her computer a forum for people to dial up, read and leave messages, and leave and copy files.

- ✔ **Service providers:** These are companies that, for a monthly fee, allow you a direct access to the many offerings of the Internet.

Taking the simple route with commercial services

Prodigy, CompuServe, America Online (AOL), and GEnie are the four major commercial online services available. These services exist for one reason: They provide a service and charge an access fee to cover the costs of that service. The good news is that, many times, the fees they charge seem rather small compared to the amount of time you spend using the services. As long as you understand the concept that this isn't the public (read: *free*) library, you should be okay.

Nothing of any great value is free, but plenty of valuable items are available for a normally moderate access charge. It's sort of like your long-distance phone bill. If you call Senator Smith in Washington every month and talk for 20 minutes about Freedonia, you know that next month's phone bill will reflect it. If you call America Online and spend the next 72 hours exploring, it's kind of like talking to Senator Smith for 72 hours. Just keep in mind what you're signing up for and think of it as a taxi with the meter running — get to what you want and then get out as soon as you can.

The next time you stop by your local bookstore, browse the computer section and you will find many, many books about these and other services. Look for IDG Books Worldwide's *America Online For Dummies,* 2nd Edition, by John Kaufeld and *CompuServe For Dummies,* 2nd Edition, by Wallace Wang, for starters. (*America Online For Dummies* includes a disk for you to experience AOL free for ten hours.) Your local computer software store can provide you with the necessary software and initial month's online time for around $25. Popping out the diskette and the manual isn't too difficult, and, for the most part, actually installing the software and getting connected the first time aren't (installing software, getting connected) that tricky, either.

The following sections provide a quick look at what's out there.

America Online (AOL)

AOL is one of the easiest services for new computer users to figure out. It's very graphical and easy to follow with points and clicks of your friendly mouse. For $9.95 a month — a real bargain — you get five hours each month on the meter, and each additional hour runs only $2.95 more.

Some of AOL's features are as follows:

- Generally excellent news coverage, featuring Reuters, UPI, *The New York Times, Chicago Tribune,* and other news outlets to keep you up to date

- User groups, where you can converse with others sharing your interests in a variety of topics: taxpayer, seniors, environmental, gay/lesbian, mental health, military/veterans, and other issues

- Searchable text from the Public Broadcasting Service (PBS) and news programs

    Forgot to watch *The McLaughlin Group* last weekend on television? AOL has the text. I did a search on Newt Gingrich, and up popped a listing of quips from the show regarding the current Speaker of the House.

    Washington Week in Review, another weekend staple, is also available. It carries a complete directory of current congressional members, addresses, phone/fax numbers, and Internet e-mail addresses, if available. You can look in this publication to find Gingrich's e-mail address at georgia6@hr.house.gov.

America Online has a Campaign '96 info center complete with message boards where you can leave messages or talk to people. It includes biographies of all the presidential candidates, copies of many of their speeches, and other useful information to help you make up your mind about which candidate to support.

CompuServe

CompuServe has been a leader for several years in the field of online services, and it offers an equally wide variety of services as AOL. For the same $9.95-a-month entrance fee, you have basic access to the system. Certain areas cost you added charges, but CompuServe informs you each time you enter one of these *premium* areas.

Some of CompuServe's features are the following:

- ✔ Excellent news coverage, featuring AP, Reuters, the *Washington Post* (perhaps the key domestic political newspaper in the nation today), and other international wire services
- ✔ User groups covering many different issues and topics, some with additional charges involved

Other services

Prodigy and GEnie are somewhat less valuable than AOL or CompuServe: Prodigy by content, GEnie by potential cost.

- ✔ Prodigy is currently working to upgrade its software, which should bring it up to par with AOL's functional screens, but the news coverage is somewhat below that of AOL and CompuServe.

  Prodigy user groups and bulletin boards are very good and provide many topics of interest. *Newsweek* magazine is a new feature, with search-and-locate abilities. If you're interested in Prodigy or have friends on Prodigy, don't give up, because the new features may bring Prodigy back among the leaders.

- ✔ GEnie is a potential gold mine of information but is limited by the high charge of access. GEnie's search and information abilities are excellent, but at rates of up to $20 per hour, you could find yourself with a very expensive new hobby. If you can get your boss at work to let the company tap into GEnie, go that route, but if you're just a home PC user, look elsewhere.

Plugging in online

It's easy to get connected, even without taking a trip to the nearest Electronic Wonderland!

America Online	800-827-6364	Dow Jones News	800-522-3567
CompuServe	800-848-8199	Lexis/Nexis	800-543-6862
GEnie	800-638-9636	NewsNet	800-345-1301
Prodigy	800-776-3449		

Other possible oracles are Dow Jones News/Retrieval, Lexis/Nexis, and NewsNet:

- ✔ If you read the *Wall Street Journal,* Dow Jones News/Retrieval is your baby.

- ✔ Lexis/Nexis is a boon for attorneys doing legal research and offers tremendous news coverage as well.

- ✔ NewsNet is news, featuring newsletters geared toward specific industries and professions.

Bulletin board systems

Perhaps one of the most controversial aspects of the online community is the plethora of small-yet-powerful electronic bulletin board systems (BBSs) that exist across the U.S. A BBS is nothing more than a computer system linked to phone lines by modems and running software that allows people who access the computer to obtain information. You can think of a private BBS as a poor man's America Online or CompuServe. A number of corporations have BBS numbers to provide software patches, updates, and the like.

For a moderate investment, you can convert a personal computer attached to a single modem and phone line into a BBS system. Check out IDG Books Worldwide's *BBSs For Dummies* by Beth Slick and Steve Gerber to find out more about BBSs, including how to set up one of your very own.

BBSs have a number of private and professional users, but it's in the shadowy world of underground politics that the BBS has grown and flourished. During California's debate on affirmative action, backers of an initiative to eliminate state affirmative action programs are using the Internet to collect the nearly 1 million voter signatures required to put the proposal on the November 1996 ballot. With the savage bombing of the Oklahoma City Federal Building, we know much more about some of the seamier political aspects of these BBS systems. Information is power. You can decide for yourself whether what you are receiving is information or propaganda.

Accessing the Internet directly

The latest craze to sweep the country (although it's been around for decades), the Internet is many things to many people. What started out as a narrowly defined connection of academic computer systems has grown and expanded into a bewildering maze of electronic connections that links just about everything in the world you've ever wanted to know (including some things you probably don't) to anybody who can connect to it via some form of network link. The Internet is organized about like a bowl of spaghetti.

To some extent, the Internet functions like CompuServe, AOL, and so on, but without the structure. The Internet is really just a collection of computers and networks of academic institutions, corporations, individuals, and so on. Unlike with phone lines — which are strung together and maintained by the phone companies — nobody is really in charge of the Internet. It's just sort of "out there."

My advice is to sit back and watch the show for a little while before plunging in. You may ask what you think is an innocent question and come back the next day to find your mailbox overflowing with electronic love letters of a decidedly negative variety. On the Internet, humanity's more primal side often comes out, and you see the true spectrum of human character and intelligence, good and bad.

Sound scary? Well, don't get too concerned, because the Internet is a lot like life in general. Some of what you see on the Internet is neat stuff. Some of it is meaningless — unless you're an interpreter for the United Nations (the Internet is multilingual, with lots of foreign-language newsgroups).

Check out *The Internet For Windows For Dummies Starter Kit* by John Levine and Margaret Levine Young or *The Internet For Macs For Dummies Starter Kit* by Charles Seiter (both from IDG Books Worldwide). Each includes the software necessary to get connected immediately. Seemingly half the books in the computer section of the bookstore these days are about the Internet, so you shouldn't have any trouble finding one that suits your needs.

Harnessing the true abilities of the Internet requires the use of different computer programs to navigate newsgroups, the World Wide Web (sounds like the plot for the next *Batman* movie, eh?), MUDs, telnet, and other nerdy things. Most Internet providers bundle the needed software together in packages that are functional for most people with a moderate amount of technical improvisation — but if you're a computer babe in the woods, go slowly with your online journey and stick with the commercial online services for a while.

Finding needles in haystacks: Usenet newsgroups

The politically fascinating part of the Internet is the newsgroups. Just as in real life, the Internet contains thousands of different areas of conversation. If you don't care to discuss the weather trends in Finland or no-fat recipes using tofu, just pass them by.

Several programs can offer you access to newsgroups. One of the most popular is WinVN, which is short for *Win*dows *V*irtual *N*ewsreader.

Learning to use newsgroups is much like browsing through a library; once you get the system down, you're sure to find topics of interest. Libraries try to organize thousands of books using the dreaded Dewey decimal system. Newsgroups are similarly organized by major categories, broken down into subtopics, and then further subtopics, and so on, all held together by periods. So, for example

- ✔ rec.humor.funny contains stuff that is recreational, humorous, and funny (hopefully).
- ✔ talk.abortion contains a discussion of abortion.

The seven major categories are as follows:

news.	Newsgroup issues
comp.	Computer issues
rec.	Recreational, hobby, and related issues
sci.	Science-related issues
soc.	Social issues
talk.	Free-wheeling, divisive issues
misc.	Everything that doesn't fit above

So you can find everything in those seven categories, right? Of course not! Read on.

Unsanctioned groups

With the growth of *Usenet* — an Internet facility that offers newsgroups, bulletin boards, and public forums — the wonderful seven basic categories of newsgroups just couldn't handle the explosion of ideas and topics that searched for homes on the Internet.

The most open, often most intellectually free, and of course most potentially offensive newsgroups belong to the *alt.* series, short for alternative. Several online services limit access to alt. groups; some groups are expressly prohibited.

The alt. groups contain all kinds of items, some very specific to a topic:

alt.fan.g-gordon-liddy	G. Gordon Liddy, conservative radio host
alt.politics.bush	George Bush

alt.politics.clinton	Bill Clinton
alt.politics.org.batf	U.S. Bureau of Alcohol, Tobacco and Firearms
alt.rush-limbaugh	Rush Limbaugh, conservative radio host

A good reference source to find the newsgroup that you're interested in is *The Internet Yellow Pages,* but look in any bookstore's computer section and you'll find other types of Internet newsgroup directories.

Usenet newsgroups are based on articles that are composed by users and then posted to the group, much like thumbtacking a message to a bulletin board. Other articles may be posted independently or arrive in response to previous postings. The new articles are posted off by themselves on the bulletin board, but the response postings are taped (so to speak) onto the original article and stretch down to the floor. These follow-ups, and follow-ups to follow-ups, form a *thread* — a Usenet conversation, like the dialog in a play.

Using the World Wide Web

The World Wide Web is the hot spot on the Internet right now, and even politicians are starting to stand up and take notice.

The Web is like a grand electronic maze, a place where each mouse click can bring you to a wonderful new experience. The Web links text, audio, and graphics into a *multimedia* (which just means a combination of two or more of those media) experience that is limited only by the imagination of those who designed the location you're exploring.

Politicians are starting to see the Web as a place where they can place their messages and let the online community explore their candidacies in ways not ordinarily possible. As we approach the 1996 presidential election, many of the Republican challengers to President Clinton have opened up home pages. The White House has a home page of its own for exploration. Even state and local party organizations are scrambling to get pages up on the World Wide Web.

Here are the Web addresses of major candidates and organizations:

Specific officials:

Lamar Alexander	http://www.nashville.net/nashville/bredesen/
Bill Clinton	http://www.whitehouse.gov
Phil Gramm	http://www.gramm96.org

(continued)

Richard Lugar	http://www.iquest.net/demiller/lugar/lugar.htm

Democrats:

Turn Left	http://falcon.cc.ukans.edu/~cubsfan/liberal.html
Digital Democrats	http://www.webcom.com/~digitals/
Democratic National Committee	http://www.democrats.org/
Senate Democrats	http://www.dsccc.org/d/dscc.html
House Democrats	http://www.house.gov/democrats/

Republicans:

Right Side of the Web	http://www.clark.net:80/pub/jeffd/index.html
Town Hall	http://www.townhall.com/
Republican presidential primaries	http://www.umr.edu/~sears/primary/main.html
GOP On-Line	http://www.gop.org/
The Christian Coalition	http://cc.org
NewtWatch	http://www.cais.com/newtwatch/

Other parties:

United We Stand	http://www.telusys.com/uwsa.html
Libertarian Party	http://www.lp.org/lp/

Nonpartisan information:

White House	http://www.whitehouse.gov
Congressional Quarterly	gopher://gopher.cqalert.com/
Thomas	http://thomas.loc.gov./
Campaign Central	http://www.clark.net/ccentral/
Project Vote Smart	http://www.vote-smart.org/

You can use the Web's search tools to find a vast array of topics. Note that searches can be very quick or can take moments or even several minutes, depending on what's going on with the Web and the nature of the query involved.

A search on "Tax Reform" brought me a veritable smorgasbord of information, some from governmental sources, some from think tanks, and some even from private citizens:

http://www.akebono.stanford.edu/ Economy/Taxes/ Information	Long-term changes to entitlement programs and tax structure
http://www.taxprophet.com/clinton.html	Comparing the Clinton 1992 campaign proposals to the actual administration
http://www.cais.com/main/sp5-11-5.html	The economic and civil liberties case for a national sales tax
http://www.emerald.net/atr/purpose.html	Americans for Tax Reform

One of the best things about the Web is that it is a living beast; people are constantly working at it and improving and changing it. Sections are under construction, being added on, and in progress. Unlike a museum, where the exhibits may change only two or three times a season, the Web is constantly putting on a new face.

E-Mailing Your Way to the White House

More and more of America is going online. One of the first aspects of going online is receiving an *e-mail address,* which is simply an electronic location where your computerized mail can be routed. Just as the U.S. Postal Service uses zip codes to sort mail more precisely, your e-mail address is a system for your electronic mail carrier to be able to deliver your electronic mail. Fortunately, most e-mail addresses are somewhat easier to understand and decipher than postal zip codes.

There are many different ways to send e-mail, and many, many different programs exist to help with this task. Even the World Wide Web can be adapted to transmit e-mail. Most e-mail packages have fairly rudimentary systems to actually write the document. Unlike in complex word processing programs such as Word, WordPerfect, and WordPro, plunking down an e-mail message is usually more like sitting down at a typewriter and pounding away on the keys.

You can correct your mistakes with the Backspace key, but formatting is a matter of hitting the Enter key and inserting spaces by hand. You want to center a line? Remember back in typing class when they told you to start in the middle and press Backspace for every two characters in the line? Well, here's your chance to use that formula once again!

Know the address

Sending out e-mail is a very simple matter. In order to send out mail, you need only two things: something to say and an e-mail address to send it to. Sending e-mail is just like faxing your views or ideas to an elected official or radio talk show host (see Chapter 5).

E-mail addresses are composed of two parts: an internal component and an external component. The two parts are separated by a period (.). The external component tells where to route your mail through the maze of complicated router tables that keep track of every provider site on the Internet. The internal component is the specific location within the larger unit of sites where a person receives mail. For example

tim@aol.com	This address is for Tim, who is an America Online user.
70000.0000@compuserve.com	This one reaches a CompuServe user; CompuServe uses numbers instead of names.
Jenna@prodigy.com	This address reaches Jenna, who uses Prodigy.

Just follow the address exactly, including spacing, and you're in business.

Some popular political e-mail addresses are

The White House	president@whitehouse.gov
Vice President Al Gore	vice-president@whitehouse.gov
Speaker Newt Gingrich	georgia6@hr.house.gov
Senate Minority Leader Tom Daschle	tom_daschle@daschle.senate.gov

The trick to sending e-mail, just like sending regular post, is knowing the address of the person you're sending it to. Many people now put their e-mail addresses on their business cards and stationery. If you want to receive mail, you should certainly make your e-mail address a regular part of your correspondence.

Don't get burned by the flames!

Arguments take place all the time on the Internet. Some are kindly, almost genial affairs. When they degenerate, you've reached the flames. *Flames* are articles that are heated, insulting, and normally dramatic attempts at one-upmanship. Flames can even spill over into electronic mail, and particularly offensive battles — or grievous offenses to Internet etiquette — can result in stacks of hateful e-mail messages piling up in your virtual mailbox.

Remember that newsgroups consist of international forums where people from all backgrounds and all over the world participate. Your comments are being watched, read, and interpreted by an audience of people from many different viewpoints. Usenet discussion groups are *not* private chitchat; they're a series of cameos on a stage where the audience may be very limited or very large in size.

Because you're going to be going up on stage, it's high time you learned how to act! Just as you learned that it's polite to establish eye contact with someone you're speaking with but very rude to engage in a stare-down, you need to learn how to communicate effectively using just the letters and symbols on your keyboard.

Evoking drama and emotion with the 256-character ASCII set is difficult, but over the years, a set of standards has evolved to help add a little spice to the otherwise bland dialogue that a keyboard can crank out. One of the biggest things to learn is how to SHOUT OUT LOUD and then how to speak softly.

Here are some tips to successful online communication:

- Don't capitalize EVERY WORD: It's the equivalent of screaming.
- Be creative: Use other methods to convey information — like a smiley :-)
- When you really want to *emphasize* something, use asterisks.
- Try adding dramatic . . . . . pauses to set tone.
- Use symbols to represent certain four-letter %@&#! words.

Part III:
Politics Is a
Team Sport

In this part...

*T*his part discusses why we have only two major parties and all sorts of minor parties and independent candidates. Look here to find out how to become a member of a political party and what happens when you do. This part also looks at special interest groups — you may be a member of one without even knowing it. This part tells how special interest groups can work for, not against, you.

Chapter 7
Partying with Politics

• •

In This Chapter

▶ Introducing America's two-party system
▶ The declining power of parties
▶ How political parties serve us
▶ How parties select their candidates

• •

A political party is a group of people who have common beliefs and goals. A party organizes to promote those beliefs and goals by electing officials who share them. Parties select candidates, raise money for their campaigns, encourage participation by eligible voters, and gain power by winning elections. Parties also influence the policies of government and serve as the loyal opposition when they're not in power.

Why We Have Only Two Parties

The United States currently has two major parties: the Republican and the Democratic. Other parties, called *third parties,* have formed in this country from time to time. Sometimes these parties are organized around a single person, such as Teddy Roosevelt's Bull Moose Party (or Progressive Party) in 1912. Sometimes these third parties form around a single issue, like segregation, as George Wallace's American Independence Party did in 1968, or the Prohibition Party, which had a candidate for president on the ballot in every presidential election for 100 years from 1876 to 1976.

Third parties, such as H. Ross Perot's United We Stand America, can occasionally make impressive showings. But third parties seldom receive many electoral votes. Perot received none in 1992. The few third-party candidates who have received electoral votes have never won. Even Teddy Roosevelt, who received more electoral votes in 1912 than the Republican nominee William Howard Taft, only succeeded in splitting the Republican vote and electing the Democrat, Woodrow Wilson.

The big-tent theory

In this country, our two major parties are essentially big tents. They allow room for many different approaches and policies all under the same banner. The parties do not enforce rigid adherence to party policies by refusing to attach the party label to those members who don't agree with everything the party says and does.

The big-tent theory of parties in this country is necessary because our electoral system discourages splinter parties. Ours is largely a winner-take-all system. We don't have proportional representation in our Congress or state legislature. Under *proportional representation* systems, parties win seats in legislatures in accordance with the percentage of the vote cast for their party. In our system, the presidential candidate who gets the most votes in every state, even if the most votes turns out to be less than the majority of votes cast, receives all the electoral votes the state has.

When in Rome . . .

Although the United States practices winner-take-all elections, the experience in other countries is different. Many other countries allow proportional representation of the political parties in their legislative bodies.

Proportional representation increases the likelihood that smaller parties will win some elections and have some officeholders. That permits smaller parties to be players. When ruling coalitions are formed to piece together a majority in the legislative body of a country, smaller parties that have won seats through proportional representation have bargaining power. That ability to have political power encourages smaller parties to continue playing the political game.

In Italy, for example, putting together a government may take a coalition of seven, eight, or more parties. Each of those parties bargains for something from the coalition leader in exchange for the party's support. The party may have a minister or two selected from its ranks for service in the new government, and so on. The parties can have influence even though they received a very small percentage of the popular vote in the election.

This system permits the formation of small, well-organized parties that advocate one issue or a small group of issues. Proportional representation and coalition building permit these parties to play a role in government and policy that isn't available in the American system.

A winner-take-all system discourages third-party candidates and third parties. It also limits the options available to the voter. Because success is limited to one of two parties, the parties must select candidates with the broadest possible appeal. Controversial candidates with bold ideas are not favored under this system. Parties seek candidates who represent the lowest common denominator of appeal to voters — that is, the broadest possible appeal with the lowest potential for alienating voters. Single-issue candidates, like controversial candidates, are disfavored.

Third parties

The odds against their winning the presidential election are so great that it's difficult for third parties to get a toehold. Campaigns are so expensive that third-party candidates must have a huge amount of personal wealth to launch a national campaign.

Ross Perot spent tens of millions of his own dollars in his effort to run for president. He managed to get about 19 percent of the votes cast for president in 1992, but he received none of the electoral votes.

Perot may have run under the banner of United We Stand, a third political party, but he was, in reality, an independent candidate. (*Independent* candidates are different from third-party candidates in that they are running purely on their own views and merits, not as representatives of an overarching group or party.) There was no organized effort to run other United We Stand candidates. The party was established to enable Ross Perot to run for president. His was an independent candidacy under the guise of a third-party movement.

The 19 percent of the popular vote received by Ross Perot is the largest percentage received by a third-party candidate for president in our history. Many political pundits regard his impressive showing, despite his on again/off again candidacy, as a symptom that the two major parties are not meeting the needs of the voters.

Many political commentators think we will see more successful third-party candidates during this era of voter alienation from the political process. But in the United States, the odds are that a third party will probably have no more to show for its efforts to elect candidates than bills. Our presidential elections are winner take all, even without a majority, and that system definitely favors the two, and only two, party system. Occasionally, an independent candidate can be elected if the circumstances are right, but that's an individual candidate, not an entire slate of candidates running under the banner of a third party (see the following section for more on independent candidates).

Dominance by two political parties does not mean that the same two political parties will always dominate. It is possible that a third party could gain momentum by advocating the right issue at the right time and eclipse one of the two major political parties. The names and perhaps the philosophies of the two political parties might change under those circumstances, but the number of major political parties would probably remain the same.

Independent candidates

Independent candidates have no party affiliation or are affiliated with a smaller political party, not the Democratic or Republican Party. Often, successful independent candidates were once affiliated with a major party. Lowell P. Weicker, Jr. was elected governor of Connecticut as an independent, but that was after he had been elected a Republican senator previously.

Being elected as an independent is considerably easier in theory than in reality. Independent candidates must build the structural support that parties provide by themselves. They must raise the money to get their message across on their own. Unless the candidate is independently wealthy, running as an independent is a very, very difficult proposition.

If all the stars, the sun, and the moon are in alignment, it's possible for independent candidates to win elections. But don't bet your farm on the outcome — you might have to move in a hurry.

Departing from the Party

Parties in America are entirely different animals than parties in other countries. Candidates, not parties, drive the American political process. The American electorate, by and large, votes for the candidate, not the political party the candidate represents.

Sometimes, if a popular candidate belongs to an unpopular political party, that candidate deliberately downplays his party affiliation. Often, the candidate's ads may not even mention which party he represents. He may refuse to appear in advertisements or printed campaign material with his party's candidates for other offices on the same ballot. Campaigns in America these days can be largely solo performances rather than team competitions.

Voters value independence

In this country, *straight-ticket voting,* voting for all of the candidates of a single party, is the exception rather than the rule (see "Straight-Ticket Voting versus Ticket Splitting", later in this chapter). Candidates relish their ability to demonstrate their independence, which can extend to becoming mavericks within their own political parties. If a candidate or an officeholder can demonstrate independence from his party, the voters view that independence as a positive, not a negative, characteristic.

An officeholder relishes nothing more than opportunities to show that he can't be ordered around by anyone. Voters value an officeholder who shows a willingness to "stand up" and go against the tide. Voters are not impressed by party discipline or being a team player.

Legislation requires cooperation

Getting elected because of your independence is one thing. Doing anything after you're elected is something else. The attitude that a candidate is her own person and not answerable to anyone, which may help her get elected, works *against* passing legislation, where the emphasis is put on teamwork.

When you're dealing with Congress, getting those majorities involves convincing quite a few representatives and senators. It takes 218 votes to pass any legislation through the House of Representatives and another 51 votes to pass anything through the U. S. Senate. For a bill to become a law, it must pass both houses of Congress, usually with a majority vote. That means that 217 other mavericks in the House and 51 in the Senate must agree with the legislation the representative is attempting to pass. If all the officeholder has done all session is demonstrate her independence by swimming against the tide, why should any other legislators bother to help her pass her legislation? Why should other Members of Congress take risks for a Member who is not willing to take risks for them?

Compromise and consensus are the essence of good legislation. No representative or senator can accomplish anything alone, other than gaining the reputation of a maverick. Any legislation needed by a district or state, any public policy sought to be enacted because it benefits voters, must have the support of a majority in both houses of the legislature.

Only Nebraska has one legislative house. All other states have two houses that must pass legislation before it can become law. Even in Nebraska, a majority of the 49 elected representatives must vote to enact legislation.

Those Were the Days

Before candidates began to use television to speak directly to you and other voters, they were identified by their parties. In your parents' or grandparents' day, parties had a much greater influence on candidates — as well as more power over them.

Television is such a pervasive part of our culture that it's difficult to imagine life without it. In the times before prime-time commercials, parties were the vehicles by which candidates communicated with other voters. Party workers contacted their constituents personally. They distributed literature to help voters make decisions. Parties needed volunteers to make those contacts, but little else.

Candidates relied on the parties to help with their campaigns. The parties provided the only effective way of reaching the people and persuading them to vote a certain way. Because candidates and officeholders needed the parties to win elections, the parties had influence with them. They could use that influence to encourage elected officials to do things voters wanted — things that the officials might otherwise be reluctant to do.

Party officials who knew the ins and outs of politics followed the actions of elected officials very closely. Those party officials knew precisely what an officeholder had to do to ensure passage of a bill. They were not fooled by the fancy footwork or doubletalk of an elected official. Parties understood the issues and the procedural maneuvers involved in passage of a bill. The parties followed what happened on important issues and took retaliatory action if officials failed to live up to their commitments.

In short, there was accountability. An elected official was directly responsible to someone other than large contributors. The "old days" (not to say the "good old days") of party bosses may have had its flaws, but elected officials were forced to make and keep commitments on what they would do once they were in office. If an officeholder failed to keep his or her commitments, the party could deny that officeholder the party's nomination for reelection.

Television and the Decline of Party Power

The advent of television in political campaigns changed the dynamic of campaigning. Today, parties are no longer monolithic structures that control political life in America. Now, with the help of the old boob tube, candidates take the issues directly *to* the voters and get their power directly *from* the voters. This creates problems.

The cost of campaigning

In today's politics, candidates can buy television time to talk directly to you. They can hold town meetings and press conferences and appear on television and radio talk shows. All these things guarantee the candidate media coverage to take his message over the heads of the party members and into the homes of the voters.

What's wrong with that, you might ask. Shouldn't candidates and officeholders communicate directly with the people who elected them? Isn't that what a democracy is all about? Of course they should. The issue is not whether they should communicate; the issue is how they communicate.

Television is one of the most effective ways to communicate, but it's also one of the most expensive. In a contest between a candidate with money and a candidate with party support, the candidate with money usually wins. He becomes the nominee of the party whether the party leaders like that fact or not.

Today, party leaders can't control who runs as their candidate, and candidates no longer need party leaders to communicate with you and other voters. Party discipline is largely a thing of the past.

Officeholders have the power of incumbency to raise large sums of money for reelection. Those large sums of money give them further insulation and protection from accountability to the political parties.

Contributors gain the upper hand

Not only has television undermined the ability of party organizations to enforce accountability, it has also tremendously increased the cost of campaigning. Candidates must spend enormous amounts of time raising money to enable them to communicate through television and radio. To raise the enormous amounts of money required, officials must court those individuals and groups that can make substantial campaign contributions.

Those individuals and groups that help the officials raise the amounts of campaign money needed seldom do it solely out of a desire for good government. These contributors do hold the officials accountable — for their own agenda of interest, that is. It is no accident that incumbents have a significant advantage in the fund-raising area. After all, if you're a contributor interested in influence, the officeholder is a proven winner. She's in a position to help the contributor's agenda, at least as long as she keeps winning.

This is accountability of a sort. Now officials are listening more to a few contributors and less to the Tom, Dick, and Mary who comprise the party organization in their districts. Ask yourself who is more likely to represent your interests on these issues and votes: wealthy contributors or Tom, Dick, and Mary?

Perhaps it's not in your interests to allow the decline of party influence to continue. Maybe it's time you and your neighbors got involved in the party of your choice.

Voters can be duped

Now you might say that all elected officials are ultimately accountable to the voters, so what's the problem? Don't the voters have the final say in this process? Isn't that the final check on abuses in the system?

In theory, that is true. However, today's society is so complex and fast moving that it's totally unrealistic to expect you, the voter, to follow each issue as closely as necessary to make officials accountable. That climate permits clever officeholders who are reluctant to take risks to have their cake and eat it, too.

Elected officials, particularly legislators, can position themselves so they can claim to have supported both sides of an issue. To do this, an official may vote on a procedural matter to kill a proposal and then vote for final passage of the measure. The official can then "legitimately" claim to one group of constituents that he was *for* the measure, and then, to another group of constituents, claim to have voted *against* the measure. Given this ploy, how can voters be expected to hold their officials accountable?

Not every elected official pulls this type of stunt, but it's much too common. An official who does try it, and who has enough money to get his message out in a campaign, will probably get away with it, too!

You can't possibly monitor all the nuances of an official's voting record on any and all issues. After all, you have enough to do already with work, home, your children, your parents, church, and Little League. Anyway, you would have difficulty getting the type of detailed information necessary to assess the importance of every vote.

Some special interest groups do track every vote of interest to the group. These groups then publish the results to their membership and sometimes to the public. Senior citizens groups, business groups, environmental groups, chambers of commerce, labor unions, citizen watchdog groups, and the like watch every procedural and substantive vote on their issues and attempt to hold elected officials accountable for their votes. If the group is large enough or influential enough in the elected official's district, accountability can be enforced.

On issues not followed by such groups, accountability is absent. Officials can talk out of both sides of their mouths without serious consequences because the parties are no longer strong enough to make elected officials accountable.

Straight-Ticket Voting versus Ticket Splitting

Perhaps as a consequence of the increasing independence of the electorate, the number of voters who vote *straight ticket* is declining. *Straight-ticket voters* vote for all the nominees in a single political party — either all the Republican candidates on the ballot or all the Democratic candidates on the ballot. They do not vote for some candidates from one party and some from the other.

Ticket splitting, where you vote for the nominees of one party for some offices and the nominees of another party for other offices, is more and more common. One recent estimate states that the number of straight-ticket voters in general elections has declined to less than 20 percent of the votes cast.

The increase in ticket splitting reflects the increasing number of voters who think of themselves as independent voters. Even among those voters who identify themselves by party, the number of straight-ticket voters has steadily declined. Republican and Democratic voters are more likely to pick some candidates from the other party to vote for.

The way it was

In the days of straight-ticket voting, political parties could nominate up-and-coming candidates for lesser political offices with the confidence that their party affiliation alone would carry those candidates to victory in the election. Voters didn't need to be educated about the qualifications and issues in these lesser offices because the party identification alone would ensure that sufficient votes were cast to elect these people on the coattails of the top of the party's ticket.

Voters identified themselves by their party affiliation and were more willing to vote for their party's choices for less important offices. That assurance permitted parties to groom the next generation of top-of-the-ticket candidates. Parties could recruit candidates with relative ease because they were in a position to guarantee election to these candidates.

The way it is

By and large, party labels alone are no longer powerful enough to guarantee election to lesser offices. Candidates are now expected to work for their own election.

Because the parties can't help as much as they used to, the parties are no longer as important to the candidates as they once were. Predictably, candidates no longer show their parties the degree of loyalty that they once showed. Voters may be independent of the political parties, but candidates are increasingly that way, too — all of which makes political parties weaker than they once were, which has its own consequences (refer back to "Those were the days," earlier in this chapter).

Political Parties Serve a Purpose

Parties provide very important civic services:

- ✔ They help conduct fair elections.
- ✔ They help register voters and make voting easier on election day.
- ✔ They provide information on candidates and issues.
- ✔ They give individual voters with similar views a means to unite and affect public policy.

Ensuring a fair election

Political parties and their supporters choose the candidates from whom you pick when you vote in the general election, but they also perform many other functions that enable elections to occur without much controversy.

Political parties are responsible for finding people to work everywhere voters cast their ballots on election day. Volunteers monitor voting places and count and record ballots. In short, the political parties provide workers to guarantee that elections are held in as open and fair a manner as possible.

Watchers

Each political party must provide *watchers* to ensure that elections are conducted according to the law. Those workers make certain that their candidates' right to an election free of fraud and intimidation is respected.

Each party is entitled to an equal number of watchers at every voting place. The precinct committeeperson for each party appoints the watchers for each voting place. Each candidate on the ballot is also entitled to a watcher at every polling place. The campaign manager for a candidate issues a piece of paper that identifies the volunteer as a watcher for a particular candidate.

Candidates are free to provide their own poll watchers for each voting place in the district in which they are running. Few candidates do so. Finding the number of volunteers necessary to cover each voting place is difficult. Having each party do it for all the party's candidates makes more sense than having 10 or 15 candidates finding volunteers to cover all the voting places necessary.

Ballot counters

The parties provide workers to count the ballots that are undisputed and to record the ballots that are disputed so that election boards or courts can determine whether those ballots should be counted.

Precinct workers have several alternatives when counting paper ballots. They may

- ✔ Agree to count a ballot because, although there may be mistakes, it's clear who the voter wanted to vote for

- ✔ Agree not to count a ballot

- ✔ Agree to count a ballot partially — that is, to count it for some offices where the voter's intent is clear but not for one or more offices where it's unclear what the voter was trying to do

If the representatives of both political parties can't agree, the ballot is disputed. State law determines whether a disputed ballot is ultimately counted or not. At the precinct level, the workers need only count the paper ballots they agree on and put the others aside. Most of the time, the workers at the precinct level resolve all the disputes as fairly as they can.

Join a party and volunteer

In order to work as a ballot counter, you have to declare a party affiliation and keep it. Neither party will want to use you for these sensitive duties if they can't be sure of your loyalty to the party's candidates. (If you don't want to have a strong party affiliation, you may still work on election day for the candidate of your choice. Contact your candidate's campaign office to volunteer your services.)

Aggressive representation for both parties insures fairness. The parties are afraid that a worker who is not a strong party person will lie down on the job in a tough or close election.

If you're interested in helping on election day, you should contact the precinct committeeperson for your political party. If you want to work on election day to help a particular candidate, call the campaign headquarters for that candidate and let the staff know that you're willing to volunteer. Your political party will be delighted to train you; there are never enough good election-day workers.

Some examples of ballots that might be disputed are

- ✔ The voter voted for two people for the same office
- ✔ A ballot contains marks that might identify the voter (all paper ballots are cast anonymously)
- ✔ The voter used a paper ballot for the wrong legislative or congressional district

Getting out the vote

In addition to ensuring a minimum of shenanigans at the voting places, parties perform what is commonly referred to as *grassroots* activities. Grassroots political activity begins with registering people to vote and continues with polling voters and making voting as easy as possible.

Registering voters

If you volunteer for grassroots activities, you may find yourself going door to door registering people to vote and identifying them as sympathetic to or opposed to your candidate or party. You don't usually get paid for performing this important function, but it's a way for you to be involved in politics and meet your neighbors at the same time.

Although government employees register voters who come into government offices, they do not provide this service in people's homes. Door-to-door registration is usually a volunteer effort by civic-minded people like you.

Polling a precinct

After registering all potential voters, conscientious party people begin to poll their precinct. *Polling a precinct* means canvassing voters in that precinct in person or by phone to determine which party's candidates the voters are likely to support.

A precinct poll is unlike a poll by professional pollsters. A precinct poll does not consist of a randomly drawn sample of registered voters from the district where demographic information, but not the identity of the individual voter, is important. A precinct poll is designed to identify each and every voter in the district by name. Party workers need to know which voters they should be encouraging to vote on election day.

Volunteers canvass by knocking on doors or calling people on the phone, identifying the party or candidate they are working for, and asking a few simple questions. The approach goes something like this:

Hi! I'm Bill Monroe. I'm your neighbor just down the street, and I'm taking a voter poll for the Democrats. Do you mind if I ask you a few quick questions?

- Are you registered to vote?

- How many others are registered to vote in this household?

- Do you consider yourself a Democrat, Republican, or Independent?

- This November 6, there will be an election to choose the mayor of our city. Do you plan to vote in that election?

- The candidates are Democrat Joe Blow and Republican Mike Smith. For whom will you vote?

Volunteers are trained on how to react to the different responses they may get when conducting a precinct poll:

- If the voter tells the Democratic pollster that he plans to vote for the Democratic candidate, the pollster asks how the other voters in the household feel. He asks whether the voter needs an absentee ballot or any assistance in getting to the voting place on election day.

- If the voter tells the pollster that she hasn't made up her mind, the pollster gives her literature about the candidate and perhaps talks to her about his party's nominee to help persuade the voter to vote for his candidate.

- If the voter tells the Democratic worker that he is a Republican who is supporting the Republican candidate, the pollster politely thanks him for his time and leaves.

Polling a precinct is a time-consuming project for which the party worker is usually not compensated. That poll can provide candidates with useful information about voters they need to persuade. It also helps the party worker do her job of turning out more voters who will vote for her party's candidates.

Making it easy to vote

Party organizations are service organizations. They want to help you, the voter, by making it easier for you to vote . . . and, in particular, to vote for their candidates. Here are some specific things political parties can do for you:

- ✔ They can tell you which district you live in and who your candidates are.

- ✔ They can tell you the location of your voting place.

- ✔ They can assist you in obtaining absentee ballots and rides to the polling places.

   Individuals who are ill, disabled, out of the state on election day, or away at college are all prospects to vote by *absentee ballot*. Such voters can mail in their ballots. Or, in the case of a shut-in voter, election representatives go to the voter's home with a paper ballot for the voter to fill in.

Not every party organization has its act together; you may ask for something and not get it. But you never know whether your local party organization can help you until you try to use it. Call a party when you have a question or need help. Most party organizations have a headquarters with telephones. If yours doesn't, find out the name and phone number of the county or city chairperson for your party and call him or her at home. If you don't ask, you won't receive!

Reminding you to vote

The party and its workers also help the candidates remind citizens to vote on election day. Motivating citizens to vote in nonpresidential elections is a difficult, time-consuming, and expensive task. The party organization can help candidates by making the person-to-person or neighbor-to-neighbor contact. These efforts can turn out an additional five or ten votes per precinct.

Providing information

Political parties can even help you decide which candidate to vote for in the election. If you want to make direct contact with a candidate, the party can tell you how to contact him or her. If you have a specific question about a candidate, the party can help you get the answer to your question. For example, parties can give you voting records of incumbents so you can judge for yourself where they stand.

Keep in mind that the information a party provides you about its candidate is drafted to persuade you to vote for that candidate. The material that parties provide voters is not objective; or, in political terms, it's *partisan*. A party's literature tells you all the good things about that party's candidates without educating you on any flaws its candidates may have. That is to be expected, but you should be aware when you read it that you're receiving only one side of the story. Before you make up your mind, ask the opponent's party to give you the other side.

A single vote *does* make a difference!

The extra votes that a party volunteer tries to squeeze out can make the difference between winning and losing an election. When John F. Kennedy was elected president in 1960, his margin of victory over Richard M. Nixon was less than one vote per precinct nationwide. The outcome of history might have been very different if the Republican precinct workers across this country had encouraged another voter or two per precinct to vote for Nixon, or if Democratic precinct workers hadn't worked quite so hard. Richard Nixon could have defeated John Kennedy if one more voter per precinct had stayed home.

Amplifying your voice

Making elected officials listen to you can be difficult if you're the only one talking. When other people join you in making noise, you're much more likely to gain attention. Political parties can turn a single voice crying in the wilderness into a chorus.

U. S. parties may not enforce rigid party discipline and require their members to support a particular ideology, but they can help to clarify issues and to simplify your choices on election day. Parties can also help you make your voice heard. They can help to focus attention on issues or policies that mean something to you.

Many Americans join or identify with political parties in order to magnify their influence on the political process. One voter on his or her own has a tough time changing policy or the political process. But that one political voice (or vote) crying in the wilderness can have an impact if others join it. Just as your modest contribution to the candidate you support can multiply when you solicit your friends, neighbors, relatives, and coworkers (see Chapter 5), your one vote can have a multiplier effect. When you join with others who feel about the issues as you do, your voice becomes loud enough to be heard. You can make your voice so loud that officeholders and candidates ignore it only at their own peril.

Of course, you can always form your own coalition of citizens who think as you do on an issue and bypass political parties. That approach requires organizational skill, time, and effort, but it is possible.

Picking the Candidates

On election day, you may ask yourself, "How did these two alternatives wind up on my ballot? How come I get to choose only the lesser of two evils?"

Party nominees

Parties in America are the main vehicles for selecting nominees for office. Parties and voters supporting political parties have the responsibility of weeding through the large number of candidates who may file for a particular elective office.

There's no real secret to candidate selection: Party people prefer to select their candidates from among those people they know and know well. Party people are no different from the rest of us. We are all more comfortable with things and people we know.

Party people get to know a candidate in one of two ways: She has either been active in the party organization itself or has been a candidate before.

Choosing one of their own

Nobody likes to nominate a candidate for important offices who hasn't earned his political spurs first. Candidates are first expected to work for the party organization performing a variety of functions, from precinct work to fund-raising. Would-be candidates are also expected to have labored in the vineyards of other campaigns. Both of these activities demonstrate to party people that the would-be candidate is *really* a Democrat or Republican. Once a candidate puts in his apprenticeship, party people recognize that it's the candidate's time to run. A common expression is: "It's his turn."

Party workers like candidates who demonstrate commitment to the party team. After all, party people value the functions performed by party organizations. Because they value the party's work, it's natural that activists would expect candidates to value that work, too. A candidate truly demonstrates her regard for the party and its work by performing some of the tasks herself, preferably for some time, before becoming a candidate for office.

Recycled candidates

Another way party activists know would-be candidates well enough to nominate them for office is when the candidate is *recycled;* that is, the candidate ran in the past, either for the office in question or another office. The level of comfort that comes with a recycled candidate encourages many of the same people to run over and over again for the same or another comparable office.

Some of the more influential party workers may be currently, or may have once been, employed by the recycled candidate when he or she was an officeholder in the past. These influential party workers have a vested interest in the candidate.

The party workers may know that the recycled candidate isn't going to set the world on fire. The recycled candidate may not be the best candidate the party could put forward, but he or she probably isn't the worst candidate, either. The party workers know what they and the voters are getting with a recycled candidate. That knowledge raises the party workers' comfort level. It's the unknown that is frightening, after all. These are the things party workers think about when choosing a candidate. See Chapter 13 for some things you might want to consider in selecting your candidates.

Term limits and recycled candidates

It isn't unusual for one person to serve at different times in different county elected offices. In a political career, a candidate may serve as county treasurer, county assessor, county auditor, and/or county clerk. Ironically, this recycling of candidates occurs because of term limits. For years, many local governments have imposed term limits on the number of times a candidate may be elected to a particular office. For example, in some jurisdictions, a person may be elected county auditor, assessor, clerk, or sheriff for only two terms. But the statutes are silent about the total number of years or terms an officeholder may have in all elected offices.

Term limits were designed to keep officeholders from becoming arrogant and complacent. Advocates for term limits believe that taxpayers receive better service from officeholders who have a definite term of office to complete their improvements on the office and make their marks as officeholders. New blood is introduced into the election process at regular intervals. These new candidates are supposed to invigorate elected offices by generating new ideas and creating fresh approaches to public service.

The goal of having citizen officeholders serve for brief, distinct periods of time as elected officials before resuming their careers in the private sector is a good one. Unfortunately, that goal hasn't been achieved. We don't have very many good citizens serving their communities for brief stints in elected offices. We don't have ordinary citizens interested in public service being nominated on anything approaching a regular basis. We have *career officeholders*. The same recycled candidates move from one position to another as the term limits expire, in an elaborate game of musical chairs.

Does the complacent county assessor who views her office as a personal fiefdom become an exemplary public servant by moving two doors down the hall in the county office building and changing her title? Of course she doesn't! The title may change, but the quality of service for the taxpayer stays the same.

Recycled candidates are more likely to be nominated by conventions or caucuses because the party activists who attend them prefer recycling. When ordinary voters like you don't participate in primary elections to select the nominees of the parties for office, the party activists who do vote have more influence because fewer votes are cast.

Candidates will continue to be recycled until you get involved and convince party activists to set their sights for candidate selection higher. See the rest of this chapter for tips on breaking into party life.

Primaries

The primary allows parties and the voters who identify with these parties to choose the candidate who will be the nominee of that party for each office in the next general election. Either directly (through primaries) or indirectly (by electing delegates in primaries), the primary determines your choices on the ballot in the next general election.

Voters increasingly use the primary to select candidates for office. When primaries were first used, they were viewed as a democratic alternative to control of the nominating process by party bosses sitting in smoke-filled rooms. Now primary selection is more common than convention or caucus selection for nominees (see the following section for more on these other methods of selection). That is particularly true for the office of president. Voters express their preference for presidential candidates by primary in 34 states (as of 1992). Nine of those 34 states have a Democratic presidential primary and a Republican caucus or convention.

Primary elections are seen as a reform because they allow more people to participate in the selection process for candidates. In primary elections, even if only 25 to 35 percent of those eligible to vote in a statewide primary do so, you're still talking about reaching hundreds of thousands of voters.

Unfortunately primaries increase the cost of campaigning significantly. Primaries are a much more expensive method of selecting candidates than conventions. If you're concerned about the rising cost of campaigns, you should be aware that primaries are one reason for the higher cost. You can decide whether the increase in the cost of a campaign is worth the opportunity for more people to participate in the nomination process.

Conventions

Those delegates you elect in primaries go to the state convention of your political party and choose the party's nominees for other, less visible statewide elected offices, sometimes called *down-ballot offices*. In states that elect an attorney general, secretary of state, state treasurer, state auditor, and so on, nominees for these offices are usually selected by the state conventions of the political parties.

Convention selection for down-ballot positions is a less expensive method of choosing candidates for less visible offices. A candidate running in a convention does not have to spend as much money campaigning to reach 1,000 or 2,000 delegate votes as he or she would have to spend to reach a majority of voters in a primary election in the entire state.

You can have a role to play in the selection of convention nominees either by running as a delegate yourself or by asking the delegate candidates, who want your vote, whom they are prepared to support at the convention. You can then vote for the delegate who will support the candidate you want nominated.

Any voter who declares his or her party affiliation can run for election as a convention delegate. See Chapter 20 to find out how you can become a delegate.

Conventions are cheaper for the candidate to run, and they are also less expensive for taxpayers. It costs taxpayers millions of dollars to conduct a statewide primary. Convention or caucus selection costs the taxpayers nothing.

The Role of Ideology in Candidate Selection

Background plays a more significant role than ideology in the selection of nominees for local offices. How candidates for county clerk feel about the balanced budget amendment or abortion is less important than how candidates for Congress feel about those issues.

Ideology doesn't have much impact at the local level, where the main function of an office is administrative. But when an office involves setting public policy, ideology plays a very important role in the selection process for both parties. Party activists choose these candidates in significant part because of their ideology, whether such a choice may cost the party support in the general election or not.

Many party people are active in politics because they feel strongly about policy issues. They have policies they want to see implemented, and they have policies they want to see undone. They do their work to elect candidates because they want to make a difference in their community, state, or nation. If you understand why many activists become, and remain, involved, you will understand that policy considerations play an important role in the selection of candidates for policy-formulating offices.

When you understand that background, you can appreciate the fact that there are certain litmus-test issues in both parties that candidates must support if they are to stand a reasonable chance to be nominated by party activists. A *litmus-test issue* is on which, by their support or rejection of that issue alone, candidates prove themselves to be ideologically in line with their party.

The parties try to enforce ideological conformity on their candidates by requiring commitments to certain, key policies supported by most party activists. The parties require these commitments even though making such commitments may not assist candidates in the general election. They require these commitments and leave the candidates to assume the risks associated with supporting these positions in the general election. The commitments are not meant to hurt their candidates' chances for election; they're required because they're important to the party activists.

To make certain that the litmus tests are few in number and reflect your views, you need to participate in the candidate selection process. The old adage is an accurate one: If you want to make sure that something is done right, do it yourself! The only way we can be absolutely confident that our alternatives on election day provide us with good choices is to choose those alternatives ourselves. You need to get involved in the selection process for candidates early.

Chapter 8
Taking Sides

• •

In This Chapter

▶ Looking at the history of the parties

▶ Joining a party — the ups and the downs

▶ Accepting the pitfalls of third parties

▶ Choosing between the Republicans and the Democrats

• •

*Y*ou are in a position to decide whether you want to associate with a political party or not. You can choose to join the Republican Party, the Democratic Party, or an independent party. You are the only one who can decide which party you should join and what joining it means for you. But reading this chapter may help you decide.

Putting Parties in Their Place

As early as the 1790s, political parties had influence on the Electoral College. In those days, the Electoral College played a much more important role than the official role it has today (for more on the Electoral College, read Chapter 22). Before long, political parties were involved in all elections.

Every president in this nation's history has had the support of one of the major political parties of his time. No candidate from a third or minor party has ever been elected President of the United States.

Although this country has had two major political parties at all times, the names and the groups supporting these political parties have changed over time. The positions the parties have taken on issues have also evolved. It's not important for you to know all of the twists and turns the parties have followed in becoming what they are today. The only two things to know, so you can casually mention them at parties, are

✔ The Democrat-Republicans of Thomas Jefferson's day became the Democrats of Andrew Jackson' s time, and that party is today's Democratic Party.

✔ The early Federalist Party became the Whig Party. Whigs and others became the Republican Party of Abraham Lincoln.

For the last 130 years, the two major parties of this country have been the Democrats and the Republicans, or GOP (Grand Old Party). These two parties compete to win elections and the support of voters.

Joining a Political Party

Joining a political party definitely has its advantages:

✔ You can have a more substantial role in selecting the candidates you get to choose from in the general election.

✔ You can vote with confidence for the candidates running under your party label, even if you don't know a great deal about them.

✔ You can help to shape issues for your party and its elected officials. Your voice is louder when you belong to a group of people who think about the issues the same way you do.

✔ As a party activist, you can begin working to restore accountability for elected officials.

So how do you become a member of a political party? You simply declare yourself a member. Call yourself a Democrat or a Republican and you are one. There's no master list of all Democratic and Republican Party members. There are no pledges to sign or membership cards to be issued, no dues or bizarre initiation ceremonies. You are what you say you are . . . with certain limitations.

✔ In some states, you will be viewed as a member of a party by voting for the party of your choice in a primary election. When you do that, voting lists in your county and state show the party for which you vote.

Some states discourage voters from voting in one party's primary one year and another party's primary the next. You should check with your county or state election board to see whether your state has any rules in this regard. You'll want to know if those rules could affect you. You never know when the other party will have a more interesting primary. You may want to vote in that one instead.

✔ Some states permit you to declare your party preference when you register to vote. If you do that, you will automatically be listed on the voter files by the party label you provided — whether you ever vote in a party primary or not.

✔ Another way to increase the likelihood of your identification with a political party is to contribute to its candidates and its party organization. Even if your contribution is too small to be listed in the campaign finance reports, the government requires campaigns and parties to keep a list of your name, address, and contribution. Once you give money, the party to which you gave regards you as one of its own!

Registering as a Democrat or Republican

When you identify yourself as a Republican or a Democrat, that disclosure has consequences for you. Is it better to play your cards close to your vest and say that you're an Independent? After all, our country has a secret ballot so that you don't have to tell anyone how you voted if you don't want to — why give hints?

Advantages

If you declare yourself a party member, chances are that a number of good things will happen. Here are some of the doors that joining a party can open for you:

✔ **Candidate literature:** During the primary election season, you may receive information from candidates eager to win your vote for the primary election. Receiving (and, of course, reading) this information makes it easier for you to cast an informed vote.

✔ **Primary elections:** You become eligible to vote in primary elections. Very few people, often as few as 25 percent of the eligible voters, vote in party primaries. If you are one of the 25 percent, your vote carries a lot of weight. It carries a lot more weight in the primary, when candidates are selected, than it does in the general election, when the candidate is elected, because the number voting in the general election is more than double that of the primary turnout. (See Chapter 20 for more about primary elections.)

✔ **Caucuses:** You also become eligible to vote in the caucuses that may be held by your party if your state uses a caucus selection system for candidates. (See Chapter 21 for more discussion of caucuses.)

- **Volunteering:** You may be asked to work at the polls on election day as a poll watcher or a get-out-the-vote volunteer. Serving as a volunteer is an easy way to become more active in politics. It provides a means for you to meet the party activists and most of the local candidates who visit the polls on election day. You have a chance to interact with these people when you attend the party's training sessions to learn your new task — and learn to function on coffee and donuts, which help fuel such activities.

- **Becoming a delegate:** You also become eligible to run for delegate to the state and national party conventions. These conventions adopt the state and national platforms for the respective parties and nominate candidates for a variety of offices, including president and vice president. (See Chapter 21 for more on delegates.)

Regardless of whether you declare a party affiliation, you are completely free to vote for whomever you like in the general election. Republicans can vote for Democratic nominees for any office and vice versa.

Disadvantages

Declaring your party affiliation also has some disadvantages:

- **Courting:** You probably won't be courted by either party's candidates. You probably won't receive direct mail or phone calls. Both parties assume you will vote the way you have declared. (Of course, you may view this neglect as an advantage!)

- **Everyone knows your politics:** Once you declare an affiliation, you have told the world, or at least the part of the world who wants to look, how your politics lean.

Many states require political balance for appointments to boards and commissions appointed by state governments. If you are seeking appointment to a board or commission, the government looks to your party preference stated by declaration or through primary voting to determine whether you are eligible.

Asserting your independence

You can choose not to affiliate with a political party. Approximately one-third of the voting public takes this approach. Being an Independent also has pluses and minuses.

Advantages

- ✔ People don't know your politics unless you want to tell them.

- ✔ The candidates from both parties woo you trying to persuade you to vote for them. You'll probably receive direct mail and phone calls from both sides.

Disadvantages

- ✔ In most states, you will probably not have a vote in the nominating process. You may find yourself choosing the lesser of two evils on the final election day.

- ✔ Your opportunities to get active politically by volunteering are limited to supporting a particular candidate. In those states where the parties count the votes on election day, you'll be unable to participate.

Joining a third party

Nationally and in many states, third parties are active. In fact, in 1992, the following third parties nominated candidates for president:

United We Stand America

Libertarian

America First

New Alliance

U. S. Taxpayers

Natural Law

Socialist Workers

La Rouche

Third parties tend to be organized around an issue or a philosophy. They are less interested in winning elections than they are in focusing attention on issues or policies of importance to their membership. Predictably, they don't generally receive many votes in any election. Our system of government is set up to accommodate only two parties — anything extra doesn't have the perks or the opportunities of a dominant party.

Advantages

- ✔ If you feel strongly about an issue — and you are more interested in making your feelings known than in winning elections — a third party may provide the answer.

- ✔ If you don't feel that either major party reflects your views, you may be more comfortable belonging to a third party.

- ✔ If you are just getting involved and think that the time has come to shake up the political process, membership in a third party may be the way to make waves.

- ✔ If you are just becoming active and want prominence and responsibility in a hurry, you may find it easier to get that prominence and responsibility in a third party.

Disadvantages

- ✔ Staying involved and working hard in election after election is difficult when it's almost a foregone conclusion that all your candidates will lose.

- ✔ Third-party members generally have no say in the selection of the Democratic and Republican presidential nominees, one or the other of whom will probably be elected president.

- ✔ Raising money for third parties that have almost no chance of winning is a very difficult proposition.

- ✔ If you support a third-party candidate who is elected president, he or she will still have to contend with a Congress consisting of Democrats and Republicans, making it difficult to get legislation enacted.

- ✔ Third parties generally form around a few ideological issues of importance to the members of the third party, but the public may not feel as strongly about these issues and may wonder why you are wasting your time and effort tilting at windmills.

Separating the Democrats from the Republicans

To understand how to separate the Democrats from the Republicans, you must understand something in general terms about their histories, their evolutions, and their memberships.

Historically, the Republican Party identified itself with supporting opportunity and voting rights for African-Americans. The Republican Party in Abraham Lincoln's day was the anti-slavery party. The GOP was against big business and for a strong federal government. The Republicans supported antitrust legislation to break up monopolies. In Teddy Roosevelt's era, the GOP was strongly pro-conservation.

The Democratic Party, on the other hand, supported states' rights. It was not at all eager to abolish slavery or provide the newly emancipated African-Americans with rights. The Democratic Party identified with the steady stream of immigrants who flooded our shores in the second half of the nineteenth and into the twentieth century.

Over time, the policies advocated by both parties changed. So did the membership of the parties. Knowing which is the chicken and which is the egg is always difficult. Did the parties change their positions to win more voters to their banners, or did the people who called themselves Democrats and Republicans change their views, leaving the parties to adjust their philosophies? Whatever the reason, there is no doubt that the two parties have changed over time.

The state and national platforms can provide insight on what the parties believe and what their goals are. The platforms are supposed to represent the views of all party members. When the parties viewed themselves as big tents, encompassing everyone who wanted to wave the party banner — including liberals, conservatives, and moderates — drafting the platforms to obtain majority support at the national and state conventions was difficult. See Chapter 20 for more on platforms.

In recent years, groups have tried to move their parties in certain ideological directions. In the Republican Party, it is the religious right that wants firmer statements of ideology and goals than some Republicans are comfortable with. In the Democratic Party, the tension comes from the liberal wing pushing the party more to the left than many members want to go. These attempts lead to spirited debates about the drafting and content of party platforms and have put more emphasis on ideological purity and less on all party members living happily under one big tent.

Why the donkey and the elephant?

Since 1831, the donkey has been the national symbol of the Democratic Party. The symbol was popularized by the famous cartoonist Thomas Nast of *Harpers's Weekly* during the 1880s. Nast first used the symbol in a political cartoon showing Andrew Jackson riding a donkey and beating it to support his veto of the U.S. Bank recharter.

The elephant was first coined as a Republican symbol by the same political cartoonist, Thomas Nast, in 1874. Nast depicted the Republican elephant stomping Tammany Hall (the New York Democratic political machine) tiger. The elephant has been used to symbolize the GOP, or Grand Old Party, ever since.

Running with the elephants

If you are considering whether to join the Republican Party, you should be aware of several general points of agreement among those who identify themselves as Republicans. Remember, not every Republican feels the same way about each issue, but this discussion should give you an overview of some basic Republican philosophy.

In today's political world, Republicans lead the charge for states' rights. They want the states, not the federal government, to manage as many issues and programs as possible, including enforcement of environmental regulations, welfare, nursing-home standards, and Medicaid. Republicans favor smaller government and want to get the federal government off the backs of the states, businesses, and individuals. They oppose gun control. They see little role for the federal government aside from foreign policy and national defense.

Republicans do see a role for the federal government in fostering family values such as sexual abstinence, prayer in public schools, taxpayer support for alternatives to public education, and restricted sex education and abortion.

There are exceptions to every rule, but here are some characteristics shared by many members of the Republican Party:

- ✔ Higher-income individuals
- ✔ Self-employed individuals
- ✔ Businesspeople
- ✔ More small-town than big-city people
- ✔ Men
- ✔ Whites
- ✔ Fundamentalist or evangelical Christians
- ✔ Protestants
- ✔ More likely to favor flat or regressive taxes

Joining the donkeys

Unlike Republicans, Democrats believe that the federal government should play a role in assisting citizens they consider to be disadvantaged: the poor, the elderly, and the disabled. Democrats are more willing to see the federal government intervene and propose solutions to problems. They don't have the same

Evolving constituencies

Certain subgroups in the population identify more with one party or the other. It's fair to say that upper-income people, businesspeople, suburbanites, college graduates, and white men are more likely to count themselves as Republicans. Lower-income people, union workers, high-school graduates, African-Americans, other minorities, and women are more likely to consider themselves Democrats.

Party identification doesn't necessarily stay constant. It can evolve over time. Women and African-Americans used to associate them-

selves more with the Republican Party. From the Civil War to Franklin Roosevelt's second term, African-Americans voted Republican. From the time women received the vote nationally in 1920 until the 1980s, women were more likely to vote Republican. These days, both groups are more likely to identify with the Democratic Party. More women identify themselves as Democrats by a few percentage points, and African-Americans overwhelmingly self-identify as Democrats.

inherent faith in the ability of state governments to manage complex problems that Republicans do and are less willing to turn over federal dollars to the states to administer.

Democrats generally favor gun control, affirmative action, and direct college loans to students. But Democrats generally have less faith than Republicans in the ability of government to foster a system of personal values in this country and prefer to leave churches and families to perform that function. Democrats are opposed to mandatory prayer in public schools. They're generally pro-choice on abortion issues and favor using public funds to pay for abortions for victims of rape and incest who are on Medicaid.

The same caveat about exceptions to every rule applies here, but here are some common Democratic traits:

- Highly educated (graduate education) individuals
- Individuals with only a high-school diploma
- Working-class citizens
- Labor union members
- Minority groups
- Women
- Urban rather than rural people
- More likely to favor progressive taxes

This list and the list for the Republicans are intended as general guides. It's not necessary for you to fit all or most of the characteristics described here. Some voters will feel more comfortable in a party where they don't fit the profile. They may determine their party affiliation on the basis of a single issue they feel strongly about and ignore the other parts of the profile. When and if you choose to join a party is a decision you should make for yourself.

Making Your Own Choice

Okay, you're sold on the advantages of belonging to one of the two major parties, but which one? How do you determine which party reflects how you feel about the issues and which party's candidates you want to see in office?

Looking at the platforms

The first thing to look at in determining which party you are more comfortable supporting is what the parties stand for. There are several places you can look to determine for yourself which party more closely mirrors your views of government.

Each state and national party drafts a party platform that their state and national conventions adopt. The national party adopts a platform every presidential election year. The state parties may adopt platforms more frequently, usually every other year.

You can request copies of these platforms from your Republican and Democratic state committees. The state committees usually have an office in the state capital. They may also have offices in the state's largest city. Call the state committees and ask for copies of the most recent state party platforms.

You can do the same with the national party committees in Washington. The addresses are

> ✔ Democratic National Committee; 430 South Capitol Street, SE; Washington, DC 20003
>
> ✔ Republican National Committee; 310 First Street, SE; Washington, DC 20003

Ask the state and national committees for copies of their platforms and ask to be put on their mailing lists. The committees will send you information and newsletters that can provide you with a great deal of insight on which issues the parties support and why. Reading the material produced by the state and national committees for both parties should assist you in choosing which party to join.

Listening to the candidates

Another way to determine which party you are comfortable joining is to watch and listen to the candidates the parties put forward for election. See which party's candidates reflect how you feel about the issues. See who else supports the candidates and determine for yourself whether you are comfortable traveling in the same circles.

When you decide which party to join, you should consider the following checklist of issues. Determining where the parties stand on these issues compared to your views can help you determine which party to associate with.

- ✔ **Tax policy:** Do you favor cuts that benefit the middle class, upper class, or the poor? Do you think tax policy should encourage other public policy like savings or education?

- ✔ **Deficit reduction:** Do you believe the country's deficit should be reduced? How do you think that reduction should be accomplished?

- ✔ **The role of the federal government:** Do you regard the federal government as your enemy? Do you believe that the federal government has little if any legitimate role to play in today's world? Or do you believe that the federal government can provide assistance in solving problems and helping those in society least able to help themselves?

- ✔ **Social issues:** Do you see a role for the government in setting values and morals? Do you think the government should be involved in issues such as abortion, prayer in public schools, and taxpayer support for parochial schools?

- ✔ **The environment:** Do you feel that government has a role to play in preserving the environment and forcing business to observe standards, or do you feel that environmental extremists have created a bureaucratic nightmare that hinders the growth of jobs and the profitability of business?

Compare your positions on issues like these with the positions of the parties and the parties' candidates to decide whom you would be more comfortable associating with.

Differences within a party

Both the Democratic and Republican parties have conservative, moderate, and liberal members. American parties don't generally conduct litmus tests for ideological purity as some foreign parties have done. In the Soviet Union under Stalin, failure to agree with Stalin's (often changing) opinions on any issue could result in being ousted from the Communist party. Democrats and Republicans may disagree among themselves, but no procedure exists for drumming a ideological maverick out of either party.

Sometimes elected officials switch and declare themselves members of the opposition party. Renunciation of party affiliation by an individual is the only way to leave a party. The parties do not have mechanisms for purging their ranks of members who are no longer in the mainstream of party ideology.

For both parties, the tent encompassing membership is very large, and the requirements of membership are very vague. (See "The big-tent theory" in Chapter 7.)

Differences between the two parties

Despite the fact that the major political parties tolerate opposing views, general differences do exist between the parties in attitude and ideology. Those differences translate into different groups that support one party rather than the other.

When you are deciding which party to join, you need to see which party, as a general rule, is closer in approach and philosophy to what you feel the role of government should be and how you feel about the important issues of the day. The only real test is whether you are comfortable with your choice. You are the only person who needs to be pleased by your selection.

Chapter 9

Joining a Special Interest Group

. . . .

In This Chapter

▶ What are special interest groups, anyway?

▶ Looking at lobbyists

▶ Playing the you-scratch-my-back-I'll-scratch-yours game

▶ PACing a punch

▶ Contributing your money to a special interest

▶ Getting the same access to politicians as special interest groups

. . . .

*R*aces for the legislature in the 50 states are financed in part by party givers (see Chapter 4). But legislative candidates also receive money from groups that are interested in the legislature and, perhaps more important, in the laws enacted by the legislatures. These groups, sometimes referred to as *special interest groups,* band together to pursue their common interest in passing, protecting, or repealing laws.

Special interest groups are large, organized groups that work together because they share common interests or goals. They exist to protect what they have *from* government action and to get more *through* government action. They lobby and exert political pressure to get what they want from elected officials:

✔ They want laws that benefit them passed.

✔ They want laws that hurt them repealed.

✔ They want the government to make decisions that help them and their causes.

Special interest groups work to find common ground with other special interest groups so they can form temporary alliances to increase their numbers and their strength on particular issues. When they are larger and more powerful, they may have an easier time getting what they want from elected officials.

Identifying Special Interest Groups

You hear much discussion about the influence of special interest groups on the political process. You think that, whoever these special interest groups are, they have more power and influence than you do, and that worries you.

Many different groups qualify for the title of a special interest group. They may be ideological groups with no personal agenda and those whose members do have personal agendas. There are so many special interest groups that you may already belong to one or more yourself. Are you

✔ An employee of a corporation or an industry that could be defined as a special interest (steel, pharmaceuticals, hospitals, nursing homes, mining, utilities, insurance)?

✔ A member of a profession that lobbies (bar association, trial lawyers, doctors, dentists, accountants)?

✔ A member of an educational group (teachers, school superintendents, school boards, universities)?

✔ A member of a consolidated group (chambers of commerce, manufacturers associations, retail associations)?

✔ A member of or contributor to groups that lobby for specific issues or programs, including

   • Not-for-profit groups, such as associations for veterans, people with mental health problems, and people who are deaf or blind or have other disabilities?

   • Groups for arts funding or public broadcasting?

   • Groups for outdoor recreation, such as bicycling?

   • PTAs?

   • State universities?

✔ A senior citizen?

✔ A union member?

✔ An environmentalist?

✔ Pro-choice or pro-life?

✔ For or against smoking rights?

✔ In favor of public funding for mass transportation, airport development, or highways?

✔ For or against gun control?

✔ For civil rights or civil liberties?

✔ For women's rights?

If so, you may have met the enemy, and it is you. Of course, you may not agree with all or even many of the policies of the group that you belong to. You may oppose what the American Association of Retired Persons does to lobby for seniors, for example. If you aren't typical of the group to which you belong, you don't view the special interest that claims you as a member as working for you. Even if you are typical, you may still view the influence of special interest groups with grave concern.

One person's membership and support may be another person's special interest. Your attitude toward special interest groups depends on whether you are giving or receiving their attentions. If you are part of an interest group that's trying to exert influence to change votes or minds, you probably see nothing wrong with their tactics. If the issue you support is being attacked by special interest groups, you may view the attack in a much different light.

Enlisting Lobbyists

Although the term *lobbyist* has a legal definition under state and federal law, generally speaking, lobbyists are people who are paid to represent special interest groups primarily before the legislative but also before the executive branches of government. Lobbyists are paid because they make it their business to know and schmooze officials and their staffs. They also know how the government works inside and out.

Special interest groups pay for the services of lobbyists in a variety of ways. Corporations and unions simply pay out of their operating budgets for lobbying services. Groups with large memberships may use a part of the fee charged to members to pay for these services. Some of the dues you send each year to organizations to which you belong may be used to provide lobbying for those organizations' legislative or political goals.

The history of lobbyists

The term *lobbyist* comes from the special interest representatives who used to gather in the lobby of the Willard Hotel in Washington, D.C., to talk to the Members of Congress who spent time there. These special interest representatives tried to persuade the members to vote a certain way.

What began as a few people's informal method of buttonholing Members of Congress to discuss pending legislation has mushroomed into a multimillion dollar industry with thousands of people registered as lobbyists before federal, state, and local governments.

What a good lobbyist does

A lobbyist working in a state legislature or Congress is familiar with the rules of procedure of the body in which she lobbies. She knows the personalities of the supporters and the enemies of the legislators, and she knows how to

- Get a bill killed
- Amend a bill to make it more acceptable
- Amend a bill to make it unacceptable to legislators
- Push the hot buttons of elected officials
- Form alliances with other special interest groups to pass or defeat a bill

In short, a good lobbyist knows the ropes much better than a freshman legislator or congressperson.

Lobbyists are paid to protect the special interest groups from laws that might hurt them. They carefully watch all the bills introduced and all amendments to those bills to make certain that nothing will have a negative impact on their clients' interests, and to sound the alarm when it does.

A lobbyist's success doesn't depend on her speaking ability or whether she looks good on television; it's determined by what passes or fails to pass a legislative body. The future clients of the lobbyist and the amount of money a lobbyist can charge are directly related to the lobbyist's success record in passing or defeating bills of interest to her clients.

It's not uncommon for a successful lobbyist to represent more than one special interest, although lobbyists avoid representing interests that may compete against each other in the legislature.

Special interests and the government

Special interests that lobby the government fall into three categories:

> ✓ **Interests that do business with the state and federal government**
>
>   Lobbying for these groups includes getting legislatures to set the most favorable reimbursement rate possible from the state or federal government for Medicaid and Medicare payments or other payments. States and the federal government are spending increasing percentages of their budgets on Medicaid and Medicare payments. The providers of Medicaid and Medicare services — nursing homes, hospitals, doctors,

POLITICAL STUFF

Conservative lobbyists and gas taxes

You can find an example of how lobbyists band together for a common purpose and look out for their clients' interests in the alliance of groups favoring highway construction.

Representatives of architectural and engineering firms, asphalt paving companies, concrete companies, and trucking companies are ordinarily pro-business and anti-taxes. In other words, they favor conservative fiscal policies by

their governments — with one big exception.

These groups regularly band together to urge states and the federal government to increase gas taxes to generate more money for road and bridge construction. That way, they support the good public policy of improving our nation's highway system and generate more business for themselves.

Using lobbyists to wipe out the competition

A special interest group pays lobbyists to get laws passed that benefit the group. The lobbyist has a legislative wish list from the group that includes legislation favorable to the group's industry, profession, or cause. If the special interest group is a company, the group may push for legislation that hurts the competition and, therefore, helps the group.

For example, a company may support tax subsidies that raise the prices of the competitor's product. The company can then come out with a substitute not affected by the subsidies that sells better because it's cheaper. If the company has been contributing heavily to

Democratic and Republican candidates and to both parties — and throwing in contributions to charities supported by the politicians, for good measure — the lobbyist will have an easy time getting the legislation passed, even though you and other consumers are hurt by the higher prices and unfair competition.

The ability of such rich and powerful special interest groups to influence legislative change should cause you concern. It gives influential companies and people the ability to improve their position at the expense of you and other voters.

and drug companies — all lobby state governments and Washington for a better rate of reimbursement for the services they provide. The higher the rate of reimbursement, the more profitable the provider's business.

(*Medicaid* is the federal program that provides health care to the poor, some of whom are elderly. The program is jointly funded by federal and state tax dollars and, with the increasing cost of health care, is more and more expensive. *Medicare* is the federal program to provide health care to the elderly.)

✔ **Interests that are funded by the state or federal government**

Lobbying for these groups includes persuading the legislators to give them more money from the state or national budgets or allowing them to raise fees or borrow money. School corporations, universities, mental health facilities, the National Endowment for the Arts, the Corporation for Public Broadcasting — all these groups lobby legislators for a bigger share of the state or federal budget.

✔ **Interests that are regulated by the government**

Special interest groups that are regulated by states lobby the legislature and state agencies for more favorable regulatory treatment. Insurance companies, utilities, banks, and other financial institutions fall into this category.

Making Political Contributions

Successful special interest groups mount campaigns on several fronts to protect and promote their interests. Lobbying, maintaining political clout, and organizing campaigns designed to rally public support for their positions are all part of successful campaigns to advance their interests. But making political contributions is one of their best known tactics.

A key factor in a politician's decision on which position to take is whether or not special interests with money to contribute care about the issue. Special interest contributions can be a big factor in a politician's analysis of what is at stake. Picking the "right" side of an issue can result in large special interest contributions. Picking the "wrong" side of an issue can mean the special interests give to the candidate's opponent or run an independent campaign to defeat the candidate.

Special interests don't contribute large sums of money to a campaign — particularly a campaign to enact certain legislation — purely out of a desire for good government. Sure, *you* may make contributions to a cause without expecting anything in return, but your contributions are relatively modest — not like the thousands of dollars that special interest groups spend when they want something in return. The "something" these contributors want usually has a direct financial benefit to them.

Sometimes special interests use their money to mail to their membership and urge those members to vote against a candidate or for her opponent. The money spent doesn't go directly into the campaigns of a candidate or her opponent, but it has an indirect effect on the outcome of the campaign if enough special interest supporters follow the advice of the special interests and vote in the election.

Getting action with PACs

Special interest groups form *p*olitical *a*ction *c*ommittees (PACs) so that they can contribute to legislative candidates and political parties. Because the federal government and a large number of states prohibit corporate contributions as well as contributions from labor funds, many corporations and unions form PACs to enable themselves to contribute to political campaigns. Not-for-profit groups generally don't form PACs or make contributions to candidates or parties.

PACs can make substantial ($5,000) contributions to federal and many other officeholders every election cycle. Some states permit PAC contributions larger than $5,000 per candidate per election. If the PACs contribute enough money to enough officeholders, they may be able to round up a majority of votes for almost any measure they want. Gifts of cash have a way of doing that.

Some states permit direct contributions from corporations to candidates and political parties. In those states, the corporate contributions are supplemented by PAC contributions.

PACs have become very common features of modern-day political campaigns, and they come in all shapes and sizes. Many PACs are formed at workplaces by employers or unions. Others are formed by people who shareviews about issues. When many small contributions are pooled to support a candidate, these small contributions can be substantial enough to get any candidate's attention.

Here are some of the reasons for which PACs are formed:

- ✔ To support women and African-American candidates
- ✔ To support the pro-life or the pro-choice cause
- ✔ To support candidates sensitive to environmental issues
- ✔ To support the anti–gun control or pro–gun control cause
- ✔ By employers or unions at workplaces to support their own causes

PACs mean big money

In 1994, PACs contributed $169,500,000 to federal candidates. In 1982, that number was $83,600,000.

PACs consist of groups of like-minded people who are often employed by the same company or are members of the same union and who pool their contributions to maximize their impact. PACs are equivalent to political labor organizations and operate under the same principle — a large number of people, when organized into a group, can speak with a louder voice and change their lives.

The larger PACs not only talk loudly — they carry very big sticks. Here are some examples of how much PACs contributed to Democratic and Republican candidates in the 1994 election cycle:

- United Parcel Service's PAC gave more than $2,500,000.

- AT&T gave about $1,300,000.

- The tobacco PACs of RJR Nabisco and Philip Morris gave about $1,500,000 combined.

Not surprisingly, candidates certainly do regard the PACs as serious political players.

("PACs Cross the Street," Business Week, *issue 3419, April 10, 1995, pp. 94–96)*

- ✔ By industries, such as the hospital and tobacco industries, to support their own causes

- ✔ By people who share views about issues to promote those issues

- ✔ By diverse groups supported by many small contributions which, when pooled to support a candidate, can be substantial enough to get any candidate's attention

If you ask around, you'll find numerous opportunities to join and contribute to PACs — and that will help you to increase your political clout.

Joining a PAC or forming your own

You may already be a member of one PAC or more through your work and community involvement. If you are a member, you can seek appointment or election to the committee of your PAC that decides how the PAC makes its contributions. The people who make those determinations for PACs can be very influential in determining who wins and who loses various races for office. Those PAC committee members have substantial political clout — now that dollar signs are attached!

You also have the option of forming your own PAC. If you care about a particular issue and have some friends who feel the same, you can create your own PAC, raise money, and decide who will receive the contributions. Keep in mind that you will also have to comply with state or federal reporting requirements for PAC activity. Your state election board and the Federal Election Commission can provide you with the information you need to comply with the law. You can find your state election board's phone number in the phone book, and you can call the Federal Election Commission at
1-800-424-9530.

PAC regulations

A federally qualified PAC is a creature of federal law. A PAC is permitted to raise money from certain sources to contribute to federal campaigns. Since the 1980s, PACs have played a significant role in financing federal elections.

In a federal campaign, each individual can give a candidate $1,000 for the primary election and $1,000 for the general election. (A *primary election* is a public election to decide who will be the nominees of the political parties in the final election. The winners are the top vote-getters for each party, or the top two vote-getters if the race is nonpartisan. The *general election* is the final election when voters choose from among the primary election winners. See Chapter 20 for more on primaries.)

Corporations are prohibited from giving to federal candidates at all. Labor unions can give PAC money, but not labor union dues money, to support federal candidates.

Each state has its own rules on who may give to state and local candidates and how much can be given. If you want to give and are unfamiliar with your state's laws, you can call your state election board or secretary of state's office and ask for a copy of your state's campaign finance laws. Your state library has a copy of them, too. This information is usually provided free of charge.

PAC money and clout

Knowing what organizations gave money and to whom is important because it helps you understand what's going on. If one of the PACs is supporting or opposing an issue that you are interested in, you need to know whether your elected official has received contributions from this PAC.

If the answer is yes, you know you will have to organize enough voters who feel as you do about the issue to counter the impact of the contribution on your elected official's behavior. You need to convince your elected official that doing the "wrong" thing, voting the way the PAC wants, will cost him votes in the next election. You need to counter the money analysis that the elected official will perform with a vote analysis that you have created (Chapter 2 explains the money/vote analysis in detail). You need to convince your elected official that it's better to lose future contributions from that PAC than all the votes you can mobilize against him at the next election. You need to demonstrate to your official that not only large contributors have political clout — voters can have political clout, too, even without the dollar signs attached. Chapter 5 tells you how to communicate your arguments to the official.

Contributing to nonlegislative candidates

Legislative candidates are not the only beneficiaries of special interest contributions. Mayors and city or county councilpeople of large cities, federal candidates, and governors also benefit. Mayors and governors can propose legislation. They can usually sign into law or veto legislation, and they make many decisions on awarding grants or funding to new or existing businesses. Theirs is usually the final word on awarding city and state contracts. Large-city mayors and governors are the types of elected officials whom special interest groups cultivate with campaign contributions and support.

You scratch my back, I'll scratch yours

Special interest groups usually see a direct relationship between their contributions and the goals they are seeking. That isn't to say that they're foolish enough to demand a commitment from a candidate to vote a certain way on a bill in return for a political contribution. That approach is too direct — and illegal. Besides, if the officeholder changes his mind, there's no way for the special interest group to enforce the commitment it had from the officeholder. No, approaches by special interest groups tend to be more subtle.

The representatives of the groups and the candidate meet to discuss matters of concern to the group and see whether there's a common understanding of the issues. The group may ask for and receive a general commitment of support, but that's all.

What the special interest groups receive in return for their contributions is all-important: They receive *access!* They know that if they give enough money, their calls will be returned. When they give election after election, their requests for meetings with officeholders are honored. That access permits lobbyists for special interest groups to make their case for or against proposed legislation directly to one or more of the officeholders casting votes to decide the issue.

If these special interest groups give to many legislators, their access increases dramatically. If they give generously to the leadership of the legislative bodies or the caucus fund-raising efforts, they can count on being received courteously at the highest levels of power.

Contrary to popular belief, access may not guarantee the special interest groups the results they want. Competing special interest groups may be exerting counterpressures on the official. Or the public outcry over the legislation may make it politically difficult or impossible for the legislators to deliver what the special interest groups want.

But, although it may not be foolproof, access is critical. The ability to make their arguments directly to lawmakers gives the special interest groups with access a leg up on the competition. That competition can include you, the average voter. (See the upcoming section.)

Getting the Same Access as Special Interest Groups

What you, as an individual, want is the same access that special interest groups enjoy to explain your position on issues of importance to you. Some access is available to you already. Your state legislator may return your phone call when you call to tell her what you think. Of course, the call may come after the vote is cast. You may even get a letter or a call from a staff person for your Member of Congress in response to your call or letter.

But getting access to the leaders of your state legislature or Congress is much tougher. You don't have the same ability as an influential lobbyist for a special interest group to call the Chairperson of the House Ways and Means Committee in Washington to get put on his calendar for lunch. In order to make your voice heard in the halls of leadership, you need to multiply your clout. See Chapter 5 for suggestions on how to do that.

It's obvious that the special interest groups that contribute can make their cases to these important people in person and you can't. Campaign contributions in large quantities translate into access for those making the contributions. That's why many special interest groups give in the first place.

Keep in mind that, if you are a member of a special interest group that has contributed generously and often, your representative may be able to have lunch with these legislative leaders even if you yourself can't. That's fine from your point of view, as long as you share the viewpoint of the special interest group to which you belong.

Are Special Interest Groups Contributing Your Money?

The answer is probably. If you buy from a corporation that can make direct contributions to political candidates, you have helped make those contributions possible. If you buy power from a utility company or insurance from a company that can make direct corporate contributions to candidates and political parties, you helped make those contributions possible.

If you participate in a PAC yourself, you are contributing your own money directly to political campaigns and political parties. If you work for a corporation that has a PAC and you make voluntary contributions to that PAC, you are contributing your own money. The PAC committee may decide how the money is spent, but *you* are contributing.

You may not realize that simply purchasing from a corporation with a PAC helps to make its contributions possible. Your money may not be used directly by the corporation to fund its political PAC, but your money can be used to pay the salaries of the management personnel of the corporation. In turn, people in management are encouraged by their bosses to participate in a voluntary corporate PAC. They are asked to make voluntary payroll deductions to fund the corporate PAC out of the salaries that your purchases helped pay.

Union PACs work the same way. If you belong to a labor union and participate in a PAC, your money is used to fund the PAC's political contributions. Some states permit unions to use a part of their union dues money for political contributions over and above union PAC contributions. If you belong to a union, you are helping to fund contributions in those states that permit the use of union dues money for political contributions, even if you don't participate in the PAC.

In short, you may be part of the financing for the special interest that you've been blaming for contaminating the political process in recent years! Well, everyone's a special interest these days. You can't avoid involvement completely, but there are a few steps you can take to try to make the PACs you are associated with reflect your views. Once you're aware of what a special interest with which you are associated is doing and don't agree with it, you can either stop your contributions or make direct contributions to the side of the issue or election that you want to support.

You can also avoid purchasing the products or stock of companies whose executives or PACs support candidates and issues with which you disagree.

Finding Out Who Contributes

When a special interest group or PAC makes a contribution to a political candidate, that information gets reported two times. The candidate must report it in her campaign finance report. (Chapter 14 has more information on campaign financing.) In addition, the special interest group PAC must report all its expenditures to the government.

Special interest groups must file federal PAC reports with the FEC in Washington. You can write the FEC to request copies of these reports, but remember, you will be charged for each copy you get. When you examine the special interest PAC report, you can find out who contributed to the PAC as well as every candidate who benefited from the PAC's generosity.

Local races

In most states, the campaign finance reports for local candidates and political parties are filed in the offices of the county clerk or the county election board. These reports tell you how much special interest money a local candidate or campaign has raised and from whom. The reports also tell you how a campaign has spent its money and how much it has left on hand as of the filing date. These reports don't tell you all the contributions a special interest has made to other political candidates, but they do tell you whether any local candidates or parties, whose reports you look at, received anything from a particular interest.

In an election year, most states require local candidates up for election and their party organizations to file several reports. These reports cover set periods in the election cycle. There's probably a preprimary or precon-vention report you can examine, as well as reports filed a month or six weeks before the election is held. Some states also require candidates to disclose large contributions received late in the campaign within a short period of time after they are received by the candidate.

State races

Many states require candidates for statewide office and state political parties to file their campaign finance reports with the state election board or secretary of state's office. In a year when the candidates are on the ballot, they must file their reports several times at key points in the election cycle. You are free to examine any of the reports for statewide candidates to see who gave money to these candidates, how much, and when. Each report you examine gives you a part of the picture on how a particular PAC is spending its money.

These reports don't give you a complete picture of how a special interest is spending its PAC money. For that, you must look at the special interest PAC reports in your state. Check out the FEC's DAP program, which reports PAC contributions (see the "Federal races" section, coming up).

Some states maintain these campaign finance reports in computer files that you can access. Contact the office in your state to find out whether the information is available by computer and to learn how to access it. Usually, all you need are a personal computer, a modem, and maybe an eight-year-old kid to show you how to use them.

Federal races

If you are interested in a race for U.S. Congress, you can check two different places for these reports:

- ✔ They're filed with the state agency responsible for keeping the records. States generally use the secretary of state's office, the state board or registrar of elections, or the lieutenant governor's office to file these records.

- ✔ The records for all federal campaigns are also kept by the Federal Election Commission (FEC) in Washington, D.C.

Fortunately, the FEC believes in making its information available by computer: It has a *Direct Access Program* (DAP) to make tracking the financial activities of federal candidates, PACs, and political parties easier.

DAP works on virtually every personal computer that has a modem and communications software. The system uses a national telecommunications network, which means that most users can dial a local phone number to make the connection. The information is accessible 24 hours a day, 7 days a week.

Getting information via DAP costs $20 per hour, with no sign-up charges, and takes ten business days to become available. To sign up, simply call the DAP representative at 800-424-9530 or write to

> DAP Program, FEC Data Systems Division, 999 E. Street, N.W., Washington, D.C., 20463.

The information the FEC has available includes

- ✔ Contributions by individuals, PACs, and party committees

- ✔ *Soft money,* or nonfederal money to national parties (see the upcoming sidebar, "Soft Money")

- ✔ Financial status reports on all federal candidates and committees, including latest total receipts, disbursements, cash on hand, and debts owed

- ✔ "Top 50" rankings by the FEC of campaign finance activities, which indicate facts such as the 50 campaigns that raised the most or spent the most or received the most PAC money

- ✔ Individual contributor searches that allow DAP users to perform searches by a contributor's name, place of business or occupation, city, state, zip code, and date of contribution

Although the FEC's DAP service costs $20 an hour, it can be a valuable tool for any citizen wanting to learn what's really going on with campaign contributions. Because the data is available in formatted and unformatted reports, you can manipulate the data by using spreadsheets or database programs for targeted research. You can find out who's giving money to the candidates you're interested in and how the special interest groups raise and spend their money. These reports can also tell you whether groups you belong to are making contributions that include your money to candidates or political parties.

If knowledge is power, using DAP can make you a pretty powerful person — which isn't bad for $20 an hour!

If the task seems too overwhelming, you can simply read and pay attention to media reports of campaign contributions. Many groups interested in campaign finance reform publish their findings from analyzing the reports of many different candidates. These groups follow the most visible and controversial special interest group contributions. Sometimes, the groups also follow the voting records on the special interest issues of elected officials who are the beneficiaries of the contributions. These evaluations can give you a greater understanding of what is going on with your elected officials and/or the special interest groups you are watching. See Chapter 12 for more on how to find this information.

Soft money

Soft money is money that can't be given legally to a federal candidate. It either exceeds the federal limit for individual contributions of $1,000 per election or the PAC $5,000-per-election ceiling, or it is direct corporate money, money from PACs that are not federally qualified, or labor union dues money.

These contributions must be donated to state and national parties rather than directly to the candidates to avoid legal limitations.

The parties then spend the money on activities that benefit the candidates.

Part IV:
It's All Marketing

In this part...

This part tells you how consultants called *handlers* package their candidates and try to sell them to you — the voter. It tells you how to separate the truth from the campaign hype. All this should help you decide which candidate to bring with you to the check-out line . . . I mean voting booth.

Chapter 10

Harry Handler Meets Carly Candidate

● ●

In This Chapter

▶ Understanding the role a candidate's handler plays

▶ Packaging and marketing the candidate

▶ Finding the message and delivering it

● ●

*T*o understand any campaign, you need to remember that it's all about marketing, pure and simple. The product is a candidate — not soap, cornflakes, or a car — but the technique is essentially the same, with one critical difference: You can purchase soap, cornflakes, or a car any time you want to (provided you have the money). But in a campaign for election, the sale and purchase of the product take place on one, and only one, day in an election cycle.

Either you make your purchase on the first Tuesday after the first Monday in November, or someone else makes the purchase for you. In some elections, the date may be different, but the principle is the same. The purchase occurs with or without your input.

It may be a little insulting to suggest that a political candidate's campaign is, in essence, the same as selling soap, cornflakes, or a car, but the analogy is accurate. A candidate is packaged, marketed, and sold to the voters. Citizens use their votes as the currency to buy the candidate of their choice. Not every voter receives his or her choice, but all the currency is spent, or it's valueless.

Handling a Campaign

Who decides how the candidate — I'll call her Carly Candidate — is packaged? Who calls the shots about marketing strategy, such as what Carly says and when she says it? In high-visibility elections for important offices, those decisions are usually made by professional political consultants, also called *handlers*.

The handler makes all the important decisions about which message the candidate conveys and how the money for the campaign is spent. (Other professionals specialize in raising the money.)

Profile of a political handler

Professional handlers usually follow similar career paths. I'll use the fictional Harry Handler for purposes of discussion.

Starting as a volunteer

Harry probably enters politics as a volunteer in a local campaign. He works for his state or national party learning the ropes of the political world, or for an elected official in his state or in Congress. (See Chapter 4 for how to volunteer your time in a campaign.)

Getting paid as a staffer

Next, Harry becomes a paid staffer in a political campaign. Harry is expected to work long hours for very little pay. He is young and, fortunately, has incredible amounts of energy — a necessary commodity for campaign work.

Working in a high-visibility campaign demands a total commitment of his time and effort. Harry has no life outside the campaign as long as the campaign lasts — no vacations, no leisurely dinners, no time for romance. Harry measures success and failure by the amount of money raised and the press coverage for a particular day; a day with the fund-raising quota met and good press coverage is a good campaign day. It's fair to say that a political campaign consumes the lives of the staffers and handlers as well as the candidate.

Some campaign staffers remain active in their state in subsequent elections. They may have other jobs that they leave to come back to campaigning. But Harry remains in politics full time, graduating to the level of handler.

Why do people do this to themselves?

Campaign workers put in their long, poorly compensated hours because they like the work. As crazy as that may seem, some individuals really enjoy the demands that a campaign imposes. They enjoy working closely with others to achieve a common, higher goal: the election of the person they view as the better candidate.

This goal, coupled with the excitement of being part of a campaign, is what initially encourages young people to get involved. It takes a certain personality type — a unique combination of ability and luck — to stay involved and make it into the small circle of successful, well-compensated Harry Handlers.

If you're thinking about becoming a handler, remember that it's a risky business. If you lose a couple of campaigns in a row, you may need to find another line of work. You also should realize that handling a campaign is seldom compatible with a healthy family life and children.

Becoming a handler

After rising from the ranks of the young, poorly paid campaign workers to the rarefied atmosphere enjoyed by handlers, Harry is now much better paid. It may still be a labor of love, but, for political handlers, campaign work is well compensated.

Harry is friendly with a lot of other handlers. He and his associates probably reside in or around Washington, D.C. Other handlers are more like nomads, wandering from state to state, working in election after election.

Moving around within the party

Many professional handlers move from state to state and campaign to campaign like migrant farm workers. But, usually, these handlers choose political sides — they work exclusively for Republican or for Democratic candidates. Party affiliation may be the only criterion for employment. They work for conservative, moderate, or liberal candidates from the party of their choice. They are particular only as far as the party label; to work for both sides of the political fence could hurt their credibility and make them less marketable.

James Carville, who was involved in Bill Clinton's 1992 campaign, and Bob Teeter, who was involved in the George Bush campaign, are examples of professional handlers who move from campaign to campaign on one side of the political fence.

Working for a common goal

The handlers for the candidates go at it tooth and nail during the campaign. Each believes in his candidate and thinks it best for the voters if his candidate wins. But all handlers share a commitment to

- Conducting hard-fought campaigns based on different approaches to issues
- Encouraging people to become involved in politics
- Respecting those who are willing to put themselves on the line as candidates and handlers
- Encouraging as much civility in politics as possible

Shared respect for the political process can overcome the antagonism that comes from being on opposite sides in an election. Witness James Carville and Mary Matalin. During the 1992 presidential campaign, Carville was a handler for Bill Clinton, and Matalin was a handler for George Bush. They may have been on opposite ends of a major political battle, but they didn't let that interfere with long-term romance. They were married once the election was over. They may be joined in marriage but not in politics. Carville still works for Democrats, and Matalin is a rock-solid Republican.

Developing a Marketing Strategy

Carly Candidate relies on her consultant, Harry Handler, to devise a strategy for winning over your votes. Harry's marketing strategy spans all facets of Carly's candidacy:

- Your reaction to the candidate's appearance
- Your image of the candidate
- The message you hear from the candidate

Checking out the candidate's appearance

When Harry Handler is brought in to manage a highly visible campaign, he looks first at the candidate's appearance to see whether improvement is necessary or possible. Does the candidate dress correctly for the image that the campaign is trying to project? For example, if the campaign wants to project the candidate as a no-nonsense businessperson, Harry may decide not to dress the candidate casually, choosing a dark business suit instead. Harry may bring in a fashion consultant to help with the dress, hairstyle, and makeup. The fashion consultant's job is to suggest clothes and hairstyles that reinforce the desired image.

Judging a book by its cover

Appearance is a very important part of any campaign. Many voters see the candidate only once or twice, for short periods of time, in the course of the campaign. First impressions may be the only impressions. They are extremely important, and so it's not surprising that a great deal of thought goes into the candidate's image.

Small changes in dress or appearance can result in subtle changes in the manner in which a candidate is perceived. Remember when Dan Rather of CBS News fame began wearing sweaters under his sports jackets on the nightly news? Some fashion consultant decided that wearing sweaters would make Dan seem more approachable and likable. If more people liked Dan, the CBS News ratings would go up — obviously, Dan and CBS News were willing to give it a try. Don't dismiss the importance of small appearance changes to a candidate's image.

But also remember that no Harry Handler, no matter how good, can make a silk purse out of a sow's ear. The changes that I'm talking about are relatively minor. Fine-tuning is the order of the day. Smoothing out rough edges is more the goal than fundamental change. Should the candidate wear contact lenses instead of glasses? Does the candidate need a hearing aid? Is a body wave for his hair appropriate? Is the hair color acceptable? Could she lose ten pounds? These are not wholesale changes. There is no way (yet) for a handler to alter the candidate's genetic makeup. No matter how much the handler would like it, the candidate is not going to turn into Paul Newman or Julia Roberts for the duration of the campaign.

Still, the press always treats these changes as newsworthy. This is true even though most of the changes a handler requests are nothing more than what you would do to get ready for your 25th high school reunion. If you go in for a makeover and change your appearance, are you being manipulative?

Opening the family album

When Harry Handler is reviewing the candidate's appearance, he also considers the appearance of the candidate's family. Does the candidate's wife wear her skirts too short? Does she otherwise dress in a way that reveals too many of her physical endowments? If the candidate is a woman, how does her husband look? How does he dress? Does he wear too much flashy jewelry? Do the candidate's daughters suffer from big-hair disease (too much hair going in too many directions all at once)? Do the candidate's sons look like the background for an MTV video?

A nice-looking family can be an asset to a candidate. It can reassure the voters that the candidate can be trusted. She's a nice, ordinary family woman just like the voter. But if the appearance of a candidate or family member strikes a discordant note, the voters may hesitate to support the candidate. That's unfair, of course — anyone who's raised teenagers knows about the constant battle to make them leave the house dressed as full-fledged members of the human race. Sometimes you just shrug and suspend hostilities in the constant war about what a teenager may wear, but even though you may be lax yourself, you expect more from your elected officials. After all, if a candidate can't manage his own family, how can he hope to manage a city, state, or nation?

Improving a candidate's image

In addition to appearance, another thing that campaign handlers concentrate on is the candidate's image. To gain our support, the candidate must come across as a leader and inspire confidence and trust. We want to be enthusiastic about our leaders. We want a good person, a person of honesty and integrity. We want to feel secure that the candidate is mentally, physically, and morally ready to hold an important government office.

Getting on TV

Handlers work to create situations that reassure voters on all these fronts. They try to arrange situations where the television coverage of a campaign event reinforces a positive image for the candidate.

Campaigns work very hard at developing those visual images because more and more of us get all our political information and news from television. Most of us trust what we see on TV more than what we read in the newspapers. That's why presidential campaigns work very hard on the free media visuals that you see on nightly news broadcasts. The campaigns also spend most of the money they raise for the campaign on television commercials. In 1992, George Bush spent 68 percent and Bill Clinton spent 51 percent of every dollar they raised to put commercials on your TV screen.

Image-boosting gimmicks

Handlers have made an art of manipulating the images of their candidates. Once you know the methods handlers employ to market candidates, you can recognize those methods when a campaign directs them at you. You can decide whether you are impressed or not. You can cut through the glitz and slick marketing devices and decide whether this is the candidate you want to support. You can see through the techniques and base your decision on issues and substance rather than good marketing strategy.

POLITICAL STUFF

Image versus reality — sometimes reality wins

Lamar Alexander, one of the Republican candidates for president in the 1996 election, often appears in public wearing a plaid shirt. Alexander's handler has decided that the warm and casual image is the one Alexander needs to convince you and other voters that you can trust him to run the country.

When George Bush was running for president, his handlers decided that they needed to show that Bush was a regular guy. They wanted to demonstrate that voters could trust him because he was just like they were. He worried about the same things and spent his time the same way they did. How did they demonstrate how regular Old George was? They put him in a pair of jeans and sent him into a bar in Texas to talk to the customers. The national news ate it up.

In 1988, when Michael Dukakis's handler decided that the Democratic nominee for president had to reinforce his image as a candidate who strongly supported the military, he had Dukakis pose for photographs in a tank while wearing a helmet. Harry misjudged the image. The picture he got was of a short, uncomfortable candidate very much out of place in a military setting.

Sometimes Harry's right. Sometimes Harry's wrong.

Whenever a handler alters his candidate's appearance or puts him in a setting where he would not normally appear, he is manipulating appearances to win you over to his candidate's side. You don't have to reject a candidate who resorts to these tactics, but you want to be aware enough to recognize them for what they are.

WARNING!

To move beyond the slick marketing, be aware of some common techniques used to market candidates:

- **Warm fuzzies:** Shots that create a happy or comfortable feeling — posing with the family or the family pet, holding a baby, speaking with an elderly person while holding her hand — all designed to make you like and trust the candidate because she values the same things you do

- **Patriotic themes:** Shots that inspire feelings of national pride — flags in the background, parades, patriotic music — all designed to make you identify the candidate with patriotism

- **Informal poses:** Shots of the candidate in a flannel shirt, with a suit jacket slung over the shoulder, or with his tie loosened, designed to persuade you that the candidate is a regular guy, just like you

- **Testimonials:** Testimonials about the candidate by relatively unknown third parties who tell you good things about the candidate's background or record, designed to reassure you that supporting the candidate is the right decision for you

✔ **Action shots:** Shots of the candidate in motion, doing things, talking to voters, seeing the manufacturing process up close, talking to children in the classroom — designed to show the candidate on the move, working for us, and working on the issues we're worried about, such as jobs and education

✔ **Staged events:** Shots of occasions where campaign staffers have worked hard to turn out as many people as possible, designed to demonstrate the candidate's popularity

The event may take place in a room that's too small, in order to make the crowd appear larger than it actually is. The staffers make signs that look as if the audience created them spontaneously. Other visuals, like balloons and red, white, and blue bunting, are used to create a festive atmosphere.

These techniques convey visual images designed to sway you into supporting the candidate. They are good marketing strategies because you think positive thoughts about the candidate when you see them.

But good marketing strategy is not a sound reason to choose an elected official. You need to recognize this strategy for what it is and move on to substance before you decide how to cast your vote. After all, most candidates have a family and some friends willing to say nice things about them. Candidates are patriotic folks, and flannel shirts are comfortable.

A candidate is free to use these marketing techniques as long as that isn't the sum and substance of her campaign. Make sure that she gives you a sound, tangible reason — something other than slick packaging and marketing — before you give her your support. (See Chapter 13 for more on how to decide which candidate to support.)

Identifying the message

Perhaps the biggest step in the marketing campaign is to identify the message. Many factors go into deciding what message Carly Candidate will spend the campaign communicating to you.

✔ Carly starts with some ideas that she wants to discuss or issues that she thinks need to be addressed.

✔ You and the voters have issues or problems that you want Carly to talk about.

✔ Carly and her opponent may have records to promote or defend.

Opponent makeover

At the same time that campaigns work to establish a positive image for their candidates, they are not above creating a negative image for the opponent.

In the 1988 campaign, Bush's consultants told him that Democrats would not vote for Dukakis if he was seen as soft on crime and unpatriotic. The Bush campaign decided to redo Michael Dukakis's image. By the time it was finished with the Willie Horton ad (an ad that concentrated on a repeat criminal named Willie Horton and the concept of jails with revolving doors) and the debate over whether schoolteachers should be required to recite the Pledge of Allegiance,

Dukakis's image was made over, and the election was decided in Bush's favor.

Another method used in the 1994 election to make over the image of the opponent was *morphing,* which is the technique of fading from the opponent's photo to a photo of an unpopular but recognizable third party. The object is to make us associate the opponent with the unpopular third party. This technique was used in many congressional races around the country by Republican candidates for the House of Representatives. The unpopular third party whose face was used was President Clinton. (For more about campaign techniques that focus on the opponent, see Chapter 18.)

✔ Groups of voters may be clamoring for positions on issues of importance to them.

✔ Even the media may have ideas about what the campaign should include.

All of this goes into the mix when Harry Handler determines Carly's message.

At most, Carly can emphasize two or three issues in a campaign. Picking the right issues can mean the difference between winning and losing the election. Harry doesn't rely on his instincts or the instincts of Carly Candidate to refine the content of the message that Carly will deliver; he checks it out with you first. Harry touches those bases with you and the other voters by conducting focus groups and polling (see the next two sections).

Harry wants Carly Candidate to be successful. You are key to that success. Harry and Carly must know what's on your mind — what you want the candidates to talk about. Harry Handler tries to find out what you think about the following:

✔ **Carly and her opponent:** This helps Harry decide how to make Carly's case and whether to attack her opponent.

"It's the message, stupid"

In the 1992 presidential campaign, Bill Clinton had a simple message. A copy of it was kept on the wall of campaign headquarters in Little Rock: "Change versus more of the same. The economy, stupid. Don't forget health care."

"The economy, stupid" mattered to the voters. They were worried about the national recession and wanted the question of jobs addressed by the presidential candidates. Clinton did; Bush didn't. Clinton's simple message carried the day.

In 1980, Ronald Reagan's message was a question. He asked voters if they were better off in 1980 than they were in 1976. The answer was no, and that answer translated into votes for Reagan on election day. Reagan defeated the incumbent Jimmy Carter with that message.

- ✔ **Carly's ideas and proposals:** This helps Harry decide which two or three of Carly's ideas or proposals to emphasize in Carly's message.

- ✔ **Proposals that Carly's opponent is making:** This helps Harry decide whether to ignore the opponent or not.

- ✔ **Carly's record:** Assuming that she has one, are there things in Carly's record that impress or offend you?

- ✔ **Her opponent's record:** Assuming that he has one, are there things in his record that impress or offend you?

Focus groups

If Harry Handler has enough campaign money, he conducts *focus groups* to discuss your responses to these and other questions in depth before or after the first poll is taken. Campaigns use focus groups to gain in-depth knowledge of the voters' concerns and attitudes. That is, they do if they can afford focus groups — which cost $8,000 to $10,000 each.

Focus groups bring in a random, representative sample of the voters in a candidate's district. The people in the sample are paid to spend a few hours discussing the candidates, the issues, and their attitudes in great depth with Harry Handler or a facilitator.

If a candidate is running for statewide office and wants to use focus groups, more than one focus group needs to be held. This is because different regions may have different ideas about the issues. For example, a focus group in the northern part of a state may list economic development and jobs as the focus group members' primary concern because a plant just closed in that area of the state, putting thousands of workers out on the street. Another area of the state may list crime as the number one issue because a vicious murder just occurred in that area. Holding more than one focus group permits the campaign to understand regional differences in emphasis. (See Chapter 5 for more on focus groups.)

Benchmark polls

Harry Handler orders a professional *benchmark poll* as early in the campaign as money and campaign research permit. (See Chapter 15 for more about benchmark polls.) Money is important because a statewide poll can cost from $15,000 to $25,000. Campaign research is important because the campaign needs to know what questions to ask in the poll.

Consider a candidate for governor who wants to talk about her program for capital improvements in the state's highways and bridges. (A *capital improvement* by government is an expenditure designed to improve long-term productivity, such as sewers or dams.) She may think that this program is an important way to appeal to voters. No candidate in a high-visibility race discusses such a program or how to pay for it without first determining through polling and, perhaps, focus groups whether the voters in the state share her ideas and are willing to vote for her because of those ideas.

For example, a poll that asks whether the state highway or bridge system could stand improvement will receive an overwhelming response of *yes.* Voters always agree that things can be improved. The trick for a pollster is to measure the depth of that support for improvement. Are the voters willing to see improvements made in highways and bridges if they have to pay for those improvements?

As I discuss in Chapter 3, sometimes voters want inconsistent things. You may want the capital improvements but not be eager to pay for them. Carly must know whether you will support a program for improvement that uses a gas tax or income tax increase. The poll also tests any other, more palatable means of financing the improvements. If the polls show that you are unwilling to pay for the improvements, Carly discards the highway and bridge improvement program. In this political climate, no candidate who wants to be elected proposes a tax increase that does not have broad, popular support.

An unscrupulous candidate may raise a proposal requiring significant new public spending even if polling shows voters do not want to finance it. When pressed for a financing mechanism to pay for the capital program, the unscrupulous candidate may duck and weave. The candidate may deliberately understate the cost of the capital program or propose a funding source that he knows is inadequate to the task.

Remember the old adage: If something appears too good to be true, it probably is. Unscrupulous politicians are not above making false promises to gain politically. There are some politicians who are modern demagogues. You need to ask yourself whether that is the type of leader you want in office. Are you willing to vote for a candidate who promises you the moon with no chance of delivering? The choice is yours.

A leader or a follower?

Harry Handler does the research, the focus groups, and the polling all to find out what you want the candidate's message to be. Harry is trying to identify those items that you want discussed and the proposals that you want to hear more about. This entire exercise is performed to capture your interest and, ultimately, your vote for Carly Candidate.

If your opinion on an issue changes, Carly Candidate can change her message. You may change your mind because events occur and receive media coverage. For example, the capital improvement program for highways that Harry Handler decided not to use as an issue may suddenly get new life when a bridge collapses and a series of news stories about the condition of the state's bridges alarms the public. Or the opponent may attack with something unanticipated that requires a response. Campaigns may have a game plan and a message, but they must remain flexible if they're going to win.

You may say that this type of candidate isn't good enough for you. You want a candidate who doesn't need to look to you and other voters to determine how she feels about an issue or what she wants to propose to improve things. You may say that you want to vote for a *leader* to represent you — not a parrot who mimics what you and the other voters are thinking and feeling. Perhaps you want an elected official who will tell you what you need to hear even when the message is unpleasant. After all, you don't want to choose someone whose only goal is to get reelected.

But just as a candidate who is merely a follower is not good enough for you, being merely a leader isn't good enough, either. Do you really want a candidate or an officeholder who doesn't pay any attention to what you and the other voters think? Are you comfortable with a candidate who is so sure of herself that she doesn't want or need input from you? Of course not; you have a right to be heard, especially since you've become politically involved and know what is going on.

A better approach is to elect a candidate who has a reason for running other than winning. You want a candidate with ideas about what needs to be done and how it should be accomplished — a leader, but not only a leader. You have a right to demand more. You have a right to demand a candidate who will lead and, at the same time, listen. You're entitled to an officeholder who doesn't think that he must be the originator of every worthwhile idea or program, someone who is aware that he hasn't cornered the market on brains or creativity, regardless of what his handler wants you to think. Someone who wants to do what you want but isn't afraid to propose ideas and suggestions of his own. Someone who knows that he was elected to represent you.

Finding that type of candidate is not easy — Chapter 13 shows you how to select a candidate. But once you absorb enough from this book to become politically aware, you'll have a better shot at recognizing a candidate of that caliber when you see him. You'll also know what to do to get him elected and what to do when he is in office to keep him on the narrow, straight path of leading and following so he can be the type of official you want and deserve.

Responding to a Handler's Controls

How should you react to the ways in which Harry Handler controls Carly Candidate's campaign? You can view them as smart marketing moves to win you over. You can view them as deceptions designed to manipulate you into voting a certain way. Or you can view them as something in between the two extremes.

- **Smart marketing moves:** Many of us don't worry too much about candidate makeovers because we do the same thing all the time ourselves. We've all changed our hairstyles. We go from long to short, from sophisticated to casual, from curly to straight hair. We may even change our hair color from time to time. We all change clothing style and eyewear. We're used to changes of this nature because we all try to look our best, and what constitutes our best changes with the styles and over time. Because you make these sorts of changes yourself, you shouldn't view them as manipulative. You should consider them good marketing or packaging techniques.

- **In between:** More of us are concerned when Carly's *image* is changed. We are more skeptical of changes like these because we don't have experience with them ourselves. Whether you view these as legitimate marketing techniques or blatant attempts to manipulate you into voting a certain way probably depends on whether you think they are sincere or not.

  Take, for example, the situation where Harry softens Carly's image. If Carly is a caring person who has a warm, loving relationship with her family, it is fair to portray her that way. Harry is trying to counter an unfair perception of Carly as a tough, self-centered person with visual evidence of the true facts. On the other hand, Harry may be trying to create an image that doesn't exist. Carly may *be* a tough, self-centered individual who doesn't have a warm, loving relationship with her family or anyone else, in which case Harry is skillfully using visual images to create a false impression in your mind to influence how you vote.

How do you decide which is which? The answer is that it isn't easy. You must be alert to these tactics. When they occur in a campaign, recognize them for what they are. When you begin seeing Carly on television night after night in warm images that aren't what you associated with her, your antennae should go up. Read about Carly and talk to people who knew her before she was a candidate. Then you can decide whether Carly is the type of person you want in a position of power.

✔ **Manipulation:** When Harry tries to control the *message* Carly delivers, we are even more worried about being manipulated. On one hand, we want Carly to talk about the issues *we* think are important. On the other hand, we want to know where Carly herself stands on issues. We don't want her to use focus groups and polling to tell us only those things that we want to hear. We want her to be responsive to us, *and* we want her to be a leader. Our fear is that Harry will control the flow of information from Carly to us, and we won't receive the type of information that we need to cast an informed vote.

If you don't hear any new ideas from Carly Candidate, you should wonder why. If she can't tell you why she is running for office, you should be skeptical. If you hear Carly identify problems but propose no solutions, you should be concerned. If Carly talks about diversions and not important and complex issues, you should listen carefully (see Chapter 16 for more about diversions). If Carly discusses issues with emotional appeal and fixes blame on a segment of the population, you should consider whether you are being manipulated.

It is up to you to determine whether a candidate's campaign is good marketing strategy or a dishonest attempt to manipulate your emotions to get you to vote for that candidate. If you decide that you're being manipulated, you should ask yourself whether you're comfortable with a candidate who is willing to use such tactics in a position of power.

Chapter 11

Selling the Candidates, Warts and All

In This Chapter

▶ Recognizing candidate warts and how campaigns disguise them

▶ Recognizing candidate beauty marks and how campaigns highlight them

▶ Defending against attacks

*N*o candidate for any office is perfect — that stands to reason, doesn't it? After all, candidates are people just like us. There is no genetic laboratory harvesting just the right combination of intelligence, appearance, personality, and ambition to create the perfect candidate. Candidates come in all shapes and sizes. Some candidates are intelligent; some aren't. Some candidates are articulate; some can't string two sentences together to complete a thought. Some candidates look great in front of a camera; some candidates have faces made for radio.

This chapter deals with how professional campaign consultants called *handlers* (see Chapter 10 for more on handlers) identify a candidate's flaws (I call them *warts*) and selling points (which I call *beauty marks*), to best market that candidate to you.

Performing Cosmetic Surgery on a Candidate's Warts

One of the most important things that Harry Handler must do to devise a campaign strategy is determine what types of problems Carly Candidate has. Now you might think that would be easy. Harry should just ask Carly what flaws she has. The problem with that approach is that Carly may not realize what a flaw is. And if she's a first-time candidate, she may be uncomfortable discussing flaws, not realizing how devastating a creative attack by an opponent can be.

If Harry can't rely on Carly for this information to devise his strategy, what does he do? The answer is *internal opposition research.* Harry finds out everything he needs to know about Carly, even things Carly's forgotten. Internal opposition research tells Harry where the attacks will come from and what he has to do to keep your support.

Personal questions

Internal opposition research for the first-time candidate relies heavily on the memory and candor of the candidate. The handler grills the candidate on a variety of issues:

- Arrest record, for both the candidate and family members
- Tax returns
- Lawsuits (either on the receiving end or the filing end)
- Ordinance violations
- Overdue debts
- Overdue property taxes
- Bankruptcy
- Published written work (even while as a student, or letters to the editor on a controversial topic)
- Anyone with private knowledge of the candidate who may bear a grudge
- Employment (Is there anything about that employment that would cause bad feelings among voters? Does the candidate operate a business that has been accused of polluting the area?)
- Relationship problems with a spouse
- Children who may cause trouble

When Harry Handler has the answers to these questions, he can devise a strategy to win and keep your support for Carly Candidate.

POLITICAL STUFF

Candidates' sex lives in politics

The Harry Handlers of old didn't have to worry so much if Carly Candidate had some secrets about her personal life to conceal. The topic of a candidate's sexual life didn't get reported in the press unless it was an unusual situation. Two notable exceptions from the nineteenth century follow:

- Andrew Jackson's wife Rachel was labeled a bigamist. Her divorce from her first husband was not finalized, as they believed, when they married. They had to remarry two years later. Her marital status was an issue in Jackson's 1828 campaign.

- Bachelor candidate Grover Cleveland was accused of fathering a child out of wedlock. He acknowledged the child, but his opponents didn't let the issue die. They used a song to remind the voters of Cleveland's misconduct: "Ma! Ma! Where's my Pa! Gone to the White House! Ha! Ha! Ha!"

Long after their deaths, it was revealed that presidents from Harding through Johnson had interesting personal lives that could have presented political problems if revealed by the press.

In the past, the press ignored rumors about candidates or officeholders unless doing so was impossible. For example, in the 1970s, stories about drinking and other activities by Congressman Wilbur Mills, Chairman of the Ways and Means Committee of the House of Representatives, didn't make the news until Representative Mills appeared on a burlesque stage and then waded in the Tidal Basin in front of the Jefferson Memorial with Fanny Foxe, his stripper girlfriend. That type of activity was too public for the press to ignore. Mills admitted having a drinking problem, was stripped of his powerful chairmanship, and did not seek reelection.

Another more recent example of changing press attitudes involved Senator Gary Hart, who was a married candidate for president in 1988. The *Miami Herald* followed Hart in an attempt to catch him spending the night with his girlfriend. Catch him they did, and Hart withdrew from the race. The *Miami Herald* justified its conduct in putting a tail on Hart by saying that he invited the scrutiny with his famous quote, "If you think I am fooling around on my wife, follow me." What the *Miami Herald* didn't tell us was that they were following Hart before he ever made that comment.

Many of the incidents involving the sexual conduct of persons in high places have been the subject of public testimony and, therefore, press coverage. The confirmation hearings of Supreme Court Justice Clarence Thomas and Senator Bob Packwood's ethical problems with sexual harassment of women staff members have both been given extensive press coverage.

Officeholder record

If Carly Candidate is an incumbent or former officeholder, Harry Handler needs to research the record of Carly's term in office. In addition to all the personal questions, he must ask these professional questions:

- ✔ When Carly was an officeholder, did she increase the size of the office staff?

- ✔ Did the budget for the office go up substantially while Carly was in office?

- ✔ Did Carly take extravagant trips to conventions or seminars at taxpayer expense?

  Even if these trips were perfectly legitimate educational seminars, can you blame taxpayers for getting upset when such trips are held in exotic or attractive locations where many of us can't afford to travel when we take vacations?

The nature of the office held, or formerly held, by Carly affects how extensive the additional internal opposition research must be.

- ✔ If the office awarded contracts or made purchases, Harry Handler takes the time to find out whether any of these were awarded to friends or contributors of Carly and then makes sure that you know about it through a media splash. Carly may not have awarded or purchased on that basis, but that won't stop the charge from being made.

- ✔ Did Carly hire the offspring of friends or contributors to work in the office? Even if the employee was perfectly qualified for the position, the hiring may be an issue that you want to consider in the campaign.

A wart that doesn't appear so bad at first blush can be made to look worse by an opponent eager for an issue. For example, a simple mistake on a campaign finance report filed by an inexperienced campaign treasurer can be made to appear much more sinister than it is by a creative and aggressive opponent. It is important to hear all sides of a charge and defense before forming any conclusions. The truth in emotionally charged campaigns is usually somewhere in between the positions of the candidates.

Illegal warts

It goes without saying that any type of illegal conduct creates substantial problems for any candidate. A conviction for tax evasion or marijuana smoking, even while the candidate was in college, can be a fatal flaw. Voters may agree that the candidate has paid the required price for her conduct, but they don't see any way to view that type of activity as an asset. No amount of cosmetics can hide the wart of a criminal history. Absent some extraordinary circumstances, a candidate with a criminal history is DOA (dead on arrival).

Legal warts

That illegal activity creates fatal warts for candidates isn't surprising. What is surprising is that *legal* conduct can do the same.

For example, candidate Barney Bankrupt had financial problems once upon a time in his career and took a perfectly legal route out — creating potentially fatal candidate warts. Barney declared bankruptcy in the past and now finds himself exposed to criticism by the opposition and the media. The argument goes something like this: "If Barney Bankrupt can't manage his own finances, how can he handle taxpayer money?" The situation may be completely different — Barney may have resorted to filing bankruptcy because of factors beyond his control. But those factors don't matter to the media or the opposition. The stigma attached to the inability to pay one's debts attaches to the candidate as well. That stigma may be sufficient in some voters' minds to torpedo the candidacy.

A candidate who is sued in a civil action may also develop substantial or even fatal warts. Even if what's at issue in the lawsuit has nothing whatsoever to do with running for office, the opposition may jump on the lawsuit allegations.

If the lawsuit claims that the candidate, a former businessperson, defrauded a consumer by selling the consumer a poor product, the opposition might create a commercial that says, "You can't trust candidate Fred Fraud. He will say or do anything to get elected. A customer of the widget store that Fred used to run says Fraud defrauded him out of $10,000 of his hard-earned money. Is this the type of person you want representing you in the state legislature? Vote for Sally Straightnarrow on election day!"

This attack by Straightnarrow on Fraud may not be fair. Maybe Fraud did owe the customer money, but then again, maybe not. These are just pleadings in a lawsuit; the allegations are not proven. It may be unfair, but it is effective. If an opponent can make a charge in 30 seconds and it takes you five minutes to explain why the charge is unfair, you have lost the debate. Too many voters listen to the charge without hearing or understanding the explanation. Unfairly or not, candidate Fraud has a substantial wart.

Some professions are wart filled

Some professions give candidates so many warts that potential candidates who recognize that fact don't even run for office. Legalized gambling, bail bonding, and performing abortions are all examples of professions that don't lend themselves to producing wart-free candidates.

One profession that's the wart-developing equivalent to kissing frogs, but produces many candidates nonetheless, is the legal profession.

Prosecutors and district or state attorneys

Prosecutors and district or state attorneys are almost guaranteed a difficult time in running for other offices. Those elected officeholders can be held responsible for everything that occurred in their offices. Every plea bargain for too small a sentence, every case lost because of poor trial preparation or poor police work can be laid at the feet of the elected prosecutor or state or district attorney. Opponents can make political hay just because cases aren't disposed of fast enough.

Most prosecutors' or district attorneys' offices plea bargain the vast majority of their cases. They *have to* plea bargain: The sheer volume of cases precludes trying them all. There are not enough lawyers, courtrooms, judges, or juries to allow all cases to go to trial. Plea bargains may be an essential part of our criminal justice system, but they have a negative connotation in today's society.

Many people think that when a prosecutor or district attorney gives plea bargains, the defendants are released from jail. In reality, many plea bargains give the defendants substantial amounts of time in prison. But just the term *plea bargains* causes problems for incumbent prosecutors and district attorneys.

Heaven help the prosecutor or district attorney who plea bargained a case and released a defendant, for whatever good and legitimate reasons, who went on to commit a heinous crime after release. The original charge that was plea bargained may not have been serious, but that fact won't matter at all. The subsequent charge will be the one generating all the publicity. The opposition — recognizing a golden opportunity — will say that the second crime was the prosecutor or district attorney's fault. If a family member of the victim will go on camera, the opposition may win on this issue alone.

Criminal defense attorneys

Criminal defense attorneys also have a difficult time getting elected to office. Fairly or not, a defense attorney can be identified with the clients she has represented in the past. An opponent may use an ad saying that accused child molesters, rapists, and murderers were put back on the street because of the criminal defense attorney's work. Such an ad is particularly predictable if the defense attorney is seeking elective office as a prosecutor, district attorney, or criminal court judge.

You may question whether this technique of identifying the criminal defense attorney with her client or the arguments she made in defense of her clients is fair. After all, you might say, the criminal defense attorney was merely doing her job, and she had an ethical duty to give each and every client vigorous representation.

If the position that the criminal defense attorney is seeking has nothing to do with criminal justice, that association is probably unfair. If she's running for county commissioner or school board official, her professional representations are beside the point. You can decide for yourself whether the candidate who raises the issue in the context of one of these types of offices is simply trying to prejudice you unfairly against the criminal defense attorney. If you conclude that that is what the candidate is doing, you can decide if you want to penalize that candidate by voting for the criminal defense attorney.

On the other hand, when you are choosing a prosecuting attorney or another officeholder associated with the criminal justice system, you may find the criminal defense attorney's background relevant information for you to consider. The criminal defense attorney can still be a good prosecutor, but many voters would want assurance that she can make the transition from defending to prosecuting easily. Many voters would consider her background in the overall decision on who would make the better prosecutor. They would not penalize the candidate raising the issue.

Why handlers worry about a candidate's flaws

Internal opposition research is tough to do. It's embarrassing for the candidate and for the candidate's family. Any candidate who goes through this type of inquiry is understandably defensive. It's very difficult to put your entire professional and personal life under a microscope and look for vulnerabilities. But as painful as this process is, it's much better for the candidate to be prepared. When a handler is aware of the worst attacks that the opponent can launch against his candidate, he can be confident that he has done the best possible job of preparing the candidate's defenses.

Anticipating the worst that the opposition can throw at a candidate may permit the handler to devise a strategy to minimize the impact of the opposition's bombs. With some creativity and preparation, the opposition's nuclear bombs may become grenades. The handler can seldom, if ever, turn a wart into an asset or grenades into confetti, but minimizing the impact of an attack can at least turn a silver bullet into pellets from a BB gun.

Perhaps you think that the handlers should ignore the flaws and concentrate on telling you about the candidate's good points. Harry Handler would like nothing better, but he knows that such an approach would cost his candidate the election.

Harry Handler knows that if Carly is seeking a prominent office, one with high visibility, whatever skeletons she has in her closet will be brought out and displayed to you and the other voters. The opposition has an interest in portraying Carly in the most unfavorable light. Candidates don't only try to make you like them; they try to make you dislike the opponent. (See Chapter 18 for more on negative campaigning.)

Harry also knows that, even if the opposition doesn't highlight Carly's skeletons, the press will probably do it instead. If these flaws are big enough or portrayed in a graphic enough fashion, you may be distracted from the issues of the campaign. Harry's fear is that you will focus only on the flaws and fail to see the good things about Carly Candidate.

Fending Off Attacks

The candidate has four ways to defend against wart-based attacks by the opposition:

- ✔ Ignore the attack.
- ✔ Reveal the other side of the story.
- ✔ Diffuse the attack.
- ✔ Attack first.

Campaigns use one or more of these defenses when the warts are exposed or about to be exposed. All these defenses are designed to prevent you, the voter, from transferring your support to the opposition.

Ignore the attack

One defense is to ignore the attack. Some campaigns take this approach because they don't know what else to do. Ignoring attacks by the opposition in a campaign is never a good idea. The opposition is attacking because polling tells the opposition's campaign that the voters find the attack persuasive.

Ignoring the attack doesn't make it go away. It just guarantees that the attack is not answered. Voters tend to believe attacks that are not rebutted. Option one in a campaign is always to do nothing. But when doing nothing means allowing the opposition to score points by highlighting a candidate's flaws, it may be tantamount to giving up the election.

Tell the rest of the story

Another option for the candidate who is under attack is a spirited defense that points out that the opponent did not tell the voters the entire story. Every issue, or wart, has at least two sides — sometimes five or six.

When Carly Candidate tells her side of the story, she can raise doubts about the opponent's credibility in your mind, either directly or indirectly. If Harry Handler and the media people producing the advertisements responding to the attack are skillful, they can succeed in muddying the waters sufficiently on the issue. When charges and countercharges are flying back and forth, many voters tune out the entire issue. The candidate's wart is lost in all the rhetoric. The issue never becomes the silver bullet for the opposition.

The danger in this approach is that, when so many charges fly back and forth, we voters become disgusted by the campaign and blame Carly. Harry Handler must weigh the risk of having us view Carly as a negative campaigner against the risk of having us believe the opponent's accusation.

Diffuse the wart

Another option for the campaign of a candidate with large warts is to diffuse the potential issue that the wart may create. The handler can diffuse the issue in one of two ways. He can take the initiative and make the issue public or attack the opposition for waging a negative campaign.

Self-disclosure

Self-exposure of a candidate's warts — that is, raising the issue before the opposition does — is a risky business. After all, the opposition may be incompetent and not find the warts. Or they may not have sufficient resources to advertise about the warts often enough to ensure that the voters are aware of them. You never want to underestimate what opposing campaigns will do to each other, but you don't want to overestimate them, either.

It must be a unique wart for this strategy to work — one that is almost sure to get out. If a candidate has such an offense in her background and it's too late to back out of the campaign, her handler may decide to acknowledge it before the opposition can attack. If it isn't too late to back out, Harry Handler may even advise Carly to get out of the race altogether and look for another career.

An example of a wart that Harry Handler would consider making public is Carly Candidate's drunk-driving conviction. Convictions are matters of public record and available to any citizens who want to find them. The odds are reasonably good that a competent opponent will find such a conviction, even if it occurred in another location. After all, Carly Candidate can't conceal her prior addresses. She has to list the college she attended and where she lived in the past on her resume or in response to media inquiries.

If Carly stays in the race, Harry might advise her to run an advertisement telling you that she has learned some hard lessons in life; one of the hardest lessons was to accept the consequences of her actions. When she was young, she made a mistake. She drank too much and embarrassed her family by being arrested and convicted for drunk driving. Now Carly asks you not to hold that youthful indiscretion against her in the election. She tells you that she took responsibility for her actions and was never so irresponsible again. For the past 15 years, she has worked hard to be a better citizen. Now she wants to put her knowledge and experience to work for the voters of the district or state.

This approach is not perfect, but it may gain some sympathy from the voters. It also may reduce the likelihood of a vicious attack on the same issue by the opponent. If Carly's disclosure is seen by the media and the voters as a courageous attempt to be honest, the disclosure may prevent the opposition from attacking on the issue. The opponent does not want to appear to be piling on a candidate who is down. And the self-disclosure presents the indiscretion in less harsh terms than the opponent would use.

It would obviously be better for Carly's campaign if it never had to deal with her drunk-driving conviction at all. Such an issue can never help a candidate's campaign; it will never win voter support. The best that Harry Handler may hope for is that you won't reject Carly because of it. Harry Handler hopes Carly's candor about her background will demonstrate to you that Carly is honest and can be trusted despite having made a mistake. Maybe, as a result of Carly's self-disclosure, the campaign will be on life support instead of at the funeral home preparing for burial.

Counterattack

The other way a handler diffuses the issue created by his candidate's wart is to attack the opposition for waging a negative campaign. The attack on the opposition goes something like this: "Candidate Sleaze doesn't want you to know that, as an elected official, he permitted his office budget to double in size. Sleaze doesn't want you to know that he took five trips a year at taxpayer expense to vacation spots you can't afford to visit. Sleaze doesn't want you to know these things about him. That's why Sleaze is attacking Carly Candidate. Sleaze thinks that running a negative campaign will divert your attention from his record. Don't be fooled by Sleaze's negative campaign!"

Harry Handler is trying to muddy the waters here. He hopes that, with charges and countercharges swirling around, you'll forget or dismiss the attack Sleaze is making on Harry's candidate Carly. Harry's strategy isn't risk free, because you may get irritated by the constant barrage of attacks. If you and the other voters blame both candidates, voter turnout may suffer, but the outcome of the election probably won't change because of Harry's approach.

Take the offensive and attack first

The final option for a campaign facing wart exposure by the opposition is to attack first. Whatever silver bullet a campaign thinks it has to fell the opposition can be used before a campaign is on the defensive. The theory in political campaigns is that the best defense is a good offense. If the opponent is forced to respond to the campaign's attack, he may change his strategy. The opposition may get so rattled by an unexpected attack that it fails to launch its own attack. Even if the opponent stays with his game plan, the message may be so muddled by the charges and countercharges that it lacks the punch it otherwise would have. If the attack lacks punch, you may not be persuaded to change your vote. This strategy has risks, too. The key one is that Carly may be labeled a negative campaigner because she went on the attack first.

Candidates should always tell the truth

Whichever alternative Harry Handler employs to deal with his candidate's warts, he'd better tell the truth. Harry's first instinct may be to deny the charges or attacks from the opposition. It's only human to try to avoid unpleasantness by denial. But if the charges are true, Harry's denial is a fatal mistake. It is morally wrong to lie, and it is political suicide. When Harry denies a charge made by the opponent, he creates an *issue*. That's another way of saying that Harry has created a factual dispute. One side is saying that something is true; the other side is saying that something is a lie. When an issue arises in a campaign about something important, the media investigates and decides who is telling the truth: the candidate or the opposition.

When that happens, the debate is no longer just charges and countercharges between campaigns. The press examines the charges and denials, determines the truth, and tells you and the other voters who is lying. If the investigation by the press supports the attack from the opposition, Harry Handler has not only his candidate's wart to defend but her credibility as well. The media may determine that the facts as presented by the opposition are true. The media may also determine that Carly Candidate has been less than candid with the voters and the media. If that happens, she may just as well draft her concession speech. The campaign is over.

 Why Carly Candidate lies or doesn't lie isn't important. What *is* important is that if she lies, and you find out, it is fair to show your disapproval by voting against her on election day. How can you trust Carly Candidate to be a good elected official when she will lie to you to obtain your vote?

Highlighting a Candidate's Beauty Marks

The process of disguising or obscuring the warts that a candidate brings to a campaign can be thought of as minimizing the negative to keep you, the voter, from defecting to the opposition. But candidates also bring *positive* characteristics to a campaign, and it's a handler's job to market these to you as well.

The first trick in marketing Carly Candidate's beauty marks, as with her warts, is to identify them. What things in Carly's background would you find most persuasive as a reason for voting for her? It isn't enough that there are positive things to say about Carly. Almost any candidate's mother will go on television to tell voters that her son or daughter would make a wonderful legislator, mayor, or Member of Congress. But the positive aspects advertised by a candidate like Carly must persuade you to choose her over the opposition, not just convince you that she's a nice person. Otherwise, spending money talking about the beauty marks is a waste of time and campaign money.

Determining which beauty marks will convert to votes for Carly Candidate takes some work on the part of Harry Handler. Harry must resort to exhaustive research to determine which things in Carly's background might be used to persuade you to select her over the opposition.

Celebrating a candidate's upbringing

The obvious place to start looking for beauty marks is Carly Candidate's upbringing. Is there a story in Carly's background that will appeal to you and show you that Carly shares your values and goals? Harry Handler can get that point across by using the simplest of messages.

For example, Carly worked through high school and college to be able to attend college. The jobs themselves may not be so important, but by working, she learned an important lesson: Some goals in life require hard work and sacrifice to obtain, but they are well worth it. Many of us had jobs to pay for college. That fact is not very remarkable, but Harry Handler's message about the lessons Carly learned will appeal to most voters. You've probably had similar revelations yourself. Harry's presentation of a rather unremarkable feat in Carly's life tells you that Carly shares your experiences and your values. You can trust her with decisions affecting your life because she is like you.

Harry Handler looks for anything in Carly Candidate's background that will appeal to us, that will show us how Carly is a regular person who thinks and feels the same as we do about life. After all, we want officeholders who will approach problems and solutions in the same manner we would. We have confidence that people who share our values and opinions can be trusted to make political decisions affecting our lives.

Making the most of a candidate's parents

Just as Harry Handler examines Carly Candidate's past, he looks for similar simple, appealing stories about Carly's parents. "Carly's father worked hard all his life. He never got anything for nothing. He worked for the same company for years. Then the company went bankrupt. After 40 years with the same company, her father has no pension to secure his retirement. Carly understands the importance of pension reform to protect our hard-working senior citizens from a similar fate. Carly can understand our anxiety about old age and self-sufficiency. She's experienced the anxiety on a personal level. She can be trusted to protect our interests."

Even if Carly Candidate was born with a silver spoon in her mouth, Harry Handler can make the silver spoon a way for us to connect with Carly. His approach could be: "Carly realizes how lucky she has been. She wants to give something back to the country that has been so good to her and her family. She won't take any raises while she's in office. She won't take any contributions over $100 from supporters. She won't be anyone's governor but yours. Carly's parents may have been wealthier than most, but she realizes that those benefits create a special obligation to us voters. You can trust Carly Candidate with your vote."

Don't let beauty marks distract you from more important stuff

Harry may hope that you will fall for an inspiring but simplistic message about Carly's upbringing or parents and not take the time to look at what she's done in office or what she stands for, if Carly's office record or message is more of a wart than a beauty mark.

Whether or not you accept Carly's portrayal of her upbringing or her parents depends on whether you think that the image she is trying to create in your mind is accurate or a blatant attempt at manipulation. Are these Carly's true values and attitudes? You can judge for yourself — based upon what you know about Carly and what people you trust know about Carly — whether you are being told the truth or being manipulated.

If you decide that Carly is really like you because she shares your values and experiences, you can decide to vote for her. If you conclude that she really feels strongly about a certain pension issue, for example, and wants to get elected to do something to protect our citizens, you can identify with her and reward her with your vote. If you conclude that this issue and her attitude are attempts at manipulating you — orchestrated by Harry Handler — you can punish Carly Candidate by voting for her opponent.

Remember: You make the decision. You cast the vote.

How important are beauty marks?

Mentioning family and upbringing are fine as far as beauty marks go. We feel more comfortable with candidates whom we know more about. It also helps our comfort level if the things we learn convince us that Carly Candidate is a real, live person with emotions and experiences similar to those we feel and have. You don't have to base your decision for whom to vote on beauty marks alone, however. You can consider all their beauty marks and still ask the candidates where they stand on particular issues of importance to you.

There are many ways to get answers to your specific questions on issues. See Chapter 5 for more information about how to get elected officials and candidates to answer your questions. You don't have to settle for the beauty marks that Harry Handler uses to persuade you to vote for Carly Candidate. You have a right to know Carly's position on specific issues of importance to you before you cast your vote.

Chapter 12
Truth in Advertising

- -

- -

Separating the wheat from the chaff in political advertising can be difficult. How do you identify the truth in the mass of charges and misinformation traded back and forth in the heat of a political campaign? And what is *truth,* as opposed to mere accuracy?

You should care about knowing the truth. The truth lets you understand the entire story behind an issue or occurrence, rather than simply giving you an accurate recitation of *part* of the facts that slants the story in a certain direction.

There is no shortage of charges and countercharges in the last days of a political campaign. Because you have decided to become politically aware by picking up this book, you're probably someone who wants to make your decisions about which candidate to support by using as much accurate information as possible.

You want to know which charges or countercharges are fair and which are not. You want your choice to be an informed one. You don't want to vote for someone who has gained your support by unfairly attacking his or her opponent. You don't want to be persuaded by underhanded tactics or manipulation. Otherwise, you might wind up believing that the opponent supports raising your taxes, legalizing cocaine, and banning kittens.

To make the all-important decision about how to cast your vote, you must sort through the attacks and responses to determine the truth for yourself. That is the only way you will be confident that you are making the right choice for you.

Truth Plus Truth Doesn't Always Equal Fact

Many times, ads for competing campaigns seem to say opposite things. One campaign says that the candidate lied on his taxes. The other campaign says that the candidate reported his taxes truthfully.

If all the information is accurate, can they both be telling the truth? The answer is yes.

Drawing a false conclusion

Even when a campaign is making truthful charges, the manner in which it presents the facts may still create a false or incomplete picture — without actually lying.

A paid advertisement shows you 1 + 1. The 1 + 1 are facts that are accurate. But the campaign doesn't stop there. The campaign's ad tries to show you that 1 + 1 = 3. The conclusion that the ad draws from two accurate facts is not accurate. That's where the ad is unfair or inaccurate.

The art of set-up legislation

In addition to drawing faulty conclusions, another way a candidate can create a false impression is by setting up a vote, in advance of an election, that is sure to win disfavor for the opponent.

For example, members of the minority party in the state legislature introduces a bill that they know will make a good campaign issue in the next election — an election in which their candidates are challenging incumbent legislators. They bring this issue to a vote to put incumbent legislators *on the record* about a particular issue. Then they use that record to campaign against the officeholders in the next election.

The case of the soft attorney

Suppose that Jane Dillon, a candidate for prosecuting attorney, attacks the incumbent's handling of a particular domestic violence case. The candidate cites the poor handling as an example of incompetence or, worse, a soft bent on crime.

Candidate Dillon describes the case this way: A woman was beaten by her husband. The police were called. No charges were filed by the prosecutor's office, so the defendant was released from jail. The defendant returned to his wife after he was released and beat her a second time. She died from the second beating, killed by the defendant who was out on the streets because charges hadn't been filed.

Candidate Dillon obtains pictures of the defendant and the victim and uses them in a television ad. Dillon comes to a very simple conclusion in her ad: If the prosecuting attorney had been doing his job, the victim would not have been killed. The prosecuting attorney failed to help the victim. The prosecuting attorney shouldn't be reelected.

Dillon has the facts right, but she's not telling you the whole story. The fault may not be entirely, primarily, or in any way the prosecutor's. Here's another side of the story in this scenario: It was the neighbors who called the police. After the defendant was arrested, the victim called the prosecutor's office to demand that charges be dropped. The victim did not want the defendant, her husband, to go to prison.

Legally, the prosecuting attorney could have compelled the victim to testify and sent the defendant to prison. Practically, he needed the victim's cooperation. If she was forced to testify against her will, she could have gone on the stand and said that she started the fight. She could have said that she and her husband were in love and that the incident would not be repeated. She could've made it clear that she didn't want the defendant to go to prison, that their children would suffer if he was incarcerated. No jury would send someone to prison with that type of testimony.

The prosecuting attorney knew that without the victim's cooperation, he would lose the case; filing the charges would have been a waste of everyone's time. So, after arguing with the victim at length, he told the court that the state didn't have a case against the defendant and that the court should let the defendant go.

The outcome of the case — the wife's death at the hands of her husband — was tragic, but it was not the prosecuting attorney's fault. He was prepared to prosecute the defendant and protect the victim from harm. He even argued with the victim to try to convince her that she was being foolish. All to no avail.

In this case, the prosecuting attorney was not at fault. But Candidate Dillon's ad implies otherwise. All her facts are accurate; what is not accurate is the conclusion that the prosecuting attorney did something wrong. What is unfair is the charge that the prosecuting attorney deserves to be defeated because he's soft on crime.

A common example of set-up legislation is when a legislator introduces a bill calling for a substantial tax cut of an unpopular tax, such as the property tax. That idea has tremendous popular appeal to voters because we all want to see our property taxes cut. But it may not be a realistic option. See the sidebar "The case of the taxing legislator" for an illustration of this point.

The case of the taxing legislator

Bill Moose, a legislator, introduces a tax-cutting bill that he knows won't pass. He knows that, if it did, the state would be unable to fund elementary and secondary education. Its passage would create tremendous fiscal problems. It would cause schools to close.

Bill knows that his bill is fiscally irresponsible, but he isn't worried, because it will never become law. Bill Moose knows that all the members of the majority party in the legislature will be forced to do the fiscally responsible thing and vote against his bill. It's not that the members of the majority party are in favor of property taxes. They would love to find a way to reduce them, if only to appeal to voters, but this measure isn't the way.

After Bill Moose and his party force the majority party members to vote against a popular bill, they use that vote to campaign against the majority party incumbents in the next election.

The pitch will be

A popular plan for property tax relief was introduced. Jan Incumbent voted against it. Jan Incumbent is opposed to property tax relief. Jan Incumbent is a tax-and-spend liberal who is willing to spend your hard-earned tax dollars. Vote against Jan Incumbent on election day.

The facts are accurate, but the conclusion may not be. The equation is

(Fact)	1	A property tax relief bill is introduced.
	+	
(Fact)	1	Jan Incumbent votes against it.
	=	
(Conclusion)	3	Jan Incumbent is opposed to property tax relief.

Jan Incumbent opposed Bill Moose's idea. That is a fact. One reason for her vote may be her opposition to property tax relief. Another, more likely, reason is that Bill Moose's bill was fiscally irresponsible. The conclusion may or may not be correct. If it is not correct, it tries to create a false impression in the voters' minds that Jan Incumbent is fiscally irresponsible with the taxpayers' hard-earned money.

The Media Can Help You

If two ads can have conflicting messages and still both be accurate, how do you know who is telling "the truth, the whole truth, and nothing but the truth, so help you, voter"? The media can provide assistance in determining the truth in political advertising. For a number of reasons, reporters are in a position to get the information they need for their analyses:

✔ They have easy access to the facts and the candidates.

✔ They can get transcripts of the commercials.

✔ They can demand and get any underlying documentation that supports or refutes a candidate's charges or claims.

✔ They can get a response from the opposition and then check out the opposition's response, too.

✔ They may have instant access to third parties — those who have no axes to grind in the political campaign. These third parties can sometimes shed a great deal of light on the claims and counterclaims made in advertisements.

Journalists don't just review the accuracy of the facts being used in an ad; they also make a judgment on the fairness of the conclusion that the ad reaches. If these journalists determine that the conclusion isn't fair, they may label the ad misleading or unfair.

The press knows where to look

For an example of how the press might investigate a political advertisement, suppose that a candidate for attorney general claims that the incumbent attorney general seeking reelection has spent more tax dollars per capita operating her office than any attorney general in the country. The press is trained to investigate the facts behind an assertion like that.

The press knows or can discover that all the attorneys general in the U.S., for example, belong to an association called the National Association of Attorneys General. This organization, like the organizations for other statewide elected officials, compiles information on the offices, budgets, staffs, and responsibilities of all the attorneys general.

The press person investigating the ad can call an organization like this and get information not easily available to the average voter. That information may support or dispute the charge made by the candidate. This press person is now in a position to determine the real facts behind the charges and the response. An investigation by the press helps you understand whether it's the charge or the response that's more credible and reliable.

Getting the media analysis you need

Some newspapers and television stations go beyond the he said/she said approach when political advertising is involved. They've begun evaluating political advertising for accuracy, an approach referred to as *media watch* or *truth in advertising*.

The newspapers and television stations that perform these services for voters research every charge and claim made in a commercial. As new television commercials appear for candidates, some journalists do independent analyses of the accuracy of the claims or attacks made. Thorough reporters examine the commercials word for word to see whether the claims or attacks in the ads have facts to back them up. If they do, the analysis concludes that they are truthful. If the claims or attacks can't be substantiated, they are labeled unfair.

When truth-in-advertising or media-watch analysis is done well, the media spells out which points are supported by the facts and which are not. Make it a point to watch these analyses during the heat of a campaign. They can really help you understand what's actually going on. When you know which facts are correct, you can decide for yourself whether the implication is fair or accurate.

The media analyzes each new ad as it goes on the air during the course of a campaign. If more than one television station or newspaper performs the media-watch or truth-in-advertising analysis, watch or read as many as you can. When you view or read more than one and each analysis makes the same points, you can be more confident that the analysis isn't just the result of the individual likes or dislikes of one reporter.

You can call your local television stations to find out whether they are reviewing the ads and when. The television stations may even promote the truth-in-advertising reviews in the teaser spots they use to drum up viewers for their nightly news shows. Newspapers may have a special box and location in the newspaper where you can always find the reviews of the advertisements.

If the media does its job well, its evaluations can help you decide whether you should pay attention to the advertising or ignore it completely. It can help you understand which candidate is playing by the rules and which isn't. The media can help you become an informed voter.

If your news media doesn't review ads, tell 'em to get on the stick!

When newspapers and television stations perform media-watch and truth-in-advertising services, they help to keep the excesses of campaigning in check. If campaigns don't have this type of analysis to fear, they will always push the envelope. That is, campaigns will always try to get away with overstating a claim or an attack. After all, they're trying to persuade you how to vote. They want to use the most powerful arguments they can to bring you over to their side. Campaigns that aren't afraid of press exposure and criticism will occasionally bend the truth to win you over. They won't lie — the risks are too great — but they may stretch the truth to make a point.

All newspapers and television stations should perform these services. It should be a priority, and a proper amount of time and resources should be devoted to it. That is the only way you can know the truth in the commercials that you see. If your television stations and newspapers aren't conducting automatic review of political ads, call them and demand that they do it.

Call the League of Women Voters, the press associations, and the association of broadcasters in your state and tell them to get on the ball. Tell them that you need help and that they should provide it or help you put pressure on those who can. If these organizations are not listed in your phone book, call or write the national headquarters and ask for a name, address, and phone number for a local contact person in your state.

The national addresses for some of these organizations are

> **League of Women Voters of the United States,** 1730 M St. NW, Washington, DC 20036; 202-429-1965
>
> **National Association of Broadcasters,** 1771 N St. NW, Washington, DC 20036; 202-429-5300
>
> **Accuracy in Media,** 4455 Connecticut Ave. NW, Ste. 330, Washington, DC 20008; 202-364-4401 or 800-787-0044
>
> **Center for Media and Public Affairs,** 2100 L St. NW, Ste. 300, Washington, DC 20037; 202-223-2942
>
> **Common Cause,** 2030 M St. NW, Washington, DC 20036; 202-833-1200

Whose Side Is the Media On?

When you're trying to figure out what's going on and which candidate to support, you may wonder whether the media reporting on candidates and issues is reliable. Does the media choose sides in elections? Is the reporting objective? Can you trust what you read in newspapers and see on the nightly news? Is the media there to assist you in making an informed choice on election day, or is it just another obstacle to making that informed choice?

The answer to each of these questions is a little of both. Many people don't have much faith these days in the media. According to some polls, Americans like the press as a profession only slightly more than used-car dealers and slightly less than the politicians the press covers. Television reporters are seen as more trustworthy than print journalists, perhaps because they appear in person in people's living rooms every night. All in all, journalism is not currently a profession that moms and dads urge their offspring to enter.

Taking the good with the bad

In reality, journalism is no different from any other profession. There are good and bad reporters. There are lazy reporters and energetic reporters. Some reporters are smart, and some aren't so smart. Some reporters like some candidates and dislike others. Some reporters can't help rooting for the under-dog and bend over backward to help give that candidate coverage (they call it *leveling the playing field*). There are reporters who like to be schmoozed by important people, including candidates and officeholders — if these reporters are treated right, they treat the candidates right.

The media is a cross section of America, the good and the bad. Reporters are no better or worse than any other groups of citizens. Most of them try to cover campaigns fairly to the best of their abilities. They try as much as possible to leave their own personal prejudices at the newsroom door. Some reporters try harder than others, and some are more successful than others in getting that done.

There is such a thing as being too objective

A problem with many journalists is that they try to be too objective. Hold on, you might say — it isn't possible for a journalist to be *too* objective. It's like a judge being too fair or a minister being too kind.

Perhaps you think that reporters should not filter the election news you receive — you want to get it all without any editing or commentary. Maybe you feel that you are better equipped to make judgments about the candidates and the issues if you have just the facts, all the facts, and nothing but the facts. You may want the reporters to keep their judgments and opinions out of your news. If they have opinions or viewpoints, they should be columnists, not news reporters.

When reporters try to be too evenhanded in their campaign coverage, they give each candidate equal time. The ideas and responses of both the candidates are given identical weight in the news story. The reporter writes a story saying that Candidate Anderson said the following about Candidate Baily. Candidate Baily responded by saying the following about Candidate Anderson. Sounds okay so far. Sounds as if the reporter is doing what you want — giving you the facts so you can make a judgment for yourself. The reporter is not filtering the information that you're receiving. You're getting it just the way it happened. It's just as if you were there.

The problem is that you *weren't* there. You don't have the benefit of knowing the candidates personally. You probably won't be as familiar with the issue and the facts as the reporter covering the campaign. You may not know that Candidate Anderson's attack is completely bogus. You may not know that the charges have no merit at all and that Candidate Anderson is just a little bit flaky. A he said/she said story is merely a reporter's regurgitation of the charges and countercharges made by the candidates or the campaigns. The reporter doesn't evaluate the charges or tell you that the issues raised by one or both of the candidates are without merit and that voters should disregard them.

Some reporters don't necessarily do an independent evaluation when a candidate makes an accusation. They feel a responsibility to report what the opposition says in answer to a charge or attack in a campaign, but that's the extent of their duty as they see it. They may not perform an investigation of the underlying facts and charges to determine for themselves and for you which has more merit, the attack or the response. They may leave the responsibility of providing the other side to the opponent, who will no doubt tell voters that if the charges are untrue or unfair.

The problem with reporters who maintain this kind of objectivity is that you lose. If the reporters don't provide any independent evaluation of the facts, you are left to sort between the charges and countercharges to find out which is true. But you, the voter, are handicapped; you may not have ready access to the information that's available to reporters. It's much more difficult for you to do an independent evaluation to determine the truth than it is for a trained professional reporter.

Knowing the truth allows you to make an informed choice. You don't want to be manipulated into voting for a candidate who doesn't share your views and values. You don't want your support going to a candidate who has suckered you into supporting her by making unfair attacks on the opposition. You want the candidate who is right for you. Knowing the facts allows you to vote for that candidate and have confidence in your decision.

If You're on Your Own

What if, despite your entreaties, the media in your community doesn't perform a media-watch or truth-in-advertising service for the voters? How do you decide on your own which of two dueling commercials is accurate and which is not? If you don't know which facts to rely on, how can you decide whether the attack or the defense is more credible?

Here are some ways to guard against getting a false impression from campaign ads:

- ✔ Listen carefully to campaign advertisements. Separate the objective facts from the conclusions drawn by the opponent in the campaign's presentation.

- ✔ Beware of any conclusions a campaign ad makes. Don't accept anyone else's conclusions based on the facts given in the ad. The ad may be conveniently leaving out other facts that support a different conclusion. Reach your own conclusions.

- ✔ Be skeptical of simplistic arguments. Things are seldom as simple as a campaign ad can make them appear. Because most ads are between 30 and 60 seconds long, there isn't time for the ad to show the complexities of the situation. It's much easier to present a complex problem as a simple indiscretion.

- ✔ Listen carefully to the explanation given by the candidate under fire.

- ✔ If the candidate being attacked doesn't give an explanation, call his headquarters and ask for one.

If it takes 30 seconds to attack and five minutes to defend, the attacker wins — unless you fight back by seeking the truth.

Listening to neutral parties

One way incumbents deal with an attack that they think is unfair or misleading is by bringing in third parties to dispute the attack. Perhaps the victim's sister is offended by having a loved one's death exploited for political advantage and is willing to inject herself into the controversy. She may appear in an advertisement for the incumbent or issue a statement to the press disputing the facts in a candidate's attack. She's in a position to know what did happen, and she isn't trying to win an election.

If a third party with knowledge of the issue comes forward, it's much easier for you to ascertain what happened and whether it should influence your choice on election day. You can judge for yourself whether a third party has a partisan interest in the outcome. If the third party is someone who is not politically involved, the information he provides is more likely to be prompted by the facts and not by partisan loyalties. If the third party is a friend or colleague of one of the candidates, you should view the information provided with a grain or two of salt.

Learning the truth yourself

The media analysis isn't available, and no third party comes forward; how do you decide who's telling the truth? The answer is that it's not easy.

You must listen very carefully to the charge and response and be very certain of precisely what each side is claiming. Then you can compare the two versions and determine where there is a discrepancy in the facts that each side alleges. The discrepancy may be either of the following:

- ✔ What happened?
- ✔ What's the significance of what happened?

Go to the newspaper

If the disagreement is about what happened, you can go to your newspaper and see whether the episode that's the basis for the ad was the subject of any independent investigation or was reported by the press at all. If it was, the reports are probably the most reliable indicator of what transpired.

If you still have questions, call the newspaper and ask to speak with the reporter. Ask her directly what you want to know.

Approach the candidates directly

If you're having trouble finding media reports of an incident that an ad is based on, call the office of the elected official in question and ask what the facts are. Ask the person you speak with for copies of the police reports or any written information that supports the claims of the elected official.

Call the candidate making the charge and ask any follow-up questions you may have. Ask the candidate who is making the accusation for written confirmation of the charges in the commercial. Don't hesitate to take the direct approach. Both these candidates are eager to get your vote. Tell them that you have some questions that must be answered before you can commit yourself. Make them work for your vote by justifying their attacks. (See Chapter 5 for more about how to communicate with your elected officials.)

Don't let cleverness distract you from the truth

If the dispute between the two campaigns is not about what happened but about what something that happened *means*, you still need to listen very carefully to the charge and the response. Don't be distracted by the visuals or cleverness of the ad. Don't let the ad's appeal to hot-button issues prevent you from hearing exactly what the opponent is alleged to have done or failed to do (see the upcoming sidebar "Pushing your buttons" for more about hot-button issues).

Call both campaigns and ask for transcripts of the ads that you have questions about. Without the pictures and music, you will be able to understand the charges and responses made in the course of each 30-second television spot. When you've done that, you can decide for yourself which side is telling the truth.

Analyze the results

After you hear the arguments both sides make in support of their positions, you need to weigh the facts presented to decide whether the attack or the response is more credible to you.

- Was the incumbent derelict in her duty?
- Is the failing sufficient reason to deny her reelection?
- Does the attack omit important mitigating facts and create a false impression that the incumbent is soft on crime?
- Is the attack fair or unfair?

These are questions you need to answer for yourself before you cast your vote.

The more time you spend analyzing the attack and the response, the closer you'll be to discovering the truth behind the charges and countercharges. After you decide which side is telling the truth, you can decide which candidate deserves your vote.

If you decide that one side was unfair

If you decide that one side's attack is unfair and that the other side is telling a more truthful story, you may still decide to support the candidate who launched the unfair attack. On balance, that candidate may be the better choice. But he should be significantly better to overcome the liability of creating a false impression about his opponent in the minds of the voters.

Don't Let Either Side Manipulate You

When you're analyzing political advertisements, you should be on the lookout for certain red flags. A candidate who makes a blatant appeal to voters on a very emotional issue is trying to manipulate you. The candidate is hoping that your emotional reaction will trigger a response in her favor without additional analysis.

Beware of straw men

A manipulative candidate has no interest in telling you why she wants your vote. She doesn't want to discuss controversial solutions to complex problems. She's not interested in discussing the important issues in the campaign; she's looking for a diversion, just like the candidate who injects the perks and privileges issues into the campaign, as I discuss in Chapter 16.

But, unlike the candidate who harps on perks and privileges, this candidate doesn't have anything to offer you as a diversion. She's not promising to give up some benefit of the office to save the taxpayers' money. This candidate is simply raising a straw man and beating it into the ground to win your vote. A *straw man* is an insubstantial, emotionally charged issue brought up to distract voters from the real issues, the ones that affect your future, your standard of living, perhaps your way of life. A couple of common straw man issues are racism and patriotism.

Pushing your buttons

Hot-button issues are those issues designed to arouse your emotions but not to promote a debate on the emotional issue. Rather, the candidate raising a hot-button issue hopes that the words and images he uses will trigger an emotional response from you and other listeners.

For example, a candidate will say that English should be recognized as America's official language. A candidate using that as a hot-button issue is not really concerned about English as the universal language of this country. He's not in a policy debate about English as the national language with his opponent. He is appealing to listeners' fear of immigrants. He's hoping that the bias many feel against foreigners who are different in appearance and language will translate into support for him.

Hot-button issues emphasize those characteristics that divide rather than unite us as a nation. They are "us against them" issues that motivate voters to vote against a candidate.

Racism

Appeals to racial prejudice, no matter how subtle, are designed to manipulate you. Television ads that play on the fears or prejudices of white citizens are manipulative. Some campaigns use African-American people in ads on crime to engender fear in voters. The appeal may be visual only, with no racial words used. The subliminal message is that a vote for the opponent will result in more African-Americans having the opportunity to commit serious crimes, which may victimize the voters or their families.

Campaigns seldom make a racial appeal openly. That's much too risky a tactic. If it's obvious what the campaign is doing, various public service groups hold press conferences and denounce the tactic. The media may condemn the practice in editorials and political columns. It could backfire big time.

Campaigns can employ buzzwords or code words to trigger an emotional reaction in voters based on racial prejudice. The emphasis here is on the word *can*. Campaigns can also raise these issues to stimulate legitimate public policy debate.

If you hear candidates use any of the following terms, listen carefully to what they are saying:

- ✔ Affirmative action
- ✔ Racial quotas
- ✔ Immigration
- ✔ English as the official language

POLITICAL STUFF

The doomed Duke campaign

An example of a racial appeal made too openly was the campaign of David Duke for governor of Louisiana in 1991. David Duke was a leader in the Ku Klux Klan who had been a Nazi sympathizer. He had used racist and anti-Semitic rhetoric in earlier campaigns for public office but said he had changed his views.

Duke ran for governor as a Republican but was publicly repudiated by President George Bush and former Republican Governor Buddy Roemer. Duke's opponent, Democrat Edwin Edwards, was very unpopular but won the election anyway because Duke's appeal to middle-income white voters was seen as too racial by the majority of Louisiana's voters, who turned out in record numbers in a nonpresidential year to give Edwards more than 61 percent of the vote.

See whether the candidates using these terms have identified a problem that you think is legitimate. Has the candidate raising the issue made specific proposals to solve a real concern affecting the quality of your life? Or do you feel that the candidate's motive in raising the issue is to manipulate you and other voters?

REMEMBER

Don't accept at face value the candidate's declaration that these issues are causing problems where you live. Ask yourself, when you hear these appeals, whether any problems in your community or state stem from affirmative action, quotas, immigration, or English's status as our official language.

SPEAKING UP

Demand to know precisely how these policies are hurting you and your neighbors. Demand to know what the candidate proposes to do instead. Tell the candidate at your next opportunity that you are concerned that he is trying to manipulate you instead of addressing important policy issues. Ask him whether you are justified in feeling that way and if not, why not. Obviously, the candidate won't admit to manipulation, but his explanation of why he brought up the issue will help you make a more informed decision. (See Chapter 5 for more about communicating with officials.)

Patriotism

Another red flag to watch out for is the use of patriotism in a campaign. Almost every candidate, like almost every voter, is a patriotic American. Each is committed to our political system and our country. No candidate has a corner on loving her country. Unless you have hard-and-fast evidence to the contrary, assume that every candidate is a patriotic American who is working to make our country a better place.

The issues to watch out for are

- ✔ Flag burning
- ✔ The Pledge of Allegiance

When a candidate talks about constitutional amendments to ban the burning of flags or to require the recitation of the Pledge of Allegiance, your antennae should go up. Is this candidate raising a legitimate problem and proposing a solution, or is she trying to manipulate the voters? No candidate wants to see the flag desecrated. Every candidate believes in the principles espoused in the Pledge of Allegiance. So why is this issue being discussed in the campaign?

When a candidate tries to corner the patriotism market, watch out. She's trying to avoid discussing the more difficult issues by making an emotional appeal. The candidate hopes that the emotional appeal will cause you to vote against her opponent. She thinks that wrapping the campaign in the American flag or patriotism will be sufficient reason for you to support her. The unstated argument is that she is patriotic, while her opponent is not.

Analyze carefully what the candidate is attempting to do. See whether there's any merit to the contention that the opponent is not patriotic. A candidate with a different approach to a certain issue isn't necessarily the same as a candidate who's disloyal or unpatriotic. If you have no proof that the candidate is disloyal or unpatriotic, disregard the advertisement.

If you don't want to be manipulated . . .

Racism and patriotism are just two of the issues that candidates use to try to manipulate voters. Other us-versus-them issues include

- ✔ Prayer in public schools
- ✔ Appeals to class warfare, pitting the rich against the poor

Whenever a candidate raises one or more of these issues in a campaign, you should analyze what he is attempting to do. These are questions you should ask yourself:

- ✔ Are these issues legitimate concerns?
- ✔ Are there differences in approach between the candidates that merit debate?
- ✔ Is the candidate using these issues as hot buttons to try to manipulate voters into an emotional response against his opponent?

If you answer No, No, and Yes, then the candidate is trying to manipulate you and the other voters. If these are not legitimate issues for a candidate to raise in an election where you live, they are attempts to make subtle appeals for support based on racial, ethnic, class, or religious prejudice.

Campaigns that rely on straw men such as racism and patriotism are hoping that the manipulation will succeed because you won't analyze what you are seeing. The campaigns want you to simply react by voting against the target of the ad. Once you know what to look for in the advertising campaigns, it will be harder and harder for campaigns to manipulate you. The more you know about what campaigns do, or try to do, the less likely you are to fall for these kinds of emotional appeals.

Make it a point to listen carefully to every ad and watch the tactics that campaigns are using. You can learn to recognize the attempt to manipulate you, and then it won't succeed.

In fact, you should give long and hard thought to supporting any candidate who would resort to such tactics in the first place. Ask yourself whether this type of person would make a trustworthy officeholder. And take a closer look at the candidate discussing the *real* issues in your local community or state or even country.

Demand that candidates discuss what you want to hear

Make candidates talk about issues of importance to you and your fellow voters. Don't let them duck and weave. You have a right to know what type of officeholder you are being asked to support. Make them tell you. Don't take no for an answer; refuse to be sidetracked by issues that don't affect the quality of your life. Of course, a candidate who doesn't know the answer to your question should be permitted to say so.

Tell candidates that you have a right to this information. You do! You shouldn't be asked to vote for a pig in a poke. You want to know what the candidates will do if they are elected. It's not unreasonable for you to ask for that information before you cast your vote — the information doesn't do you much good after the candidate is elected.

Don't be nervous about holding candidates to account. After all, with your newfound political savvy, you're going to hold them accountable as officeholders. You might as well get them used to your demands early. Read Chapters 5 and 6 for more discussion about communicating with candidates and officials and letting them know what's important to you. Read Chapter 16 for more about what issues you want the candidates to discuss.

Chapter 13
Making Your Purchase

. . . .

In This Chapter
▶ Following your party line
▶ Consulting with others to make your decision
▶ Getting information on the candidates
▶ Evaluating a candidate's campaign

. . . .

You've got only one vote to cast, and your choice is nonreturnable — at least until the next election. How do you decide which candidate you want to support? What do you look for in a candidate? How do you know who will make a good officeholder?

Odds are that you won't know every candidate intimately by election day. With a little effort and a little reading on your part, though, you can know *something* about all of them.

Looking to Others Can Help You Decide

When people are confronted with big decisions, they often turn to close friends, colleagues, or authorities for help. It's just human nature. Even though your vote is your own, there's nothing wrong with consulting with others to make your decision.

Voting by party

If you haven't read or seen enough about some of the candidates to answer all your questions about them and comfortably make your selection, you have two alternatives:

 ✔ You can decide not to vote in some of the races.

 ✔ You can rely on the party affiliation of the candidates as a guide in making your decision.

 If you're comfortable thinking of yourself as a Republican, and all things are otherwise equal, vote for the Republican you don't know rather than the Democrat you don't know. If you think of yourself as a Democrat. . . . Well, you know the drill.

When you vote by party, you are trusting that the party label means that the candidate you have selected will be closer to you philosophically than her opponent. It's not a foolproof method of selection, but it beats throwing darts or relying on the political consulting firm of Eenie, Meenie, Minie, and Mo.

If you're truly an independent and don't register as a Democrat or Republican or vote by party in a primary, you're out of luck! Of course, you can always vote only for the candidates you know and leave the rest alone.

If you decide not to vote, others will make the hiring decision for you. The office will be filled with or without your input. When you haven't participated in the selection, you have no right to complain if you don't like the results!

If Frank likes this guy . . .

One way to make the decision of whom to vote for is to rely on the judgment of people you trust. If a candidate has the support of other individuals — particularly nonpolitical people — whom you know and trust, that's a good sign. Friends and coworkers of yours and of the candidate can provide insight. So can individuals who have known a candidate in a different context. Perhaps the candidate coached softball or was active in the PTA or United Way campaign. Perhaps people you know have children in the same school as the candidate's children. You can learn whether the candidate takes his duties as a parent or member of the community seriously.

The insight you can glean about a candidate's earlier experiences can be more valuable in understanding the candidate than anything you can learn while that candidate is running. During the campaign, you can be sure that the candidate will be on her best behavior. Learning how the candidate behaves when her guard is down can help you understand what this candidate is truly like.

When you rely on the opinions of people you trust, you should discount the endorsements of other elected officials. Except in very rare cases, the nominee of a political party enjoys the support of all the elected officials in that party. It's the 11th commandment of politics that one Democrat or Republican does not speak ill — at least not publicly — of another Democrat or Republican.

However, if your local Republican mayor endorses the Republican nominee for governor, it's hardly newsworthy. If the local Republican mayor refuses to endorse the Republican nominee for governor, or endorses with less-than-anticipated vigor, or — even more intriguingly — warmly endorses the *Democratic* candidate, that is an item worthy of note. In other words, don't simply pay attention to what they say; listen for what they *don't* say!

Checking out endorsements

You can also rely on the endorsements of groups to which you belong or are sympathetic. Various groups — from labor unions to chambers of commerce to teacher and police organizations to individual businesses and environmental groups — have *political action committees* (see Chapter 9 for more discussion of PACs). These committees interview the various candidates in races of interest to them and then decide which candidate to endorse and how much money to contribute.

Support of or opposition to a candidate by groups whose goals you share can provide insight into which candidate you will be comfortable supporting. Conversely, support or opposition by those groups whose objectives you oppose can help you decide whom not to support.

Making Up Your Own Mind

If you aren't content to rely on the opinions of others, you can form your own opinion of the candidates in a given race. When you're deciding which candidates should get your votes, think of the selection process as if you were interviewing and hiring the candidates for jobs. After all, that's exactly what you are doing: You're hiring candidates to work for you by representing you. Think of each vote as a hiring decision.

- ✔ Which candidate would you enjoy working with? ·
- ✔ Which candidate demonstrates a better work ethic?
- ✔ Which candidate would fit in better at your workplace?
- ✔ Which candidate would you feel more comfortable introducing to your parents?

Candidate selection checklist

If you're deciding whether or not to vote for Carly Candidate, here are some things to look for:

✔ Does Carly Candidate appear intelligent, or does she give the impression that she's just filling the suit?

✔ Is Carly Candidate qualified by education and experience for the job?

✔ Do you like Carly Candidate's programs and ideas?

✔ Is there anything in Carly Candidate's background that causes you concern?

✔ Are you comfortable with the groups and individuals who support Carly Candidate?

✔ Can you trust Carly Candidate? Does she pass the elevator test? (If an elevator door opened in front of you and getting on meant you would ride alone with the candidate, would you get on?)

Gathering information

The more information you seek before choosing a candidate, the more comfortable you'll be with your decision. A number of sources can provide the answers to your burning interview questions for each candidate:

✔ Attend any meetings scheduled by civic groups to provide voters opportunities to meet the candidates. Many times, when you go to these events, you'll have the opportunity to ask questions of the candidate directly.

✔ Watch debates between the candidates for a particular office.

✔ Request any position papers on issues that the candidates may have. (*Position papers* are writings that candidates release to give their positions on issues in much greater detail than news coverage provides.)

✔ Write to the candidates and inquire about their positions on issues of importance to you. You won't always get responses, but sometimes the failure to respond speaks volumes.

✔ You probably receive pamphlets or direct mail about the candidates' ideas and backgrounds. Take a few minutes to read them. Save them so you can remember the candidates' names and the offices for which they are running.

✔ Television news covers most of the campaigns as election day approaches. Take the time to watch the reports.

✔ Newspapers profile the candidates prior to election day. Be sure to read these profiles.

Newspapers submit questionnaires on many issues to each candidate for responses in the weeks before an election. The newspapers publish these responses or the lack thereof. These questionnaires can provide you with specific information on the candidates' backgrounds and positions.

None of this preparation takes very long, and it increases your comfort level in choosing which candidates to support.

Looking to the campaigns

One important factor to consider when you're deciding which candidate to support is the type of campaign the candidate is running.

- ✔ Do the printed materials and television and radio advertisements of the candidate give you any indication of what that person will do if elected?

- ✔ Is all the information provided to voters warm and fuzzy, appealing to emotion, or do issues or specific ideas on the improvement of the office sought play a role in the campaign?

- ✔ Is the campaign largely, if not completely, an attack on the opponent?

- ✔ Do the attacks focus on matters that generate heat but very little light?

The type of campaign a candidate runs can provide you with valuable insight into the type of person that candidate is. Once you know what type of person she is, you can predict the type of officeholder she will become. We're all more comfortable when we know what we're getting.

Making your choice

When you're making voting decisions, don't be afraid to trust your instincts. Your gut feelings can be a valuable guide. But having enough information can help you be sure that your gut feeling isn't just indigestion.

Ask yourself whether you are choosing the candidate based on looks. Remember what your mother always told you: You can't judge a book by its cover. That's true with a candidate, too. If you want your decision to be reliable, it has to be based on something more than a candidate's hairstyle, orthodonture, or fashion sense. (See Chapter 10 for more information on the image that a candidate presents.)

A match made in heaven?

Here are some things to consider when you're choosing a candidate:

✔ Do you normally feel more comfortable supporting one particular political party? If the answer to that is yes, you should look to that party's candidates first when you are deciding whom to support.

✔ Are you satisfied with the way things are being run in a particular office? If the answer to that is no, you should look to the outsider candidate (either the nonincumbent or the opposition party candidate) as a starting point in your decision making. If you are satisfied, stay with the incumbent or the party of the incumbent, if the incumbent is not seeking reelection.

✔ Which candidate is working harder to win your support? Have you been contacted by one or both of the candidates in person or on the phone? If the district is too large for personal contacts, is the candidate trying to meet as many voters as possible? The candidate who wants the office enough to work at getting elected will probably work hard at being a good officeholder.

✔ If you had an opportunity to meet or hear both candidates, did one of them impress you more than the other? Your gut instincts on these things are usually reliable.

✔ If the candidates haven't debated each other or appeared together, is it because one of the candidates is reluctant to participate in such an event? If a candidate is reluctant to appear, ask yourself whether you are willing to support a candidate with so little self-confidence that she will not give you a chance to compare the candidates for yourself. Candidates should debate (maybe not every day of the campaign, but once or twice) to give you ample opportunity to listen and make your comparisons.

Here are some important things to watch out for if you want the type of candidate who will pay attention to you and the other voters and be a leader at the same time. Look for a candidate who

✔ Makes specific proposals for solving problems

✔ Admits he doesn't have all the answers

✔ Doesn't agree with you about everything

✔ Doesn't promise quick, easy, and painless solutions to complex problems

✔ Isn't afraid to tell you that you will have to sacrifice to make things better and is willing to participate in the sacrifice

✔ Expects you to have a role in solving problems

✔ Can give you a convincing reason to vote for her

✔ Will tell you more about his finances than he is obligated by law to do

✔ Will promise not to accept free lunches, gifts, and trips from special interests that are trying to influence her official duties

✔ Understands that public office is a public trust

✔ Is willing to embrace new ways to improve our system and make it more responsive to voters

When you find a candidate who can do all or most of these things, don't just vote for him — get involved in his campaign! Read Chapters 7 and 8 for ways to work in helping to elect this person to office. A candidate like this is precisely the type of candidate we need. If he wins the election, he will work to make our political system and government more responsive. With your newfound political savvy, you can help him be successful.

When should you make your decision?

The obvious and correct answer to the question of when to make up your mind on how to vote is *when you are ready.* You should decide when you have enough information to be comfortable with your decision. It's a personal decision that you need to make for yourself. If you are not completely sure about whom to support, you might consider waiting at least until you've done the following:

✔ Received information — whether written, oral, or through the media — about the candidates and the issues from both sides, or all sides if there are more than two candidates

✔ Had the opportunity to observe and/or listen to all candidates, preferably in person, but at least on television or radio

✔ Seen what type of campaigns all the candidates are waging (see Chapter 18 for more on how to recognize negative campaign tactics)

✔ Heard which groups or individuals you know (and do or don't respect) are supporting which candidate

✔ Had an opportunity to read media interviews or questionnaires from the candidates published in the newspapers

Many of these events don't take place until shortly before the election. Obviously, if you have supported one candidate in the past or you know one of the candidates personally, you will be comfortable making your decision earlier in the campaign. If not, you may want to keep an open mind until just before the election so you will have as much information as possible to make an informed choice.

Part V:
Let the Campaigns Begin!

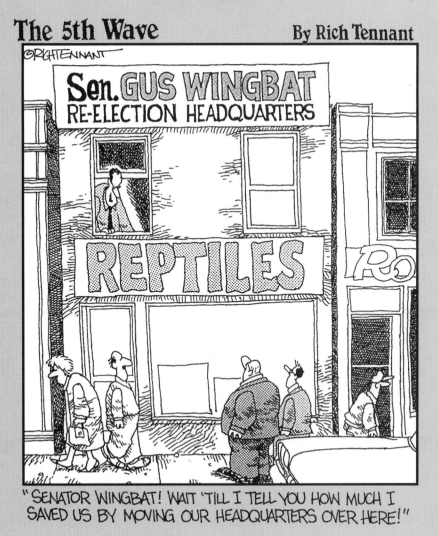

The 5th Wave   **By Rich Tennant**

"SENATOR WINGBAT! WAIT 'TILL I TELL YOU HOW MUCH I SAVED US BY MOVING OUR HEADQUARTERS OVER HERE!"

In this part...

This part explores campaigns at the local, state, and national levels. Discover where all that campaign money comes from and where it all goes. Find out why polling is so important to a successful campaign and why candidates ignore certain issues even when the polls show that the public wants to hear about them. This part also takes a walk on the dark side of politics — the truth behind negative campaigning and the reforms needed for politics to clean up its act.

Chapter 14

Who Says Talk Is Cheap?
(Where Your Contribution Goes)

In This Chapter

▶ How local campaigns use your contribution

▶ How national campaigns use your contribution

▶ Why political campaigns need so much money in the first place

▶ What your contribution won't pay for

▶ Looking past the money

*Y*ou've decided to get involved. You've made up your mind to contribute to a campaign. You've even decided which candidate to give your money to. You're about to write out your check, but, before you do, you wonder how your candidate plans to spend your hard-earned dollars. Your question is not unreasonable. After all, you're new to this thing called politics. You have a right to know where your money goes.

Campaigning at the Local Level

For the most part, the level of the office you are supporting determines how your campaign contributions are spent. A campaign for a local officeholder, city councilperson, state legislator, or county commissioner is run pretty much on a personal level. Most of the individuals involved with campaigns at the local level are volunteers; paid political consultants are rare at this level of politics. This is the type of race where the level of contact between the candidate and the voters is shaking hands or kissing the baby.

Going door to door

One of the best tactics that a candidate can use on the local level is knocking on every door in the district and asking each voter personally for support. Of course, if the race involves hundreds of thousands of households, or even millions of them, this method isn't practical. Door-to-door campaigning works only when the number of votes cast is small enough for a candidate to get to all of the doors during the election season.

The downside

Although it's a very effective method of reaching and persuading voters, going door to door is also very time-consuming. It occupies weeks and months of the campaign. Day after day, through the heat of summer, despite the rain and the dogs, candidates must be energized and interesting as well as interested in what the voters have to say. Door-to-door campaigning wears out numerous pairs of shoes in addition to the wear and tear it puts on the candidate.

Keep in mind that going door to door may not be practical for a candidate who isn't physically able to do all that walking, either because of age or disability. It goes without saying that you shouldn't hold this against a candidate.

The upside

As difficult as it is, there is no more effective method of communicating with voters than person-to-person contact. Door-to-door campaigning has the additional virtue of being an inexpensive means of campaigning — it doesn't put a strain on the campaign coffers.

The only expenses likely to be incurred in a door-to-door effort are for literature about the candidate that the candidate personally distributes on her visits and sends to the homes later for follow-up contact. In many state-of-the-art campaigns, the candidate is accompanied by an assistant who carries a handheld computer containing the street order walking list of registered voters. The assistant can tell the candidate if the person they are about to visit is a registered voter, how frequently the voter votes, and the party, if any, with which the voter identifies.

Because the voter list is on the computer, there is no confusion about whether the person being visited is registered or not. If you are not on the list, you need to be registered. The assistant can register you on the spot, as part of the campaign's well-honed, to-your-door service.

What to do when opportunity knocks

Even though going door to door is effective and inexpensive, some candidates who run in districts suited to door-to-door campaigning (and who are able to do it) are too lazy or undisciplined to subject themselves to the rigors of an extended door-to-door campaign. Some candidates are in districts that make their elections a virtual certainty, and they don't need to work that hard to ensure election. But sometimes candidates just aren't willing to work that hard to win.

If your district is small enough for door-to-door campaigning and you get a knock on your door, you should give serious consideration to voting for the candidate on the other side of that door. That candidate cares enough about what you think to make that extra effort to speak with you directly. That concern should count for something, even if he interrupted a crucial episode of *One Life to Live.*

When the candidate comes to your door, you can use the opportunity to bring your concerns to the candidate's attention. Tell the candidate what you want from an officeholder. Don't hold back! Tell the candidate what issues are important to you and ask what he can do about them.

Meeting face to face with a candidate is the best way to find out whether this is the type of person you want to support. Bring your concerns and views to his attention. If you have decided to become more involved, you can determine whether this campaign is the type you would like to be involved with. Do you think this is the type of candidate you would give your hard-earned money to? Is this the kind of candidate you would be willing to volunteer to help? Use this opportunity for conversation to see whether this is the candidate who meets your standards. Consider this a job interview — and you're the employer.

If you just want to be left alone, tell the candidate that you are supporting the opponent and that nothing he can say or do will change your mind. Chances are that the campaign will leave you alone after that — and no doubt will take pains to avoid reminding you to vote.

Follow-up letters

Many candidates follow up their visits with personalized letters. The assistant or the candidate makes notes on issues that you raise during the visit, and those notes are fed into the computer to generate a number of form letters. For example, Mr. Smith at 100 Pine Lane wants a stop sign at the next corner. Ms. Jones at 102 Pine Lane thinks property taxes are too high. The campaign sends personalized letters to Mr. Smith and Ms. Jones on the issues they raised. An efficient campaign makes certain that Mr. Smith and Ms. Jones receive letters from the candidate within a day or two following the personal contact, espousing their staunch support for more stop signs and lower property taxes.

If you aren't at home when the candidate comes to visit, you may still receive a personalized "sorry I missed you" letter. Most people like receiving this personalized mail because it demonstrates that they're important enough for the campaign to contact them directly.

Thousands of other voters probably receive similar letters. On the other hand, the candidate is concerned enough about your views and your vote to go to this trouble to try to win you over.

Alternative contacts

In local races, your money may be used to buy handouts — nail files, magnets, cards with emergency phone numbers — with the candidate's name on them. It may also be used for yard signs and newspaper, radio, and television ads that are designed to bring your candidate to the attention of the voters.

Television ads

Sometimes a local campaign produces cable television spots by itself without professional help. Such spots can be filmed at many cable television studios using the workers at the cable stations. The quality of the commercial may leave something to be desired, but the message can still be effective.

These cable spots can cost as little as several hundred dollars — as opposed to thousands of dollars for a professional spot — to create. That leaves a limited-resources campaign with a lot more available cash to get its message out to you and other voters. Because cable television advertising is so inexpensive, more and more local candidates are using campaign money to put their families on cable.

As inexpensive as it is, though, it's not free, and neither are the other kinds of advertisements. Your contributions can be used to pay for radio and television time and for the production costs associated with the advertisements that your candidate is putting on the air.

Radio advertising

Depending on the office and the district, radio can be a much more effective tool for communicating than TV or even cable TV. Most radio spots are 60-second ads. Those ads can be produced in the radio studio for very minimal cost. Knowing what to say in these ads is a function of the campaign's polling. Candidates or their volunteers often use a trial-and-error method to write their scripts.

Direct mail

If the district is too large for the candidate personally to contact all the necessary voters, your contribution can be used to send mail directly to the voters. Sometimes, a well-financed campaign sends direct mail in addition to the personal contact. Direct mail is a very effective method for reaching the voters who need to be persuaded; it is also expensive.

To have the desired impact, a campaign must send several pieces of direct mail to each household that the candidate is trying to persuade. If the candidate needs to persuade 10,000 voting households to vote her way, 40,000 to 50,000 pieces of mail may be needed to get that job done.

Campaigns send their mail bulk rate, but the postage and printing for that volume of mail could cost between $15,000 and $20,000! And that's just to say "Hello, how are ya?" and "Hey, look me over." You can see why campaigns need your money.

A sample campaign budget

The following is an example of a campaign budget for a gubernatorial candidate in a midsized state. The population range for this state is 4,500,000 to 5,500,000. States like New York and California with several times that population could have gubernatorial campaign budgets several times this large. States with smaller populations. . . . Well, you get the idea.

Net income $3,500,000: This figure is the fund-raising total minus all expenses associated with raising the money in the first place (for example, the proceeds for direct-mail soliciting minus the expense of creating the letters and mailing to potential contributors). All fund-raising costs that aren't paid by the host or hostess of the fund-raising event are paid by the campaign.

From the $3,500,000 net fund-raising income, the campaign must estimate all the expenses that will be incurred in selling its candidate.

Here are the expenses for this example:

Staff: A statewide campaign has a professional handler, a fund-raiser, a press person, and a couple of support staff people to answer phones, coordinate volunteers, and get things done.

Total budget for staff: $200,000

Rent: The candidate has to have a campaign headquarters unless her state party has enough room to provide a headquarters for her. The headquarters will probably be open for one year. This figure includes the phone bill, which can be substantial in a statewide campaign.

Total budget for rent: $54,000

Equipment: The candidate tries to get as much equipment through contributor donations as possible but still needs desks, phones, computers, and copying machines.

Total budget for equipment: $18,000

(continued)

(continued)

Travel: The cost of moving the candidate around the state with a car and a driver and some airplane travel for the candidate.

Total budget for travel: $20,000

Polling: The candidate conducts focus groups and polls at the beginning of the campaign and several other times during the course of the campaign. Right before the election, she probably also tracks her own popularity and voters' familiarity with her message and her opponent's message. The candidate signs a contract with a professional polling company for this work.

Total budget for polling: $250,000

Direct mail: The candidate wants to do some direct mail to segments of her constituency where television is not an efficient method of communicating or where her message should particularly appeal to voters. If the candidate is an incumbent legislator, she mails all her constituents several times during her term in office using state funds if she is a state legislator or the franking privilege (free mail) if she is a U.S. representative or senator. Using taxpayer-financed mail during a campaign is frowned upon and in some cases an ethical violation, so incumbents do their taxpayer-financed mailings before the campaign heats up.

Total budget for direct mail: $225,000

Printed materials: Party workers want information on the candidate to hand out to voters at various times (door-to-door canvassing, county fairs, party events). They also want bumper stickers and buttons to give to supporters.

Total budget for printed materials: $15,000

Television production: This covers the cost of filming and producing the TV commercials for the candidate. The media consultants hired by the candidate produce these commercials without too big a markup. The media consultants make their money by receiving a percentage of the television buy — usually 15 percent.

Total production costs: $125,000

Television time: The candidate wants to be on the air from Labor Day until the election. This figure includes 11–12 weeks of television and the cost of buying the time. This is the most effective method of communication with the voters of this state; the vast majority of campaign resources are spent in marketing the candidate to you and the other voters.

Total television costs: $1,493,000

National and Statewide Campaigns

Campaigns for higher-level offices spend their money somewhat differently. Candidates for most congressional, senatorial, gubernatorial, and other statewide offices (those for which everyone in the state votes) have professional consultants in addition to volunteers helping with the campaigns. Your contribution may help pay the salaries of these professional consultants, who perform a variety of functions, all of which cost money. These consultants manage the campaign and decide what message the candidate should communicate, how the message is communicated, and what is the best strategy to win votes and support for a candidate.

You have to see it (on TV) to believe it

With a statewide office, television is the preferred method of communicating with you and the other voters. It reaches the most people in the most cost-effective manner. When a candidate is trying to persuade all the voters of a state, he needs to reach millions of people. Direct-mail communication with numbers in the millions is too expensive for the average statewide campaign. Television is the way most statewide candidates get their messages to you and the other voters.

If voters don't see ads for a statewide candidate on television, they don't believe that there is a campaign. It doesn't matter how hard the candidate is working, how many miles the candidate has walked, or how many speeches a candidate has given. Without television advertising, the candidate and campaign are invisible. With television, the candidate is recognized and has credibility. Television advertising helps reinforce everything else the campaign is doing.

Your contribution and those of many others can help your candidate get his message on television among all the beer and deodorant commercials. If you and other contributors have been generous enough to permit it, a candidate hires another professional to produce the ads and buy the television time.

Buying the time

Producing professional ads for television and buying time are very expensive propositions. How expensive depends on the location. Buying television time in New York City, Los Angeles, or Chicago requires very deep pockets — pockets that contain millions of dollars. The pockets don't have to be quite as deep in Des Moines, Iowa, or Harrisburg, Pennsylvania. In less expensive television markets, hundreds of thousands of dollars for television may be sufficient.

When a candidate goes on television with campaign advertising, being on once or twice or for a short period of time isn't enough. Every campaign's goal is to stay on television until the end of the campaign. But just airing its ads until the end of the campaign isn't enough, either — the campaign must try to get more television time than its opponents. Doing so can cost a campaign the vast majority of all the money it has raised, but it can't effectively reach millions of voters any other way.

Successful statewide campaigns pour the vast majority of every dollar raised into television advertising. If you are giving to a statewide race and your candidate wants to have a good chance of winning, chances are that your contribution will be used for television advertising.

Cheap TV

Campaigns on a limited budget can avoid professional media buyers and buy their own time from the cable networks in the candidate's district. They tell the cable stations the type of person they are trying to persuade with their message and ask which programs they need to buy time on to reach that audience.

The candidate or campaign volunteers can write the commercial. They need to know what message they want to get across to voters — if they have polled, they should have ideas on what the most effective message is (see Chapters 10 and 15). Then they have to write a script to communicate the message in less than 30 seconds. That is the usual length of a campaign commercial on television. Sometimes ads can be 60 seconds, but buying time for 60-second ads is twice as expensive as for the normal 30-second spot.

If you've decided to volunteer for a campaign and end up trying to write a script that very concisely (in 30 or 60 seconds) communicates the message, be aware that it's a tricky proposition. Don't despair if you aren't producing award-winning spots immediately. You'll get the hang of it with a little practice.

Getting Out the Vote

Going into the election, a campaign has to worry about your mood and that of the other voters. Is there enough interest in the campaign to ensure a reasonable voter turnout? If you and the other voters couldn't care less about the election, does the campaign have sufficient funds to whisper sweet somethings and get you to come out and vote?

Campaigns spend significant resources encouraging you and voters sympathetic to their campaigns to come out to vote. *Get out the vote,* or GOTV, is a very important part of any campaign. A candidate who convinces a majority of potential voters that she is the best candidate still loses if she fails to get these supporters to come out and vote.

As a potential voter, you are reminded by mail, phone calls, and advertisements to vote. All of these reminders cost money. Mail sent in volume can cost 25 cents for each letter. Phone contacts for GOTV can cost 50 cents to 60 cents per call. In races for higher office, these calls are made by professional vendors, not volunteers. The volume of necessary calls is too great for volunteers to complete them during the few days before an election. Vendors with hundreds of phones and employees assisted by computer dialing cost the campaigns money.

Radio and television advertisements targeted at you and different segments of the voting population reminding you about the election and encouraging you to vote are very expensive. Millions of people vote in statewide elections, a couple of hundred thousand in a congressional election, tens of thousands in a state senate race, and several thousand in a state assembly race — all of these people need reminders to get out and vote, and it takes a lot of increasingly expensive stamps and touch-tone pounding to get to the eyes, ears, and feet of the voting public.

Most of the public is motivated to vote in the greatest numbers in presidential election years and is less likely to vote in nonpresidential elections. Non-presidential elections are wars of *turnout,* or numbers of voters. Whichever party or campaign is more successful in getting the public to turn out and vote will probably win. GOTV is a silent but important part of any successful candidate's strategy. It is designed to get voters to do something that they're not likely to do if left on their own.

Where Your Money Won't Go

You can rest assured that your campaign contribution probably will not be used to hire private detectives to follow the opposition around and get dirt on the opponent. The campaign may want to do this kind of snooping, but the risks are too great. If a reporter uncovers that type of shenanigan, the campaign's plan backfires. He's suddenly earned the campaign the kind of extensive news coverage and publicity that money can't buy — or correct.

Successful campaigns don't take those kinds of risks, despite what Hollywood may think. Some ground rules for acceptable campaign conduct are usually followed.

You can be confident that your contribution goes toward persuading other voters to support the candidate you've already backed with your hard-earned dollars. Your money is not ordinarily used for some nefarious purpose; indiscretions have an uncanny way of coming back to haunt the candidate.

Campaigns Never Say, "Enough!"

Campaigns have an almost insatiable need for money. Spending more is never a challenge. They want more money even when there's a substantial risk that they can't spend what they have effectively. Whether the campaign is for a local, state, or national office, the point when the campaign staff says it's raised enough money never comes.

Of course, the campaign must always be concerned about what will happen next. Given the secrecy that surrounds political strategy, a campaign can never be certain what its opposition has planned. It makes decisions about its own tactics in almost complete ignorance of what the opposition is doing — and how much the opposition is spending to do it.

Fund-raising wars

In the battle for your vote, a campaign has to consider what its opponent will say or do. All of these questions play a role in how much money a campaign needs to raise:

- ✔ How successful is the opponent's fund-raising?
- ✔ Will the opponent start advertising on television first?
- ✔ Is the opponent sending direct mail?
- ✔ Will the opponent attack the campaign's candidate?
- ✔ What information does the opponent have, and what form will the attack take?
- ✔ Will you find the opposition's message more persuasive?
- ✔ Will you believe the opponent's attack on the campaign's candidate?
- ✔ Does the opponent have enough money to get her message out to you?
- ✔ If you hear the message enough, will you change your vote?

Secrecy, spying, and surprise

Obviously, opposing campaigns do not share this type of information with each other. In fact, they often leak incorrect information (*disinformation*) to confuse their opponents. This disinformation may concern the success of fund-raising, the results of polling, or campaign tactics.

A campaign facing a credible opponent doesn't necessarily know what's coming, how it will come, or when it will come — which is why political campaigns are considered the leading cause of paranoia in even-numbered years.

The element of surprise can be crucial in the war for your vote. Each side wants to catch the other off guard. When a campaign is surprised, it may make a mistake. If a campaign fails to respond or responds in the wrong way, you may question whether you're supporting the right candidate. All the secrecy, plotting, and campaign tactics are about getting your vote on election day.

If a campaign resorts to military tactics like spying or paying for information, and those tactics are uncovered, its candidate is guaranteed to lose. Talk about flying blind!

Campaigns generally don't know how much money the opposition has to launch the attack and make the charge stick in the your mind. Despite this lack of any real information, a campaign must worry about whether and how to respond. It can't afford to let a charge go unanswered — you may begin to believe the charge! The campaign must convince you that the charge is unfair, or at least distract you, if the campaign has any hope of keeping or winning your vote. A campaign has to figure on having the resources to let you know the candidate's side of the story.

You can easily understand why no campaign is ever confident that it has raised enough money to meet every possible circumstance. A campaign is expected to fight a war when it doesn't know when the war will begin, what type of weapons the enemy has, or how large its army is.

Winning your vote

Remember that this war is all about you and your vote. You, and others like you, are the prize each side is seeking to win. Money plays a very important role in this war. Without money, a campaign can't respond to an attack or distract the voters — it is merely adrift on the ocean, being pounded by waves from all sides, without the power to get to the winning port, and no doubt rendered violently ill on election night.

When you see a candidate with enough money to go on television first, you know that that candidate has won the fund-raising war. When you receive direct mail from one candidate and not the other, you can be sure that it isn't because the candidate who didn't write you is taking your vote for granted. He probably doesn't have enough money to send direct mail at all or as much as his opponent. (See Chapter 17 for a discussion of direct mail.)

Looking beyond the money

If you aren't going to be persuaded by money alone, you need to view these overtures for your vote with a grain of salt. Listen to the arguments from the candidate with enough money to contact you, but try to find out what the candidate without the money would say to you if she had the dollars and stamps to contact you. In other words, spend some of your time and effort to discover what the other candidate's position or point of view may be before you decide whom to support. Think for yourself.

Because money *is* the single most important determinant in deciding who wins and loses elections, you may want to consider contributing to a candidate of your choice whose campaign appears to be underfunded. Your campaign contribution can

- Defray the cost of creating and mailing letters
- Help pay for the literature that the candidate distributes
- Assist a candidate in getting input from real, live voters like you
- Help to personalize campaigning, at least for local races

The candidate with the most money doesn't *always* win but does win much more often than not. That's why fund-raising is such an important part of any campaign. You won't know whether the losing candidate was the better candidate if the campaign lacked the money to get that message to you effectively.

Chapter 15

For Whom the Campaign Polls

In This Chapter

▶ The role of pollsters

▶ Pollsters want to know what you think

▶ Are you hearing the message?

▶ Why is your mailbox full of campaign mail?

*O*ne evening in the summer months before an election, you answer your telephone, and the voice on the other end of the line asks if you are willing to answer a few questions. The person says that she's with XYZ Public Opinion and that she's taking a survey. You have been selected as a target for a polling firm for one of the candidates or parties in the upcoming election.

Why you? You were just minding your own business, watching *Jeopardy!* What did you do to deserve this type of treatment?

Pollsters are the marketing experts of a campaign. They get the information from you and other voters to focus their campaigns. The results of the campaign's polling decide when, how, and to whom the message gets out as well as what the message is.

You were called so that the campaign can use your responses to shape its message and to determine the most effective way to communicate it. Your responses help determine whether to use direct mail, what to say in it, and who receives it; what television shows to advertise on and how much time to buy; whether the benefits of a last-minute phone drive overcome the wrath of voters like you who vigorously object to negative campaigning.

If money is no object, campaigns also sample voters by means of focus groups. These groups permit campaigns to go into detailed interviews with a few specially selected representative voters to understand how these voters view the candidates and the issues. See Chapter 10 for more about what focus groups are and how campaigns use them.

The Role of Polls

Most campaigns for high-profile offices employ professional pollsters. Many of the prominent polling firms that specialize in political campaigns are located in Washington, D.C., and New York City, but polling firms exist in most large cities. They are hired to perform polls that the *handler* (that is, the campaign consultant) and the candidate need and for which they can afford to pay. (See Chapter 10 for more on handlers.)

Like handlers, pollsters may work for a variety of candidates running in many different states for many different offices, but they generally stay on one side or the other of the political fence — Republican or Democrat.

Who gets polled?

Scientifically conducted polls randomly select the voters interviewed. Randomness is the factor that permits a few hundred people to speak for all the voters within a statistical margin of error. In other words, you are as likely as any other voter in the district to be asked to participate in the poll. No sample is perfectly random, but pollsters try to make their survey as close to random as possible because that's the way the sample is most reliable.

Methods to their madness

Random digit dialing is one technique used to ensure a sample's accuracy. In *random digit dialing*, telephone numbers are randomly connected to each working telephone exchange. This method is especially accurate and has the benefit of reaching voters with unlisted numbers, but it's expensive because the pollsters charge for the numbers they dial that aren't working or aren't the numbers of registered voters.

If the area being polled doesn't have clear exchange boundaries, like a city where different legislative districts represent people in the same exchange, random digit dialing may not be cost effective. That's because there is no way to separate out the phone numbers of people in the district of interest to the poller. If the poll is for a primary race with low turnout, random digit dialing may not be cost effective either because the pollster will reach so many people who don't plan to vote in the primary.

When random digit dialing doesn't work, pollsters use voter file lists that have been *phone matched*. This method may not be as accurate as random digit dialing because some groups of voters don't have phones in proportion to the number of people in the group who vote. Older voters, mobile voters, rich voters, and young voters tend to be undersampled when this method is used.

No method of selecting the voters to be polled is perfect, but pollsters try very hard to make the sample as representative as possible. After all, the candidate makes important decisions based upon the answers you give.

Fitting a certain profile

If you get called for a poll, it's probably because your number came up at random. On the other hand, you may have been selected because you fit a certain profile. You may still have been selected at random, but from a small subgroup of the voting population.

For example, suppose that Harry Handler thinks a position taken by the opponent will anger women under the age of 50. Harry may believe that publicizing this position will lose the opponent votes among that age and gender group. He wants to test that theory before spending any resources getting the word out to voters. It's not worth spending the money if the opponent won't lose votes.

Your name may have been selected from among those who fit the profile of the interested subgroup — women under 50. The answers you give to the pollster's questions tell the handler whether or not to spend money getting the word out to other voters like you.

If you get that call . . .

Only a few hundred people are asked their opinions on these questions. Those few hundred people have a significant impact on the message and strategy for the campaign. Their answers help decide which programs a candidate supports or opposes during the campaign. They tell a candidate whether her message is getting through or needs to be refined.

As Chapter 3 discusses, no campaign will spend money finding out what you think if you are not a registered voter. If you want an opportunity to shape political campaigns, make sure that you're registered to vote when that pollster calls you.

If you are polled and take the time to respond, you can shape the approach and content of a campaign. You are one of only a few hundred people in your congressional district or state who get to speak about a broad range of issues while the candidate listens. You are in a position of influence. The candidate wants to know what you think. The candidate is paying the pollster good money, and lots of it, just to hear your views. You are a political pooh-bah. And all you did was register to vote and answer your phone! Of course, you also missed *Jeopardy!* — but now real folks, not just the television set, have had the benefit of your wise answers to questions.

Who polls?

Any campaign with sufficient money uses polls these days. The level of the office being sought doesn't matter — county and legislative candidates use polls, too. Polling is advisable whenever an office involves policy or a campaign is going to be anything more than "I'm Carly Candidate; vote for me!" A well-run, well-funded candidate tests his message before he spends money communicating it.

Sometimes candidates for less visible offices pool their resources and poll together. Sometimes party organizations pay some or all of the costs. Occasionally, special interest groups use polling to convince candidates or officials of the wisdom of supporting the special interest position on an issue. (Turn to Chapter 9 if you're not sure what a special interest group is.) Special interest groups use polls to show candidates that their ideas are popular or that an issue they are opposing is unpopular.

Polls Are Expensive

One of the reasons campaigning for office costs more now than in the past is the increasing use of professional polls to find out what you and other voters want and think. (See Chapter 14 for other reasons campaigning costs are on the rise.)

But the candidate's *handler* — the campaign consultant who shapes and directs the entire campaign — knows how important polling is. Even though professional polls cost thousands of scarce campaign dollars, the Harry Handlers of the world spend that amount gladly in an attempt to contact you and learn what you are thinking.

Harry Handler uses polls throughout the campaign process:

- He does a benchmark poll (see the discussion later in this chapter).
- He goes back in the field with polls when he begins his television commercials to see whether you are responding to the message.

✔ He also polls when the opponent begins his television advertising to see whether you are persuaded by the opponent's message.

✔ If Harry intends to attack the opponent or believes the opponent will attack his candidate, he polls in advance to test your response to the attacks and the anticipated defenses.

✔ Harry also polls you during the attacks to see whether you are inclined to change your vote.

Each of these polls costs thousands of dollars! Why would a well-funded, professionally run campaign spend that kind of money on polling? Think of it as an investment to monitor your reaction to the campaign as it goes along. If your reaction is not what Harry Handler hoped, he adjusts the campaign strategy to win you over.

Size of the sample

The cost of polls is determined primarily by the sample size — the greater the number surveyed, the more expensive the poll. But to get within a certain acceptable margin of error for their determinations, pollsters have to complete a given number of surveys.

In a statewide poll, the range of the sample is 600 to 800 completed calls. In a congressional district, the desirable number of completed surveys is in the 400 to 600 range. Generally speaking, bigger is better. Bigger sample sizes permit more accurate looks at different subgroups in the polls, such as elderly or minority voters.

But above a certain minimum size, bigger isn't always worth the price in terms of statistical accuracy. For example, the margin of error for a sample of 1,200 is only one percentage point less than the margin of error for a sample of 600.

The *margin of error* is the range of statistical accuracy for a poll. For example, a sample of 400 has a margin of error of 4.9 percent. That means that the totals could vary either way by up to about five percentage points. In other words, a poll that shows Carly Candidate tied with Opus Opponent could be inaccurate by as much as Opus Opponent leading by five points or Carly Candidate leading by five points.

Pollsters need to contact more voters than the 600 to 800 needed in a statewide contest to complete that many surveys because they have to make up for calls placed to answering machines and people who do not take kindly to being interrupted. The pollster tries to minimize the lack of completed calls and the hostility of the voter by calling after dinner (but not too late) on the days of the week when people are more likely to be home — Sunday through Thursday.

Length of the poll

The amount of time that the pollsters must spend on the telephone for each survey also affects the cost of polls. The longer the time spent asking questions, the more expensive the poll. Pollsters don't ask any extraneous questions; they don't waste time asking questions when they already know the answers.

An example of a useless question that pollsters wouldn't waste their time on is whether convicted felons should do prison time. The answer to that question would be an overwhelming *yes*. The real question is whether voters are willing to spend $100,000,000 to build the new prison necessary to make certain that all convicted felons do prison time.

It's not uncommon for pollsters to ask 60 to 80 questions once you agree to be interviewed. That may seem like too many, but most of the questions are quick. The pollster tries not to take more than 20 – 30 minutes of your time. That's about how long it takes you to go to your polling place and vote on election day — and answering these questions can have a much more profound impact on the course of a campaign than your one vote can ever have.

Benchmark Polls

A *benchmark poll* is a lengthy professional public opinion survey taken very early in a campaign. It's the poll that determines campaign strategy and planning. Benchmark polls measure some important items, *benchmarks,* to compare with measurements taken later in the campaign in order to chart the campaign's progress or lack of progress.

Before a campaign conducts a benchmark poll, it finishes its internal opposition research and its external opposition research. (For more discussion of internal and external opposition research, see Chapter 11.) In other words, Harry Handler now knows all there is to know about the opposition and his own candidate before taking a benchmark poll. Harry Handler first identifies matters in the candidate's and the opposition's backgrounds that might be persuasive to the voters. This poll tests how good, or bad, Harry's instincts were.

The object of the benchmark poll, taken so many weeks and perhaps months before the election, is to determine what the outcome of the election will be if the campaign unfolds as expected. If you listen carefully to the questions the pollster asks you, you can determine what message the campaign will use to persuade you to vote for the candidate. You can also guess what attacks the campaign may use to persuade you to vote against the opponent.

What to expect

Benchmark polls usually follow some variation on the following format:

```
Do you know the two candidates?
Do you feel favorably or unfavorably about the two
          candidates?
```

Answers to these first two questions tell Harry Handler how many voters he must persuade to win the election.

```
This November, there will be an election for governor between
          Democrat Carly Candidate and Republican Opus
          Opponent; for whom will you vote?
```

Answers to this question tell Harry where the election stands now, before the campaign's message is delivered.

```
What do you feel is the most important issue in this campaign
          (for example: education, crime, taxes, unemploy-
          ment)?
How do you feel about specific programs Carly Candidate has
          proposed (for example: a road construction pro-
          gram, an educational program)?
Do you feel good about the direction your state is headed or
          not?
If you knew the following good things about Carly Candidate,
          would you be inclined to vote for her?
```

The answers to these questions tell Harry Handler which of Carly's many accomplishments should be used in the message to bring you around to supporting her.

```
This November, there will be an election for governor
          between Democrat Carly Candidate and Republican
          Opus Opponent; for whom will you vote?
```

Harry asks this question to discover whether you find the positive facts about Carly Candidate persuasive enough to support her.

```
If you knew the following bad things about Opus Opponent,
        would you be less inclined to support him?
```

Answers to this question tell Harry Handler whether attacks on Opus Opponent will persuade you to vote for Carly Candidate.

```
This November, there will be an election for governor between
        Democrat Carly Candidate and Republican Opus
        Opponent. For whom will you vote?
```

Asking this question again tells Harry whether his anticipated attacks on Opus Opponent will cause you to change your vote for governor.

```
Some people say that Carly Candidate is too liberal with
        taxpayer money. Her office budget has increased
        40 percent during her six years as attorney gen-
        eral. Others say that Carly Candidate is a fiscal
        conservative who has refused a pay raise and that
        her office budget has gone up only because her
        office is doing more for the taxpayers by not
        hiring outside attorneys who charge large fees to
        represent the State in court. With whom do you
        agree?
```

Answers to this question tell Harry Handler whether his responses to Opus Opponent's attacks will work and persuade you to vote for Carly Candidate.

Learning from the pollsters

If you listen carefully to the questions a pollster asks, you can tell who is taking the poll. The candidate taking the poll asks questions about her own characteristics and record in an attempt to determine what positive message to communicate to you and the other voters. The candidate taking the poll also spends a fair amount of time on questions testing the opponent's weaknesses to decide which attacks work.

You can also learn what facts in her own record the candidate taking the poll is concerned about. You can learn what issues the candidate taking the poll would be willing to use in the campaign, provided that you are persuaded by them. In fact, listening carefully to the pollster's questions can tell you much more about the records of both candidates than the campaign itself will ever disclose.

The candidate taking the poll will only use a few of the most persuasive positive factors in his own background and a few of the most persuasive negative factors in his opponent's record in her campaign. (See Chapter 10 for more information on how the message of a campaign is determined.) But if you listen to all the questions that the pollster asks, you can tell what other issues are out there that the campaign decided not to use.

Telling pollsters which arguments persuade you

Polls ask you questions about the candidate as well as her opponent. They test positive items in the candidate's background to see whether these items persuade you to support the candidate. They test anticipated attacks by the opposition and the candidate's rebuttal. Your responses to these questions help the handler decide which method to use to disguise whatever warts the candidate may have. (Alternative approaches are discussed in Chapter 11.) Your answers tell the handler which disguise for the warts will be most effective.

When you answer a pollster's questions, you are determining the course of a campaign. If you're opposed to negative attacks, your answers to poll questions should be consistent with that view. You cannot both oppose negative campaigns and allow yourself to be persuaded by them. If you tell the pollster that the attacks on Opus Opponent's record will persuade you to vote for Carly Candidate, Harry Handler will attack Opus Opponent — even if you tell the pollster that negative ads turn you off.

Is the Candidate's Message Getting Through?

Harry Handler must constantly evaluate whether the campaign's message is getting through to you and monitor the effect of the opponent's message on you. The opponent's message may be more persuasive than Harry bargained for. He may need to try another approach to disguising Carly Candidate's warts, or her message may not be as persuasive as Harry hoped. Harry may need another message or another approach to the message that he is using to get through to you. Subsequent polls help Harry make the necessary midcourse corrections that keep Carly's campaign on target to victory.

A campaign is fluid: It's all about moving the undecided voters into one or another candidate's corner. When the purpose of a campaign is to change minds, and the inflexible deadline of election day is looming, a handler had better be able to adapt and change course quickly. If a campaign has spent three weeks and hundreds of thousands of dollars on television telling voters what the candidate has done for them, and the poll reveals that the voters still don't know what the candidate has done, the message isn't penetrating, and the campaign must go to Plan B.

Chapter 16
Dodging the Issues

*W*hen ads appear on your favorite television programs, they are examples of how important gaining your support is to the success of the various campaigns. But you may wonder about the messages contained in the advertisements. (Chapter 15 discusses how candidates poll voters to determine which items should be part of a candidate's message.)

The message and marketing are designed to get your attention. All this research and scientific information-gathering is done at great time and expense to campaigns. You know all this already. What you don't know is why the campaigns decided on the message you are seeing. Why are they talking about a trivial matter instead of something you have identified as important?

The next time you hear an advertisement talking about an issue that you feel is unimportant, ask yourself why the candidate chose that message. What issue or issues is the candidate avoiding? Be careful of candidates who aren't willing to tackle discussions of complex problems when asking you for your vote. If they aren't willing to talk about these issues during campaigns, chances are that they won't want to deal with them when in office, either.

Tough versus Trivial Issues in a Campaign

If you observe election campaigns long enough, you'll notice that candidates avoid certain issues at all costs and spare no expense to harp on others. Unfortunately, the issues they avoid may be the ones you're interested in hearing about, while the issues they champion may seem petty.

Here are some tough issues that candidates try to avoid discussing:

- ✓ Abortion
- ✓ Gun control
- ✓ Whether taxes are unfair and how they should be changed
- ✓ What programs must be cut to balance the federal budget
- ✓ Steps to take to reduce the growth in Medicare (the federal health program for the elderly)
- ✓ Steps to take to keep Social Security solvent
- ✓ Why our children perform poorly in today's schools and how we can correct that

Instead candidates talk about these issues:

- ✓ Renouncing the perks and privileges of office
- ✓ The need for campaign finance reform . . . at some point in the future
- ✓ Term limits — under a definition that allows this candidate to spend his entire career as an officeholder
- ✓ The moral decline of society and the need for prayer in schools to counter it
- ✓ A balanced budget constitutional amendment — which will require some future Congress to make the tough choices to cut federal spending or raise taxes
- ✓ A constitutional amendment to ban flag burning
- ✓ Extending the death penalty to unpopular crimes as a means of reducing crime

You can't hide from everything

Some issues of importance are impossible for candidates to avoid. Candidates must take positions on them regardless of the potential for risk and controversy. For example, it will be difficult, if not impossible, for congressional candidates to avoid taking positions on Medicare during the 1996 elections.

The future of this program is the subject of daily press speculation and debate in Congress. Every senior citizens' group and every journalist will ask where candidates stand on this issue. As much as candidates would like to avoid the subject, they will have to speak out. If you are concerned about this issue for yourself or your parents, you'll have an opportunity to learn where your congressional candidates stand before you vote in November 1996.

To win, a candidate must build support

Say, for example, that you and a solid majority of the voters indicated in a poll that the most important issue in the legislative campaign is property taxes. Yet neither campaign is talking about the issue, or the challenger is attacking the increase in property taxes without offering any solutions. Why?

The answer is that there is no answer. The problem of escalating property taxes may not have an easy solution. Proposals for changing the tax base of any community always work to the advantage of some groups and to the disadvantage of others. Anytime a candidate makes a proposal to change taxes, most people think that they'll lose out. They never believe that tax reform will benefit them because it usually doesn't — tax reform seems to be just a tax increase in disguise.

When taxes are changed, even if the move is revenue neutral, most people think that they're paying more. A *revenue neutral* measure is one in which no more total money is raised through taxes, but the way the money is raised may be changed. Governments may be willing to substitute revenue sources, but they are seldom in a position to abolish a tax that provides a significant amount of revenue without replacing it with another. Property taxes in most states fund public education. They provide much of the money for local law enforcement, fire protection, and other essential government services. As onerous as property taxes may be, governments can't afford to abolish them, or even lower them, without finding alternative sources of revenue.

Once candidates start talking about substituting one tax for another, they lose votes. Voters may agree that they want something done about property taxes, but they don't agree what that something is. They are fundamentally skeptical that any change will work to their advantage. Voters are just regular people, not eager to make tough choices. They also have zero confidence that politicians will make the right tough choices for them.

A candidate who wants to win builds support. She wins by convincing as many people as possible to vote for her. When a candidate begins talking about something as complicated as property tax substitutes, she raises doubts in the minds of some voters. Those doubts can fracture the fragile coalition of support that a candidate has worked to build. Building support is difficult when doubts about a candidate's program or judgment surface in a campaign. Fractures can erode a candidate's winning majority.

Proposing change is risky

Proposing any change is risky. Proposing substantial change may be foolhardy. Winning elections in this day and age is all about avoiding as much risk as possible. A candidate hesitates to propose anything that doesn't already have the strong backing of a majority of the electorate. Anything new or — heaven forbid — radical is out of the question.

However, a candidate must have a platform or a message to communicate to the voters. A candidate has to say something besides "vote for me," after all. A candidate does have to give you a reason to choose him over the opponent. The message or platform is as uncontroversial as possible — as plain vanilla as the electorate and media permit.

Voters may say they want something done about property taxes, but unless voters agree what that something is, no candidate will make a proposal to do anything about the problem. Instead, you find the candidates discussing issues that you may regard as less important or discussing the need for change without any specific suggestions for how to change.

Sticking to symbolic issues

A candidate looks for an issue that appeals to you and other voters but isn't complex and controversial. An example of this may be a candidate's refusal to use the car paid for by the taxpayers, which has traditionally been a perk of the office. Taxpayer-provided cars symbolize all that voters dislike about politics. A vehicle paid for by tax dollars is a perk or privilege that few, if any, of the rest us receive. It's a symbol of how elected officials are out of touch with average citizens.

The symbol could just as easily be use of a taxpayer-provided credit card for official duties, taxpayer-provided travel to conferences, or a pay raise. Any of these issues can strike a chord with voters. Any of these issues can provide voters with a reason to choose one candidate over the other.

Issues like these are particularly potent when a candidate refusing to take these perks or privileges runs against an officeholder who has taken her share and then some. The smart candidate uses the refusal to take the perks and privileges of the office as the reason that you should elect her and retire the current officeholder.

Voters pay attention to issues like these. These symbols — though unlikely to make a difference in the quality of their lives — are easy to understand. They may not have anything to do with the important issues in an election; they may say nothing about property taxes and what government can do to lower them. But they do give us insight into how much a candidate wants to represent us and why. They tell us that the privileges of the office are more important to some candidates than others. That, by itself, can be useful information.

Beware, however, of candidates who invoke straw man issues such as racism or patriotism. (See Chapter 12.)

Using Diversions to Avoid Risks

A creative candidate may take the symbolic issue of turning down a perk even further. She may argue that refusing a pay raise, car, credit card, or travel will lower the cost of government. Lowering the cost of government will reduce the need for more property taxes. That argument is a very ingenious way to turn the property tax debate, an issue for which the candidate has no program, into a perks or privileges debate, an issue for which the candidate does have a program.

A thinking voter knows that cutting all the perks and privileges will not affect property taxes one iota. Taking this line does, however, give the candidate something to say when property taxes come up in debates or question-and-answer sessions.

- ✔ A candidate can't say that she hasn't thought about property taxes when the overwhelming majority of voters has identified property taxes as the number-one issue in the campaign.

- ✔ The candidate can always say that property taxes are too burdensome. Voters will agree with that gem of wisdom. But that answer exposes the candidate to the inevitable follow-up question: "What are you going to do about them if you are elected?" The candidate wants to avoid giving a real answer to that question at all costs.

- ✔ The last thing that a candidate wants to admit is that he doesn't want to propose alternatives to property taxes because he's afraid of losing votes. It may be true, but the voters and the media will have no patience with the answer. The diversion permits the candidate to say something responsive to the question about high property taxes without much risk.

Dodging with diversions

By resorting to a diversion, the candidate can sympathize with the problem and propose an uncontroversial "solution" to help deal with it. She can say that taxes are too high and that an alternative fund source for local governments needs to be explored. She may even propose something uncontro-versial that, on closer analysis, probably won't work.

For example, the candidate may propose providing property tax relief by using part of an existing source of revenue. The candidate may say that a percentage of the state's lottery revenue should be used to provide property tax relief. However, most states quickly spend every cent that their lotteries net. There is no large pot of lottery revenue sitting in a bank waiting to be spent for property tax relief or anything else. If lottery money is spent to solve the property tax problem, some other, equally worthy cause will be left short of funds. That shortage may need to be replaced with another source of revenue.

The candidate views that as someone else's problem. She isn't looking at the big picture. We're talking about trying to get elected, not governing. The candidate can simply say that sufficient revenue exists or that something else, less important than property taxes, has to be cut. She has answered the question — the solution may not work, but she gets away without having to propose a real program that will provide property tax relief but also risk losing the candidate votes.

The candidate will not propose new revenue sources, because increasing or adding new taxes is very risky in today's political climate. The candidate can recognize the problem and give a mealy-mouthed suggestion for a solution — such as changing the issue to a perks-and-privileges debate. All of these alternatives are designed to avoid taking positions that may solve real problems but can cost candidates elections.

A candidate talks about unimportant items instead of real issues to reduce the risks to himself. A candidate wants to give you a risk-free reason for voting for him. He'll do that as long as you let him get away with that approach. If you aren't willing to let him have a risk-free campaign, keep on reading. Later in this chapter, I talk about how to make candidates discuss the issues you want to hear about.

Diversions may not build support, but they don't jeopardize it, either

No voter ever refused to support a candidate for turning down the perks and privileges of an office. Voters are sick and tired of officeholders with lucrative salaries, the ability to bounce checks without penalty, and pension plans that won't quit. They are tired of officeholders who don't understand what it means to lose health care coverage or have the company you have worked for all your life go under and take the pension plan you were counting on for your retirement with it.

To put it another way, the diversion might work to diffuse a controversial issue and to gain the candidate some votes. But if it doesn't work, it won't fracture the coalition that the candidate is building to win election. The candidate doesn't lose any ground if the strategy is unsuccessful. She simply has to find another approach to winning over enough voters like you to be successful.

Stick to Your Guns!

The candidates may not like it, but you still want them to talk about what they will do to control the growth in property taxes. How do you find out what, if anything, they propose to do if they are elected? How do you make candidates talk about the issues that you want to hear about? How do you make them take the very risks that they're trying so hard to avoid?

The answer is persistence.

Speak up at local forums

Candidates for local office appear in forums sponsored by the League of Women Voters or neighborhood associations. These forums include a session for questions from the audience. Ask your questions, but do so artfully. Anticipate the diversion. Put it in your question. Something like this would be good:

> "Carly Candidate, you have said that you will refuse the car, credit card, and raise that come with the office you seek. I commend you for your stand, but we all know that those steps to hold down the cost of government, while good, don't affect the growth in property taxes that we are facing. What else would you propose to do to bring property taxes under control?"

That question doesn't permit the candidate to use her stock, risk-free answer. It gets the discussion beyond the perks and into the tough choices that have to be made to bring property taxes under control.

If the candidate disagrees and tells you that refusing these perks will reduce property taxes, tell her publicly that that's hogwash! The entire amount involved in her proposal won't total $25,000 annually. What is she going to do about the rest of the hundreds of millions of property taxes collected in your community each year?

Tell her that her unwillingness to give your question the attention it deserves must mean that she doesn't treat the issue of rising property taxes seriously or has no solution to offer. Tell her how difficult it is to treat a candidate seriously who hasn't thought enough about such an important issue to discuss it intelligently. After all, if this candidate wants your support, you have a right to know her positions before you give it.

Although you should make candidates take stands on the issues that you want to hear about, remember that they may not have all the answers to your questions on the spot. Allow for the possibility that a candidate may not be trying to duck and weave. Ask her whether she or her associates can get back to you later with an answer. Then see whether the opposition has anything to say on the issue.

Getting help from the media

If you can't attend forums with questions and answers, or if they aren't held where you live, ask the press to get the answers for you. The media covers press conferences and speeches given by candidates for important, and not-so-important, policy offices. Call the reporters who cover the races you're interested in and voice your questions. Ask the reporters to help you learn where the candidates stand on a particular issue. Tell the reporter what the candidate's stock, risk-free answer is and ask the reporter to get beyond it so you can cast an informed vote.

Newspapers and television stations are examining their coverage of election campaigns. They are attempting to find out — through polls and focus groups — what voters want to know about the candidates and finding ways to get that information and report it to voters.

Don't wait until your local newspaper and television station call you — call them and tell them what you want to know. Ask them to find out the answers to your questions so you can make an informed choice on election day.

You can voice your concern through letters to the editor to your newspaper. If you provide a reasoned, thoughtful letter, you may provoke a response from the candidate. You may also interest the editors or news reporters for the newspaper to follow up on the points you have made.

Several television stations also encourage letters to the editor and read them in whole or in part on the air. Many of these stations also have Internet addresses, so you can use your computer to make contact. See Chapter 6 for more information on using your computer to be heard.

Candidate questionnaires

Another way to get the information you want is through *candidate questionnaires.* Many newspapers routinely send questionnaires to candidates for many offices. The questionnaires include background information solicited from candidates as well as the candidate's views on important issues. Ask the newspaper to include your question in its questionnaire. The newspaper may not use your wording, but it may include some questions on the subject matter that you want the candidate to discuss.

Newspapers publish the results of these questionnaires shortly before election day. Read the results and determine how the candidates stand on the matters you care about. If the candidates don't answer the questions, consider that fact in deciding whom you can trust with your vote.

Many organizations also send candidates questionnaires that probe issues of importance to the organization. The results are sent to the organization's members. Neighborhood organizations, senior citizens' groups, the League of Women Voters, labor organizations, and chambers of commerce all use candidate questionnaires to obtain the type of information you are interested in having. You can ask an organization or its members to give you copies of the candidates' answers so you can read them for yourself.

Even if you're not a member, many of these organizations will still share this information with you in hopes that you'll see the value of membership and join someday. Anyway, it never hurts to ask for the information. All they can say is no.

You may already belong to a group that uses candidate questionnaires. If you do, you can volunteer to serve on the committee drafting the questionnaires to make sure that your questions are included. If you don't belong already and don't want to join any of these organizations, you can still approach any of these groups about including your questions in their questionnaires.

The questionnaires are usually compiled by the political action committees (PAC). If you belong to such an organization and want to participate, ask the head of your organization who is in charge of questionnaires and how you can participate.

When all else fails, don't forget the direct approach

Don't overlook the obvious. You can always use the direct approach to information gathering. Call the candidate and ask your question — what he or she proposes to do about property taxes, for example. If you can't get the candidate on the telephone, write a letter asking for the candidate's views on steps that can be taken to control the growth of property taxes or whatever other issue you are interested in knowing about. See Chapter 5 for more on how to contact elected officials.

 When you receive a letter back from a campaign asserting the candidate's views, you have a right to rely on that information. Keep a copy of the letter. You may have to remind the candidate or the media of his position at a later date.

Remember, the shortest distance between two points is always a straight line. You may just get a response and the information you are seeking. Stranger things have happened in politics!

 The moral: Don't be shy. If you want to know something, ask and ask often. If you are polite and persistent, you will learn enough information to make reasonably informed decisions on which candidate you would rather see win. It's the squeaky wheel that gets the oil. Fortune, like informed politics, favors the brave, the curious, and the tenacious!

Chapter 17

Campaigning for Your Vote

. . . .

In This Chapter
▶ Direct mail campaigns
▶ Advertising onslaughts
▶ Phone calls during dinner

. . . .

Republicans are roughly one-third of the voting electorate. So are Democrats. Independents or undecided voters are the third who hang in the balance and decide elections. The percentages may vary by state and by district, but thinking of the electorate in terms of thirds is a useful approach. Except in districts or states that are overwhelmingly one party or another, a candidate must appeal to a majority of the independent or undecided voters in order to win. This category of voters, by definition, is waiting to be convinced by one campaign or the other which candidate to vote for.

If a campaign is not convincing the voters with one approach and message, it needs to try another — quickly. Once a campaign really starts getting its message out, the time to an election is counted in days or, at most, weeks. A timetable like that does not permit much reflection or any indecision. When the countdown is in days, and it takes days for a message to get through, a campaign must act quickly if it's going to persuade you to vote for its candidate in time.

Launching a Direct Mail Campaign

Sometimes, sending good, old-fashioned letters, called *direct mail*, can be a campaign's best approach. Campaigns use the information gathered through polls to target groups of receptive individuals and send them literature on issues likely to persuade them to vote for a particular candidate.

You can tell a great deal about a candidate from the direct mail he sends out, including

- ✔ which subgroup he wants to target
- ✔ which issues he wants to discuss
- ✔ which hot buttons he wants to press

When you receive the direct mail, look at these items critically. See whether you think the approach the candidate is using is fair to his position and that of his opponent. See whether this candidate is the type of person you are comfortable having in elected office. That will help you decide how to vote.

Freedom from scrutiny

Direct mail is good for making more negative attacks on opponents than a campaign may be comfortable making on television. Some television stations and newspapers have started analyzing the accuracy of the campaign advertising they carry. If a candidate has to justify every word she uses in an attack, the candidate is more careful.

Little if any monitoring is done of direct mail until after the fact. Candidates can hit their opponents harder and lower with direct mail attacks than they can on television or radio.

Advantage of the delayed reaction

Candidates also use direct mail because it takes the opposition longer to respond. When a candidate makes an attack on television, the opponent has instant access to the commercial. The opponent knows just what is being said and how often the commercial is on television. The opponent even knows the minimum duration that the advertisement will run — that is, if the candidate bought time for a week or more.

By law, television stations must allow access to records of political advertisement time purchased. Those records show anyone, including the campaign being attacked, how much money the campaign making the purchase spent station by station in a media market. In other words, when a campaign uses television, the opponent knows the current scope of the war and can decide how to respond.

A candidate using television to respond can produce and air a response advertisement in 36 to 48 hours. If the candidate anticipated the attack, the response advertisement may already be produced. If it is, the response can be on the air as soon as the campaign gets the commercial and the check to the television stations. The televised rebuttal can be on the same day or the next morning at the latest.

It's very important for a candidate to respond to an attack ad as soon as possible. When an ad goes unanswered, it is more likely to strike a chord with voters.

Direct mail, on the other hand, can torpedo a campaign. The candidate being attacked by direct mail may hear from someone who heard from someone else that there's direct mail being sent. He can't just turn on the television and hear what is being said. The candidate being attacked must take some time to get a copy of the material from someone who received it.

The victim of the attack doesn't know who else received the mail, so formulating a response can be tricky. A candidate doesn't want to publicize something negative about himself to voters who may not have received the attack letter; he wants to respond only to those voters who did. No candidate wants to spend time and resources repeating and responding to an attack unless it's necessary.

In addition, direct mail takes many days or weeks to arrive. The material must be drafted, printed, and mailed bulk rate to thousands of voters. Responding by direct mail is much more time-consuming than responding by television. But direct mail does permit the candidate to restrict the scope of those receiving the response to only those who received the original attack, assuming he can determine who those are.

Targeting the right voters

Campaigns give a great deal of thought to which groups of voters should receive a campaign's direct mail. The object is to mail to those voters who can be persuaded with a message that is so compelling that they will vote for a candidate. Sometimes there is a unique issue in a campaign that appeals to only one group of voters.

Most direct mail campaigns are more general. In direct mail efforts that don't target subgroups, the handler decides which large groups of voters should receive the direct mail. Members of this group then receive three or four positive pieces on the campaign's candidate and one or two comparative or negative pieces that focus on the opponent.

An issue with limited appeal

An example of an issue with limited but potent appeal is a proposal to increase the property tax exemptions of senior citizens. A candidate may propose to increase the exemption once she is elected to the state legislature, or one of the candidates may have voted against such a proposal in the state legislature. Either way, this is an issue with tremendous appeal to senior citizens.

The candidate proposing this exemption increase uses direct mail to communicate to property-taxpayers over 65 years of age in her district. The candidate feels that this issue alone will provide those voters with a reason for choosing the candidate over his or her opponent.

Or, if the case is that the candidate's opponent voted against this proposal, the candidate communicates the opponent's negative vote to senior property owners in the district as a reason for those senior property owners to vote against the opponent.

Why is your mailbox full of political mail?

Why you? Why does your mail include one of these direct mail pieces every other day for a week or so? You checked with your neighbors on both sides, and they haven't received any. You, on the other hand, have received three or five or seven of these multicolored, self-folding, slick brochures. What list are you on to be so lucky?

The answer is simple: You are getting direct mail because a campaign has decided that it wants your vote and can get it — you are seen as a voter who can be persuaded.

- ✔ First, you are registered to vote.
- ✔ Second, your household probably consists of more than one voter. When a wife and her husband both fall into the persuadable category, the campaign can reach two voters with one copy of all the direct mail pieces. The campaign can kill two birds with one stone!

The computer list generated to produce the mail is sorted by household, not by voter. That permits the campaign to reach more voters without duplication. A campaign can get more bang for the precious campaign buck by mailing to the Jones Household on Pine Street rather than separate pieces to Mary Jones and Paul Jones. Check the label on your mailing and see for yourself.

Independence makes you popular

If you are getting direct mail from one candidate for an office, chances are you will receive it from the other candidate for that office, too. You have probably been identified by one or both of the campaigns as an independent. If a campaign has money to contact the independents or persuadable voters, in addition to whatever is done on television or radio, it will do so.

You may be classified as an independent because you received a phone call during the campaign asking for whom you are likely to vote. If you indicated that you have not decided, you are put in the category of persuadable voters and targeted to receive direct mail.

If the campaigns don't have the volunteers or money to call all voters and ask how they will vote, the campaign assumes that all nonprimary voters and those who switch their primary voting from one party to another are independents or persuadables. If the number of households in this category is too large, and therefore too costly, to mail to, the campaign may cut down the number by making assumptions based on where you live.

For example, you don't vote in primaries and are an independent, but you live in a precinct that's 90 percent or better Republican. The campaign may eliminate you from the mailing assuming that you are a Republican, even though you haven't declared yourself to be one by answering phone polls in that manner or voting Republican in primaries.

If the number is still too high, the handler may eliminate voters in 80 percent-Republican precincts, and so on until the number of households is manageable. Campaigns do the same in heavily Democratic precincts.

The method isn't foolproof, but it is rational. The campaign doesn't have enough money to do all the mailings that it would like, so the number of households must be reduced. This method makes more sense than simply mailing the list in alphabetical order until the campaign runs out of money or throwing darts at a map of the district and mailing where the darts hit.

Those voters who identify with the Republican or Democratic parties are important, too. But the campaigns assume that the vast majority — 80 to 90 percent — of the voters who identify themselves by party will support the candidates whom their parties have nominated. The campaigns spend some resources reminding these voters to vote on election day. But, unless there is a particular reason to do so, the campaigns do not send them direct mail to persuade them which candidate to support. If they vote, the self-identified party supporters will probably vote for their party's candidate. They don't need convincing. They are already persuaded.

Still stumped?

The campaign may further reduce the number of households it mails to based on the likelihood of voting. For example, a household that votes every election has higher priority than one that votes sporadically. Persuading someone who is going to vote anyway to vote for a particular candidate is easier than motivating someone to vote in the first place. If money is tight in a campaign, and it almost always is, the campaign eliminates mailings to independent voters who aren't sure bets to vote on election day.

So why didn't your neighbors on either side of you get the same direct mail that you did? Well, maybe they voted in primaries, or maybe they don't vote regularly and therefore aren't a good target for the campaign, economically. There is an even more shocking alternative: Your neighbors may not be registered to vote at all! Shame on them! When you are finished reading *Politics For Dummies,* you may want to lend them the book. Better yet, tell them to buy their own copies.

Carefully read the material that the campaigns send you. It may provide some insight into the types of elected officials that these candidates would be. The information can help you decide which candidate to support with your vote. After all, the campaigns spent a great deal of time and money getting this information into your hands. They must think that the information they are mailing you is persuasive. See if you think so, too.

"And Now a Word from Our Sponsors . . ."

Around the same time that your mailbox is stuffed with propaganda from both sides in a campaign, you are bombarded over the airwaves with the candidates' messages. In the weeks leading up to an election, candidate advertisements seem to fill up all the ad time on television. There is so much of it that you long to see the ads for your favorite beer or perfume, just for variety. You may hear the same commercials when you listen to morning radio on your drive to work. Why is the message coming at you from so many directions at once? What have you done to deserve the full-court press that you're experiencing?

The answer is that you are paying attention. The total onslaught of news coverage, mail, and advertising has made you aware that there is an election coming up. Most voters begin paying attention to an election only a few days or weeks before it is held. The campaigns try to make the most of your interest by timing their messages to arrive in your mailbox or on your television or radio during the time that you are paying attention to politics.

The timing of political advertising is also geared to cost. The Federal Communications Commission (FCC) requires television stations to give political advertising the most favorable commercial rate for 60 days before a general election and 30 days before a primary election. Those rates represent a significant savings for campaigns. The lower rates enable a campaign to show you its ads a few extra times.

When and how candidates advertise on TV

Once a campaign makes the decision to advertise on television with a message (see Chapter 10 for more on the message), the campaign still needs to determine when and how to advertise. It hires the most effective media handlers to produce and film the commercials to win your support. (See Chapter 8 for more on television and campaigning.)

The candidate wants to reach the right people often enough to get her message through. The media handler has the responsibility for determining which television shows the candidate's commercials must appear on to get that job done.

The media handler is responsible for buying the television time. Polling for the campaigns has already told the media handler who the candidate needs to reach to be successful. The fund-raiser has told the media handler how much money has been allotted to get the candidate's message out on television. The media handler now has to decide how to spend the money available as wisely as possible to reach the maximum number of voters.

The media handler decides which shows to buy advertisements on by who watches the shows. Part of that analysis is how many viewers a show has, but that's only part of it. From a political campaign's perspective, the show with the highest ratings is not always the smartest buy. For example, a show that appeals to those viewers under the age of 35 is usually not a good buy for a campaign. The percentage of voters under the age of 35 who vote is very low.

On the other hand, the percentage of voters over the age of 50 who vote is high. A media handler may decide that a show whose appeal is to a smaller number of older voters is a better buy. Most of those older voters already plan to vote. Because it is easier to persuade someone who's coming to the polls anyway to vote for your candidate than someone who is not so disposed, the older audience is a good one to target.

Older voters tend to watch the news, so you see many political commercials on news shows and shows that air adjacent to news shows. Campaigns with more limited budgets avoid prime-time shows because they are more expensive and reach too many younger people who are not likely voters.

Remember that political campaigns pay for advertising based on the number of people reached, not the number of voters reached. The media handler is looking for voters like you, not viewers. He is not selling a product that will be purchased equally by all viewers. He is selling the equivalent of Centrum Silver vitamins. That's why you'll see more political ads appearing with products that older voters would purchase and fewer political ads on shows where Guess jeans advertise. Older, or more mature, voters are more likely to vote; younger ones are less likely. The media handler will target the more mature audience every time, hoping to reach the most citizens who take their responsibility to vote seriously.

Are you a target?

If political ads are appearing on your favorite shows, it probably demonstrates that you fit the profile. It is another piece of evidence that you are being targeted. You are not paranoid! They really are after you.

You are registered, are likely to vote, and watch television shows that your peers also watch. Your tastes are typical. Because the campaign is trying to convince you and others like you to choose a particular candidate when you go to the polls, the campaign is spending its money wisely.

Advertising on the programs that you like is just another example of how important you are to the electoral process. Campaigns are spending huge amounts of campaign resources trying to get your attention. The advertisements are designed to appeal to you and persuade you to vote for a particular candidate. Rather than viewing the ads as an annoyance, you should see them as examples of how much political clout you have if you are a registered voter.

Attack of the Killer Phone Calls

Another tactic is increasingly common in the final days of a hard-fought campaign: If you are a persuadable voter with a listed phone number, you may receive a "persuasion" call. These phone calls deliver a message about the opponent that usually is very negative. It can be so negative that the campaign arranging the calling does not want any public scrutiny by the media of the message.

These telephone attacks, also called *killer phone calls,* occur so late in the campaign — often the weekend before the election — that it is impossible for the candidate being attacked to respond in time and set the record straight.

The attack may be grossly unfair and easy to respond to, but the election will occur before the candidate can get the word out. By then, the damage has already been done.

Sometimes the callers say they represent an organization whose name you have never heard before. That organization probably does not exist. The campaign paying for the call does not want to risk the backlash that may come from paying for very pointed and perhaps vicious attacks on the opposition. The campaign uses another name to deliver the negative message both to avoid the possible backlash and to give the attack more credibility with you. The theory is that you expect attacks from the opposition and therefore discount those attacks. When third parties make charges about a candidate, they are more likely to be believed by the unsophisticated voter than an attack made by the candidate's opponent.

These last-minute, vicious attacks are becoming increasingly common. Be on the alert for any calls that you receive immediately before an election if these calls do anything other than urge you to vote and vote for a particular candidate. Ask yourself: If this information is so good and so persuasive about the opponent, why is it being brought out only hours or days before the election? If the information is *that* solid, wouldn't the opponent have made it public early enough to ensure that every voter heard it? You'd better believe it. The only explanation for the delay is that the information is not that credible. Don't be persuaded to vote against a candidate by one of these last-minute, underhanded types of killer phone calls.

Chapter 18

Negative Campaigning — The Dark Side of Politics

*Y*ou hear it all the time as election day nears: "I'm sick and tired of negative campaigns. I don't want to turn on my television and see any more mud-slinging ads. Why can't these candidates run positive campaigns?"

Understanding why campaigns resort to negative advertisements and being able to recognize when a negative advertisement goes over the line are important steps to take if you want to discourage negative campaigning.

The More Things Change . . .

People tend to think of negative campaign tactics as a recent development. They believe that campaigns today are more vicious than they used to be. But you should realize that attacking an opponent in a political campaign in this country is nothing new. Some of the most vicious, most highly personal attacks occurred in political campaigns of the last century.

Slinging mud in the 1800s

The election of 1800 between President John Adams and Thomas Jefferson was a bitterly fought contest. Jefferson may have been Adams's vice president, but Adams was not above predicting the ruin of the country if Jefferson were elected president. Figure 18-1 shows a sample poster used in the election of 1800.

Republicans
Turn out, turn out and save your country from ruin!
From an Emperor — from a King — from the iron grasp of a British Tory Faction —
an unprincipled banditti of British speculators. The hireling tools and emissaries of his majesty
king George the 3rd

Figure 18-1:
This 19th-century poster shows that negative campaigning is nothing new.

have thronged our city and diffused the poison of principles among us.
DOWN WITH THE TORIES, DOWN WITH THE BRITISH FACTION,
Before they have it in their power to enslave you, and reduce your families to distress by heavy taxation.
Republicans want no Tribute-liars — they want no ship Ocean liars — they want no Rufus King's for Lords — they want no Varick to lord it over them — they want no Jones for senator, who fought with the British against the Americans in time of the war —
But they want in their places such men as Jefferson & Clinton

(*The American Heritage History of the Presidency*, 1968, p.139)

The election of 1828 between John Quincy Adams and Andrew Jackson was one of the most negative campaigns in American history. "Coffin handbills" were distributed by the Adams forces accusing Jackson of murdering six militiamen under his command. He was also accused of bigamy and adultery for having married his wife Rachel before she was legally divorced from her first husband.

For his part, Jackson gave as good as he got. He accused Adams of stealing the election of 1824 when Jackson received more votes than any candidate but lost to Adams in the decision by the House of Representatives.

In the 1884 election, Grover Cleveland's personal life became an issue. Cleveland was accused of fathering an illegitimate child. His Republican opponents thought that this accusation would kill the presidential campaign of the Democratic reformer. The negative campaign failed to work; Cleveland admitted the child might be his, and the sympathetic public elected him president.

The point is that negative campaigning is nothing new. It's been around for more than 200 years, and it's no more unpleasant now than it used to be. So why has it suddenly become an issue with voters and commentators?

Negative advertising: Johnson versus Goldwater

An example of a classic negative ad was used against Barry Goldwater, the Republican nominee for president in 1964. The television ad, which only ran once, caused an uproar across the country. It pictured a little girl picking daisies in a field. The screen then showed a nuclear explosion. The ad did not even mention Barry Goldwater's name, but the implication was that a vote for Lyndon Johnson's opponent was a vote for nuclear war.

Joining the TV generation

The use of television in political campaigns has changed campaigning in many ways (see Chapter 7 to find out some of the other ways). One of the most noticeable changes is that television forces you to view more negative advertisements in political campaigns than you ever wanted to see. You can't miss the negative message of a well-funded campaign. You see it, like it or not, every time you watch your favorite TV show.

Campaigns no longer rely only on handbills and word of mouth to bring their attacks to your attention. You see the attacks whenever you turn on your TV, not to mention hearing the attacks whenever you turn on the radio and reading the attacks when you open your mailbox and find direct mail from the campaigns. Because information is communicated so efficiently and effectively these days, it seems as if you're drowning in a sea of negative campaign commercials and mail each time an election is near.

Research on presidential campaigns from 1960 to 1988 suggests that the percentage of negative television commercials versus positive television commercials in presidential campaigns has not changed much. If anything, the research suggests that, as a percentage of political television advertising, negative commercials have decreased. In 1964, 40 percent of the commercials broadcast were negative. In 1976, the percentage decreased to 24 percent. In 1988, it rose but only to 37 percent of the total commercials. (Linda Lee Kaid and Anne Johnston, "Negative versus Positive Television Advertising in U.S. Presidential Campaigns, 1960-1988," *Journal of Communication,* Summer 1991.)

Of course, because so many campaigns now use television advertising, the fact that the percentage of the total advertising budget of any one campaign has decreased is no consolation. So many more campaigns are using television advertising that those smaller percentages of many more campaigns add up. The total volume of negative advertising that you're exposed to in a campaign cycle has increased.

You're tempted to throw up your hands and ask, "Why is politics so consumed with mud-slinging? Why can't campaigns talk about issues? Why can't they tell me positive reasons to vote for a candidate?" Before you wash your hands of politics and wonder whether the country is on the slippery slope to ruin, you should remember that our founding fathers engaged in a very rough-and-tumble brand of politics. In many ways, the campaign tactics employed in earlier presidential campaigns make today's methods seem like a tea party!

Two Principles of Campaign Communications

In order to recognize a negative commercial for what it is, you need to remember the two principles of campaign communications:

- ✔ A candidate communicates with the voters to persuade them that he cares about the same things that the voters do.
- ✔ A candidate communicates with the voters to convince them that she's a better person than her opponent for the job.

Candidates try to make you like them

The first principle of campaign communications deals with what most people think of as a positive campaign. When a candidate tells you that he cares about the same things you do, he first tells you things about himself that you'll like: his background, family, education, and qualifications, for example. The candidate also communicates on the two or three issues that polling and focus groups have identified as the most important issues in the campaign (see Chapters 3 and 15 for more on polls and focus groups).

All the communications under the first principle — whether television, radio, or direct mail — are designed to make the candidate likable to you. Political consultants believe that you will vote for the candidate with whom you are most comfortable. If the communication under the first principle can reassure you that one candidate is qualified by education, experience, and ideas to hold the office and you identify with the candidate, you will be more likely to vote for the candidate on election day.

That theory is fine as far as it goes. When a campaign is communicating in a vacuum, you are persuaded by a campaign following the first principle of campaign communications — as long as the opposition is silent. A problem arises when the opposition does the same thing. What happens when the opponent also follows the first principle of campaign communications? What happens when the opponent is also making herself likable to you and the other voters?

If both candidates have nearly equal campaign money to get their messages out, you're presented with two "likable" candidates. If both campaigns have done their jobs, the candidates and the issues they discuss in their advertisements are designed to appeal to you for your vote and are doing so very effectively. You have two seemingly well-qualified, likable candidates on the ballot. How do you decide which one to choose? That's where the second principle of campaign communications comes in.

Candidates try to make you dislike the opponent

After the candidate has given you reasons to vote for him, in a competitive campaign, he gives you reasons not to vote for the opponent. This is the area of campaign communications that gives rise to charges of negative campaigning. I discuss what makes an ad negative a little later. For now, just look at why campaigns try to make voters dislike the opponent.

If a campaign can give you a reason for choosing one candidate over the other, a reason that you will find persuasive, it does so. After all, campaigns are in the business of winning elections. Campaigns are all about convincing you to vote for a certain candidate. When contrasting the two candidates gives you a convincing reason to choose one candidate over the other, campaigns will do it in a heartbeat!

Just think about it for a minute. Campaigns would much rather provide you with a clear choice between two candidates. To do that, they look at all kinds of things to contrast the two candidates. Most of the items campaigns explore to develop the contrast are fair game. The general rule about what is fair game is reasonably simple. For example, if a candidate is an incumbent with a record, anything in that record can be brought to the attention of the voters. Any part of that record can be compared and contrasted with the opponent to make the choice between the candidates clearer. (For more specifics on what's fair game and what's not, see the next section, "Separating the Good from the Bad.")

Candidates on the receiving end of this comparison and contrast may scream foul. They may protest to the media that the opposing campaign is engaging in dirty politics and label the opponent a negative campaigner. But with fair-game ads, that label is what is really unfair.

What kind of system would we have if every candidate were free to create a picture of what she stands for, and that picture was never subjected to challenge by the opponent? All candidates should be forced to explain and justify their records. If the record of a candidate is different from the positions that the candidate is taking in the campaign, shouldn't you know that before you vote? Don't you have a right to know what a candidate has done, not just what a candidate says she wants to do? Comparing the record of a candidate with her positions in the campaign can really help you understand what she's likely to do if elected again. So any advertisement that does this comparison for you can really help you decide which candidate you want to support.

Campaigns make these comparisons to show that their candidate is better than the opponent for the job he's seeking. The comparisons help define the choice you face on election day. The process of comparing and contrasting the candidates is designed to make you feel better about the candidate you ultimately choose by making the opponent less acceptable. The hope is that you will no longer like both candidates the same; you will like one candidate more.

Separating the Good from the Bad

The $64,000 question of modern campaigning may be, "What makes a campaign negative?" Campaigns are always quick to tell us that the opposition is running a negative campaign. Sometimes people apply that label to the campaign that goes on the attack first. Sometimes one particular ad or issue is so offensive that it overshadows the entire campaign and labels it a negative one. Sometimes it's the amount of time and money spent communicating a negative or a contrast instead of a positive message that makes you label a campaign negative.

Some of the more outrageous examples of negative campaigning are easy to recognize and condemn. Some others may be labeled negative by the person being attacked but are not criticized as negative by more-objective analysts. How do you know which is which? Following some general principles can help you decide which commercials step over the line and which candidate to blame for mud-slinging.

Above-the-belt ads

Many voters define any advertisement that mentions an opponent in a critical way as a negative ad. These voters think that a candidate should talk only about himself, not the opponent. Even if you accept this definition of a negative ad, you should still be aware of the degrees of negative campaigning. Not every negative ad is or should be viewed by the public or the media in the same light.

The general rule is that anything contained in a public record is fair game. Ads containing information that is readily available to any citizen who wants to look for it may be negative, but they're not below the belt.

Public records are just that — records available to any member of the public. These are records that require no influence or underhanded methods to obtain. Examples are voting records, budgets, speeches, newspaper articles, comments from third parties who know the candidate, campaign finance reports, arrest records, lawsuits, property tax records, and financial disclosure statements required by law.

If a candidate has voted for or against tax increases, that is above-the-belt, fair-game material for ads. If a candidate has increased or reduced her office staff or office budget, that is fair game. If a candidate has taken positions on important issues like education funding, choice in reproductive rights, gun control,

---

Negative ads can actually help you cast an informed vote

Sometimes negative campaigning is necessary to give you critical information you need to make an informed decision on which candidate to support. Suppose, for example, that a candidate for state treasurer discovers that his opponent was sued by clients in her private business for mishandling their money. Suppose that those clients won the case because a jury found that the opponent was an incompetent money manager.

For the candidate to bring that information to your attention would require the candidate to air a negative advertisement. It would be a negative ad because it would mention the opponent. It would also be above the belt, because the jury verdict is a matter of public record. That ad would tell you that the jury had decided the opponent was an incompetent money manager.

Are you opposed to the candidate running a negative advertisement? Wouldn't you like to know that one of the candidates was found by a jury to be incompetent as a money manager before you vote for a state treasurer to manage your tax dollars?

campaign finance reform, and so on, all of these issues can be a productive source of contrast between two candidates. Candidates can air an ad mentioning an opponent's record based on any part of the public record and be assured that, even if the ad *is* considered negative, it will not be considered a below-the-belt attack — unless it distorts the record (see the next section).

Below-the-belt ads

There are negative ads, and then there are negative ads. A negative ad can cross the line and become a below-the-belt blow in a number of ways. Here are some of the most common methods:

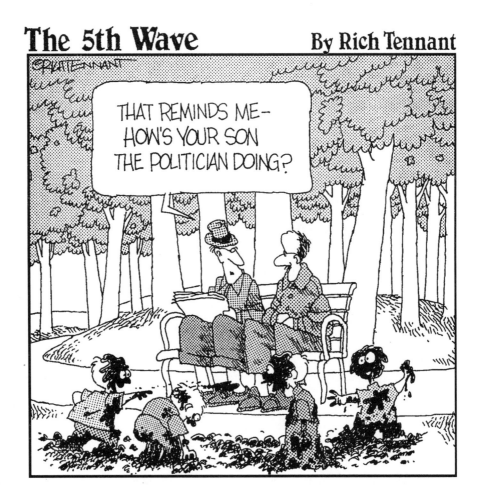

The 5th Wave   By Rich Tennant

THAT REMINDS ME — HOW'S YOUR SON THE POLITICIAN DOING?

- ✔ Distorting a candidate's record or background

- ✔ Using information obtained by underhanded methods

- ✔ Anonymous attacks on an opponent

- ✔ Using bogus groups to do the dirty work of attacking in a campaign

- ✔ Altering a candidate's photo or using an old one

- ✔ Wedge issues — emotional appeals designed to make you hate a candidate

If you determine for yourself that a candidate has engaged in below-the-belt negative campaigning, you should ask yourself whether you would be comfortable voting for that candidate. Do you really want an officeholder who either doesn't understand the difference between above-the-belt and below-the-belt punches or doesn't care?

Sneaking around

What is not fair game and is below the belt is any information that can't be obtained except by underhanded means. Any information obtained by private detectives or wiretaps or any other secret means is subject to a charge of below-the-belt negative tactics.

Normally, confidential communications with any government agency should not be the subject of campaign advertisements or attacks. Any dealings that a candidate has with the Internal Revenue Service or other government agency are not public information, unless they resulted in a lawsuit being filed. An opposing candidate should not use these dealings in a campaign unless he's willing to engage in a below-the-belt negative campaign.

Distorting the facts

Any charge that distorts the opponent's record or plays fast and loose with the facts is properly labeled negative and below the belt.

For example, say that an officeholder is justly proud of his record on children's issues. Over a ten-year period, he authored or sponsored a dozen pieces of important legislation to provide quality child care, immunizations, and funding for at-risk children (children from poor homes who are more likely to fail in school and life without additional help). His support for legislation improving the lives of children is a source of pride to him.

His opponent runs an ad claiming that a vote he cast was anti-child. The ad implies, but does not say, that the officeholder is an enemy of poor children. It is not, strictly speaking, false. But the ad is designed to create a false impression. The fact is that the officeholder cast the vote in dispute, but the vote was on an irresponsible piece of legislation that would have busted the budget. The opposition introduced the measure to force the officeholder and others to vote against it so they could use the issue in an upcoming election. The opposition had no hope of passing the legislation and no desire to have it pass.

The charge that the opponent is making with this advertisement is correct, to a point, but it goes way too far. The impression that the opponent is trying to create in your mind and the minds of the other voters is false. The officeholder cast the vote in question, but he is not an enemy of poor children — quite the contrary. Introducing a bill that you don't think should be passed to provide ammunition for an upcoming campaign is a negative campaign tactic.

Blatant lying

It goes without saying that lying about an opponent's record is a negative campaign tactic. Because catching a candidate who does something as blatant as lying is so easy, this kind of campaigning seldom happens. Negative tactics must be more subtle than that if they hope to succeed and win elections. When they *are* more subtle, like the vote-manipulation example, they have a kernel of truth in them. That kernel of truth makes the charge much easier to launch and much more difficult to defend against.

Any candidate who wants to attack his opponent had better have documentation to support the attack. If a candidate can't document his attacks, the attacks will be considered below-the-belt negative tactics, even if based on the public record.

Personal attacks

In a campaign, there are also areas of discussion that the public generally reacts unfavorably to and considers negative campaigning and below the belt even if they are based on public information. Any discussion of a candidate's personal life is generally viewed by the public with extreme disfavor. You don't want to hear that a candidate was indiscreet in her personal life, that she smoked pot while in college. You don't care how many times or whether she inhaled. Anything that comes under the heading of a personal attack on the candidate or the candidate's family is very likely to backfire on the candidate making the accusation. It is also very likely to label the candidate making the attack a negative campaigner who hits below the belt.

Anonymous literature

Attacking an opponent anonymously and using bogus groups to do the attacking are methods that occur very late in campaigns. Unethical campaigns that don't want to be blamed permit or encourage supporters to distribute leaflets attacking an opponent anonymously. These leaflets accuse the opponent of all sorts of things, most or all of which are baseless. These anonymous attacks occur so late in a campaign, usually within days of the election, that there is no time for the person being attacked to get to the bottom of this tactic. By the time the victim discovers the attack and tries to rebut it, the election is over.

Some campaigns produce the leaflets themselves, but most encourage others to do it because doing it themselves and failing to put the disclaimer language on the flyer is a violation of election law. All written material is supposed to have a disclaimer that tells people who authorized and paid for the information you are reading. If you receive information without that disclaimer, throw it away. Better yet, bring the leaflet to the attention of the media or the candidate being attacked.

Groups that want to make accusations anonymously can't be very sure of their information or position. If they are not certain enough of their charges to defend them publicly, why should you put any stock in them at all?

Killer calls

A similar negative tactic involves the use of fictitious groups that make telephone attacks on the opponent. These groups have good-sounding names, like Citizens for the Environment, or Neighbors against Crime. But they do not exist. The names are used in telemarketing attacks on an opponent in the final days of the campaign and are financed by a campaign or a party. (See "Attack of the Killer Phone Calls" in Chapter 17.)

The callers tell you that they represent these groups and are calling because they are concerned about the opponent's record or positions on issues of concern to the group. The issues are important to you, too. That's why the group carries the name it does — polling has told the campaign that this issue will get your attention and your vote.

If you receive one of these calls, ask yourself why the group waited until 72 hours before the election to communicate this important information to you. The answer is the group doesn't exist. When a phony group attacks publicly in advance of an election, its credentials are questioned. The group is exposed as a front for a campaign. That's why the campaign waits until days or hours before the election and uses telephones to communicate the message.

What you are receiving is a disguised attack by the other candidate, who doesn't want to be blamed. The campaign paying for this tactic doesn't want you to associate its candidate with negative campaigning — that could make you vote for the candidate being attacked instead. The campaign making the call also hopes you will find an attack by a third party more persuasive than a last-minute attack by an opponent, persuasive enough to make you vote a certain way.

Even using unaltered photos can sometimes be negative

Sometimes campaigns use a real photograph of the opponent to accomplish the goal of creating a negative impression with the voters. For example, in the 1994 campaign, the opponent of Republican Representative J. C. Watts of Oklahoma used a photo of Watts that was more than ten years old. Most of us would be happy if an older photo were used, but Watts had a large Afro hairstyle in those days. That hairstyle presented a decidedly different appearance than the close-cut hair Representative Watts sported in 1994.

As we all know, styles change. Hair and clothing styles that were once commonplace look ridiculous when we look at them years later. The image that the opponent wanted to put in the voters' minds was of Watts as a radical. By using the old photo, the Democratic candidate was trying to create a distorted and negative image of Watts for the voters to consider. The tactic failed to convince the voters to vote against Watts.

Altering the opponent's photo

Another technique that a negative campaign uses is altering the opponent's photograph for television commercials or direct mail. Sometimes the alterations are subtle. The candidate may have a five o'clock shadow added to an official photo. Or the official photo's smile may be turned into a scowl when the opposition uses it. The object is to alter the photo so that the opponent looks sinister or untrustworthy but can still be recognized by the voters. Negative campaigns have also recently employed a new technique called *morphing*, where a candidate's photo is changed on camera into the photo of another person. The new photo is of a person who is expected to create a negative image in the minds of voters like you who see the advertisement. The idea is to get you to associate the negative feelings you may have toward the person in the second photograph with the candidate who is being morphed.

Wedge issues

Wedge issues are emotionally charged issues that are used in campaigns to fracture an opponent's base of support. They produce a strong reaction among segments of the electorate and divide a candidate's traditional base of support into different groups, pitting those groups against each other. The candidate is forced to choose sides in an emotional conflict that will cost him votes, votes that he would normally be able to count on for support.

Wedge issues are seldom substantive issues. They appeal to emotions, not intellect. A classic wedge issue is race, which has been used to divide the base support of Democratic candidates, particularly in the South. Since Franklin Roosevelt's second election in 1936, African-Americans have voted Democratic in overwhelming numbers. Working-class white voters are also an important part of the Democratic core vote. Appeals to racial prejudice are designed to pit African-American Democrats against working-class white Democrats.

The case of Willie Horton

Race was used as a wedge issue very effectively in the 1988 presidential campaign. An ad ran blaming Governor Michael Dukakis, the Democratic candidate, for the release of Willie Horton from a Massachusetts prison. The photo of Willie Horton showed that he was African-American. The ad implied that Dukakis was soft on crime and claimed that Dukakis permitted Horton to be released to rape and murder American citizens. The subtle message was that a President Dukakis would permit African-American criminals to be released to rape and murder whites.

White working-class Democrats voted against Dukakis and for Bush. No one can say for certain whether this ad was the only reason or even the primary reason for the defection of a part of the Democratic core vote; however, it was clearly an example of a wedge issue, and there were defections in the Democratic base vote.

The case of Pamela Carter

The Willie Horton wedge issue worked for George Bush. But wedge issues can backfire if campaigns use them too obviously. An example is the 1992 Indiana attorney general's race. Democrats nominated Pamela Carter, a well-qualified, first-time candidate who happened to be African-American. Republicans nominated a white male candidate named Timothy Bookwalter. Bookwalter was convinced that if the voters in many parts of Indiana realized that Carter was African-American, she would lose the election on the issue of her race alone. African-American voters in Indiana make up only about 8 percent of the voting population.

Bookwalter had life-size cutouts of Carter made and took them from courthouse to courthouse in most of the 92 counties in the state. Each local newspaper ran a story about his visit complete with a photo of the cardboard cutout. The Bookwalter campaign achieved one goal — by election day, most voters realized that Carter was an African-American. But the strategy backfired on Bookwalter. Voters saw the move as an overt appeal to racial prejudice and elected Carter.

The case of Harold Washington

Race was also used as a wedge issue in the 1983 Chicago mayor's race. Harold Washington, the Democratic candidate, was an African-American. His opponent, Bernard Epton, ran ads telling voters to vote for him for mayor "before it's too late." The ad implied that the election of a black mayor would be the end for the city of Chicago. The slogan was also too blatant an appeal to racial prejudice. It backfired, Washington won, and Chicago is thriving.

Selling Negativity

Attacks are more likely to be viewed as negative when they only attack, as opposed to comparing or contrasting the two candidates. These attack ads simply tear down the opponent. They are not designed to make you feel slightly better about the candidate who is doing the comparing or the contrasting. The only goal of these attack ads is to make you dislike the candidate being attacked. They are so negative that the candidate making the attack does not want to risk even being in them for comparison or contrast.

Even though these attack ads may deal with matters of public record, voters react more unfavorably to them. The way the information is presented to the voters is unpleasant. The tone of the advertisement is designed to shock and offend you into rejecting the candidate being attacked. These ads are generally unpleasant to watch. Even though they don't violate the simple rule that public matters are fair game, the tone of the ads may be enough by themselves to label a candidate a negative campaigner.

Product comparisons

Voters are much more likely to accept negative information if it is presented in comparison form because of all the commercial advertising that comes in this format. Most people know the ads that compare Chevy to Ford pick-up trucks and the campaigns where viewers choose Coke over Pepsi, General Mills over Kellogg, or McDonald's over Burger King, and vice versa. Heaven knows we've seen enough Sprint or MCI versus AT&T ads to appreciate this type of comparison advertising.

Attack advertisements without comparisons, on the other hand, are used only in the political context. No commercial advertisement tells you not to buy Coke or not to buy Pepsi without offering an alternative. Chevy doesn't pay for advertisements that only attack Ford's product, and vice versa. Because these attack ads are used only in politics, you're probably more skeptical of them.

Laughter covers faults

When a candidate uses an attack ad, he sometimes tries to soften the delivery of the attack by using humor to deliver a tough message. If voters laugh when they see the ad, they are more likely to remember the ad as positive rather than negative.

Consultants are aware that you and other voters are tired of negative campaigning, so they try to vary the approach. They believe that making you laugh with an attack ad permits the campaign to get the attack message out without the risk that you will be angry at the campaign doing the advertisements. Humor can be a devastatingly powerful weapon. Once voters begin laughing at a candidate, the candidate is finished in an election. He won't be taken seriously again. The attack is still made, but the humor distracts you from the negative approach of the message.

An example of this was Senator Mitch McConnell's campaign against Senator Dee Huddleston in Kentucky. McConnell ran for the U. S. Senate in 1984 using a commercial that featured bloodhounds searching for incumbent Senator Huddleston in vacation spots where he collected speaking fees while the Senate was in session. The use of bloodhounds tempered a negative attack on Huddleston with humor and permitted McConnell to make the attack successfully.

Why Use Negative Advertising?

If a campaign takes risks in going beyond comparison advertisements or stepping over the line in talking about matters that are not public record, why do they do it? The answer is they want to win your vote.

The public may resent the negative ads, but negative ads still work. People are more prone to vote *against* something or someone than *for* something or someone. Hate is still a more potent force than love. Subtle distortions of an officeholder's record can create a false picture in voters' minds and win elections for opponents willing to use such tactics.

Besides, despite the risks, it's easier for a campaign to give you a reason to vote *against* someone in 30 seconds than it is to give you a reason to vote *for* someone in the same time frame.

Polling on the issues tests the strength of the attack in moving your support from one candidate to the other. The polls tell a campaign which attack you and other voters find the most compelling, and that is the issue that a campaign uses to attack the opponent. Remember, all negative campaigning is just designed to persuade you to vote for one candidate and not the other.

Countering Negative Campaigns

So what can you do to eliminate or reduce negative campaign tactics? As an informed voter, you can have an impact on the types of campaigns candidates run. You can do several things to reduce the amount of negative campaigning and encourage candidates to take the high road.

- Watch the marketing of the candidates carefully to determine whether anyone is engaged in negative campaigns tactics.
- Contact candidates who are running positive campaigns and compliment them.
- Write letters to the editor of your local paper criticizing negative tactics of candidates and praising candidates who are positive.
- Withhold your vote from a candidate who wages a negative campaign.

You can decide for yourself when a campaign for your vote has become too negative. Judge for yourself whether the comparison between the two candidates helps you make an informed decision or is unfair to the candidate being compared. Recognize a wedge issue for what it is — a subtle attempt to appeal to the worst in all of us. And use your voting power to punish those candidates who go over the line of fairness. Once you understand what candidates are trying to do to win your vote, you can decide whether to give it to them or to their opponents. Remember that you are in control because you are the only one who can cast your vote on election day.

Preventing negative campaigning from discouraging good candidates

In many ways, holding elective office today is more difficult than at any time in our country's history. To many voters, the word *politician* is a completely negative word. Voters think that election campaigns are more and more negative, and they don't like it. Our attitude toward politics and politicians is reflected on late-night talk shows, talk radio, and programs like *The Simpsons*. A reasonable person looking at the election process and the attitude of many voters might well let the opportunity for serving in elective office pass.

Any person willing to put herself forward for public office risks having every aspect of her life made public in the press. Some people persist in finding conspiracies in the most innocent of events and try to make a mountain out of a molehill to win a political advantage. A candidate may find herself explaining that mistakes she made were just that and not something much more sinister.

In this type of political climate, it is even more important that informed voters like you speak up and be heard. If you see a good person running a positive campaign, help him. Volunteer your time. Make a contribution. Vote for him and try to persuade your neighbors, friends, and relatives to get involved too. He needs all the help he can get. Tell him that he's precisely the type of person who should be running for office and that you're glad to see him doing it. Give him the encouragement he needs to get through he election process successfully.

When you see a candidate who deserves to be the butt of the late night television jokes, work against him. Tell people who will listen to you why they shouldn't support him. Go to public meetings and speak out about the negative campaign tactics he's using in this campaign. Don't hesitate to call him to account for his actions. Don't let his negative campaign tactics get your vote.

As long as voters are persuaded by negative campaign ads to change their votes, candidates will use negative tactics. Complaining about negative campaign tactics isn't enough. Voters like you must recognize a negative campaign for what it is and vote against it. When using negative campaign tactics costs candidates elections, candidates will stop using them. You are the key to increasing the positive nature of political campaigns.

Give 'em a pat on the back

Whatever the reason or the motive, it is a tribute to the strength of our democratic system that so many people are willing to take the risks that come with public service. When you see a politician who is doing a good job, tell her so.

- ✔ Walk up to the officeholder or write her a note and say thank you for doing a job well for the average citizen.
- ✔ When a good candidate for office asks you to volunteer or contribute, give the idea serious consideration.
- ✔ Don't forget to vote yourself.

A little appreciation in this process can go a long way toward encouraging the type of public servants we would all like to see run for and hold elective office. It can also go a long way toward keeping good officials running for the offices after they've been elected. All of us like approval; if the officeholder deserves your thanks, don't forget to give it now and again.

Chapter 19

Is Reform Possible?

● ●

In This Chapter

▶ Reducing the influence of money on political campaigns

▶ Getting more good people involved

▶ Winding up with more and better choices on election day

● ●

*W*hen most of us think about what's wrong with politics, the first thing that comes to mind is money. We think candidates are too dependent on it. It's everywhere and it makes our political system go 'round. Most Americans believe that

✔ Campaigns cost too much

✔ Special interests and their money play too big a role in politics

✔ Candidates and officeholders spend too much time raising money

Campaigns Cost Too Much

You know that a huge amount of any candidate's time is spent raising money. In today's political climate, legislative races can cost tens of thousands of dollars. Congressional races can cost hundreds of thousands of dollars. Races for U. S. Senate and governor can cost millions of dollars. What bothers you is that, in order to raise the necessary campaign finances, candidates must spend time with groups and individuals who can afford to give substantial campaign contributions.

Contributors get better access to politicians

The problem with the time candidates spend fund-raising is that, because they solicit from those who can afford to give, they spend time with the same contributors. That time gives contributors the opportunity to get to know the candidate and establish a relationship with her. The relationship big contributors form with candidates means access to the candidates when decisions are made that affect those big contributors and the rest of us.

The fact that big contributors have access does not affect every decision an elected official makes or every vote she casts. Most of those decisions are influenced by a variety of factors. (See Chapter 2 for more on the vote/money analysis.)

- ✔ Party loyalties determine how many decisions are made. The party leaders ask legislators to support the position taken by their political party to support a particular policy or to gain a public advantage.

- ✔ Legislators have friendships with other legislators. Sometimes those friendships have an effect on voting. If a colleague votes for a measure a legislative friend wants one day, he may ask the friend to return the favor another day on another vote.

- ✔ When legislators are elected, they bring their own attitudes, points of view on issues, upbringing, friendships, and political promises with them to elected office. All those factors influence how a legislator casts her vote.

The access to elected officials available to large contributors may have a role to play in how officials make decisions, but it isn't the only factor. If money could be removed completely as a factor in campaigns, these other factors will still have an impact on how a candidate behaves when he is an elected official.

If you think campaign contributions are the sole factors in determining elections, think again. In fact, 8 of the 20 most successful fund-raising candidates for Congress in 1994 lost their elections.

Voters end up paying

Although large contributions don't necessarily affect the way elected officials behave, the impact of money on politics is still of concern to you:

- ✔ Some excellent candidates decide not to run out of fear that they won't raise enough money to be competitive. When fewer good candidates seek elective office, we have fewer good candidates from which to choose on election day.

- ✔ Candidates spend a great deal of time and effort fund-raising. The time spent fund-raising is time not spent discussing issues and meeting voters.

  The more time spent with individuals and groups that can afford substantial campaign contributions, the less time a candidate has to spend with average voters like you. There are only so many hours in a campaign. You want to see candidates spending more of those hours telling you why you should vote for them. You'd like more opportunities to hear the candidates speak and to get to know them. When so much of a candidate's time is spent fund-raising, you won't have as many opportunities to get to know the candidates.

You can't remove money as a factor in politics. But you can take some steps to minimize the importance of money in political campaigns. You urge politicians to support policies that encourage as many candidates for office as possible. You can support measures to reduce the cost of campaigns.

If the cost of campaigns declines or continues to rise but more slowly than in the past, fund-raising may not consume as large a portion of the candidate's time and energy, and candidates with less experience fund-raising may be willing to run.

Campaign Finance Reform

Every so often, somebody starts a movement to reform the way campaigns and parties raise and spend money. Many ideas have been suggested to reduce the influence of money on the political process. Sometimes the debate centers on reducing the cost of campaigns themselves. Sometimes the debate concerns who should be permitted to give money and how much. Will changing the way the campaigns raise money or spend money make any difference to you?

Federal campaigns

In the 1970s, significant changes were made in the way federal elections are financed. Congress imposed limits on individual contributions of $1,000 per election, imposed an aggregate limit of $25,000 for an individual to all federal candidates in an election cycle, and imposed a limit of $5,000 per election on PAC contributions. (I discuss PACs, or _political action committees,_ in Chapter 9 of this book.)

Since the 1976 election, presidential campaigns have been publicly financed. For the general election, nominees of each _major_ party — defined as any party that won more than 25 percent of the vote in the last presidential election — have complete public financing. Complete public financing means that they cannot raise any money themselves for the fall campaign. The federal government gave the Republican and Democratic nominees $55.24 million dollars each in 1992. (H. Ross Perot did not seek federal funds.) In return, the nominees agree not to accept any direct contributions to their campaigns.

Money to fund the grants to candidates comes from taxpayers who check a box on their federal tax returns authorizing a dollar to be used for this purpose. The theory behind public funding of presidential campaigns is to reduce the reliance by candidates on wealthy contributors and the importance of fund-raising in general.

Public funding also made the amounts that each presidential candidate spends on campaigning more nearly equal. That provided an advantage to the Democrats, who were traditionally outspent by the Republicans. Public funding benefited the two major parties because minor parties either did not qualify for funding at all or qualified for only partial funding.

Loopholes

The idea behind all this campaign finance reform was to get the candidates off fund-raising and onto the issues. The campaigns would spend more time telling you what they would do if they won and less time asking wealthy individuals and groups for money. The theory was good. Unfortunately, Congress left two very large loopholes in the system: independent expenditures and soft money.

- **Independent expenditures:** Under the law, presidential candidates can spend money to get elected, and money can be spent two other ways to help elect a president: expenditures by independent committees and by state and local party organizations.

  Independent expenditures are made by individuals or committees that support the election or defeat of one or more of the candidates. They cannot be made in coordination with the campaigns that benefit from their activities, but they can be made. Their money must be federally qualified (that is, it is subject to contribution limits, and it can't include corporate or labor union dues money), but these individuals and committees can raise and spend an unlimited amount. In 1988, these independent expenditures totaled more than $13 million.

- **Soft money:** The party expenditures can be *soft money* (see the "Soft money" sidebar in Chapter 9). Candidates can spend soft money in certain ways to benefit their campaign or get out the vote. In 1988, the soft money expenditures in presidential campaigns totaled more than $47 million.

In the 1992 presidential race, the total of independent expenditures declined by more than two-thirds, but the soft money expenditures by national parties rose significantly, up more than 40 percent to almost $68 million.

As you can see, those two loopholes in the campaign finance laws for presidential campaigns are large enough to drive an armored truck or two through. The candidates help raise the money for the state and local party organizations to spend on these activities. Candidates for president curry favor from the same wealthy contributors and groups that they did before. The checks are simply made out to a different entity. The givers still have the same access to the powers-that-be as they did when making the contributions directly to the candidates.

Matching funds

Candidates for each party's nomination for president also receive matching funds in the presidential election year, if they raise money in a certain way. Public funding of presidential primary campaigns is available to candidates who raise money in smaller contributions from many givers. When candidates who are competing for their parties' nominations want to be eligible for federal matching funds, they must do several things:

- ✔ Establish functioning committees (committees that are doing something and not just existing on paper) in at least 20 states

- ✔ Raise at least $5,000 in every state in contributions of no more than $250 each

- ✔ Agree to limits on expenditures in primary states

- ✔ Receive at least 10 percent of the vote in at least one of their two most recent primaries

The money provided by taxpayers for candidates competing to be nominated only supplements the money that they raise themselves, which is substantial. The Federal Election Commission reports that Republican presidential hopefuls spent $10.6 million between January and March 31, 1995. That is nearly three times the previous high for the first three months on a presidential election cycle. That's right — $10.6 million is *three times* the previous record for the same period in the election cycle. And that amount was spent almost a full year before the choosing of the first delegate to the national conventions.

State campaigns

States have experimented with many different types of campaign finance reform. All the experiments are designed to reduce the influence of money on the political process. The four basic categories of political contributors to state campaigns are

- ✔ Corporations
- ✔ Individuals
- ✔ Political Action Committees (PACs)
- ✔ Unions

As you might imagine, there are as many approaches to regulating political contributions as there are states. The fact that so many states have taken action indicates that most states recognize problems with campaign financing. Although most states see problems, they don't all see the same problem. Interestingly, some states take one approach, and others take the opposite.

Table 19-1 shows some of the approaches that states are taking.

Table 19-1   State Approaches to Campaign Finance Reform

Approach Taken	Some of the States Taking It
Contribution limitations in all four categories	Washington, Michigan
No campaign limitations in any category	Colorado, Utah
No corporate or labor contributions	Wisconsin, Arizona
Corporate and labor contributions allowed but with an aggregate limit	Indiana
Higher aggregate limits for corporations than for individual contributors	Nevada
No corporate contributions but unlimited labor contributions	Kentucky, Tennessee
No corporate contributions, but unions can make larger contributions than any other category of giver	Massachusetts
PACs can give more than any other category of giver	Vermont, New Jersey
No limit on PAC contributions, but individuals limited to $1,000	Wyoming
Unlimited contributions but stringent reporting requirements, including public disclosure of large contributions immediately before an election	Virginia, Colorado
State parties limited in how much they can give to certain types of candidates	Minnesota, Delaware

The bans and limits imposed in many of the states seem to indicate that those states see problems with corporate and labor contributions. But notice that a state such as Nevada permits higher aggregate limits for *corporations* than for individual contributors (just the opposite of Indiana) and that still more, such as Kentucky and Tennessee, prohibit corporate contributions but permit unlimited labor contributions.

Some states, such as Minnesota and Delaware, limit the amount that state parties can give to certain types of candidates to prevent the flow of restricted money to the candidates indirectly through the state parties. State parties are usually subject to different limits for contributions because they help many candidates. When campaign finance laws limit the ability of state parties to give to certain candidates, the restrictions imposed on candidates have more teeth to them.

All of these variations on campaign finance law are attempts by the states to deal with the influence of money on the political process. The fact that states are taking contradictory steps to deal with campaign finance shows that they either don't view the problem in the same way or have radically different ideas about how to solve the problem of money and political influence.

You can judge for yourself whether the campaign finance reforms adopted in your state have made a difference. Have they changed how campaigns are financed to any degree? Examine the reports of candidates for state and local office or read the reports of the media or watchdog groups to see if the reforms have changed the sources for candidate funding or the size of the average gift.

You and other voters can urge your state representatives and state senators not to raise money from lobbyists while your state legislature is in session, and immediately before and after the session. Don't be hesitant to tell them such fund-raising makes voters like you uneasy about the access of the special interest lobbyists to the legislators and the influence they wield over legislative decisions. Tell your legislators that you aren't reassured when they raise money from lobbyists indirectly during these periods when legislation is being debated. Tell them that you won't feel any better about this practice if the money goes to their party's legislative caucus and not directly to them.

When you see a fund-raising practice you don't like, speak up. Tell the office-holder why you don't like it. Write a letter to the editor. Call into your favorite radio talk show and condemn the practice. Let your elected officials know that you are paying attention and encourage your friends and coworkers to do the same. The best way to discourage elected officials from raising campaign contributions in ways that make you skeptical about politics is to convince them that such practices will cost them more votes than the money they raise is worth. The practices you don't like will only change when you make your displeasure known and convince the elected officials that you and many others are willing to act on that displeasure.

Getting More Good People Involved

In addition to campaign finance reform, another way to improve politics is to get more good people like you involved. The first way to get more good people involved is to encourage them to register to vote. The Motor Voter Law (See Chapter 3 for more information and Appendix A for the form to register yourself) makes it very easy for us to register to vote. It's designed to encourage participation by citizens.

Each time in our history that we have removed barriers to voting, more citizens voted — as you can see in Table 19-2. The three states that have same-day registration (Maine, Minnesota, and Wisconsin) and the one state that has no registration requirement (North Dakota) vote in significantly higher percentages than the rest of the country. In fact, in 1992, 70.34 percent of these states' eligible voters actually voted. Only 54.28 percent of eligible citizens in the remaining states voted in the same election.

Table 19-2   The Results of Making Voting Easier
(Numbers represent percentage of voting-aged citizens who voted)

Year	States with Same-Day Registration	States without Same-Day Registration	Difference
1992	70.34%	54.38%	15.96%
1988	62.80	49.52	13.28
1984	64.64	52.41	12.23
1980	66.54	51.70	14.84
1976	66.88	52.73	14.15

CRS Report for Congress, Congressional Research Service, Library of Congress, January 6, 1994.

If you think it's good to get more people involved, you should support laws that make it easier for citizens to do their duty and vote. And you should support candidates who agree with that goal. You should identify every potential barrier to participation and eliminate them one by one.

Registering and voting are two very important steps you can take to get more good people (namely you) involved. Voting is the threshold test of political involvement, but it's not all you can do.

- ✔ You can encourage your friends, family, and coworkers to register and vote, too.

- ✔ You can use your newfound political savvy to support good candidates by volunteering or contributing. (See Chapter 4 for more on how to do it.) And you can encourage good people to do the same.

- ✔ You can urge good people to run for office and actively support them if they decide to do so. You might even consider running for an office yourself.

When you notice an officeholder who is doing a good job, pat him on the back and thank him. Tell him his efforts have not gone unnoticed. If an officeholder has just made a tough decision that you think is the right decision, tell her so. One way you can encourage good people in politics is to make certain that those elected officials who meet that definition stay in public service. That's more likely to happen when they know their efforts are appreciated.

You Can Improve the System

The more you can encourage government to reduce the cost of campaigns and the more you can encourage good people to become involved in politics, the greater the number of good choices you'll have to select from on election day. The more good options you have to select from, the more likely you'll be to find a quality elected official to represent you. The more quality elected officials are representing you, the more responsive the government will be to you and other voters like you.

Making officials more responsive and reducing the impact of money on politics also increases your faith in the system. When you have more faith in the system, you'll feel better about being involved and encouraging others to be involved.

Our system of government and politics is not perfect, but it's the best in the world. You should recognize that it can be improved, but you should also recognize that it's your responsibility as an American to work to put those improvements in place. After all, this is a government of, by, and for the people. And you are one of the people. If you don't demand these improvements, who will see that they happen? If you're not willing to fight to make our system of politics and government better, do you really think someone else will do it for you?

Part VI
Presidential Politics

In this part...

This part takes you from the New Hampshire primary to the national party conventions to the electoral college. Turn here to find out what actually goes into electing a president.

Chapter 20

Throwing Their Hats in the Ring

● ●

In This Chapter

▶ Visiting New Hampshire — the first primary

▶ Staying in the spotlight

▶ Straw polls

▶ Profile of a nominee

● ●

*W*hen Teddy Roosevelt was asked whether he would seek the Republican presidential nomination in 1912, he replied: "My hat is in the ring." Over the years, the expression *throw your hat in the ring* has come to symbolize any candidate's announcement to run for office.

Running in the primaries is how today's presidential candidates throw their hats in the ring. To be nominated for president, a candidate has to receive a majority of votes cast by delegates to his party's national convention. (See Chapter 21 for more on national conventions and delegates.) And the most common way for presidential candidates to win national delegate votes is by winning presidential primaries in the many states that hold them between February and June of the presidential election year. (See Chapter 3 for more on primaries.) How well presidential candidates do in state presidential primaries determines the percentage of the state delegates to a party's national convention who are pledged to vote for that candidate.

Welcome to New Hampshire

Ever since it held its first primary in 1920, New Hampshire has played an important role in the presidential selection process — a much more important role than its numbers would suggest.

New Hampshire has considerably fewer than one million registered voters and only a couple dozen delegates to the national convention of either party. It has four electoral votes to cast for president; only seven states and the District of Columbia have fewer electoral votes. New Hampshire's size certainly doesn't make it a major player in the nominating process for president, but in politics, like in many things, timing is everything.

Being the first

New Hampshire is a significant player in presidential politics because it's the first state to hold a presidential primary in every presidential election season. The 1996 primary, for example, falls on February 20. The only delegate-selection events before New Hampshire are the Iowa caucuses on February 12. (See Chapter 21 for more on caucuses.)

The New Hampshire primary is the first opportunity for candidates of the major parties to win or lose delegate votes that will be cast at their parties' conventions. A candidate who does well in New Hampshire can gather momentum going into other primaries and win more votes than expected, perhaps the nomination itself.

New Hampshire is also the first step in the elimination of candidates leading up to the choice of the parties' nominees at their conventions. As the grueling selection process continues, the number of candidates for president in both parties dwindles. Weaker candidates are eliminated, and the voters and the parties are left to choose from the two or three strongest candidates. If a candidate can demonstrate surprising strength in New Hampshire, he can keep himself alive as a contender for the nomination when others are eliminated from contention.

During the New Hampshire primary, candidates can demonstrate their abilities and their appeal to voters while the national media is guaranteed to be paying attention. Voters and the press are watching with great interest. They want to know who the candidates are, what they stand for, where they come from, what they're discussing, who will win.

Because New Hampshire is the first presidential primary, it gets more attention than it would ordinarily receive given its number of delegates. The results of the New Hampshire primary may be good indicators to other voters around the country of which candidates have more appeal to average voters. If you see a candidate in New Hampshire who does better than expected, watch him carefully to see what is was about him that appealed to New Hampshire voters. It may also appeal to you.

New Hampshire spells opportunity for presidential wannabes. It's become the first step on the journey to nomination.

Who goes to New Hampshire?

Who goes to New Hampshire? Presidential wannabes go. Anyone who thinks that he could or should be nominated and/or elected President of the United States (and who has the price of the car fare) goes early and often to New Hampshire. Remember that no candidate looks in the mirror and sees a loser. That is particularly true of those who long to sit in the Oval Office. They have convinced themselves that they are intelligent enough, hardworking enough, and honest enough — just what you and I and the rest of the country need in a president.

Sometimes candidates travel to New Hampshire early in the presidential cycle to lay the groundwork for the presidential election in five or six years — not the upcoming presidential election. They go representing a candidate who is running in the upcoming election. Their travel helps the candidates they are supporting and helps their own ambitions. Many of the activists they meet will still be on the scene for the next presidential election cycle and will be in a position to help them later.

For many politicians, travel to New Hampshire is part of a carefully thought-out strategy to keep all options open and viable. No candidate can ever be sure that the time will be right to run for president, but all want to be sure that if the time does come, they are ready!

When an undeclared candidate goes to New Hampshire for the first time, maybe as early as two years before the presidential election, the wannabe gives some other reason for going: to discuss foreign policy, to get input from voters on welfare reform, to speak to a party group — even just to see the scenery or take a vacation. Undeclared candidates give all kinds of different reasons to explain why they go. The real reason is for the exposure to voters. New Hampshire provides candidates with their first opportunity to appeal to rank-and-file voters.

New Hampshire can make or break a presidential wannabe. Getting through New Hampshire, doing well, and getting credit for that showing make up a true test of the ability of a candidate to run a national campaign for president.

Getting off to a good start

Going to New Hampshire is the way presidential candidates show that they're serious about seeking the nomination. It's the time-honored method of getting attention and coverage from the national media.

New Hampshire is small enough and has few enough registered voters who participate in the presidential primaries that it is possible for each candidate seeking primary support to personally meet every voter. Think about it: Each and every candidate shakes hands with each and every primary voter. A candidate with the stamina and the time can make enough contacts to be a contender in the election without much more in the way of resources. That is why candidates, particularly long-shot candidates, go to New Hampshire early and often.

Lesser-known candidates try to develop support among the voters in New Hampshire before the better-known and better-funded candidates arrive. They want the voters to know them and remember their names when the pollsters and the media start taking surveys. The candidates know that if their names are mentioned often enough, the press will begin paying attention to their campaign.

If a campaign gets media coverage and looks like it's gaining support, it will gain contributors. Many large contributors look upon their contributions as investments in a candidate. They are not eager to contribute if the candidate is not going to be around for the long haul. They want to back a winner. They would particularly like to be one of the first to identify and back a long-shot winner.

Who pays for the trips?

The candidates have to raise the money to pay for the early trips through normal campaign contributions. The presidential matching funds discussed in Chapter 19 don't become available until January of the election year. The trips occurring a year or two years before the primary must be financed in the usual ways that federal candidates use to raise money. See Chapter 4 for more about fund-raising.

But because candidates hope to receive federal matching dollars in January of the election year, they try to raise small contributions to fund the early days of the presidential campaign. Getting many small contributions helps the candidates fund the campaign before federal matching funds are available and also qualifies them for federal matching money when the time comes. The federal government matches contributions of up to $250 for every individual contributor with an equal amount. Therefore, contributions of $50 from ten different individuals are worth more to a candidate than $500 from one political action committee.

The battleground after New Hampshire consists of states with many more delegate votes, where the emphasis must be on campaigning by television rather than person-to-person contact. And many states, in different regions of the country, hold primaries on the same day, which makes personal contact as a method of generating support impractical. Candidates have to compensate with television, which requires money — money that they hope to get after a strong showing in New Hampshire, even if they don't actually win their primary.

Candidates who think of themselves as presidential material go to New Hampshire to earn their stripes, to build momentum in a small state where it is possible to compete on limited resources. The candidates hope that the momentum will bring them enough publicity, support, and money to enable them to compete in states where they'll need greater resources.

Staying in the Spotlight

When a candidate runs in the New Hampshire primary, the opportunity for media coverage is there, win or lose. The media, particularly the national media, is obsessed with analyzing politics in terms of horse races. Who is winning? Who is losing? Did so-and-so do better than expected? Did she do worse than expected? A candidate who succeeds in diminishing the media's expectations for her performance in New Hampshire and then exceeds those expectations may get more media attention than the candidate who wins!

Getting a bounce

The media attention in New Hampshire is very important to the future success of presidential wannabes. If a candidate does better than expected, he can get what's called a *bounce* out of New Hampshire. That means that the media does stories about him and begins speculation that this candidate has a real chance to win the nomination. Doing especially well in New Hampshire usually means finishing an unexpected first or second.

A candidate who does particularly well in New Hampshire has the opportunity to gain many things in addition to a modest number of delegate votes at the national convention. A candidate can use the momentum he gains in New Hampshire to

✔ Raise additional money from campaign contributors

✔ Add new givers to his list of contributors

 ✔ Obtain endorsements from party officials in other states

 ✔ Gain national media attention

 ✔ Increase local media coverage in other states

Because New Hampshire is the first primary, it attracts the most serious contenders for the nomination. A strong showing in New Hampshire can even help candidates who lose in the primary — that is, as long as that strong showing is stronger than the media expected to see, in which case those results may be interpreted as a moral victory for the losing candidate.

Pat Buchanan, George Bush's competition for the Republican nomination in 1992, benefited from such a moral victory in New Hampshire. The stories that followed Buchanan's strong showing in New Hampshire helped his fund-raising and helped portray him as a serious opponent to the incumbent president. The stories about Buchanan's strong showing got as much or more play than the fact that George Bush won the primary.

The media can also hurt

The media attention in New Hampshire can also undermine a campaign if the publicity is unfavorable. The unfavorable publicity can occur if a candidate does more poorly than expected. The key word here is *expected*.

Early on in the process, the media asks the candidate what vote percentage would make him happy in the primary. If the candidate doesn't get as many votes as he predicted he would, the press does a negative story. On the other hand, the candidate who gets more votes than she predicted gets favorable publicity. The strategy of making such predictions is risky, but as the expression goes, no guts, no glory! To be credible, the candidate must convince the media that he or she is the candidate to watch, the one who has to win before the primary is held. It does no good to spin the media after the fact. The national press has heard it all before. (See Chapter 1 for more about spin doctors and their roles in campaigns.)

A campaign can also be undermined if the media plays up the showing of the opposition. In other words, Carly Candidate wins the primary, but the next day's headlines are all about Kyle Candidate's strong showing. The lead stories on television and the headlines in the newspaper are all about Kyle Candidate, speculating that Kyle Candidate is coming on strong, a real possibility to win the nomination. Kyle Candidate may be the one.

A day at the races

The media spends a substantial amount of time in any campaign speculating on who will win and who will lose the election. That speculation is called *the horse race question.* Who is winning a campaign and who is losing is news. Voters don't want to waste their votes on a candidate who has no chance to win the election. But too much speculation on the horse race question can harm the process. If the press reports early in the campaign that Carly Candidate is way behind and would have a tough time winning, that report can become a self-fulfilling prophecy. In other words, the report of Carly's slim chances can kill Carly's chances.

Contributors shy away from wasting their money on a candidate who can't win. Volunteers may look for another candidate who is in the running to work for. Voters and the press won't pay much attention to Carly's suggestions for change or ideas for improvement because she isn't really in contention. As a result, you may not get all the information you might otherwise need to help you make your choice for a candidate in a closely contested race.

When you see horse race stories reported early in the campaign process, take them with several shakers of salt. If you think the newspapers and television stations are not giving you enough coverage of Carly and her opponent's ideas, call them and complain. If you want more information on substance than you've been getting, go out and get it. See Chapters 5 and 6 for ideas about how to do that.

The media covers the first events in the presidential election season very thoroughly. It helps to create front-runners and raises the expectations for candidates' performances. The media emphasis on horse-race stories, which candidate is ahead and which candidate is gaining, can lead to early identification of a candidate as a front-runner — although front-runners sometimes finish last (see the upcoming sidebar).

The print and television media can have a significant influence on which candidates are still in the hunt for the nomination after the early primaries and caucuses. Their positive or negative reporting on candidates can make or break fragile campaigns. In many ways, the media performs the function that used to be performed by the party, screening the candidates to reduce the number. From the huge number who may begin the presidential selection season, the process cuts most out for one reason or another, leaving usually the most able of the bunch, and they become the nominees.

Front-runners sometimes finish last

Early identification as a front-runner used to be the key to winning the nomination. A *front-runner* is someone who is sufficiently ahead in the polls that the election is seen as his to lose. He has to make some mistake to enable another candidate to win.

From 1936 through 1968, candidates who were ahead in polls at the beginning of the election year went on to win their parties' nominations. Recently, this has not been true for Democratic candidates. In fact, for a Democratic candidate who is not an incumbent president, being ahead in the polls going into the heat of the presidential nominating process has been almost the kiss of death for any hopes of securing the nomination. Check out the following list of recent front-runners for the Democratic nomination at the beginning of each election year:

1972   Edmund Muskie

1976   Hubert Humphrey

1988   Gary Hart

1992   Jerry Brown

None of these front-runners went on to win the party's nomination for president.

Being the most "able" of the bunch doesn't necessarily mean having the kinds of qualities that you might like to see in your friends or next-door neighbors. The ability to succeed in presidential politics means having characteristics that may not seem like attributes to most of us. Candidates do have to be hardworking, intelligent, and articulate, to varying degrees, but they also have to be single-minded, ruthless, good at raising money, and thick skinned. Remember that you are selecting the leader of one of the largest, most powerful nations in the world, not your next dinner companion, through this process.

Straw Polls

In addition to getting media coverage in New Hampshire, another way candidates gather momentum behind their campaigns is by winning *straw polls,* which are unofficial, unscientific surveys. Straw polls are informal, nonbinding trial votes taken at party functions in certain states. Anyone who pays a set amount, usually $25, can vote in a straw poll. Many times voters don't even have to live in the state. Participants in a straw poll are asked which of their party's candidates for president they prefer from a list of candidates willing to compete in the straw poll.

State parties are increasingly using the straw poll for presidential candidates as a fund-raising device because the party gets to keep the money participants pay to vote. A straw poll is not a scientific indication of the strength of the candidates in a state. In fact, presidential candidates, eager to win a straw poll, often bus or fly in supporters and sometimes even pay their fees to vote. If winning a straw poll has any significance, it shows that the winning candidate is the best-organized and funded candidate in the state. It does not necessarily demonstrate that the winner is the most popular candidate with the voters.

Winning straw polls gets candidates favorable stories in the media. The winning candidate then uses these favorable stories to motivate people to contribute to his campaign. If you read about a presidential candidate's victory in a straw poll, don't give that victory much thought. The winner may be better organized and funded than his opponents, but you want to know what he thinks about issues of importance to you.

Introducing the Nominees

Do political nominees have anything in common besides a good self-image and a healthy dose of ambition?

The answer is yes. Most of the nominees of both parties in the last 20 years have been current or former officeholders who generally come from one of three places: the presidency, the vice presidency, and state governors' offices. The U.S. Senate was also a source of presidential nominees before 1976 and may be again, 20 years later: The 1996 Republican candidates include four senators.

Governors have been favored as nominees in recent years. It may be because they have experience in running state governments and making the tough decisions on how to balance the budgets of their states. It may be because voters have more confidence these days in their state and local governments than they do in their national government. It may also be because such candidates are not "tainted" by being part of the problem that many voters view Washington as being. Whatever the reason, there has been a governor or former governor on the ballot for president in every election since 1976.

Presidents and vice presidents continue to be key sources of nominees for both political parties. In fact, in the 60 years from 1932 to 1992, an incumbent president or vice president has been on the ballot for every election but one — 1952, when Harry Truman declined to run again, and his 75-year-old Vice President, Alben Barkley, was denied the nomination at the convention.

Table 20-1 shows the presidential ballot from 1976 to 1992 and illustrates how the executive branch — at both the national and the state levels — has been well represented.

Table 20-1	Recent Presidential Nominees and Their Prenomination Occupations			
Year	*Republican*	*Occupation*	*Democrat*	*Occupation*
1976	Ford	President	Carter	Governor
1980	Reagan	Governor	Carter	President
1984	Reagan	President	Mondale	Vice President
1988	Bush	Vice President	Dukakis	Governor
1992	Bush	President	Clinton	Governor

Candidates without elective-office experience have sought the nominations of both parties unsuccessfully. For example, Jesse Jackson sought the Democratic nomination in 1988, and Pat Buchanan sought the Republican nomination in 1992 — neither had elective-office experience. H. Ross Perot, running as an independent in 1992, lacked such experience as well.

Chapter 21

National Party Conventions

*B*oth major parties hold conventions during the summer of a presidential election year. Delegates to each convention ratify the party's choice for president and nominate the choice for vice president.

Independent candidates for president don't go through the nominating process at all; after all, independent candidates don't represent a party. Because they don't have to secure a party's nomination for president, they don't enter primaries, caucuses, or conventions.

Sending Delegates to the National Convention

The national conventions are held every four years in the summer of the presidential election year. The party to which the current president belongs has its convention in August; the other party — the *out party* — traditionally has its convention in July. In 1996, however, both parties' conventions are in August. The national committee of each party decides where to hold its convention.

The national committees of both parties consist of party officials from the 50 states and representatives of other groups within the party organizations. Each state party decides how it selects its representatives to the national committee, subject to national party rules.

Democratic and Republican party representatives, called *national delegates,* meet at the party's national convention to choose the nominees for president and vice president. Each state has a number of delegates allocated to each party based on the population and the relative strength of each party in the state.

The total number is different for each party. Getting the Republican nomination for president means getting a majority of the more than 2,000 Republican national delegates to vote for you. Getting the Democratic nomination for president in 1996 means getting a majority of the more than 4,000 Democratic delegates to vote for you.

Table 21-1 lists the number of delegates to the Republican and Democratic national conventions for U.S. states and territories for 1992. The numbers vary a bit for each presidential election year.

Table 21-1   U.S. State and Territory Delegates for 1992

State	Republican	Democrat	State	Republican	Democrat
Ala.	38	62	Alaska	19	18
Ariz.	37	47	Ark.	27	43
Calif.	201	383	Colo.	37	54
Conn.	35	61	Del.	19	19
Fla.	97	160	Ga.	52	88
Hawaii	14	26	Idaho	22	24
Ill.	85	183	Ind.	51	87
Iowa	23	57	Kans.	30	42
Ky.	35	61	La.	38	68
Maine	22	30	Md.	42	79
Mass.	39	106	Mich.	72	148
Minn.	32	87	Miss.	33	45
Mo.	47	86	Mont.	20	22
Nebr.	24	31	Nev.	21	24
N.H.	23	24	N.J.	60	117
N.Mex.	25	33	N.Y.	100	268
N.C.	57	93	N.Dak.	17	20
Ohio	83	167	Okla.	34	53
Ore.	23	53	Pa.	91	188

State	Republican	Democrat	State	Republican	Democrat
R.I.	15	28	S.C.	36	49
S.Dak.	19	20	Tenn.	45	77
Tex.	166	214	Utah	27	28
Vt.	19	20	Va.	55	92
Wash.	35	80	W.Va.	18	39
Wis.	35	91	Wyo.	20	19
D.C.	14	30	Amer. Samoa	0	4
Democrats Abroad	0	9	Guam	4	4
Puerto Rico	14	57	Virgin Islands	4	4

The methods of selecting these delegates are a combination of party rules and state statutes. Most are now selected by primaries. (Chapter 20 talks more about primaries.) Two-thirds of the Democratic delegates and three-fourths of the Republican delegates are selected that way.

Democrats also have *super-delegates* — people who are automatic delegates to the national convention by virtue of their office or position. Super-delegates include all sitting governors, Members of Congress, and Democratic National Committee members. Super-delegates account for about 18 percent of the delegates to the Democratic National Convention.

Conventions don't choose presidential nominees

That's right. The national conventions don't choose the nominees anymore. Voters voting in presidential primaries and party people in caucus states determine which candidates have enough votes to be the nominees. The voters and party people in the states choose the nominees. The conventions simply ratify those choices.

The national conventions rubber-stamp the primary, caucus, and convention selections that occur in each state from February to June of the election year. The trend in this country in the last 25 years has been toward primary selection for the national delegates based on the primary showings of the presidential candidates. In some states, voters express their preference for presidential candidates, and the delegates are selected later through a different selection process. In other states, voters vote directly for the delegates. The ballot may or may not indicate which candidate the delegate is supporting.

Conventions historically chose the nominees

George Washington was elected president twice with no process in place for nominating him. No one disputed him as a choice. Each member of the Electoral College simply cast two votes for president, and Washington was chosen unanimously. That was the last time there was unanimity behind any choice for president.

A nominating process became important after Washington, when there were alternative candidates for president. Our nation experimented with a couple of methods of nominating national candidates before the parties began holding national conventions.

The national conventions gave party leaders control of the selection of presidential nominees. *Brokered conventions,* where party leaders traded support for a candidate for other considerations, were the norm.

Over time, particularly since 1968, the influence of the party leaders on the nomination process has diminished as primaries have increased in importance. The deals and compromises in the selection of nominees that were commonplace in the last century have ended. Because primaries are the key way to select nominees and delegates, more people participate in the selection process now than at any time in our history.

The selection process varies from state to state and from party to party within the same state. For example, in 1992, Democrats used the primary in states where the Republicans used a caucus or state convention to choose their delegates. In 1968, only 17 states chose their delegates by primary. In 1996, more than 40 states are using this method.

Because the national conventions ratify the choices of voters and party people, those voters participating in the primaries, conventions, and caucuses play a much more important role in the selection of the presidential nominees than ever before. By voting in your presidential primary or participating in your party's caucus or convention, you have an important role to play in who will be the next President of the United States.

These days, most delegates go to a convention committed to vote for a certain candidate on the first ballot. That is particularly important because all the nominees of both parties have been selected on the first ballot ever since the time Democrats required three ballots to nominate Governor Adlai Stevenson of Illinois for president.

POLITICAL STUFF

What in heaven's name is a caucus?

The term *caucus* comes from a Native American word that means to speak or to counsel. It has several meanings in politics:

- A meeting of residents of a district who are of the same political party to elect state and national convention delegates and vote on party platforms and policies (for example, the *Iowa caucuses*)

- A meeting of individuals of the same party who share an interest in an issue or have ethnicity or race in common to promote policies favored by the caucus (for example, the *Congressional Black Caucus*)

- A group of elected officials of one party that meets behind closed doors to plan strategy and elect its own leaders (a *legislative caucus*)

- A meeting of party leaders of one political party to fill vacancies on the ballot or vacancies in office caused by the death or resignation of certain types of officeholders

A lot of meanings for one little word!

What happens at the national conventions?

The national conventions play a less important role than they once did in selecting nominees, but they still perform other very useful functions:

- ✔ Approve the selection of the presidential nominees
- ✔ Approve the selection of the vice presidential nominees
- ✔ Adopt party platforms
- ✔ Adopt the rules that govern the parties for the coming four years
- ✔ Showcase the candidates and future candidates of the parties
- ✔ Rally the troops for the fall campaign

Selecting the vice president

No method is in place for the general public to choose candidates for vice president. The choice of vice president is in the hands of the convention delegates. The conventions traditionally defer to the nominee for president to choose a running mate, who is then presented for nomination to the convention.

POLITICAL STUFF

When the convention chose the running mate

The last time there was a real battle for the vice presidential nomination in either party was the 1956 Democratic National Convention, when Adlai Stevenson, the Democratic nominee for president, left the choice of a running mate to the convention. He did not ask the convention to ratify his choice — he let the convention choose. For two dramatic ballots, Senator John Kennedy of Massachusetts ran neck and neck with Senator Estes Kefauver of Tennessee before Kennedy lost the nomination on the third ballot.

The convention and the excitement of the balloting for vice president were carried on national television. The exposure that Kennedy received during the 1956 convention helped him to secure the presidential nomination itself in 1960.

Presidential nominees have to consider the wishes of the delegates because the delegates have the right to reject the presidential nominee's choice if it meets with disfavor. Occasionally, presidential candidates generate excitement and a spirited campaign by throwing the nomination of a vice presidential candidate to the delegates to choose. See the "When the convention chose the running mate" sidebar for details.

Sometimes the choice of a running mate provides the only element of suspense in the convention proceedings. The delegates don't know the nominee's choice for a running mate until the convention actually begins. George Bush made his surprise announcement of Senator Dan Quayle as his choice for vice president as the Republican National Convention began in New Orleans in 1988.

Adopting platforms

Conventions adopt *platforms* — declarations of principles and policies — for the national parties and thereby develop a consensus approach to important issues of the day. The platforms define who the parties are and what they stand for. The platform can also serve as a framework for discussing the issues to be debated in the fall election campaign.

Unifying the party

Each party's convention adopts the rules for governing the party for the next four years and resolves questions about how to run the party. It serves to focus party members' attention on the opposing party and candidates rather than on rifts within the party itself.

The various factions of the parties that supported losing candidates through the nominating season are encouraged to focus on what unites them rather than on what divides them. The convention showcases the party nominees, calls attention to the party's rising stars, and unifies the party faithful.

National conventions serve to unite the Republicans or Democrats in a common cause: electing a national ticket. Parties spend a great deal of time and money organizing these conventions. In fact, each political party received $10,600,000 — apiece! — from federal matching funds to run the 1992 conventions and raised many millions more from private sources.

The Politics of the Conventions

At national conventions, everything is organized. The organizers want nothing left to chance. Even the placement of the state delegations is the subject of much debate and jockeying. Every delegation wants to be seen on television. Every delegation wants to be immediately in front of the stage to be able to see the nominees and other dignitaries up close and personal.

Who gets to address the conventions and what the speakers get to say are also rigidly controlled matters. With the possible exception of former presidents, speakers must submit their remarks in advance to those party people in charge of the convention and receive clearance for what they want to say.

If you watch conventions on television, you see many floor demonstrations. Delegates march around the floor waving signs and chanting. These demonstrations appear to begin spontaneously in the crowd and spread through the hall, gathering force as they go. Those "spontaneous" demonstrations are actually carefully orchestrated. Delegates are told not only when to demonstrate but which signs to wave.

The convention organizers distribute many signs of different shapes and colors during the convention. Delegates may be told to wave the red, square signs at one point and the blue, rectangular ones at another.

Creating the right effect

Campaigns leave nothing to chance at their national conventions because appearance is very important when the national media is watching closely and some cable networks are providing gavel-to-gavel coverage. If the event is staged properly, it can emphasize the unity of the party and its enthusiasm for its candidates. A successful convention can set the mood for the fall campaign and project an image of confidence.

A poorly executed convention can have a negative impact on a party's chances in November. In 1992, the Republican Party heavily emphasized family values and religion. The speeches at the convention appealed to Republican delegates sitting in the audience but irritated the less partisan voters, particularly women, watching the convention at home. Many convention follow-up stories cited public opinion research that showed voters' uneasiness by what was viewed as an exclusionary message of the Republican convention.

Concentrating partisan energies

Although everything is carefully scripted, the conventions are great unifying and energizing forces for Democrats and Republicans alike. When the delegates leave the convention, they are part of something bigger than themselves. That something the delegates are part of has a clearly defined objective: victory in November.

The delegates leave eager to get home and accomplish the objective. The conclusions of the conventions unleash a flood of energy that flows across the country into every state in the union. The timing of the floodgate's opening is also important because the conclusion of the national conventions signifies the start of the fall campaign.

Playing Your Role as a Voter

Today, more people — voters, *regular* people — have the opportunity to participate in presidential selection because more states are using the primary selection method. Millions of Americans participated in selecting the nominees of both parties in 1992, but the overall percentage was still very low. Only 19.6 percent of the voting-age population in primary states bothered to vote in the 1992 presidential season. Less than one in five of those who could vote spent the 15 minutes it takes to cast their ballots to choose the nominees for the most powerful position on Earth.

Whatever the reasons, it is important that more people participate in the selection process. Democracy works well only when people inform themselves about the issues and the candidates and make their wishes known. Reading this book is a great way to get informed about the process and ready to participate on every level, including helping to choose the next President of the United States.

If you don't like the alternatives, change them. Run for office yourself or persuade good people to do so. Work for their election. Tell your neighbors and friends to vote for them. Contribute to their campaigns. Get off your duff and make things better. See Part II for how to do it.

If you think money plays too big a role in politics, get campaign finance reform laws passed in your state. Start a movement to change the campaign finance laws on the federal level. Don't let yourself be what Spiro Agnew, Richard Nixon's former and very undistinguished vice president, used to call a "nattering nabob of negativism." Every journey begins with a single step. You can start a movement to improve our democracy. That's a pretty good legacy to leave your children.

Chapter 22
Electing a President

• •

In This Chapter

▶ What's different about a presidential campaign, and what's the same

▶ Researching the candidates

▶ Graduating to the Electoral College

▶ Does your state swing?

▶ Volunteering for the presidential campaign

• •

*T*he conventions are over. The Democratic and Republican parties have their nominees for president and vice president. If there's a third party or independent candidate for president, her name is on the ballot in all 50 states. The process has weeded out any unfit candidates and left only candidates qualified to be president by virtue of experience, background, intelligence, and stamina. The preliminaries are over. The campaign has begun. But you can still get involved in the process.

The presidential election campaign involves every corner of this country. Some corners are more important in the strategy than others (I discuss which ones later in this chapter, under "The Electoral College and You"). But, because the election is national, you have plenty of opportunities to get involved if you want to. You also have many ways to become more knowledgeable about the process. You'll cast an informed vote if you do, and you'll be able to impress your friends at cocktail parties with your political savvy.

Contributing to the Party, Not the Nominee

Thanks to federal funding of presidential campaigns, money is not *as* important in the general election of presidential nominees as it is in every other campaign. Note the emphasis. Money still plays a role because the campaigns have to make choices every day on how to spend the money available to maximize the votes for their nominees.

The difference in a presidential race is that candidates — once they become official nominees and accept federal funding — can't raise money for themselves. Nominees who qualify for federal money can't ask you to contribute to their campaigns at all once they are the nominees.

Although nominees cannot raise money for their campaigns, the national parties can still raise money to spend on the election — and the nominees can help out in this fund-raising. The direct mail solicitations you receive may use the name of your party's nominee in the message, but the difference is that the checks are made payable to the national parties — the Democratic National Committee, the Republican National Committee, or a third-party committee — not the nominee's campaign.

If you are so disposed, you can respond with contributions to the party of your choice. Those contributions help the parties raise additional *soft money,* which they use to fund the campaign in a presidential election year. Each of the two major parties raised and spent $40,000,000 in soft money in 1992.

Soft money is money contributed to state and national political parties that the parties can use for the election of their candidates. Parties are not limited in the amount of soft money they can raise, but they are limited in how they can spend soft money. The FEC (Federal Election Commission) establishes rules for how soft money can be spent by political parties. Soft money cannot be contributed directly to any federal candidate because it's not federally qualified money. It may include corporate or labor union dues money or contributions from individuals or PACs in excess of the federal limit on contributions.

You can also donate to a third party or an independent candidate who is not eligible for or does not accept federal funding, if that is your preference. Any of these alternatives increases your involvement in the presidential campaign.

Getting Your Message to the Candidates

Because presidential nominees don't spend as much time fund-raising, they have more time for courting you and the other voters. They spend their time meeting voters, speaking to groups, debating the issues, and seeking support from voters. They don't spend as much time with well-heeled contributors seeking contributions to run their campaigns.

Who gets federal campaign funds?

The Democratic and Republican nominees are entitled to receive federal funds for presidential campaigns. They each receive the same amount, and that amount is set by the FEC, the Federal Election Commission.

Minority parties that received between 5 and 25 percent of the vote in a prior presidential election are also eligible for money in advance of the presidential campaign.

Independent candidates for president are not usually entitled to federal funds for the campaign, but sometimes the FEC can treat an independent candidate as a representative of a party. For example, John Anderson ran as an independent candidate for president in 1980. After the election, the FEC determined that Anderson's supporters were a party within the meaning of the federal funding law and awarded campaign funds based upon the percentage of the popular vote Anderson received in the 1980 election.

Brand-new third parties don't have a track record for the FEC to make a determination of the amount of money they are entitled to receive in their presidential campaign. New third parties that wish to qualify must raise their own campaign money before the election. They must observe the overall limitation on spending imposed by the FEC, and the candidate can't use more than $50,000 of his own money in the campaign. If the new third party follows the requirements and receives more than 5 percent of the popular vote, the FEC will award the third party federal funds after the election.

Fund-raising may not be as crucial in a presidential election campaign as in other campaigns, but the message is every bit as important. By the time the conventions are over, the candidates have polled and used focus groups extensively (see Chapter 15 for more on polls and focus groups). The nominees for president are just as eager to know which issues you care most about as your candidates for the House of Representatives, the Senate, and the state legislature are.

Sending the right message

In 1992, Bill Clinton's campaign staff put up a sign in campaign headquarters that read, "Change versus more of the same. The economy, stupid! Don't forget health care." The purpose was to remind the campaign staff and the candidate to stay focused on the issues that the consultants had identified as the winning ones.

The polling and focus groups that the Clinton campaign conducted convinced the campaign consultants that, in 1992, voters were most worried about the economy of the country. The Clinton campaign decided to focus primarily on that issue. The sign reminded the campaign workers to keep their focus. No matter what the national press, George Bush, or Dan Quayle wanted to talk about, Bill Clinton and Al Gore had to keep talking about the economy.

Finding the right message and sticking with it are critical to a campaign's success. A candidate has to repeat her message over and over and over again until she almost gags when she speaks it. Only at that point can her message penetrate the barrage of information that the voting public receives each and every day.

Identifying issues in your region

Polls and focus groups also alert the nominees to specific issues of importance in regions around the country. For example, grazing on federal land may be an important issue in Wyoming and Montana. If it is, any presidential nominee campaigning in those states had better be prepared to answer questions about it. Grazing on federal land is not an issue in Florida, but immigration may be.

Keeping candidates abreast of change

A candidate must constantly evaluate his message and whether it is getting through. If a candidate isn't flexible enough to change his message when such an action is warranted, he will lose.

As an example of how key issues can change, look at the 1980 campaign between Jimmy Carter and Ronald Reagan. Early in the campaign, no one realized the prominent role that the American hostage situation in Iran would play; few voters would have mentioned it in polls or focus groups before it became the subject of nightly news broadcasts. As the election unfolded, it may not have been the deciding issue — inflation and the economy may have been more important — but it was a big issue.

The Primary Message May Not Be the Final Message

Just as leaves change color in autumn, the message that a candidate for the party nomination communicates to primary voters or caucus participants in his own party may not be the same message that he needs to use in the fall campaign.

To win the nomination of either major party, a candidate has to give the party regulars something to be excited about. In each party, that attempt pushes the candidate to one end of the political spectrum or the other. The pressure on Democratic candidates pushes them to be more liberal; for Republicans, more conservative (that is, more liberal or more conservative than the voting population as a whole). The candidates have to respond to the party's pressure if they are to win the nomination. They have to energize the true believers among the party faithful. They have to inspire these people to work for their nomination.

But the message candidates use to win the nomination may not help them win the general election. In fact, the nomination message can actually hurt a candidate's chances for victory in November. A winning candidate in November has to be a consensus builder who inspires the confidence of a broad range of voters. These voters don't want candidates to take controversial stands on issues.

Look at what happened to Walter Mondale in 1984. He took a controversial position and called for a tax increase to deal with the federal deficit. He was soundly defeated. No one can say for certain whether this issue alone caused his defeat, but it was mentioned by voters who didn't vote for him in interviews after the election.

Nowadays, voters seem to tune out those candidates who take specific positions on controversial issues. Campaign consultants urge candidates to say as little of substance as possible. After all, candidates can't be heard saying one thing to the party faithful during the nomination stage of the campaign and repudiating those same things later. Flip-flopping on an issue of importance can make a candidate seem to voters at best indecisive and at worst a liar. You and the other voters will assume the worst from such an abrupt change of heart. That is why campaign consultants try to package the most plain-vanilla message they can on the issues and concentrate on other things.

When candidates discuss and define the issues, with input from us, they can generate a national consensus about an issue or a problem. When a national consensus forms, it is easier to enact the necessary laws to deal with the issue or problem. Voters become aware of the problem and agree that something needs to be done. That attitude on our part helps to shape the legislative agenda in our states and in Washington.

Getting the Information You Need to Vote for President

You can make it a point to follow what the presidential candidates are saying about important issues. See if you can distinguish the differences in approach to problems among the candidates.

One way to tell the differences among candidates is to watch the debates sponsored by the Commission on Presidential Debates. These events, and there's usually more than one in a campaign, are a unique way to view the nominees in an extended give-and-take on important issues. Watching one or more of these debates gives you a good opportunity to see what you like and dislike about the candidates and helps you become a more informed voter.

The media loves a presidential campaign

It's easier for you to learn about presidential candidates and their positions than about candidates for less-visible offices because everything presidential candidates do is reported. They can't sneeze in a campaign without making the national news. Reporters follow presidential candidates like flies follow honey. They hang on the candidate's every word hoping for a mistake or misstatement that will make a good news story. Presidential nominees can compete successfully with train wrecks and hurricanes for time on the national news.

Candidates for local offices or for Congress can call press conferences or release position papers during a campaign and get little or no response from the press. This is particularly true when they are explaining their ideas on programs or policies that are important but not controversial. A well-used adage for television reporting is: "If it bleeds, it leads." In other words, an item has to be gory or sensational to warrant television coverage. Releasing position papers may provide insight on a local or state candidate's views, but it isn't sexy or exciting, so it doesn't get on the television news.

Presidential nominees don't have that problem. Virtually everything they do makes news. That gives the nominees a distinct advantage over other candidates in making their case directly to you and other voters. The nominees may not always like the coverage they get from the media, but at least they can't complain that they don't get coverage.

Turning to nontraditional media

Lately, candidates have been dissatisfied with the way the press reports their messages. They feel that traditional network news, political talk shows, and newspapers interfere with their ability to talk directly to voters, that reporters are too cynical. The response from the press is that candidates are annoyed because they can't hoodwink professional reporters. Whatever the reason, candidates tried a new approach in 1992.

A number of candidates for president developed an approach to talk directly to you and other voters using free television and radio but without permitting reporters to interfere with the message. They did that through appearances on television and radio talk shows that were not simply political shows.

This method of communication was easier on the candidates. The interviewers were less hostile than the national media. The interviews were more conversational. The *Larry King Live* show was one vehicle for this unconventional approach by the candidates. These shows allowed the candidates to speak directly to voters without the filter of the national media's interpretation of what was being said. (See Chapter 12 for more about the media's role in campaigns.)

All this means that there are many new and different ways for you to find out which candidate you are comfortable supporting. You may also have additional ways to get your questions in front of these candidates: You can call in or apply to be in the audience for talk shows. You can even contact the Commission on Presidential Debates to see if there's an opportunity for you to be in the audience. The commission has a recommended reading list for voters who want to increase their knowledge of presidential politics. You can contact the commission at

> **Commission on Presidential Debates**, 601 13th St. NW, Washington, D.C. 20005; 202-872-1020.

The Electoral College and You

In most elections, the object is simply to get more votes than any opponent. In fact, the object in most races is to get 50 percent of the votes plus one more vote. A candidate who can do that wins the election. Every vote cast is equally important in coming up with that 50-percent-plus-one margin. That is true in every election under our system but one: the presidential election. The winner of a presidential election is almost always the person who receives the most votes — almost, but not always. That's because voters don't elect the president and vice president directly. Instead, the Electoral College does the electing.

Our founding fathers were leery of the passions of the populace — you and me. (Actually, the founding fathers weren't worried about me because they never thought that women would be given the vote at all.) They had their reasons for creating the Electoral College. We are no longer concerned about why the Electoral College was created. The fact is that it's there and it has an impact on the way campaigns for president are run. (See the "Large versus small states" sidebar for more information on the reasons behind the Electoral College.)

The road to 270 electoral votes

To understand the fall election strategy, you need to understand exactly how you elect the president and vice president. Every four years, in the presidential election year, you vote for a slate of electors. The *electors* elect the president and the vice president by casting *electoral votes* for the presidential candidate who carries their state.

So, rather than one national election for president, there are 51 separate presidential elections (the 50 states and the District of Columbia). A candidate must win enough of these 51 separate contests to supply the magical 270 electoral votes.

In 1992, a candidate for president could lose 39 states and the District of Columbia and still win — that is, if the 11 states he won were the 11 most populous: California, New York, Texas, Florida, Pennsylvania, Illinois, Ohio, Michigan, New Jersey, North Carolina, and Georgia.

Winning the election is all about getting a majority of the 538 electoral votes that are cast. The winner of the popular vote in each state and the District of Columbia gets all the state's electoral votes. Whichever candidate receives the most votes cast in any state, even if not a majority (as might be the case in a tight three-way race), gets all that state's electoral votes.

For the most part, electoral votes are not allocated proportionally. The only states that are exceptions to the winner-take-all electoral votes are Maine and Nebraska. That means that a candidate who comes in a very close second in a state gets no electoral votes at all. A candidate can receive 49.9 percent of the votes cast in a state and have nothing to show for it.

The winner-take-all Electoral College rules have a big impact on how the candidates conduct themselves in the fall campaign. They must always ask themselves where they can do the most good in gaining electoral votes. In states with strong competition between the candidates, the candidate may operate a grassroots campaign to register and turn out all possible voters who support the candidate. All these decisions are made in terms of a strategy to win a majority of the 538 electoral votes at stake.

All votes cast are not equal under this system. Some votes are more important than others. The idea that some votes cast are more important than others flies in the face of what we think a democracy is all about. But some votes are more important to the presidential candidates.

A vote cast to put a candidate over the top for a majority in one state is more important than a vote cast to give that same candidate 60 percent of the vote in another state or 40 percent of the vote in a third state. (Of course, in a three-person race, 40 percent of the vote might be enough to carry the state.) That's because the vote to put that candidate over the top for a majority also gives her that state's electoral votes. The vote to make her total more overwhelming is only icing on the cake. The vote to make her total 40 percent, but a losing 40 percent, doesn't matter in the larger scheme of things.

The candidate versus the party

The need to develop winning margins in enough states to win an electoral majority drives the fall campaign. Candidates concentrate their resources and their campaigning in the states with large numbers of electoral votes that are *swing states*. A *swing state* is one that could go either way on election day. Candidates will make only token appearances and devote only token resources to those states where they are sure to win or sure to lose.

Concentrating on swing states often puts the presidential campaigns at odds with state parties and with state and local candidates. When a presidential candidate is so popular in a state that he will carry that state handily, the local candidates and the state party want that presidential candidate to come to their state often. A popular presidential candidate can energize the party workers and encourage some voters who might not vote to turn out.

In states where a particular presidential candidate is almost certain to lose, the state party may still pressure the campaign to make appearances and to help in registering and turning out voters. The candidate may be unpopular with a majority of the voting population, but she will still have appeal to the party faithful.

Large versus small states

The Electoral College was a compromise between the large and small states and between the states and the federal government. Small states were guaranteed a minimum of three electoral votes to reflect their two senators and one congressperson. On the basis of population alone, some states would qualify for only one or two electors. State legislatures selected the electors in their states, according to their own rules, guaranteeing them a role in presidential selection. This method reassured the states that they were an important part of the national government.

Small states were given another advantage. Today, if the election went to the House of Representatives to be decided, each state still has only one vote. That means California and Wyoming have an equal say over the choice of a president, despite the fact that California has around 30,000,000 people and Wyoming has less than 1,000,000.

The method of choosing electors is left up to the states. In the earliest days of the Electoral College, electors cast their votes for individual candidates. They weren't committed to a candidate. Nowadays, parties choose slates of electors pledged to vote for their party's nominee if he carries their state.

Every state provides for popular election of electors. When you vote for president, you are actually voting for electors pledged to vote for a party's presidential candidate. The Democratic and Republican parties in each state choose their slates of electors. Each side has a slate equal to the number of representatives and senators that its state has in Congress. The position of elector on a party's slate is an honor usually reserved for party activists with many years of volunteer service to the party.

Some states list the names of the electors on the ballot along with the presidential candidates. Some states simply list the presidential candidates. All the electoral votes in a state go to the candidate who wins the most votes in the election in that state. It is winner-take-all except in Maine and Nebraska, which award some of their electoral votes on the basis of who wins each congressional district within the state. In those two states, more than one candidate could receive electoral votes.

Theoretically, a rogue elector could vote for a candidate other than the one who carried her state. That happened most recently in 1976, but it has never made a difference in an election. Twice in our history, the person winning the most popular votes was not the person elected by the Electoral College. When the national media declares a winner within a few hours of the polls' closing on election night, the chances of the Electoral College doing anything other than ratifying the voters' choice are slim to none.

The candidate may not want to come to a state she can't win, but the local party people want her to come. The size of the losing margin makes all the difference for victory or defeat for a party's statewide and local candidates. Their chances for victory are much better if the presidential candidate loses by a small rather than a large margin.

Presidential campaigns are frequently at odds with state parties and state and local candidates because their interests and objectives are different.

A Game of Strategy

When a candidate decides where to spend his time and resources, he and his campaign look at two things:

- ✔ Where the electoral votes are

- ✔ Which states are *one-party states* (that is, states whose electoral votes historically go just to Democrats or just to Republicans) and which are *swing states* (those whose historic voting records vary between Democratic and Republican)

When the polls showed George Bush behind in the final days before the 1992 election, he concentrated his efforts on five states, three of which were in the Midwest: Ohio, Michigan, and Missouri. The campaigns look at the past performances of states and decide which states can't be won and which states can't be lost. For example, New Hampshire goes Republican in virtually every presidential election. If a Democratic candidate for president carries New Hampshire, it is a landslide Democratic year. So Democratic nominees don't use valuable time and resources trying to change history; they cede New Hampshire to their opponents.

As for the Republican candidates, they have the luxury of taking New Hampshire for granted. They know they'll carry the state and win its four electoral votes, so they don't spend any money there, either.

Candidates put the most emphasis on the electoral-rich top 11 states. These states have demonstrated some ability to swing back and forth in their support for the two parties in presidential elections. So many electoral votes are at stake in each of these states that candidates need to devote time and resources to them.

Sometimes the strength or message of a particular candidate causes a campaign to test whether history will continue to hold true. Republican candidates for president enjoyed great support in the South in 1984 and 1988. No Southern state voted for the Democratic presidential candidate in 1984 or 1988. With the

Swing states

After the campaigns identify which states are swing states in an election, they still have to decide which of these states to target. Two areas of the country have been important swing regions in the last few elections:

✔ **Midwest states:** Ohio, Illinois, Michigan, and Missouri with a total of 72 electoral votes

✔ **Middle Atlantic states:** New York, New Jersey, and Pennsylvania with a total of 71 electoral votes

all-Southern ticket of Bill Clinton and Al Gore, Democrats decided to take a run at the South in 1992. As a result of those efforts, Clinton carried five Southern states.

Each side goes over a map of the country and does this type of analysis state by state. After they identify the sure winners, the campaigns keep polling to make sure these states stay won. The sure losers are also listed. Candidates make no more appearances and spend no more resources in either of these categories than they absolutely must to keep the party from open rebellion.

Game plan

A campaign has to piece together a game plan to win 270 votes. The game plan must strive for a combination of electoral votes from one-party states and swing states. The candidate has to persuade swing state voters to do two things:

✔ Turn out to vote on election day

✔ Vote for her

When a candidate decides which swing states she can win and comes up with a game plan to do it, she's guessing. Sure, polls and focus groups make those guesses educated ones, but they are guesses nonetheless. A campaign has to leave room for error.

A game plan can't target enough electoral votes to reach just 270 votes. It targets enough to reach, say, 300 or 325 votes. The extra votes can give the candidate a cushion if something happens in a target state or if she and her consultants guessed wrong about her ability to win one or more of the swing states.

You are the target

Once the campaign agrees on a game plan, the action begins. If you live in a swing state targeted by one or more of the candidates, you start to notice many visits by the candidates to your state. Presidential candidates give speeches and hold town meetings in your state. Debates may be scheduled in your city. You see their commercials on your favorite television show. You hear them on your radio programs.

You can be confident that the campaigns have set their sights on you. They are going to do everything humanly and financially possible to convince you to vote and to vote a certain way. They are after you!

Candidates have decided that you hold the key to victory. The game plan has determined that you and others like you will decide the next presidential election. Rather than be bothered by all the attention, you should be flattered that you are so important.

The key is to remember that the strategy, the game plan, the trips, and the advertising are all designed to get your attention and your vote. The candidates are appealing to you — trying to win you over. You are a very important part of any presidential campaign. You can be even more important if you are willing to get involved, regardless of where you live.

Volunteering in a presidential campaign

Presidential campaigns offer ample opportunities for you to get involved as a volunteer. These campaigns use many volunteers because volunteers are free. The less a presidential campaign has to pay for staff, the more money it has to get its message on television.

Volunteering in a swing state

If you have the time and the inclination to become more involved and you live in a swing state, you'll find almost endless ways to help out:

- ✔ Every time a presidential or vice presidential candidate visits, the campaign needs hundreds of volunteers to build an enthusiastic crowd for television cameras.
- ✔ Campaigns need volunteers to register voters so they can vote on election day.

> ✔ Campaigns need volunteers to call voters to persuade them to vote for your candidate.
>
> ✔ Campaigns need volunteers to distribute literature.
>
> ✔ Campaigns need volunteers to get the voters out to vote on election day.

See Chapter 4 for more information on becoming a campaign volunteer.

Volunteering in a one-party state

If you are not in one of the key swing states targeted by some candidate's game plan, it's probably because your state's tradition of voting one way or another in presidential elections is too well established for campaigns to challenge.

If you want to help as a volunteer but do not live in a swing state, you can help circulate petitions to put your candidate on the ballot in the primary election (that is, if you live in one of the 40 states that have a primary for president). States require the signatures of a set number of registered voters before a candidate's name is placed on the ballot in the primary. Presidential campaigns are always hungry for volunteers willing to go door to door to obtain the necessary signatures in the early months of a presidential election year.

Qualifying in good order for the presidential primary in each affected state demonstrates how well organized a candidate is. On the other hand, if a candidate has to scramble to make the ballot, the media sees that as the mark of a disorganized or ineffective campaign. Bad news stories will be the result.

You can also volunteer to go to a swing state to work for a set period of time. Even a week or two can be a big help to overworked and understaffed campaign organizations in key swing states. If you have the time, energy, and inclination, go for it. It doesn't matter where you live — if you're willing to become involved, there is a place for you and the things you want to do.

Just because your state is not a swing state doesn't mean that you are less important as a voter. You will still vote to elect all your state and local candidates. It is just that most of the voters in your state are too predictable in presidential elections. So much so that one side has written you off, and the other side can afford to take you for granted.

Part VII
The Part of Tens

In this part...

This is the famous ...*For Dummies* part that's all lists. Here are the ten things you need to teach your kids or yourself about politics, the ten commandments of politics, the ten most common political mistakes, and ten quotes straight from the politicians' mouths.

Chapter 23
The Ten Commandments of Modern Politics

• •

*P*olitics, like many other areas of life, has ten commandments that people find apply from generation to generation, periodically forget, and then (usually through some scandal) spectacularly rediscover. These are the tried-and-true realities of politics that apply wherever you are.

All Politics Is Local

Tip O'Neill, former Democratic Speaker of the House of Representatives from Massachusetts, was famous for saying, "All politics is local." This quote aptly expresses the notion that all political campaigns are decided at the grassroots level by volunteers working with their neighbors and friends to encourage them to vote for a particular candidate.

You Can't Beat Somebody with Nobody

No matter how weak a well-known candidate is, he still wins the election if his opponent is unknown and unfunded. It may not be fair, but a great candidate who is unknown is a nobody. A somebody candidate, no matter how unpopular, beats a nobody candidate every time.

Dance with the One Which Brung Ya

Once a candidate is elected, she must remember who helped her win. After the candidate wins, many newfound friends want to become close to her. They offer support and encouragement. She needs to remember which individuals and groups were with her when she most needed them — before she was elected. She can't forget those people who were with her before being with her was popular. She needs to dance with the ones which brung her.

Never Say Never

Candidates get into trouble all the time by taking absolute positions: The candidate won't run for a certain office. The candidate won't seek reelection.

Experienced politicians learn that situations change. Experienced politicians learn never to say never.

The Three Most Important Things in Politics: Money, Money, and Money

Robert Kennedy said it right. Money plays the most important role in modern politics. It's not only the most important factor but the second and third most important factors as well. Without money, any campaign is at a tremendous disadvantage. Money doesn't necessarily guarantee victory, but the absence of it will certainly contribute to defeat. That's why the three most important things in politics are money, money, and money.

It's Not Over 'til It's Over

Politicians can win or lose elections in a matter of hours or days. Your mood and that of the other voters can change as the election approaches. A good candidate does not rest on poll results taken the week before the election, because his lead can evaporate. A good candidate campaigns hard right up until the time the polls close, not taking anything for granted. After all, it's not over 'til it's over.

The Harder You Work, the Luckier You Get

Sometimes we tell ourselves that whether something happens or not is simply the luck of the draw. We say it's better to be lucky than smart. We're telling ourselves that our success or failure is the result of forces beyond our control. It doesn't matter what we do; luck or the lack of luck will determine the outcome.

Good politicians learn that luck, if there is such a thing, is something over which you may have some control. The best way to insure good luck in politics is to work hard for the outcome you want. The harder you work, the luckier you get.

Go Negative on Your Opponent Before He Goes Negative on You

Attack ads are part of modern politics. If a candidate is sure that her opponent is going to attack her through the media, her usual approach is to attack her opponent first and put him on the defensive. The candidate goes negative on her opponent before he goes negative on her.

You're Never Too Far Ahead

Like the modern expression "You can never be too rich or too thin," you can never be too far ahead in a campaign. This fits with the commandment "It's not over 'til it's over." A lead that looks insurmountable two weeks before an election can be overcome. Most voters don't make up their minds about whom to support until just before they cast their ballots. When voters make their decisions so late in the campaign, anything can happen. That's why no candidate can ever be too far ahead.

Most Political Wounds Are Self-Inflicted

If a candidate is wounded and begins receiving flak from the press or the electorate, he should look in the mirror before he points a finger at his opponent or anyone else. If you have any doubt that most political wounds are self-inflicted, just ask one of these characters:

- Former Senator Bob Packwood — with his sexual harassment, diaries, and deals for his ex-wife's employment
- Former Senator and former candidate for president, Gary Hart — for daring the press to follow him around and find out about his extracurricular activities
- Senator, and former candidate for president, Joe Biden — for forgetting that plagiarism is frowned upon
- Former Representative Mel Reynolds — for forgetting that sex with a minor is against the law

Chapter 24

Ten Things to Teach Your Children about Politics

• •

*Y*ou should tell your children some facts about politics. Who knows — maybe some or all of it will sink in. Your kids may not look like they're paying attention, but they may remember. After all, someday, when you suddenly go from being the dumbest parent in the world to being okay (if only by comparison to the even dumber parents of your kids' friends), some of these points may have an impact on your children.

If You're Not Registered, You're Irrelevant and Have No Right to Complain

The first thing you need to know is that politics is not a sport for Monday-morning quarterbacks. The very least that a democracy requires is for all responsible adults to familiarize themselves with the issues and the candidates and cast informed votes in each election. Excuses such as

- ✔ My vote doesn't make a difference.
- ✔ It doesn't matter who wins, the candidates are all the same.
- ✔ I don't know the candidates.
- ✔ Politicians are all corrupt.
- ✔ I'm too busy.
- ✔ I just don't want to get involved.

just don't cut the mustard. None of these is a legitimate reason for not doing your duty, making your voice heard, and voting.

Public Service Is a Good and Honorable Profession

When you hear the talk show hosts and comedians complain about government bureaucrats, remember that many good people work for government because they want to make our country a better place for us and our children. We don't pay these people very much. Many of us don't treat them well, either. When you meet a government employee who goes out of his way to help you or be accommodating, don't forget to thank him and tell him that you appreciate his courtesy. Everyone likes to be appreciated, and government employees are no different from the rest of us.

Never Pin Your Future to the Outcome of the Next Election

If you decide to become active in politics yourself, that's fine and dandy. Just remember that politics is an uncertain profession. It's tough to have your mortgage or rent payment dependent on the outcome of an election. You need training and contacts outside politics to make certain that you can support yourself if the political tide goes against you or your candidate.

You also need some savings in the bank so you won't have to call Mom and Dad to make the rent payment when you lose your job after you lose an election.

There's a relationship between financial security and political independence. This doesn't mean rich people always make better officeholders. It does mean that officeholders who don't fear temporary unemployment are more likely to do the right thing.

Never Trust Anyone Who Would Lie to You, Including a Politician

You've always been told to tell the truth. You've been told that little tiny lies are neither little nor tiny. You know that trust is a difficult thing to develop and an easy thing to lose. You expect people to trust you because they can count on you to be truthful. In turn, you should give your trust only to people who tell you the truth.

Don't trust anyone who lies to you. Politicians are no different from anyone else. You should hold them to the same standard. If they lie to you about little things, they'll lie to you about big things, too.

Democracy Is the Best System of Government

Our democracy is the best example of representative government ever. People all over the world wish they had a system like we have, where the majority rules with respect for the constitutional rights of a minority they don't necessarily agree with.

But someone is always complaining that our country is going to hell in a handbasket. When your grandfather was your age, people told him that our experiment with democracy was going down the tubes. When your children are the age of your grandfather, people will be telling them the same thing.

Our system is the best and will continue to be the best as long as good people stay involved. That doesn't mean that it can't be improved. It can and should be. But it's still better than any other alternative. So don't listen to people who say that our country is on a slippery slope to decline and decay. Tell them that if they don't like how things are, they should stop wringing their hands and get busy to make a change.

Avoiding Politics Makes You More to Blame for Its Failures, Not Less

You and other good people can't refuse to vote and participate in politics and then complain that politics is corrupt or unresponsive. If good people refuse to involve themselves in politics, who does that leave? If things need to be improved, you have a responsibility to work to make things better. The system can be improved. No matter how tough a task reforming politics looks to be, the longest, toughest journey begins with a single step.

Learn the Facts and Form Your Own Opinions

Never trust anyone else to think for you. You owe it to yourself to find out the facts and draw your own conclusions. Don't let gimmicks and slogans prevent you from thinking an issue through and deciding what outcome is best for you and your community or country.

Just as you've learned not to accept at face value every advertisement claim you hear, don't accept at face value everything a candidate tells you. Ask for proof; ask what the other side says. Think for yourself. No one else can do it for you.

You Have to Wait 'til 18 to Vote, but You Don't Have to Wait 'til 18 to Help Others Vote Wisely

You have to wait until you're 18 to vote because if you could vote earlier, the kid in your class who thinks that William Henry Harrison played lead guitar for the Beatles could vote, too. But you don't have to wait until you're 18 to learn the facts, form your own opinions, and think for yourself. You can also use your energy and enthusiasm to work for the party or candidate of your choice. Learn what politics is all about by working in campaigns and getting hands-on experience. If you're willing to work hard, you can make a difference before you're old enough to cast your first ballot.

Politicians Are Just Like the Rest of Us

The younger you are when you become involved in politics, the sooner you'll learn that politicians are just people. There are smart ones and dumb ones. There are honest ones and dishonest ones. There are brave ones and cowardly ones. They are people just like we are, with virtues and shortcomings. Many of them are worthy of your support. Some of them aren't and should be defeated. But just as you can't write off the whole human race because there are some bad people, you shouldn't write off politics because there are a few bad politicians.

When someone tries to tell you that all politicians are crooks, remind him that Thomas Jefferson, Davy Crockett, Abraham Lincoln, Teddy Roosevelt, John F. Kennedy, and Shirley Chisholm were all politicians — good politicians. Sure, there were some others who dishonored the offices they held. But many others performed brilliantly and made us proud to be Americans. You shouldn't permit yourself to believe that all politicians are crooks, because that may mean that only crooks will become politicians.

When a Politician Makes You a Promise, Make Sure That You Want What He's Promising

Nikita Khrushchev, a famous politician in the former Soviet Union, once said, "Politicians are the same all over. They promise to build a bridge even where there is no water."

Listen when a politician makes promises. Ask yourself whether what she's promising to do is right and good, not just for you but for your community and country. Ask who has to give something up so that the politician can please those she's promising.

One of the greatest things about America is that we are a country of many different backgrounds, religions, and cultures united by our love for this nation of immigrants, this land of opportunity. We are all willing to make sacrifices to see this country grow and prosper. Be wary of politicians who promise that your government can constantly give you things without asking for anything in return. If something looks too good to be true, it generally is.

Chapter 25
Ten Common Political Mistakes

• •

*I*f there's one thing that politicians can do for their own peace of mind —
as well as for the good of the country — it's learn from the mistakes of those
who have come before them. Take a look at some of these common gaffes,
which seem to be repeated over and over again in the world of politics.

Thinking Anything Is Secret

In this day and age, I'm amazed that elected officials still think that they can
have secrets. When tabloids pay money and publish the most sordid, intimate
details of an official's private life, politicians had better start with the notion
that everything about them is public information.

Giving a Reporter an Interview "Off the Record"

A candidate should never give a reporter an interview that she isn't prepared to
see on the front page of a newspaper. If the story is important enough, it will be
discussed. Sooner or later, other reporters or the candidate's opponents will
figure out that she is the source of the information. If she isn't prepared to be
associated with the story by name, she shouldn't talk at all.

Failing to Answer an Opponent's Attack

As much as a candidate wants his campaign to stay positive, the failure to
answer an attack by his opponent could cause him to lose the election. Many
voters who hear the attack without hearing the candidate's side will believe the
attack. Voters will think the attack is true because there is no response.

Promising Not to Run for Reelection

Candidates get ahead of themselves sometimes and make promises that later they don't want to keep. Take Teddy Roosevelt, for example. He became president when William McKinley was assassinated in 1901. Once he became the first vice president to succeed to the presidency and be elected in his own right in 1904, he renounced a third term. After he became angry at his successor, William Howard Taft, he decided to run again. In 1912, Roosevelt ran on the Bull Moose ticket and split the Republican vote, permitting Democrat Woodrow Wilson to be elected.

Not Taking a Poll

In modern political campaigning, not taking a poll is political malpractice. The candidate must poll to see what's on the voters' minds, to know what issues voters want discussed. The candidate must know how the voters see her and her opponent.

Taking a Poll and Ignoring the Results

Even worse than not polling at all is polling and ignoring the results. If a poll tells the candidate that voters want him to discuss a particular topic and he doesn't do so, he's making a big political mistake. He has spent the money to take a professional political poll but isn't following the advice that the poll provides.

Not Knowing When to Retire

Perhaps the most common political mistake is not knowing when to say enough. Sometimes politicians take polls that tell them they've been in office too long, and then they still run in one more election. It's much more fun to go out on a positive note by knowing when to say when.

Thinking Public Officials Can Have a Private Life

As Gary Hart and countless others can attest, there is no such thing as a totally private life for any visible public official. Even activities that don't directly affect their public service will be the subject of press scrutiny and television talk-show speculation for visible elected officials.

Putting It in Writing

Just when you think you've heard it all, something happens to make you scratch your head and wonder what gets into people. You wouldn't think that someone would keep a written record of his own potentially embarrassing conduct. Guess again!

A perfect case in point is the revelation that former Senator Bob Packwood kept a diary. This diary included accounts of his sexual approaches to women employees of the Senate as well as his discussions about finding his ex-wife a job with a lobbyist in order to reduce his alimony payments. He also included his observations about ways he and others discussed to circumvent the campaign finance laws in his last Senate campaign. Senator Packwood's attempt to alter his diary to erase his own record of his unfortunate conduct was in good part his political undoing. Needless to say, it's a big political mistake to create a written record of items that would spell your political death if they became public.

Failing to Follow the Strict Letter of the Law

As several would-be high-level Clinton appointees can testify, a potential appointee who submits her name for confirmation to the U. S. Senate had better be sure that every i is dotted and t crossed in terms of compliance with federal employment and tax laws. Many high-level appointees of the federal government require a vote of the Senate to confirm their presidential appointment. Failing to pay Social Security taxes for domestic employees or hiring illegal aliens in a household can be a big political embarrassment, not to mention a good way to jeopardize the appointment, as was the case for a number of Clinton nominees.

Failing to comply strictly with the law can also be an embarrassing problem for candidates. Ask Governor Pete Wilson of California, who made immigration a key issue in his campaign for the Republican presidential nomination only to be embarrassed when it was revealed that an employee of his and his former wife's was an illegal alien.

Chapter 26
Ten Quotable Quotes

• •

*O*ver the years, politicians have given hundreds of thousands of speeches. Some of their most memorable quotes have survived long beyond their tenure in elected office. Here's some political rhetoric worthy of note.

On Politics

"Being in politics is like being a football coach. You have to be smart enough to understand the game and dumb enough to think it's important." –Senator Eugene McCarthy

On Being President

"In America, any boy may become President, and I suppose that's just the risk he takes." –Adlai Stevenson

"Mothers all want their sons to grow up to be President, but they didn't want them to become politicians in the process." –John F. Kennedy

Did I Really Say That?

"If you think I've been fooling around on my wife, follow me." –Gary Hart

"I've looked on a lot of women with lust. I've committed adultery in my heart many times. This is something that God recognizes I will do." –Jimmy Carter

"I was recently on a tour of Latin America, and the only regret I have was that I didn't study Latin harder in school so I could converse with these people." –commonly attributed to Dan Quayle, though actually this "quote" began as a Dan Quayle joke

"I am not a crook." –Richard Nixon

On Leaving Politics

"You won't have Richard Nixon to kick around anymore." –Richard Nixon, after losing the California governor's race in 1962

"If nominated, I will not run; if elected, I will not serve." –General William Tecumseh Sherman

On the Press

"I won't say the papers misquote me, but I sometimes wonder where Christianity would be today if some of those reporters had been Matthew, Mark, Luke, and John." –Barry Goldwater

Appendix

Voter Registration

• •

*A*t the back of this book is your very own voter registration form. This appendix explains how to fill out the registration form the way your state wants you to, lists the requirements you must meet in order to register in your particular state, and tells you where to send the form.

When you're ready, follow these steps to register to vote in any election in the United States:

1. **Rip the voter registration form out of the back of this book.**

2. **Fill out boxes 1 through 5 of the form, following the general instructions at the beginning of this appendix.**

3. **Look up your state in this appendix (as easy as a, b, c) for specific instructions on filling out boxes 6 through 8.**

4. **While you're there, confirm that you meet all your state's requirements for registering to vote.**

5. **Address the form, using the mailing address listed under your state in this appendix.**

6. **Seal the form, removing the adhesive strip and folding the form into a self-mailing envelope.**

7. **Put a stamp on your form and drop it in the nearest mailbox.**

   Congratulations! You're on your way to becoming a registered voter.

The following instructions come straight from the government national mail-in registration form — word for word — so don't expect a literary masterpiece.

Who Can Use This Application

If you are a U. S. citizen who lives or has an address within the United States, you can use the application in this booklet to

- ✔ Register to vote in your State,
- ✔ Report a change of name to your voter registration office,
- ✔ Report a change of address to your voter registration office, or
- ✔ Register with a political party.

Exceptions

- ✔ **Arkansas,** by law, cannot accept this form until after Jan. 1, 1996.
- ✔ **New Hampshire** town and city clerks will accept this application only as a request for their own absentee voter mail-in registration form.
- ✔ **North Dakota** does not have voter registration.
- ✔ **Virginia,** by law, cannot accept this form until after Jan. 1, 1996.
- ✔ **Wyoming** will not let you use this application for registering to vote in that state.

Please do not use this application if you live outside the United States and its territories and have no home (legal) address in this country, *or* if you are in the military stationed away from home. Use the Federal Postcard Application available to you from military bases, American embassies, or consular offices.

How to find out whether you are eligible to register to vote in your state

Each State has its own laws about who may register and vote. Check the information under your State in the State Instructions.

Note: All States require that you be a United States citizen by birth or naturalization to register to vote in federal and State elections.

Also Note: You **cannot** be registered to vote in more than one place at a time.

When to register to vote

Each State has its own deadline for registering to vote. Check the deadline for your State on the last page of this booklet.

How to fill out this application

Use both the Application Instructions and State Instructions to guide you in filling out the application.

First, read the Application Instructions. These instructions will give you important information that applies to everyone using this application.

Next, find your State under the State Instructions. Use these instructions to fill out Boxes 6, 7, and 8. Also refer to these instructions for information about voter eligibility and any oath required for Box 9.

How to submit your application

Mail your application to the address listed under your State in the State Instructions. Or deliver the application in person to your local voter registration office.

If you were given this booklet in a state agency or public office

If you have been given this booklet in a State agency or public office, it is your choice to use the application or not.

If you decide to use this application to register to vote, you can fill it out and leave it with the State agency or public office. The application will be submitted for you. Or you can take it with you to mail to the address listed under your State in the State Instructions. You also may take it with you to deliver in person to your local voter registration office.

Note: The name and location of the State agency or public office where you received the application will remain confidential. It will not appear on your application. Also, if you decide not to use this application to register to vote, that decision will remain confidential. It will not affect the service you receive from the agency or office.

Application Instructions

Box 1 — Name

Put in this box your full name in this order — Last, First, Middle. Do not use nicknames or initials.

Note: If this application is for a change of name, please tell us in **Box A** *(on the bottom half of the form)* your full name before you changed it.

Box 2 — Home Address

Put in this box your home address (legal address). Do *not* put your mailing address here if it is different from your home address. Do *not* use a post office box or rural route without a box number.

Note: If you were registered before *but* this is the first time you are registering from the address in Box 2, please tell us in **Box B** *(on the bottom half of the form)* the address where you were registered before. Please give us as much of the address as you can remember.

Also Note: If you live in a rural area but do not have a street address, *or* if you have no address, please show where you live using the map in **Box C** *(at the bottom of the form)*.

Box 3 — Mailing Address

If you get your mail at an address that is different from the address in Box 2, put your mailing address in this box.

Note: If you have no address in Box 2, you *must* write in Box 3 an address where you can be reached by mail.

Box 4 — Date of Birth

Put in this box your date of birth in this order — Month, Day, Year. *Be careful not to use today's date!*

Box 5 — Telephone Number

Most States ask for your telephone number in case there are questions about your application. However, you do **not** have to fill in this box.

Box 6 — ID Number

Many States use an ID number for record-keeping purposes. To find out what ID number, if any, you need to put in this box, see item 6 in the instructions under your State.

Box 7 — Choice of Party

In some States, you must register with a party if you want to take part in that party's primary election, caucus, or convention. To find out if your State requires this, see item 7 in the instructions under your State.

If you want to register with a party, print in the box the full name of the party of your choice.

If you do **not** want to register with a party, write "no party" or leave the box blank. Do **not** write in the word "independent" if you mean "no party," because this might be confused with the name of a political party in your State.

Note: If you do not register with a party, you can still vote in general elections and nonpartisan (nonparty) primary elections.

Box 8 — Race or Ethnic Group

A few States ask for your race or ethnic group, in order to administer the Federal Voting Rights Act. To find out if your State asks for this information, see item 8 in the instructions under your State. If so, put in Box 8 the choice that best describes you from the list below:

- ✔ American Indian *or* Alaskan Native
- ✔ Asian or Pacific Islander *not* Native Hawaiian
- ✔ Black, *not of* Hispanic Origin
- ✔ Hispanic
- ✔ Multi-racial
- ✔ Native Hawaiian
- ✔ White, *not of* Hispanic Origin
- ✔ Other

Box 9 — Signature

Review the information in item 9 in the instructions under your State. Before you sign or make your mark, make sure that:

- ✔ You meet your State's requirements

  and

- ✔ You understand **all** of box 9

Finally, sign your **full** name or make your mark, and print today's date in this order — Month, Day, Year.

Box 10 — Name of Assistant

If the applicant is unable to sign, put in this box the name, address, and telephone number (optional) of the person who helped the applicant.

State Instructions

Alabama

6. ID Number: Your social security number is requested (by authority of the Alabama Supreme Court, 17-4-122).

7. Choice of Party: You do not have to register with a party if you want to take part in that party's primary election, caucus or convention.

8. Race or Ethnic Group: You are required to fill in this box; however, your application will not be rejected if you fail to do so. See the list of choices under the Application Instructions for Box 8.

9. Signature: To register in Alabama you must

- be a citizen of the United States

- be a resident of Alabama and your county at the time of registration and be 18 years old before any election

- not have been convicted of a felony punishable by imprisonment in the penitentiary (or have had your civil and political rights restored)

- not currently be declared mentally incompetent through a competency hearing

- swear or affirm to "support and defend the Constitution of the U.S. and the State of Alabama and further disavow any belief or affiliation with any group which advocates the overthrow of the governments of the U.S. or the State of Alabama by unlawful means that the information contained herein is true, so help me God"

Mailing address

Office of the Secretary of State
P.O. Box 5616
Montgomery, AL 36103-5616

Alaska

6. ID Number: Your social security number is requested. This information is kept confidential. Having this information assists in maintaining your voter record and may assist in verifying your identity (Title 15 of the Alaska Statutes).

7. **Choice of Party:** You must register with a party if you want to take part in that party's primary election, caucus, or convention (unless otherwise permitted by a political party).

8. **Race or Ethnic Group:** Leave blank.

9. **Signature:** To register in Alaska you must

- be a citizen of the United States

- be at least 18 years old within 90 days of this registration

- not be a convicted felon (unless unconditionally discharged)

- not be judicially determined to be of unsound mind, unless the disability has been removed

- not be registered to vote in another State

Mailing address

Division of Elections
State of Alaska
Region II
800 East Diamond Blvd. #3-580
Anchorage, AK 99515

Arizona

6. **ID Number:** The last 4 digits of your social security number and your Indian Census number (if you have one) are requested.

7. **Choice of Party:** You must register with a party if you want to take part in that party's primary election, caucus, or convention.

8. **Race or Ethnic Group:** Leave blank.

9. **Signature:** To register in Arizona you must

- be a citizen of the United States

- be a resident of Arizona and your county at least 29 days preceding the next election

- be 18 years old on or before the next general election

- not have been convicted of treason or a felony (or have had your civil rights restored)

- not currently be declared an incapacitated person by a court of law

Mailing address

Secretary of State/Elections
1700 W. Washington, 7th Floor
Phoenix, AZ 85007

Arkansas

6. **ID Number:** Your social security number and/or driver's license number are requested. These numbers will remain confidential and will not be disclosed to anyone other than voter registration officials. These numbers will not be published on any voter registration lists.

7. **Choice of Party:** You do not have to register with a party if you want to take part in that party's primary election, caucus, or convention.

8. **Race or Ethnic Group:** Leave blank.

9. **Signature:** To register in Arkansas you must

   - be a citizen of the United States

   - live in Arkansas at the address in Box 2 on the application

   - be at least 18 years old on or before the next election

   - not be a convicted felon (or have completely discharged your sentence or been pardoned)

   - not claim the right to vote in any other jurisdiction

Note: Arkansas, by law, cannot accept this form until after Jan. 1, 1996.

Mailing address

State of Arkansas
Office of Auditor
230 State Capitol
Little Rock, AR 72201

California

6. **ID Number:** Leave blank.

7. **Choice of Party:** You must register with a party if you want to take part in that party's primary election, caucus, or convention.

8. **Race or Ethnic Group:** Leave blank.

9. Signature: To register in California you must

- be a citizen of the United States

- be a resident of California

- be at least 18 years of age at the time of the next election

- not be imprisoned or on parole for the conviction of a felony

- not currently be judged mentally incompetent by a court of law

Mailing address

Secretary of State
1500 11th Street
Sacramento, CA 95814

Colorado

6. ID Number: Your social security number is requested.

7. Choice of Party: You must register with a party if you want to take part in that party's primary election, caucus, or convention.

8. Race or Ethnic Group: Leave blank.

9. Signature: To register in Colorado you must

- must be a citizen of the United States

- be a resident of Colorado 30 days prior to the election

- be 18 years old

- not to be confined as a prisoner or serving any part of a sentence under mandate

Mailing address

Secretary of State
c/o Elections Officer
1560 Broadway, Suite 200
Denver, CO 80202

Connecticut

6. ID Number: Your social security number is requested on a voluntary basis. It will be used by election officials to prepare accurate lists of electors, but no official may disclose it to the public (Conn. Gen. Stat. § 9-23g).

7. **Choice of Party:** This is optional, but you must register with a party if you want to take part in that party's primary election, caucus, or convention.

8. **Race or Ethnic Group:** Leave blank.

9. **Signature:** To register in Connecticut you must

- be a citizen of the United States

- be a resident of Connecticut and of the town in which you wish to vote

- be 18 years old on or before the next election

- not be convicted of a felony, except conviction for the crime of nonsupport (or have had your civil rights restored)

- not currently be declared mentally incompetent to vote by a court of law

Mailing address

Secretary of State
Elections Division
30 Trinity Street
Hartford, CT 06106

Delaware

6. **ID Number:** Your social security number is requested. Your social security number is used as necessary for administrative purposes related to voting, including to identify you as a registered voter, to ensure no individual is registered in more than one place, to verify address, voting districts, and other information and may be used for any other lawful purpose. The registration application containing your social security number will become part of the registration records of your county (Title 15, Sec. 1302, Del. Code and 5 U.S.C.A., Sec. 552a [Sec. 7 of the Privacy Act of 1975]).

7. **Choice of Party:** You must register with a party if you want to take part in that party's primary election, caucus, or convention.

8. **Race or Ethnic Group:** Leave blank.

9. **Signature:** To register in Delaware you must

- be a citizen of the United States

- be a resident of Delaware for 1 year preceding the election, a resident of the county for 90 days, and a resident of the election district (hundred) for 30 days

- be at least 18 years old on the date of the next general election
- not be a convicted felon
- not be mentally incompetent

Mailing address

Commissioner of Elections
32 W. Lockerman Street
Suite 203
Dover, DE 19901

District of Columbia

6. **ID Number:** Your social security number is requested. We use your social security number for ID purposes only. It will not be available to the public or used in any reports (Federal Privacy Act, PL 930579).

7. **Choice of Party:** You must register with a party if you want to take part in that party's primary election, caucus, or convention.

8. **Race or Ethnic Group:** Leave blank.

9. **Signature:** To register in the District of Columbia you must

   - be a citizen of the United States
   - be a resident for 1 year preceding the election, a resident of the county for 90 days, and a resident of the election district for 30 days
   - not be a convicted felon
   - not be mentally incompetent

Mailing address

District of Columbia Board of Elections & Ethics
441 4th Street, N.W., Suite 250
Washington, DC 20001-2745

Florida

6. **ID Number:** Your social security number is requested. The disclosure of your social security number is voluntary. It is being requested pursuant to Section 97.052(2)(k), Florida Statutes. Although your social security number will only be used for registration purposes, it will be open to public inspection (§ 99.052 [3][d], Fla. Stat.).

7. **Choice of Party:** You must register with a party if you want to take part in that party's primary election, caucus, or convention.

8. **Race or Ethnic Group:** You are requested to fill in this box. See the list of choices under the Application Instructions for Box 8.

9. **Signature:** To register in Florida you must

- be a citizen of the United States

- be a legal resident of both the State of Florida and of the county in which you seek to be registered

- be 18 years old (you may pre-register if you are 17)

- not now be adjudicated mentally incapacitated with respect to voting in Florida or any other State

- not have been convicted of a felony without your civil rights having been restored pursuant to law

- not claim the right to vote in another county or state

- swear or affirm the following:

  "I will protect and defend the Constitution of the United States and the Constitution of the State of Florida, that I am qualified to register as an elector under the Constitution and laws of the State of Florida, and that I am a citizen of the United States and a legal resident of Florida"

Mailing address

State of Florida
Department of State
Division of Elections
Room 1801, The Capitol
Tallahassee, FL 32399-0250

Georgia

6. **ID Number:** Your social security number is required. Your social security number will remain confidential and will not be disclosed except as required by law. The number will be used to identify and verify the identity of voters (Georgia Election Code, O.C.G.A. Ch 21-2).

7. **Choice of Party:** You do not have to register with a party to take part in that party's primary, caucus or convention.

8. **Race or Ethnic Group:** You are required to fill in this box. See the list of choices under the Application Instructions for Box 8.

9. **Signature:** To register in Georgia you must

- be a citizen of the United States

- be a legal resident of Georgia and of the county in which you want to vote

- be 18 years old to vote

- not be serving a sentence for having been convicted of a felony

- not have been judicially determined to be mentally incompetent, unless the disability has been removed

Mailing address

Office of the Secretary of State
P. O. Box 105325
Atlanta, GA 30348-5325

Hawaii

6. **ID Number:** Your social security number is required. It is used to prevent fraudulent registration and voting. Failure to furnish this information will prevent acceptance of this application (Hawaii Revised Statutes, Section 11-15).

7. **Choice of Party:** A "choice of party" is not required for voter registration.

8. **Race or Ethnic Group:** If you are of Hawaiian ancestry and desire to register to vote in Office of Hawaiian Affairs elections, please write "Hawaiian" in this box. HRS § 11 states that a Hawaiian is "any descendent of aboriginal peoples inhabiting the Hawaiian islands which exercised sovereignty and subsisted in the Hawaiian islands in 1778, and which peoples thereafter have continued to reside in Hawaii."

9. **Signature:** To register in Hawaii you must

- be a citizen of the United States

- be a resident of the State of Hawaii

- be at least 16 years old (you must be 18 years old by election day in order to vote)

- not be in jail for a felony conviction

- not be "non compos mentis"

Mailing address

Office of the Lieutenant Governor
State of Hawaii
P. O. Box 3226
Honolulu, HI 968-1

Idaho

6. **ID Number:** Your social security number is requested. It will be used for administrative purposes only (§ 34-411, Idaho Code).

7. **Choice of Party:** You do not have to register with a party if you want to take part in that party's primary election, caucus, or convention.

8. **Race or Ethnic Group:** Leave blank.

9. **Signature:** To register in Idaho you must

- be a citizen of the United States
- have resided in Idaho and in the county for 30 days prior to the day of election
- be at least 18 years old
- not have been convicted of a felony, and without having been restored to the rights of citizenship, or confined in prison on conviction of a criminal offense
- not be under guardianship

Mailing address

Secretary of State
State Capitol Bldg.
Boise, ID 83720-0080

Illinois

6. **ID Number:** The last four or six digits of your social security number are requested.

7. **Choice of Party:** You do not have to register with a party if you want to take part in that party's primary election, caucus, or convention.

8. **Race or Ethnic Group:** Leave blank.

9. **Signature:** To register in Illinois you must

- be a citizen of the United States
- be a resident of Illinois and of your election precinct at least 30 days before the next election
- be at least 18 years old on or before the next election
- not be in jail or on parole for a felony conviction
- not claim the right to vote anywhere else

Mailing address

State Board of Elections
1020 S. Spring Street
Springfield, IL 62704

Indiana

6. **ID Number:** Your social security number is requested but is not required. It will be used for administrative purposes and may be disclosed to the public (Indiana Code 7-3-9).

7. **Choice of Party:** Leave blank.

8. **Race or Ethnic Group:** Leave blank.

9. **Signature:** To register in Indiana you must

- be a citizen of the United States

- have resided in the precinct at least 30 days before the next election

- be at least 18 years of age on the day of the next general election

- not currently be in jail for a criminal conviction

Mailing address

State Election Board
302 West Washington Street
Room E032
Indianapolis, IN 46204-2738

Iowa

6. **ID Number:** Disclosure of your social security number is voluntary. It is requested by authority of Iowa Code Section 48A.11. If you provide your number, it will be used to help avoid multiple voter registration records for a single individual. The number may be publicly disclosed. If you do not provide your number, that fact will not affect your right to register to vote, or to vote.

7. **Choice of Party:** You may, but do not have to, register with a party in advance if you want to take part in that party's primary election. You may change or declare a party affiliation at the polls on primary election day.

8. **Race or Ethnic Group:** Leave blank.

9. **Signature:** To register in Iowa you must

- be a citizen of the United States

- be a resident of Iowa

- be at least $17^1/_2$ years old (you must be 18 to vote)

- not have been convicted of a felony (or have had your rights restored)

- not currently be judged "mentally incompetent" by a court

- not claim the right to vote in more than one place

- give up your right to vote in any other place

Mailing address

Elections Division
Office of the Secretary of State
Hoover State Office Building
Second Floor
Des Moines, IA 50319

Kansas

6. **ID Number:** Your social security number is requested but not required. It will be used for administrative purposes and may be disclosed to the public (KSA 25-2309).

7. **Choice of Party:** You must register with a party if you want to take part in that party's primary election, caucus, or convention.

8. **Race or Ethnic Group:** Leave blank.

9. **Signature:** To register in Kansas you must

- be a citizen of the United States

- be a resident of Kansas

- be 18 years of age by the next statewide general election

- not be imprisoned for conviction in any state or federal court of a crime punishable by death or imprisonment for one year or longer (or have had your civil rights restored)

- not claim the right to vote in any other location or under any other name

- not be excluded from voting for mental incompetence by a court of competent jurisdiction

Mailing address

Secretary of State
Second Floor, State Capitol
300 S. W. 10th Ave.
Topeka, KS 66612-1594

Kentucky

6. **ID Number:** Your social security number is required. It is used for administrative purposes only and is not released to the public (KRS 116:155).

7. **Choice of Party:** You must register with a party if you want to take part in that party's primary election, caucus, or convention.

8. **Race or Ethnic Group:** Leave blank.

9. **Signature:** To register in Kentucky you must

   - be a citizen of the United States

   - be a resident of Kentucky

   - be a resident of the county for at least 28 days prior to the election date

   - be 18 years of age on or before the next general election

   - not be a convicted of a felony, your civil rights must have been restored by executive pardon

   - not have been judged "mentally incompetent" in a court of law

   - not claim the right to vote anywhere outside Kentucky

Mailing address

State Board of Elections
140 Walnut Street
Frankfort, KY 40601

Louisiana

6. **ID Number:** Your social security number is required. Neither the registrar nor the Department of Elections and Registration shall circulate the social security numbers of registered voters on commercial lists (R.S. 18:104[a][16]).

7. **Choice of Party:** You must register with a party if you want to take part in that party's primary election, caucus, or convention.

8. **Race or Ethnic Group:** You are requested to fill in this box. See the list of choices under the Application Instructions for Box 8 (on page 2).

9. **Signature:** To register in Louisiana you must

- be a citizen of the United States

- be a resident of Louisiana

- be at least 17 years old, and be 18 years old prior to the next election vote

- not currently be under an order of imprisonment for conviction of a felony

- not currently be under a judgment of interdiction for mental incompetence

Mailing address

Dept. of Elections and Registration
P. O. Box 17179
Baton Rouge, LA 70898-4179

Maine

6. **ID Number:** Leave blank.

7. **Choice Of Party:** You must register with a party if you want to take part in that party's primary election, caucus, or convention (unless otherwise permitted by a political party).

8. **Race or Ethnic Group:** Leave blank.

9. **Signature:** To register in Maine you must

- be a citizen of the United States

- be a resident of Maine and the municipality in which you want to vote

- be at least 17 years old (you must be 18 years old to vote)

- not under guardianship because of mental illness

Mailing address

Elections Section
Bureau of Corporations, Elections, and Commissions
State House Station #101
Augusta, ME 04333-0101

Maryland

6. ID Number: Leave blank.

7. Choice of Party: You must register with a party if you want to take part in that party's primary election.

8. Race or Ethnic Group: Leave blank.

9. Signature: To register in Maryland you must

- be a citizen of the United States

- be a resident of Maryland and the county in which you want to vote

- be at least 18 years old before the next general election

- not be under sentence or on probation or parole following conviction for an infamous crime (that is, any felony, treason, perjury, or any crime involving an element of deceit, fraud or corruption)

- not have been convicted more than once of an infamous crime, without a pardon

- not be under guardianship with respect to voting

Mailing address

State Administrative Board or Election Laws
P.O. Box 231, 11 Bladen Street
Annapolis, MD 21404-0231

Massachusetts

6. ID Number: Leave blank.

7. Choice of Party: You must enroll with a party if you want to take part in that party's presidential preference primary. If you do not designate a party in this box, you may still enroll at the polling place on primary election day.

8. Race or Ethnic Group: Leave blank.

9. Signature: To register in Massachusetts you must

- be a citizen of the United States

- be a resident of Massachusetts

- be 18 years old

- not have been convicted of corrupt practices in respect to elections

- not be under guardianship with respect to voting

Mailing address

Secretary of State
Elections Division, Room 1705
One Ashburton Place
Boston, MA 02108

Michigan

6. ID Number: A driver's license or state personal ID number is requested.

7. Choice of Party: You must declare a "political party preference" if you want to take part in that party's presidential primary election.

8. Race or Ethnic Group: Leave blank.

9. Signature: To register in Michigan you must

- be a citizen of the United States

- be 18 years old by the next election

- be a resident of the city or township in which you are applying to register

- not be confined in a jail after being convicted and sentenced

Mailing address

Bureau of Elections
P. O. Box 20126
Lansing, MI 48901-0726

Minnesota

6. ID Number: Leave blank.

7. Choice of Party: You must enroll with a party if you want to take part in that party's presidential preference primary. If you do not designate a party in this box, you may still enroll at the polling place on primary election day.

8. Race or Ethnic Group: Leave blank.

9. Signature: To register in Minnesota you must

- be a citizen of the United States

- be a resident of Minnesota for 20 days before the next election

- be 18 years old by election day

- not be convicted of treason or a felony, or have had you civil rights restored

- not be under guardianship of the person or found legally incompetent

Mailing address

Secretary of State
Data Processing Section
555 Park Street, Suite 402
St. Paul, MN 55103

Mississippi

6. **ID Number:** Your social security number is requested. It may not be copied except for official purposes and is exempt from the provision of the Mississippi Public Records Act (Miss. Code Ann. § 23-15-47 [1972]).

7. **Choice of Party:** You do not have to register with a party if you want to take part in that party's primary election, caucus, or convention.

8. **Race or Ethnic Group:** You are requested to fill in this box. See the list of choices under the Application Instructions for Box 8.

9. **Signature:** To register in Mississippi you must

- be a citizen of the United States

- have lived in Mississippi and in your county (and city, if applicable) 30 days before the election in which you want to vote

- be 18 years old by the time of the general election in which you want to vote

- have not been convicted of murder, rape, bribery, theft, arson, obtaining money or goods under false pretense, perjury, forgery, embezzlement, or bigamy, or have had your rights restored as required by law

- not have been declared mentally incompetent by a court

Mailing address

Secretary of State
P. O. Box 136
Jackson, MS 39205-0136

Missouri

6. **ID Number:** Your social security number is requested. Any taped printouts or mailing labels provided under this section shall not include the telephone numbers and social security numbers of voters (115.157 RSMO).

7. **Choice of Party:** You do not have to register with a party if you want to take part in that party's primary election, caucus, or convention.

8. **Race or Ethnic Group:** Leave blank.

9. **Signature:** To vote in Missouri you must

   - be a citizen of the United States

   - be a resident of Missouri

   - be at least 17^1/$_2$ years of age (you must be 18 to vote)

   - not be on probation or parole after conviction of a felony, until finally discharged from such probation or parole

   - not be convicted of a felony or misdemeanor connected with the right of suffrage

   - not be declared incompetent by any court of law

   - not be confined under a sentence of imprisonment

Mailing address

Secretary of State
P. O. Box 778
Jefferson City, MO 65102

Montana

6. **ID Number:** Leave blank. However, your election administrator may request an ID number at a later date.

7. **Choice of Party:** You do not have to register with a party if you want to take part in that party's primary election, caucus, or convention.

8. **Race or Ethnic Group:** Leave blank.

9. **Signature:** To register in Montana you must

   - be a citizen of the United States

   - be at least 18 years old on or before the election

   - be a resident of Montana and of the county in which you want to vote for at least 30 days before the next election

- not be in a penal institution for a felony conviction
- not currently be determined by a court to be of unsound mind
- meet these qualifications by the next election day if you do not currently meet them

Mailing address

Secretary of State's Office
P. O. Box 202801
State Capitol
Helena, MT 59620-2801

Nebraska

6. ID Number: Leave blank.

7. Choice of Party: You must register with a party if you want to take part in that party's primary election, caucus, or convention.

8. Race or Ethnic Group: Leave blank.

9. Signature: To register in Nebraska you must

- be a citizen of the United States
- live in the State of Nebraska
- be at least 18 years of age or will be 18 years of age on or before the first Tuesday after the first Monday of November
- not have been convicted of a felony, or if convicted, have had your civil rights restored
- not have been officially found to be mentally incompetent

Mailing address

Nebraska Secretary of State
Suite 2300, State Capitol Bldg.
Lincoln, NE 68509-4608

Nevada

6. ID Number: Your social security, Nevada driver's license, or ID card number is required. The social security number will be used for administrative purposes. Registration records, including social security numbers are available for public inspection (NRS 293.507[4A]).

7. **Choice of Party:** You must register with a party if you want to take part in that party's primary election, caucus, or convention.

8. **Race or Ethnic Group:** Leave blank.

9. **Signature:** To register in Nevada you must

- be a citizen of the United States

- have attained the age of 18 years on the date of the next ensuing election

- have continuously resided in the State of Nevada, in your county, at least 30 days and in your precinct at least 10 days before the next ensuing election

- not currently be laboring under any felony conviction or other loss of civil rights that would make it unlawful for you to vote

- not be determined by a court of law to be mentally incompetent

- claim no other place as your legal residence

Mailing address

Secretary of State
Capitol Complex
Carson City, NV 89710

New Hampshire

New Hampshire town and city clerks will accept this application only as a request for their own absentee voter mail-in registration form. You need to fill in only Box 1 and Box 2 or 3. The application should be mailed either to your town or city clerk at your zip code or to:

State House, Room 204
Concord, NH 03301

It should be mailed in plenty of time for your town or city clerk to mail you their own form and for you to return that form to them by 10 days before the election.

New Jersey

6. **ID Number:** Leave blank.

7. **Choice of Party:** You do not have to register with a party if you want to take part in that party's primary election.

8. **Race or Ethnic Group:** Leave blank.

9. **Signature:** To register in New Jersey you must

- be a citizen of the United States

- be a resident of this State and county at your address at least 30 days before the next election

- not be serving a sentence or on parole or probation as the result of a conviction of any indictable offense under the laws of this or another state or of the United States

Mailing address

Office of the Secretary of State
Election Division
CN 304
Trenton, NJ 08625-9983

New Mexico

6. **ID Number:** Your social security number is required. This registration card containing your social security number will become part of the permanent voter registration records of your locality, which are open to inspection by the public in the office of the county clerk. Computerized listings of limited voter registration (without social security number or birth date) are available to the general public, and are furnished upon request to incumbent election officeholders, candidates, political parties, courts and non-profit organizations promoting voter participation and registration, for political purposes only (§1-5=19B, NMSA 1978).

7. **Choice of Party:** You must register with a party if you want to take part in that party's primary election, caucus, or convention.

8. **Race or Ethnic Group:** Leave blank.

9. **Signature:** To register in New Mexico you must

- be a citizen of the United States

- be a resident of the State of New Mexico

- be 18 years of age at the time of the next election

- not have been denied the right to vote by a court of law by reason of mental incapacity or felony conviction

Mailing address

Bureau of Elections
State Capitol, Room 419
Santa Fe, NM 87503

New York

6. **ID Number:** Leave blank.

7. **Choice of Party:** You must enroll with a party if you want to vote in that party's primary election or caucus.

8. **Race or Ethnic Group:** Leave blank.

9. **Signature:** To register in New York you must

- be a citizen of the United States

- be a resident of the county, or of the City of New York, at least 30 days before an election

- be 18 years old by December 31 of the year in which you file this form

   (***Note:*** You must be 18 years old by the date of the general primary, or other election in which you want to vote)

- not be in jail or on parole for a felony conviction

- not currently be judged incompetent by order of a court of competent judicial authority

- not claim the right to vote elsewhere

Mailing address

NYS Board of Election
Swan Street Bldg., Core 1
6 ESP Suite 201
Albany, NY 12223-1650

North Carolina

6. **ID Number:** Your driver's license, or Department of Motor Vehicles ID number is requested.

7. **Choice of Party:** You must register with a party if you want to take part in that party's primary election.

8. **Race or Ethnic Group:** You are required to fill in this box. However, your application will not be rejected if you fail to do so. See the list of choices under the Application Instructions for Box 8.

9. **Signature:** To register in North Carolina you must

- be a citizen of the United States

- be a resident of North Carolina and the county in which you live for at least 30 days prior to the election

- be 18 years of age by the day of the next general election
- have your rights of citizenship restored if you have been convicted of a felony
- not be registered or vote in any other county or state

Mailing address

State Board of Elections
P. O. Box 2169
Raleigh, NC 27602

North Dakota

North Dakota does not have voter registration.

Ohio

6. **ID Number:** Your social security number is requested. Providing this number is voluntary. This information allows the Board of Elections to verify your registration if necessary (O.R.C. 3503.14).

7. **Choice of Party:** You do not register with a party if you want to take part in that party's primary election, caucus or convention. Party affiliation is established by voting at a primary election.

8. **Race or Ethnic Group:** Leave blank.

9. **Signature:** To register in Ohio you must

- be a citizen of the United States
- be a resident of Ohio for at least 30 days before the election
- be 18 years old on or before election day. If you will be 18 on or before the day of the general election, you may vote in the primary election.
- not be convicted of a felony and currently incarcerated
- not be found incompetent by a court for purposes of voting

Mailing address

Secretary of State of Ohio
30 E. Broad Street — 14th floor
Columbus, OH 43266-0418

Oklahoma

6. ID Number: Your Oklahoma driver's license number is requested.

7. Choice of Party: You must register with a party if you want to take part in that party's primary election, caucus, or conventions.

8. Race or Ethnic Group: Leave blank.

9. Signature: To register in Oklahoma you must

- be a citizen of the United States and a resident of the State of Oklahoma

- be 18 years old on or before the date of the next election

- have not been convicted of a felony, for which a period of time equal to the original sentence has not expired, or for which you have not been pardoned

- not now be under judgment as an incapacitated person, or a partially incapacitated person prohibited from registering to vote

Mailing address

Oklahoma State Election Board
Box 528800-8800
Oklahoma City, OK 73152

Oregon

6. ID Number: Leave blank.

7. Choice of Party: You must register with a party if you want to take part in that party's primary election.

8. Race or Ethnic Group: Leave blank.

9. Signature: To register in Oregon you must

- be a citizen of the United States

- be a resident of Oregon

- be at least 18 years old by election day

Mailing address

Secretary of State
Elections Division
255 Capitol Street, N. E.
Salem, OR 97310-0722

Pennsylvania

6. ID Number: Leave blank.

7. Choice of Party: You must register with a party if you want to take part in that party's primary election.

8. Race or Ethnic Group: You are requested to fill in this box. See the list of choices under the Application Instructions for Box 8.

9. Signature: To register in Pennsylvania you must

- be a citizen of the United States

- be a resident of Pennsylvania and your election district at least 30 days before the next election in which you wish to vote

- be at least 18 years old on the day of the next ensuing primary or election

Mailing address

Office of the Secretary of the Commonwealth
Room 302
North Office Bldg.
Harrisburg, PA 17120-0029

Rhode Island

6. ID Number: Leave blank.

7. Choice of Party: You must register with a party if you want to take part in that party's primary election, caucus, or convention.

8. Race or Ethnic Group: Leave blank.

9. Signature: To register in Rhode Island you must

- be a citizen of the United States

- be a resident of Rhode Island for 30 days preceding the next election

- be 18 years old by election day

- be neither serving a sentence, including probation or parole, for which you were imprisoned, upon final conviction of a felony imposed on any date; nor serving any sentence, whether incarcerated or suspended, on probation or parole, upon final conviction of a felony committed after November 5, 1986

- not have been lawfully judged to be mentally incompetent

Mailing address

Rhode Island State Board of Elections
50 Branch Ave.
Providence, RI 02904-2790

South Carolina

6. **ID Number:** Your social security number is required. It is required by the South Carolina Code of Laws and is used for internal purposes only. Social security number does not appear on any report produced by the State Election Commission nor is it released to any unauthorized individual.

7. **Choice of Party:** You do not have to register with a party if you want to take part in that party's primary election, caucus, or convention.

8. **Race or Ethnic Group:** You are required to fill in this box. However, your application will not be rejected if you fail to do so. See the list of choices under the Application Instructions for Box 8.

9. **Signature:** To register in South Carolina you must

   - be a citizen of the United States
   - be at least 18 years old on or before the next election
   - be a resident of South Carolina your county and precinct
   - not be confined in any public prison resulting from a conviction of a crime
   - never have been convicted of a felony or offense against the election laws, or if previously convicted, have served your entire sentence, including probation or parole, or have received a pardon for the conviction
   - not be under a court order declaring you mentally incompetent
   - claim the address on the application as your only legal place of residence and claim no other place as your legal residence

Mailing address

State Election Commission
P. O. Box 5987
Columbia, SC 29250-5987

South Dakota

6. **ID Number:** Your driver's license number is required. If you have no such number, your social security number is requested. Your social security number will be used for administrative purposes but will be available to the public (ARSD 5:02:03:01).

7. **Choice of Party:** You must register with a party if you want to take part in that party's primary election, caucus, or convention.

8. **Race or Ethnic Group:** Leave blank.

9. **Signature:** To register in South Dakota you must

   - be a citizen of the United States

   - reside in South Dakota

   - be 18 years old by the next election

   - not be under a sentence of imprisonment for a felony conviction

   - not have been adjudged mentally incompetent by a court

Mailing address

Elections, Secretary of State
500 E. Capitol
Pierre, SD 57501-5070

Tennessee

6. **ID Number:** Your social security number is required. Social security number, if any, is required for purposes of identification and to avoid duplicate registration (TCA 2.2.116).

7. **Choice of Party:** You do not have to register with a party if you want to take part in that party's primary election, caucus, or convention.

8. **Race or Ethnic Group:** You are requested to fill in this box. See the list of choices under the Application Instructions for Box 8.

9. **Signature:** To register in Tennessee you must

   - be a citizen of the United States

   - be a resident of Tennessee

   - be at least 18 years old on or before the next election

   - not have been convicted of a felony, of if convicted, have had your full rights of citizenship restored (or have received a pardon)

   - not be adjudicated incompetent by a court of competent jurisdiction (or have been restored to legal capacity)

Mailing address

Coordinator of Elections
Secretary of State's Office
500 James K. Polk Bldg.
Nashville, TN 37343-0309

Texas

6. **ID Number:** Your social security number and Texas driver's license number or personal ID number (issued by the Texas Department of Public Safety) is requested. The disclosure of all of these numbers is voluntary. It is solicited by authority of Sec.13.122 of the Texas Election Code and will be used to maintain the accuracy of the registration records. The application is open to the public.

7. **Choice of Party:** You do not have to register with a party if you want to take part in that party's primary election, caucus, or convention.

8. **Race or Ethnic Group:** Leave blank.

9. **Signature:** To register in Texas you must

- be a citizen of the United States

- be a resident of the county in which the application of registration is made

- be at least 17 years and 10 months old (you must be 18 to vote)

- not be convicted of a felony or have been pardoned or otherwise released from the resulting disabilities

- have not been declared mentally incompetent by final judgment of a court of law

Mailing address

Office of the Secretary of State
Elections Division
P. O. Box 12060
Austin, TX 78711-2060

Utah

6. **ID Number:** Your date of birth serves as your ID number, and is required. Write in this box or in Box 4.

7. **Choice of Party:** You must register with a party if you want to take part in that party's primary election.

8. **Race or Ethnic Group:** Leave blank.

9. **Signature:** To register in Utah you must

- be a citizen of the United States

- have resided in Utah for 30 days immediately before the next election

- be at least 18 years old on or before the next election

- not be convicted of treason or crime against the elective franchise, unless restored to civil rights

- not be found to be mentally incompetent by a court of law

Mailing address

Office of the Lieutenant Governor
203 State Capitol
Salt Lake City, UT 84114

Vermont

6. **ID Number:** Leave blank.

7. **Choice of Party:** Vermont does not require party registration to participate in any election.

8. **Race or Ethnic Group:** Leave blank.

9. **Signature:** To register in Vermont you must

- be a citizen of the United States

- be a resident of Vermont

- be 18 years of age on or before election day

- solemnly swear (or affirm) that whenever you give your vote or suffrage, touching any matter that concerns the state of Vermont, you will do it so as in your conscience you shall judge will most conduce to the best good of the same, as established by the Constitution, without fear or favor of any person [Freeman's oath, Vermont Constitution, Chapter II, Section 42]

Mailing address

Office of the Secretary of State
Director of Elections
109 State Street
Montpelier, VT 05609-1101

Virginia

6. ID Number: Your social security number is required. Your social security number will appear on reports produced only for official use by voter registration and election officials and, for jury selection purposes, by courts. Article II, §2, Constitution of Virginia (1971).

7. Choice of Party: You do not have to register with a party if you want to take part in that party's primary election, caucus, or convention.

8. Race or Ethnic Group: Leave blank.

9. Signature: To register in Virginia you must

- be a citizen of the United States

- be a resident of Virginia and of the precinct in which you want to vote

- be 18 years old by the next election

- not have been convicted of a felony, or have had your civil rights restored

- not currently be declared mentally incompetent by a court of law

Note: Virginia, by law, cannot accept this form until after Jan. 1, 1996.

Mailing address

State Board of Elections
200 N. 9th Street, Suite 101
Richmond, VA 23219-3497

Washington

6. ID Number: Leave blank.

7. Choice of Party: You do not have to register with a party if you want to take part in that party's primary election, caucus, or convention.

8. Race or Ethnic Group: Leave blank.

9. Signature: To register in Washington you must

- be a citizen of the United States

- be a legal resident of Washington State, your county and precinct for 30 days immediately preceding the election in which you want to vote

- be at least 18 years old by election day

- not be convicted of infamous crime unless restored to civil rights

- not be judicially declared mentally incompetent

Mailing address

Secretary of State
Voter Registration by Mail
P. O. Box 40230
Olympia, WA 98504-0230

West Virginia

6. **ID Number:** The last four digits of your social security number are requested.

7. **Choice of Party:** You must register with a party if you want to take part in that party's primary election, caucus, or convention (unless you request the ballot of a party which allows independents to vote)

8. **Race Ethnic Group:** Leave blank.

9. **Signature:** To register in West Virginia you must

- be a citizen of the United States

- live in West Virginia at the above address

- be 18 years old, or be 17 years old and turning 18 years old before the next general election

- not be under conviction, probation, or parole for a felony, treason or election bribery

- not have been judged "mentally incompetent" in a court of competent jurisdiction

Mailing address

Secretary of State
Building 1, Suite 157-K
1900 Kanawha Blvd. East
Charleston, WV 25305-0770

Wisconsin

6. **ID Number:** Leave blank. However, if you submit the application on election day, you will be asked to provide a form of identification.

7. **Choice of Party:** You do not have to register with a party if you want to take part in that party's primary election, caucus, or convention.

8. **Race or Ethnic Group:** Leave blank.

9. **Signature:** To register in Wisconsin you must

- be a citizen of the Untied States

- be a resident of Wisconsin for at least 10 days

- be 18 years old

- not have been convicted of treason, felony or bribery, or have had your civil rights restored

- not have been found by a court to be incapable of understanding the objective of the electoral process

- not make or benefit from a bet or wage depending on the result of an election

Mailing address

State Elections Board
132 E. Wilson Street, 3rd Floor
P. O. Box 2973
Madison, WI 53701-2973

Wyoming

Wyoming will not let you use this application for registering to vote in that state.

State Registration Deadlines

To register in time to vote in any upcoming election, your application must be postmarked (or delivered to your *local voter registration office*) by the deadline listed below

Alabama: 10 days before the election.

Alaska: 30 days before the election.

Arizona: 29 days before the election.

Arkansas: 21 days before the election.

California: 29 days before the election.

Colorado: 30 days before the election. If the application is received in the mails without a postmark, it must be received within 5 days of the close of registration.

Connecticut: 14 days before the election.

Delaware: 20 days before any general election.

District of Columbia: 30 days before the election.

Florida: 29 days before the election.

Georgia: The fourth Friday before any general primary, general election, or presidential preference primary. The ninth day after the date of the call for all other special primaries and special elections.

Hawaii: 30 days before the election.

Idaho: 25 days before the election.

Illinois: 29 days before the election.

Indiana: 29 days before the election.

Iowa: 10 days before the election, if it is a state primary or general election; 11 days before all others. Registration forms which are postmarked 15 or more days before an election are considered on time even if received after the deadline.

Kansas: Delivered 15 days before the election.

Kentucky: 28 days before the election.

Louisiana: 24 days before the election.

Maine: 15 days before the election (or delivered *in-person* up to and including election day).

Maryland: 9:00 P.M. on the fifth Monday before the election.

Massachusetts: 20 days before the election.

Michigan: 30 days before the election.

Minnesota: Delivered by 5:00 P.M. 21 days before the election (there is also election day registration at polling places).

Mississippi: 30 days before the election.

Missouri: 28 days before the election.

Montana: 30 days before the election.

Nebraska: The fourth Tuesday before the election (or delivered by 6:00 P.M. on the second Friday before the election).

Nevada: 9:00 P.M. on the fifth Saturday before any primary or general election. 9:00 P.M. on the third Saturday before any recall or special election. However, if a recall or special election is held on the same day as a primary or general election, the registration closes at 9:00 P.M. on the fifth Saturday before the day for the elections.

New Hampshire: In New Hampshire, this application may be used only as a request for a State voter registration application, which must be received by your city or town clerk by 10 days before the election.

New Jersey: 29 days before the election.

New Mexico: 28 days before the election.

New York: 25 days before the election.

North Carolina: 25 days before the election.

North Dakota: North Dakota does not have voter registration.

Ohio: 30 days before the election.

Oklahoma: 25 days before the election.

Oregon: 21 days before the election (there is no deadline for applications for change of name, change of address or to register with a party).

Pennsylvania: 30 days before an election or primary.

Rhode Island: 30 days before the election.

South Carolina: 30 days before the election.

South Dakota: Delivered 5 days before the election.

Tennessee: 30 days before the election.

Texas: 30 days before the election.

Utah: 20 days before the election.

Vermont: Delivered to the town clerk before 12:00 noon on the third Saturday before the election.

Virginia: Delivered 29 days before the election.

Washington: 30 days before the election (or delivered in-person to the local voter registration office 15 days before the election).

West Virginia: 30 days before the election.

Wisconsin: 13 days before the election (or completed in the local voter registration office 1 day before the election or completed at the polling place on election day).

Wyoming: Wyoming will not let you use this application for registering to vote in that state.

Index

(continued)

(continued)

• T •

• *W* •

Notes

Notes

IDG BOOKS WORLDWIDE REGISTRATION CARD

RETURN THIS
REGISTRATION CARD
FOR FREE CATALOG

Title of this book: Politics For Dummies

My overall rating of this book: ❏ Very good [1]   ❏ Good [2]   ❏ Satisfactory [3]   ❏ Fair [4]   ❏ Poor [5]

How I first heard about this book:

❏ Found in bookstore; name: [6]   ❏ Book review: [7]

❏ Advertisement: [8]   ❏ Catalog: [9]

❏ Word of mouth; heard about book from friend, co-worker, etc.: [10]   ❏ Other: [11]

What I liked most about this book:

_____

_____

What I would change, add, delete, etc., in future editions of this book:

_____

_____

Other comments:

_____

Number of computer books I purchase in a year: ❏ 1 [12]   ❏ 2-5 [13]   ❏ 6-10 [14]   ❏ More than 10 [15]

I would characterize my computer skills as: ❏ Beginner [16] ❏ Intermediate [17] ❏ Advanced [18] ❏ Professional [19]

I use ❏ DOS [20]   ❏ Windows [21]   ❏ OS/2 [22]   ❏ Unix [23]   ❏ Macintosh [24]   ❏ Other: [25]_____
                                                                                                    (please specify)

I would be interested in new books on the following subjects:
(please check all that apply, and use the spaces provided to identify specific software)

❏ Word processing: [26]   ❏ Spreadsheets: [27]

❏ Data bases: [28]   ❏ Desktop publishing: [29]

❏ File Utilities: [30]   ❏ Money management: [31]

❏ Networking: [32]   ❏ Programming languages: [33]

❏ Other: [34]

I use a PC at (please check all that apply): ❏ home [35] ❏ work [36] ❏ school [37] ❏ other: [38] _____

The disks I prefer to use are ❏ 5.25 [39] ❏ 3.5 [40] ❏ other: [41]_____

I have a CD ROM: ❏ yes [42]   ❏ no [43]

I plan to buy or upgrade computer hardware this year: ❏ yes [44]   ❏ no [45]

I plan to buy or upgrade computer software this year: ❏ yes [46]   ❏ no [47]

Name: _____   Business title: [48] _____   Type of Business: [49] _____

Address (❏ home [50] ❏ work [51]/Company name: _____)

Street/Suite# _____

City [52]/State [53]/Zipcode [54]: _____   Country [55] _____

❏ **I liked this book!** You may quote me by name in future
   IDG Books Worldwide promotional materials.

My daytime phone number is _____

IDG
BOOKS

THE WORLD OF
COMPUTER
KNOWLEDGE

☐ **YES!**

Please keep me informed about IDG's World of Computer Knowledge.
Send me the latest IDG Books catalog.

SECRETS™

...FOR DUMMIES™
COMPUTER
BOOK SERIES
FROM IDG

MACWORLD
MW
AUTHORIZED
EDITION

AUTHORIZED
PC WORLD
EDITION